# Research Infrastructures for Open Science in Social Science Research

Giovanni Cerulli • Emanuela Reale
Editors

# Research Infrastructures for Open Science in Social Science Research

## Lessons from the FOSSR Case

Springer

*Editors*
Giovanni Cerulli
CNR-IRCrES
Roma, Italy

Emanuela Reale
CNR-IRCrES
Rome, Italy

ISBN 978-3-032-29574-3 ISBN 978-3-032-29575-0 (eBook)
https://doi.org/10.1007/978-3-032-29575-0



This Springer imprint is published by the registered company Springer Nature Switzerland AG
The registered company address is: Gewerbestrasse 11, 6330 Cham, Switzerland

# Foreword

This volume "Research Infrastructures for Open Science in Social Science Research: Lessons from the FOSSR Case" deals with research infrastructures, which have become a central component of contemporary scientific systems. Over the last two decades, they have progressively transformed the way knowledge is produced, shared, and applied across disciplines.

In the social sciences and humanities, this transformation has been particularly significant. The growing availability of large and complex datasets, advances in computational methods, and the global movement towards Open Science have created new opportunities to study social and economic phenomena with greater depth, transparency, and collaborative capacity.

Within this evolving landscape, the FOSSR project (Fostering Open Science in Social Science Research) represents a major initiative aimed at strengthening the infrastructure supporting social science research in Italy and connecting it to the broader European research ecosystem. Funded within the framework of the Italian National Recovery and Resilience Plan (PNRR) under the NextGenerationEU programme, FOSSR seeks to develop a national research infrastructure capable of enabling open, integrated, and interdisciplinary research in the social sciences.

The volume offers a comprehensive reflection on the role that research infrastructures can play in enabling new forms of knowledge production, facilitating data sharing, collaborative research, advanced computational analysis, and the development of new analytical tools capable of addressing complex societal challenges.

The structure of the book reflects this multidimensional perspective. The first part situates research infrastructures within the broader context of Open Science and European Research Area, exploring the conceptual foundations of infrastructures, the role of FAIR data principles, and the ethical dimensions of open social science research. The second part presents the specific contributions of FOSSR across a variety of research domains, including probabilistic surveys, panel data on societal values, behavioural experiments, policy learning tools for evidence-based policymaking, and new datasets for the study of industrial and innovation systems.

The third part explores methodological and theoretical perspectives, including collaborative research models and the emerging field of computational social science. Together, these contributions illustrate how infrastructures can support new forms of interdisciplinary research and generate innovative approaches to understanding social and economic transformations.

The publication of this volume is closely aligned with the mission of the Department of Social Sciences and Humanities, Cultural Heritage (DSU) of the National Research Council of Italy (CNR). In recent years, the Department has undertaken a process of strategic reorganization aimed at strengthening coordination among its research institutes, enhancing synergies across disciplines, and fostering new areas of research within the broad domain of the social sciences, humanities, and cultural heritage. This renewed vision emphasizes the central role of the social sciences in addressing major societal challenges and supporting sustainable and inclusive development.

Indeed, contemporary societies face profound transformations: demographic change, economic restructuring, technological innovation, environmental pressures, and growing social inequalities. Understanding and governing these complex dynamics requires robust scientific knowledge, interdisciplinary collaboration, and access to reliable data and analytical tools. Research infrastructures play a crucial role in enabling these conditions. They provide shared resources that allow researchers to collaborate across institutional and national boundaries, develop new methods, and generate evidence capable of informing public policy and societal debate.

Also, the objectives pursued by FOSSR are fully consistent with both European and international priorities. The development of open, interoperable, and sustainable research infrastructures contributes directly to the goals articulated in the European Open Science agenda and to the broader vision of science as a global public good. At the same time, such infrastructures support the achievement of the Sustainable Development Goals of the United Nations, particularly those aimed at reducing inequalities, promoting inclusive institutions, and fostering knowledge-based development.

Beyond its technological and methodological components, FOSSR represents an important institutional experiment in collaborative research. It involves universities, research institutes, and international partners working together to build a shared infrastructure that will serve the scientific community over the long term. The experience described in this volume therefore provides valuable lessons not only for the Italian research system but also for the broader international community engaged in the development of research infrastructures for the social sciences.

This book is the result of the collective effort of many scholars, researchers, and technical experts who contributed their knowledge and experience to the FOSSR project. Their work demonstrates the potential of research infrastructures to transform the way social science research is conducted and to strengthen the connection between scientific knowledge and societal needs.

It is my hope that this volume will serve both as a reference for scholars interested in the development of research infrastructures and as a source of inspiration for future initiatives aimed at advancing open and collaborative social science research.

Department of Social Sciences and Humanities, Cultural Heritage (DSU)
National Research Council of Italy (CNR)
Roma, Italy

Salvatore Capasso

# Contents

# Contributors

**Giulia Andrighetto** CNR-ISTC (Institute of Cognitive Sciences and Technologies), National Research Council of Italy, Rome, Italy

**Massimiliano Assante** CNR-ISTI (Institute of Information Science and Technologies), National Research Council of Italy, Pisa, Italy

**Maria Bigoni** University of Bologna, Bologna, Italy

**Federico Brogi** ISTAT (National Statistical Institute of Italy), Rome, Italy

**Daniele Bruschi** CNR-DSU (Department of Social sciences and humanities, cultural heritage), National Research Council of Italy, Rome, Italy

**Cinzia Caporale** Interdepartmental Center for Research Ethics and Integrity, National Research Council (CID Ethics-CNR), Rome, Italy

**Loredana Cerbara** CNR-IRPPS (Institute for Research on Population and Social Policies), National Research Council of Italy, Rome, Italy

**Miguel Ceriani** CNR-ISTC (Institute of Cognitive Sciences and Technologies), National Research Council of Italy, Roma, Italy

**Giovanni Cerulli** CNR-IRCrES (Research Institute on Sustainable Economic Growth), National Research Council of Italy, Rome, Italy

**Mario Ciampi** National Research Council of Italy, Institute for High-Performance Computing and Networking (CNR ICAR), Naples, Italy

**Massimo Gaetano Colombo** Politecnico di Milano School of Management, Milan, Italy

**Diana d'Alterio** CNR-ISMED (Institute for Studies on the Mediterranean) National Research Council of Italy, Naples, Italy

**Emanuele Damiano** National Research Council of Italy, Institute for High-Performance Computing and Networking (CNR ICAR), Naples, Italy

**Giulio Ecchia** Alma Mater Studiorum – University of Bologna, Bologna, Italy

**Serena Fabrizio** CNR-IRCrES (Research Institute on Sustainable Economic Growth), National Research Council of Italy, Rome, Italy

**Fabrizio De Fausti** ISTAT, National Statistical Institute of Italy, Rome, Italy

**Alessia Fava** CNR-IRCrES (Institute for Sustainable Economic Growth), National Research Council of Italy, Rome, Italy

**Dario Germani** CNR-IRPPS (Institute for Research on Population and Social Policies), National Research Council of Italy, Rome, Italy

**Lorenzo Giammei** INAPP – National Institute for Public Policy Analysis, Roma, Italy

**Rita Giuffredi** CNR-IRCrES (Institute for Sustainable Economic Growth), National Research Council of Italy, Rome, Italy

**Daniela de Gregorio** CNR-ISMED (Institute for Studies on the Mediterranean) National Research Council of Italy, Naples, Italy

**Barbara Guardabascio** Department of Economics, University of Perugia, Perugia, Italy

**Massimiliano Guerini** Politecnico di Milano School of Management, Milan, Italy

**Carmelo Fabio Longo** CNR-ISTC (Institute of Cognitive Sciences and Technologies), National Research Council of Italy, Catania, Italy

**Antonio De Lorenzo** CNR-ISMED (Institute for Studies on the Mediterranean) National Research Council of Italy, Naples, Italy

**Letizia Mencarini** Bocconi University, Milan, Italy

**Pier Giuseppe Meo** National Research Council of Italy, Institute for High-Performance Computing and Networking (CNR ICAR), Naples, Italy

**Elisa Molinaro** CNR-ISTI (Institute of Information Science and Technologies), National Research Council of Italy, Pisa, Italy

**Misael Mongiovì** CNR-ISTC (Institute of Cognitive Sciences and Technologies), National Research Council of Italy, Catania, Italy

**Andrea Giovanni Nuzzolese** CNR-ISTC (Institute of Cognitive Sciences and Technologies), National Research Council of Italy, Bologna, Italy

**Rocco Paolillo** CNR-IRPPS (Institute for Research on Population and Social Policies), National Research Council of Italy, Rome, Italy

**Claudia Pennacchiotti** CNR-IRPPS (Institute for Research on Population and Social Policies), National Research Council of Italy, Rome, Italy

**Francesco Poggi** CNR-ISTC (Institute of Cognitive Sciences and Technologies), National Research Council of Italy, Bologna, Italy

**Ilaria Primerano** CNR-IRPPS (Institute for Research on Population and Social Policies), National Research Council of Italy, Fisciano, SA, Italy

**Emanuela Reale** CNR-IRCrES (Research Institute on Sustainable Economic Growth), National Research Council of Italy, Rome, Italy

**Salvatore Riegler** Independent Researcher, Naples, Italy

**Ferruccio Biolcati Rinaldi** University of Milano Statale, Milan, Italy

**Erica Rizziato** CNR-IRCrES (Institute for Sustainable Economic Growth), National Research Council of Italy, Rome, Italy

**Maria Elisa Rosati** CNR-ISTC (Institute of Cognitive Science and Technology) National Research Council of Italy, Rome, Italy

**Massimiliano Saccone** CNR-DSU (Department of Social sciences and humanities, cultural heritage), National Research Council of Italy, Rome, Italy

**Michele Santurro** CNR-IRPPS (Institute for Research on Population and Social Policies), National Research Council of Italy, Rome, Italy

**Giulia Sciolli** Interdepartmental Center for Research Ethics and Integrity, National Research Council (CID Ethics-CNR), Rome, Italy

**Domingo Scisci** DASSI - Data Archive for Social Sciences in Italy, Dept. of Sociology and Social Research, University of Milano-Bicocca, Milan, Italy

**Mario Sicuranza** National Research Council of Italy, Institute for High-Performance Computing and Networking (CNR ICAR), Naples, Italy

**Andrea Simone** Department of Law, University of Palermo, Palermo, Italy

**Andrea Orazio Spinello** CNR-IRCrES (Research Institute on Sustainable Economic Growth), National Research Council of Italy, Rome, Italy

**Marco Sprocati** CNR-IRCrES (Institute for Sustainable Economic Growth), National Research Council of Italy, Rome, Italy

**Sonia Stefanizzi** DASSI - Data Archive for Social Sciences in Italy, Dept. of Sociology and Social Research, University of Milano-Bicocca, Milan, Italy

**Alessandra Maria Stilo** CNR-IRCrES (Institute for Sustainable Economic Growth), National Research Council of Italy, Rome, Italy

**Elisa Storace** CNR-UVR (Technology transfer office), National Research Council of Italy, Rome, Italy

**Luciana Taddei** CNR-IRPPS (Institute for Research on Population and Social Policies), National Research Council of Italy, Fisciano, SA, Italy

**Giusy Giulia Tuccari** CNR-ISTC (Institute of Cognitive Sciences and Technologies), National Research Council of Italy, Catania, Italy

**Valentina Tudisca** CNR-IRPPS (Institute for Research on Population and Social Policies), National Research Council of Italy, Rome, Italy

**Emanuela Varinetti** CNR-IRCrES (Institute for Sustainable Economic Growth), National Research Council of Italy, Rome, Italy

**Salvatore Vassallo** Department of the Arts, University of Bologna, Bologna, Italy

Carlo Cattaneo Institute Research Foundation, Bologna, Italy

**Cristiano Vezzoni** University of Milano Statale, Milan, Italy

**Eva Vriens** CNR-ISTC (Institute of Cognitive Sciences and Technologies), National Research Council of Italy, Rome, Italy

**Guglielmo Weber** University of Padua, Padua, Italy

**Roberta Martina Zagarella** Interdepartmental Center for Research Ethics and Integrity, National Research Council (CID Ethics-CNR), Rome, Italy

**Antonio Zinilli** CNR-IRCrES (Institute for Sustainable Economic Growth), National Research Council of Italy, Rome, Italy

**Sara Zuppiroli** CNR-ISTC (Institute of Cognitive Sciences and Technologies), National Research Council of Italy, Bologna, Italy

# List of Abbreviations

| | |
|---|---|
| ABM | Agent-based Modelling |
| AC | Associated Countries |
| AI | Artificial Intelligence |
| AND | Author Name Disambiguation |
| API | Application Programming Interface |
| ARS/ARSs | Action Research Session(s) |
| ASEAN | Association of South East Asian Nations |
| AUSSI | Australian Social Survey International |
| AUTNES | Austrian National Election Study Online Panel |
| BC | Bibliographic Coupling |
| BDI | Beliefs-Desires-Intentions |
| BMC | Business Model Canvas |
| BVC | Bank-Affiliated Venture Capital |
| CAPI | Computer-Assisted Personal Interviewing |
| CARE | Collective benefit, Authority to Control, Responsibility, Ethics |
| CATE | Conditional Average Treatment Effect |
| CAWI | Computer-Assisted Web Interviewing |
| CC | Critical Chain |
| CCPM | Critical Chain Project Management |
| CESSDA | Consortium of European Social Science Data Archives |
| CIDOC-CRM | Conceptual Reference Model of the ICOM International Committee for Documentation |
| CIVES Observatory | Observatory on Civicness and the Evolution of Society |
| CLARIN | Common Language Resources and Technology Infrastructure |
| CLAVAS | CLARIN Vocabulary Alignment Service |
| CMDI | Component Metadata Infrastructure |
| CMM | CESSDA Metadata Model |
| CNR | National Research Council of Italy |
| CODATA | Committee on Data of the International Science Council |

| | |
|---|---|
| COM | Communication |
| COVID-19 | CoronaVIrus Disease 2019 |
| CQs | Competency Questions |
| CRIS | Current Research Information System |
| CRONOS/CRONOS-2 | Cross-National Online Survey |
| CVC | Corporate Venture Capital |
| CWTS | Centre for Science and Technology Studies |
| DARIAH | Digital Research Infrastructure for the Arts and Humanities |
| DDI | Data Documentation Initiative |
| DM | Decreto Ministeriale (Ministerial Decree) |
| DMP | Data Management Plan |
| DNSH | Do No Significant Harm |
| DOI | Digital Object Identifier |
| DPIA | Data Protection Impact Assessment |
| DSU | Department of Humanities and Social sciences, cultural heritage |
| EC | European Commission |
| ECTS | European Credit Transfer and Accumulation System |
| EDI | Equality, Diversity and Inclusion |
| EFIL | European dataset of public R&D funding instruments |
| ELSST | European Language Social Science Thesaurus |
| EOSC | European Open Science Cloud |
| EP | Extended Partnerships (PNRR) |
| EPOS | European Plate Observing System |
| EQF | European Qualifications Framework |
| ERA | European Research Area |
| ERGM | Exponential Random Graph Models |
| ERIC | European Research Infrastructure Consortium |
| E-RIHS | European Research Infrastructure for Heritage Science |
| ERP | Enterprise Resource Planning |
| ESFRI | European Strategy Forum on Research Infrastructures |
| ESOMAR | European Society for Opinion and Marketing Research |
| ESS | European Social Survey |
| ETER | European Tertiary Education Register |
| EU | European Union |
| EU-LGBTI II | European Union Lesbian, Gay, Bisexual, Transgender and Intersex Survey II |
| EuroHPC JU | the European High Performance Computing Joint Undertaking |
| European-DTO | European Digital Twins of the Ocean |
| EVS | European Values Study |
| FAIR | Findable, Accessible, Interoperable, Reusable |
| FAO | Food and Agriculture Organization of the United Nations |
| FIPA | Foundation for Intelligent Physical Agents |

| | |
|---|---|
| FOSSR | Fostering Open Science in Social Science Research |
| FP | Framework Programme |
| FTP | File Transfer Protocol |
| GAL/TAN | Green Alternative Libertarian/Traditional Authoritarian Nationalist |
| GBARD | Government Budget Allocations or Outlays for R&D |
| GDP | Gross Domestic Product |
| GDPR | General Data Protection Regulation |
| GEA | Gestione iniziativE progetti di ricercA |
| GGP | Generations and Gender Programme |
| GGS | Generations and Gender Survey |
| GUIDE | Growing Up In Digital Europe |
| GVC | Government Venture Capital |
| H2IOSC | Humanities and Cultural Heritage Italian Open Science Cloud |
| HE | Horizon Europe |
| HOLIO | Horizontal Leadership and Integrated Organisations |
| HPC | High Performance Computing |
| HTTP | Hypertext Transfer Protocol |
| ICDI | Italian Computing and Data Infrastructure |
| ICSC | Italian Center for Super Computing (Italian Research Centre on High Performance Computing, Big Data and Quantum Computing) |
| ICT | Information and Communication Technologies |
| INAF | National Institute for Astrophysics/Istituto Nazionale di Astrofisica |
| INFN | National Institute for Nuclear Physics/Istituto Nazionale di Fisica Nucleare |
| INGV | National Institute of Geophysics and Volcanology/Istituto Nazionale di Geofisica e Vulcanologia |
| IOPP | Italian Online Probability Panel |
| IOPP | Italian Online Probability Panel |
| IRCrES | Research Institute on Sustainable Economic Growth/Istituto di Ricerca sulla Crescita Economica Sostenibile |
| IRPPS | Institute for Research on Population and Social Policies/Istituto di Ricerche sulla Popolazione e le Politiche Sociali |
| ISCED | International Standard Classification of Education |
| ISO | International Organization for Standardization |
| ISTAT | Italian National Institute of Statistics/Istituto Nazionale di Statistica |
| ISTC | Institute of Cognitive Sciences and Technologies/Istituto di Scienze e Tecnologie della Cognizione |
| ITSERR | Italian Strengthening of the ESFRI RI RESILIENCE |
| IVC | Independent Venture Capital |

| | |
|---|---|
| KEIs | Key Engagement Indicators |
| KETs | Key Enabling Technologies |
| KGs | Knowledge Graphs |
| KPIs | Key Performance Indicators |
| LEAD | LLM-enhanced Engine for Author Disambiguation |
| LISS | Longitudinal Internet Studies for Social Sciences |
| LLMs | Large Language Models |
| LS | Label Spreading |
| LS | Life Sciences |
| LS/LSs | Learning Session(s) |
| M4C2 | Mission 4 "Education and Research" Component 2 "From Research to Enterprise" |
| M5S | Five Star Movement (Italian political party) |
| MAS | Multi-Agent Systems |
| MIPF | Multiple Iterative Proportional Fitting |
| ML | Machine Learning |
| MoU | Memorandum of Understanding |
| MS | Member States |
| MUR | Ministry of University and Research |
| NACE | Nomenclature statistique des activités économiques dans la Communauté européenne/Statistical Classification of Economic Activities in the European Community |
| NATPRO | National Research Projects |
| NGEU | Next Generation EU (Europe) |
| NGOs | Non-Governmental Organizations |
| NIDI | Netherlands Interdisciplinary Demographic Institute |
| NRRP/PNRR | National Recovery and Resilience Plan (Piano Nazionale di Ripresa e Resilienza) |
| NSSS | National Smart Specialisation Strategy/SNSI Strategia Nazionale di Specializzazione Intelligente |
| OA | Open Access |
| OAI-PMH | Open Archives Initiative: Protocol for Metadata Harvesting |
| OAIS | Open Archival Information System |
| OECD | Organization for Economic Co-operation and Development |
| OI | Open Innovation |
| ONU | Organizzazione delle Nazioni Unite (United Nations) |
| OPERAS | Open scholarly communication in the European Research Area for Social science and humanities |
| OPL | Optimal Policy Learning |
| OPT | Optimized Production Technology |
| ORCID | Open Researcher and Contributor ID |
| ORP | Online Research Panel |
| OTC/OTCs | Online Training Course(s) |

| | |
|---|---|
| PAPI | Paper-and-Pencil Interviewing |
| PE | Physical Sciences and Engineering |
| PhD | Philosophiae Doctor |
| PHIDIAS | PytHon Interactive Declarative Intelligent Agent System |
| PID | Persistent Identifier |
| PLP | Policy Learning Platform |
| PMO | Project Management Office |
| PNIR | Piano Nazionale Infrastrutture di Ricerca (National Plan for Research Infrastructures) |
| PNR | Programma nazionale per la ricerca (National Research Programme) |
| PNSA | Piano Nazionale per la Scienza Aperta (National Plan for Open Science) |
| POLAT | Spanish Political Attitudes Panel |
| PREF | Analysis of national Public REsearch Funding, by theme and by type of allocation |
| PRIN | Progetti di Rilevante Interesse Nazionale |
| PRINWINNERS | dataset on projects funded under PRIN |
| PS/PSs | Participatory Session(s) |
| PSU | Primary Sampling Unit |
| PTA | Piano Triennale di Attività (CNR) |
| QA | Quality Assurance |
| R&D | Research and Development |
| R&I | Research and Innovation |
| RAISE | Resource for AI Science in Europe |
| RDA | Research Data Alliance |
| RDF | Resource Description Framework |
| RDM | Research Data Management |
| RESILIENCE | REligious Studies Infrastructure: tooLs, Innovation, Experts, conNections and Centres in Europe |
| RFOs | Research Funding Organizations |
| RI/RIs | Research Infrastructure(s) |
| RISIS | Research Infrastructure for Science, Technology and Innovation policy Studies |
| RO | Research Object model |
| RoP | Rules of Participation |
| RRF | Recovery and Resilience Facility |
| RRI | Responsible Research and Innovation |
| RS3- | Regional Smart Specialisation Strategies |
| S&CI | Social and Cultural Innovation |
| S4P | European Science for Policy |
| SCP | Swedish Citizen Panel |
| SDGs | Sustainable Development Goals |
| SDMX | Statistical Data and Metadata eXchange |
| SDS | Social Data Science |

| | |
|---|---|
| SEMAS | SEmantic Multi-Agent System |
| SERISS | Synergies for Europe's Research Infrastructures in the Social Sciences |
| SHARE | Survey of Health, Ageing and Retirement in Europe |
| SIO | Semanticscience Integrated Ontology |
| SIPER | Science and Innovation Policy Evaluation Repository |
| SKA | Square Kilometre Array |
| SLA | Service Level Agreement |
| SME | Small and Medium Enterprises |
| SOP | Standard Operating Procedure |
| SPARQL | SPARQL Protocol and RDF Query Language |
| SPG | Synthetic Populations Generator service |
| SRIA | Strategic Research and Innovation Agenda (EOSC) |
| SSH | Social Sciences and Humanities |
| SSHOC | Social Sciences & Humanities Open Cloud |
| STEM | Science, Technology, Engineering and Mathematics |
| STIP | Science, Technology and Innovation Policy |
| STS | Science and Technology Studies |
| T2B2T | Triples-to-Beliefs-to-Triples protocol |
| TEI | Text Encoding Initiative |
| TERGM | Temporal Exponential Random Graph Models |
| TFEU | Treaty on the Functioning of the European Union |
| TOC | Theory of Constraints |
| TRASE | Transformative Systemic Evolutionary Training |
| TRL | Technology Readiness Levels |
| UNECE | United Nations Economic Commission for Europe |
| UNESCO | United Nations Educational, Scientific and Cultural Organization |
| UO | Operational Unit |
| UX | User Experience |
| VIAF | Virtual International Authority File |
| VLab | Virtual Laboratory |
| VLO | Virtual Language Observatory |
| VRE | Virtual Research Environment |
| WP | Work Package |
| XD | Extreme Design |
| XML | Extensible Markup Language |

# Part I
# Infrastructures and Open Science in Social Science Research: An Overview

# Chapter 1
# Research Infrastructures: Concepts and Roles

**Giovanni Cerulli and Emanuela Reale**

## 1.1 Introduction

Research infrastructures are one of the most important developments that gained a momentum with the diffusion and implementation of the Open Science movement and the new directionality of the European policy toward improving collaborative efforts in science and technology to address the complex problems raised by pursuing sustainable development goals for economy and society.

This introductory chapter provides a foundational overview of Research Infrastructures (RIs) in social science research, examining their emergence, role, and impact within the broader Open Science movement. It introduces key theoretical perspectives on RIs, tracing their historical evolution and their increasing relevance in social sciences. The chapter systematically presents the contents of the book whose aim is to show how RIs facilitate data sharing, collaboration, and the production of high-quality research, while also addressing challenges related to sustainability, governance, and accessibility.

## 1.2 The Research Infrastructures in Social Sciences

The literature highlights that RIs began to gain importance in the 1940s, with large-scale, costly, and complex instruments like particle accelerators and nuclear reactors, which were crucial for both scientific advancement and military applications (Cramer & Hallonsten, 2020).

G. Cerulli · E. Reale (✉)
CNR-IRCrES (Research Institute on Sustainable Economic Growth), National Research Council of Italy, Rome, Italy
e-mail: giovanni.cerulli@cnr.it; emanuela.reale@cnr.it



G. Cerulli, E. Reale (eds.), *Research Infrastructures for Open Science in Social Science Research*, https://doi.org/10.1007/978-3-032-29575-0_1

After the second World War, the need for shared, high-cost, and advanced equipment led to the development of international research organizations and collaborations. The European Commission has played a key role in developing and coordinating RIs to foster innovation, competitiveness, and scientific excellence across Europe. The European Strategy Forum on Research Infrastructures (ESFRI) was in fact created to facilitate the development and optimal use of RIs across the continent (EC, 2016; Hallonsten, 2020).

From the 2000s the approach of the European Commission toward research infrastructures went under an important turning point, which bring a reconsideration of the role of RIs as means to optimize their coordination within the emerging European Research Area. Because of this new vision, RIs are not only "providers of scientific services and research resources. But it also considered the ability of RIs to connect Europe and its research landscape with lasting effects on Europe as a transnational space of science and technology" (Cramer & Rüffin, 2025).

Infrastructures are therefore considered key means to support EU policies, particularly to foster innovation and achievements that can address the *Grand Societal Challenges* identified in Horizon 2020 and the sustainable development goals of the Agenda 2030 (Schipper & Schot, 2011). In this period the most important RIs in social science research become consolidated and their use gain importance producing effects and changes in the processes that govern the production of new knowledge in that specific research domains (Spinello, 2017).

In the words of the European Commission "Research Infrastructures are facilities that provide resources and services for research communities to conduct research and foster innovation. They can be used beyond research e.g. for education or public services and they may be single-sited, distributed, or virtual. They include major scientific equipment or sets of instruments, collections, archives or scientific data, computing systems and communication networks, any other research and innovation infrastructure of a unique nature which is open to external users" (https://research-and-innovation.ec.europa.eu/strategy/strategy-research-and-innovation/our-digital-future/european-research-infrastructures_en).

The definition is broad and flexible enough to include different forms of RIs in different fields and remain valid beside their evolution and to the changing role that the EC attributes to them. However, we can identify at least four key components of an infrastructure over time, that are a) the provision of resources and services to different types of users beyond the research communities, b) to be included in the open science paradigm, c) the presence of an infrastructure of unique nature, not necessarily a scientific equipment, d) a mission primarily devoted to be conducive of collaborative research and foster innovation.

However, RIs have nowadays expanded beyond physical equipment to include digital and virtual infrastructures, often distributed between different actors in different counties and sites, such as data networks and archives, which support research across all scientific fields. All these changes design the complexity of the environment where RIs operates, and a transformation also of their structure and nature, which might resemble more as ecosystems.

According to APRE (2026) RI ecosystem is "a dynamic collaboration between research infrastructures which has been developed around a set of shared strategic objectives and provides, supports or coordinates services and/or activities at the level of the RI collaboration, while the individual RIs remain responsible for their own governance, strategy and business". The meaning is clear: RIs are moving away from isolated, single-site operation to interconnected, heterogeneous, and distributed models. The ecosystems consist of data platforms, software, human capital, and governance structures rather than just physical equipment. Developing these systems requires new funding models, clear data/access agreements, and integration into national and international strategies (OECD, 2025: APRE, 2026). The mentioned transformation has several consequences at organizational level, because it requires new competences, responsibilities, funding and governance. (Ribeiro, 2021).

OECD (2025) refers that an RI ecosystem is determined by a "dynamic collaboration between research infrastructures which has been developed around a set of shared strategic objectives". Furthermore, it is supposed "to provide, support or coordinate services and activities between infrastructures themselves, while the individual RIs remain responsible for their own governance, strategy and business". The Report also formulates ten recommendations, each of which requires actions from a variety of actors.

In this vein, OECD has also promoted some work to deepen the structure and opportunities of RIs for addressing societal grand challenges. Moving from the COVID-19 crisis (OECD, 2023) and looking forward on the future of RIs, OECD pointed out the pivotal role of RIs. "However, individual RIs do not host all the equipment and resources required to tackle complex scientific or societal challenges, particularly when these are multi- or inter-disciplinary in nature. The development of integrated RI ecosystems offers new opportunities for enhancing the scope, impact and efficiency of individual RIs, but requires significant incentives to overcome the practical challenges that hinder their creation and sustainability." (OECD, 2025). The RIs ecosystems make even more complex the organizations of the access to data and information, the integration and/or coordination of different research infrastructures, and fostering stricter and durable academia-industry collaborations (OECD/Science Europe, 2020).

## 1.3 Research Infrastructures in the Open Science Perspective

RIs are by their very nature integrated into the principles of open science. Nowadays RIs are one of the most important mean to realize the transformative purpose of Open Science as to changing the mode of scientific knowledge production because of the services provided, because of the rules for transnational access, because they assure portability, analysis and federation of data, produce new scientific literature, define thematic science priorities and can become a way to support community engagement (UNESCO, 2021).

Therefore, in accordance with the principles of Open Science, RIs must a) make scientific knowledge openly available, accessible and reusable for everyone, b) they increase scientific collaborations and the sharing of information for the benefits of science and society, and c) open the process of scientific knowledge creation, evaluation and communication to societal actors beyond the scientific community (Di Donato, 2026; UNESCO, 2021). The case study this book presents demonstrates how FOSSR, which operates in the domain of social science sesearch, can develop resources to be used for studying the economic and social change –demography and society, social behaviours, structure of the economy, public policies with a special focus on research and innovation policies, providing a set of resources that should enable new research questions, more interdisciplinary approaches and collaborations between scholars and stakeholders.

It may be useful to recall that the open science practices have been the subject of discussions as far as the issue of reproducibility in the fields of social science research is concerned. This point has a relevance also for RIs since one of the advantages deriving from the availability of shared data and resources is to improve the reproducibility of scientific results. However, social science research has some peculiarities with respect to other scientific domains.

Ferguson et al. (2023) conduct "a survey of a sample of social scientists, which includes scholars published in top 10 journals and graduate students in top 20 ranked North American departments, across four major fields: economics, psychology, political science, and sociology." They concentrate the interest on the practices of posting data or codes in online archives and pre-registering hypotheses and analyses. The survey was directed to measure scholars' self-reported lifetime use of practices (at least once) and private attitudes toward open science practices, and their perceptions of their field's norms regarding these practices.

Results highlights that "lifetime usage of open science practices, on average, is high." Furthermore, the favour toward open science practices remains high for both author that have already published papers in scientific indexed journals and graduates, for all the fields of science. The support for open science practices is predictive of lifetime usage. Nevertheless, posting data and codes is reported more favourable that support for pre-registration, with some variations between fields of science (sociologists appear less supportive than scholars in the other fields). Interesting also that "the lifetime prevalence of open science practices has increased over the past decade from 49 to 87%, according to social scientists' recollections of when they first used an open science practice."

This example is useful to understand that the distance between principles and actual practices and attitudes is still large, and the movement toward open science implies a deep transformation of the culture of producing and disseminating scientific results that needs time and cumulative efforts (Chubin, 1985; Gong, 2022).

Davies (2011) presented one further interesting perspective. Speaking about open data initiatives, the author distinguished between "the infrastructure that supports the widest possible range of uses, and the ecosystem in which specialised communities of use emerge, it has shown that open data initiatives frequently need to adopt strategies of co-ordination to provide a stable infrastructure, and strategies of collaboration and community building". This is precisely the challenge that RIs in social science must face.

## 1.4 Benefits and Challenges of RIs for Studies on Economy and Society

As said, the contribution that this comprehensive scientific book wants to provide is to shed light on research infrastructures (RIs) for open research in the broad domain of social sciences. To this aim, it incorporates theoretical foundations, practical insights, and a thorough examination of RIs using the case of the FOSSR project funded under the Italian National Plan of Recovery and Resilience—PNRR EC Next Generation EU. The book is articulated in three main parts that illustrate from different perspectives the benefits that RIs can provide to the studies on economy and society as well as the challenges (organization, sustainability and impact) that they pose.

**Part I** of the book is devoted to set the scene of RIs for social science research in Europe and the linkages with the principles of Open Science to understand the context where data and resources are developed by the different communities of scholars and then provided to the wide community of users. Part I is composed by three chapters which deal with three important topics: the RIs within the Open Science Roadmaps, the fairness and FAIR principles of data, and the ethical issues pertaining the research in social sciences.

In Chap. 2 the policy frameworks that shape research infrastructures in Europe and beyond are analyzed. The authors focus on global and European actors such as EOSC, examining their role in fostering Open Science initiatives. The chapter also discusses national-level policies, particularly the Italian National Plan of Recovery and Resilience (PNRR), and its investment in RIs. Sustainability strategies and the development of Open Science roadmaps are explored to contextualize the evolution of RIs within policy landscapes.

Chapter 3 delves into the FAIR (Findable, Accessible, Interoperable, and Reusable) principles as applied to social science data. It puts in context the role of FAIR principles in ensuring high-quality, ethically compliant research data management. Specific attention is given to case studies where FAIR principles have been successfully implemented, as well as the challenges faced by researchers in adopting these standards within social science research infrastructures.

Based on a scoping literature review that aimed to identify critical ethical issues, existing practices, research gaps and implications for the creation and management of a Research Infrastructure for empirical social sciences, Chap. 4 addresses the ethical aspects of open social science research and discusses measures for guidelines that can ensure responsible open science. It also includes ethical considerations and recommendations for the management of the risks connected to the possibility of indirect identification of research participants in open data.

**Part II** is devoted to depicting FOSSR aims, structure and organization. The different research focus areas allow us to understand how innovation in knowledge creation can be sustained and enabled using FOSSR resources to address different issues in social science research.

Chapter 5 introduces the FOSSR project, outlining its objectives, structure, and key research areas. It positions FOSSR within the larger landscape of Open Science initiatives and explains how it aligns with the goals of the PNRR, particularly in fostering sustainable development and advancing social science methodologies. The chapter also presents the major research themes explored within FOSSR, including societal and economic change, policy design and evaluation, migration, health across the life cycle, and new knowledge production methods. Overall, the chapter overviews the challenges and opportunities associated with these research areas, highlighting the potential innovative contributions of FOSSR.

Chapter 6 addresses the topic of monitoring social and economic change through probabilistic surveys, including longitudinal ones. From this perspective, reference to the Life Course Observatory is essential, as it represents a central infrastructure for comprehensively addressing issues of health, the life cycle, and social change from a unique perspective that considers the different components of the social structure (youth, families, adults, and the elderly).

Along the opportunities and challenges linked to research carried out using panels, Chap. 7 presents the potential of representative research panels to obtain real-time longitudinal data on the opinions of the Italian population on issues affecting society and its development, such as political orientation and geopolitical risk, issues related to civicness, education and scientific research, climate change, economic growth, and inequalities. The triplet of panel resources is completed by Chap. 8 which presents the state of the art and the limitations related to the studies on social behaviors and the new possibilities linked to the POOLPO network of laboratories developed within FOSSR.

Chapters 9 and 10 enter the opportunities of creating new tools and new sets of integrated data to address issues related to the economic and social change. The former chapter presents the opportunities linked to the development of two tools within FOSSR (Policy Learning Platform-PLP and FORECAST) for studies on policy learning to improve the ex-ante assessment of policy instruments supporting an optimal policy allocation of research resources. The latter chapter starts recalling the changes affecting the modes of knowledge production of contemporary research and demonstrates how integrating new and existing datasets and secondary data can improve the capability to investigate issues related to the production of scientific research addressing societal challenges and sustainability.

Chapter 11 discusses the existing data and tools to investigate the structure of the industrial systems using resources provided by FOSSR and the advantages of opening data to scholars for research investigations.

The next three chapters of Part II of the book deal with organizational and technological issues related to the building and maintenance of one RIs. Chapter 12 outlines the technological and organizational architecture of FOSSR. It discusses key components such as data interoperability, security, scalability, and integration with existing research infrastructures. Special attention is given to the design of platforms that support open science principles. Chapter 13 examines the governance model of FOSSR, focusing on multi-stakeholder collaboration. The description of the FOSSR ecosystem points on the decision-making processes, the risk management strategies, and strategies that are likely to ensure the long-term sustainability and impact of FOSSR.

Part II ends with two chapters demonstrating how important training, dissemination and community building are to shape the environment of one research infrastructure devoted to social science research. Chapter 14 explores the training and capacity-building initiatives within FOSSR. It highlights the role of research infrastructures in developing the next generation of social scientists, with a focus on equitable and balanced participation. Chapter 15 details the strategies used to engage the research community and the public with FOSSR. It covers key performance indicators (KPIs) for assessing the project's impact, as well as innovative approaches like action research for fostering community participation.

**Part III** of the volume presents the most important developments as to methods, models and techniques provided by FOSSR. The aim is to highlight the importance of addressing new research questions by using RIs resources that allow for using large sets of integrated data and innovative data treatments. Two chapters are included in this part of the book.

Chapter 16 explores interdisciplinary collaboration within social sciences. It examines best practices (based on the example of Virtual Research Environments-VRE) for fostering partnerships across disciplines and highlights case studies where research infrastructures have facilitated successful collaborative projects.

Chapter 17 delves into the interdisciplinary field of Computational Social Science and how FOSSR as a meta-infrastructure can be beneficial to the discipline. It shows a series of experiences and services developed in FOSSR that encompass various aspects of Computational Social Science, closing with some reflections on the promises and challenges ahead for the project to contribute to this growing field.

The conclusion of the book situates FOSSR within the broader trends of Open Science at the global and national levels. It identifies key challenges in implementing and maintaining research infrastructures for social sciences. It explores technological barriers, societal adoption issues, and the next-generation developments in data platforms and Open Science methodologies. Lessons learned from FOSSR and from other research infrastructures for ensuring the long-term sustainability of open research initiatives are also discussed. We trust that the case presented in this book can contribute to strengthening the implementation of research infrastructures in the social sciences sector.

## References


APRE. (2026). *Fostering research infrastructure ecosystems for addressing complex scientific and societal challenges*. RICH workshop, Rome 25–26 February. Accessed March 11, 2026, from https://apre.it/wp-content/uploads/2026/03/I_Session_1_Sgard.pdf

Chubin, D. E. (1985). Open Science and closed science: Trade-off in a democracy. *Science Technology and Human Values, 10*(2), 73–81.

Cramer, K., & Hallonsten, O. (2020). *Big science and research infrastructures in Europe*. Edward Elgar.

Cramer, K. C., & Rüffin, N. V. (2025). The EUropeanisation of research infrastructure policy. *Minerva, 63*, 45–68. https://doi.org/10.1007/s11024-024-09544-0

Davies, T. (2011). *Open data: Infrastructures and ecosystems*. Open Data Research. Accessed March 11, 2026, from https://d1wqtxts1xzle7.cloudfront.net/96946765/Social_Life_of_Data_Infrastructure_and_Ecosystem_Paper

Di Donato, F. (2026). Open Science and the role of social sciences research infrastructures and data. In L. Taddei & M. Paolucci (Eds.), *Longitudinal data infrastructures in Europe*. Springer. https://doi.org/10.1007/978-3-032-07005-0_1

European Commission. (2016). *European charter for access to research infrastructures. Principles and guidelines for access and related services*. EU Publication.

Ferguson, J., Littman, R., Christensen, G., Paluck, E.L, Swanson, N., Wang, Z., Miguel, E., Birke, D., Pezzuto, J.H. (2023). Survey of open science practices and attitudes in the social sciences. Nature Communications, 14:5401 doi:https://doi.org/10.1038/s41467-023-41111-1.

Gong, K. (2022). Open Science. The science paradigm of the new era. *Cultures of Science, 5*(1), 3–9.

Hallonsten, O. (2020). Research infrastructures in Europe: The hype and the field. *European Review, 28*(4), 617–635.

OECD. (2023). *COVID-19 and policy for science*. OECD Science, Technology and Industry Policy Papers, 152, OECD Publishing, Paris. https://doi.org/10.1787/8f86e60b-en

OECD. (2025). *Fostering research infrastructure ecosystems for addressing complex scientific and societal challenges*. OECD Science, Technology and Industry Policy Papers, 184, OECD Publishing, Paris. https://doi.org/10.1787/34797721-en

OECD/Science Europe. (2020). *Optimising the operation and use of national research infrastructures*. OECD Science, Technology and Industry Policy Papers 91, OECD Publishing, Paris. https://doi.org/10.1787/7cc876f7-en

Ribeiro, M. (2021). Towards a sustainable European research infrastructure ecosystem. In H. P. Beck & P. Charitos (Eds.), *The economics of big science. Essays by leading scientists and policymakers* (pp. 7–14). Springer.

Schipper, F., & Schot, J. (2011). Infrastructural Europeanism, or the project of building Europe on infrastructures: An introduction. *History and Technology, 27*(3), 245–264. https://doi.org/10.1080/07341512.2011.604166

Spinello, A. O. (2017). *Il cambiamento nel modo di produzione della conoscenza. Un'esplorazione degli effetti delle infrastrutture di ricerca nel lavoro degli scienziati*. Doctoral dissertation. https://tesidottorato.depositolegale.it/handle/20.500.14242/90757

UNESCO. (2021). *UNESCO recommendation on open science*. Accessed March 11, 2026, from https://unesdoc.unesco.org/ark:/48223/pf0000379949.locale=en

# Chapter 2
# Research Infrastructures and the Open Science Roadmap: European and Italian Strategies and Policies

**Massimiliano Saccone, Daniele Bruschi, Marco Sprocati, and Alessandra Maria Stilo**

## 2.1 Introduction

Research Infrastructures are facilities, resources, and services of a unique nature, used by the scientific and innovation communities to conduct and support top-level research across all scientific domains, fostering innovation, without restrictions of institutional or national affiliation.

European Research infrastructures are strategic assets to boost R&I, scientific discoveries and deep-tech developments at regional, national and European levels. They have a strong role in increasing the R&I potential of academia and industry in local and regional ecosystems, thus enhancing competitiveness, innovation in strategic areas, and overcoming fragmentation. The Council conclusions on strengthening the competitiveness of the EU and overcoming the fragmentation of the European Research Area, encouraged better use and deployment of Research Infrastructure facilities and services by academia and industry, including Small and Medium-sized Enterprises (SMEs) and start-ups across the entire EU.

This chapter systematically analyses—within the open science conceptual framework—the strategies, policies, plans, programs and main system initiatives at the European and Italian levels aimed at strengthening research infrastructures (RI), promoting and facilitating through them the systemic implementation of Open Science and Open Innovation policies and practices, broadening access to and use of

M. Saccone (✉) · D. Bruschi
Department of Social Science and Humanities, Cultural Heritage—CNR (DSU-CNR), National Research Council of Italy, Rome, Italy
e-mail: massimiliano.saccone@cnr.it; daniele.bruschi@cnr.it

M. Sprocati · A. M. Stilo
Institute for Research on Sustainable Economic Growth—CNR (IRCrES-CNR), National Research Council of Italy, Rome, Italy
e-mail: marco.sprocati@cnr.it; alessandramaria.stilo@cnr.it





G. Cerulli, E. Reale (eds.), *Research Infrastructures for Open Science in Social Science Research*, https://doi.org/10.1007/978-3-032-29575-0_2

RI in an open, secure, effective and sustainable manner not only for the benefit of the scientific communities, but also, more broadly, for the benefit of other stakeholders in the European and national research and innovation system, including enterprises, third sector, policy makers, public administrations and civil society.

## 2.2 European Strategic Guidelines for RIs Policies

European research and technology infrastructures, by design, strengthen transnational cooperation and institutional alignment. As highlighted in the Council Recommendation (European Commission, 2025a), they are regarded as "cornerstones of the European Research Area" and as key instruments for promoting "cohesion, resilience, and openness." At a time when European integration is confronted with both internal and external challenges, research infrastructures represent a long-term investment in unity, interoperability, and shared capacities.

Moreover, these infrastructures uphold core EU values, including the open and secure circulation of knowledge, researchers, services, and capital—as articulated in the Horizon Europe legal framework and in the ESFRI Roadmaps. They also contribute to reducing digital and data divides among Member States. This is especially relevant for the social sciences, which must navigate fragmented statistical ecosystems, heterogeneous data practices, and uneven regulatory environments.

The European Commission plays a central role in defining, assessing, and implementing strategies and instruments to ensure that Europe is equipped with world-class, sustainable Research Infrastructures. In doing so, it works closely with EU Member States and with countries associated with Horizon Europe—the EU's key funding programme for research and innovation—while ensuring that research infrastructures remain open and accessible to all researchers in Europe and beyond.

The Key Objectives of the coordinated and multilevel actions to strengthen Research Infrastructures, implemented by the European Commission and Member States, focus on:

- reduce fragmentation within the research and innovation ecosystem;
- avoid duplication of efforts;
- improve coordination in the development and use of Research Infrastructures;
- establish strategies for new pan-European Research Infrastructures as well as for mature intergovernmental or national initiatives;
- join forces at the international level to build and operate large-scale, complex, or costly infrastructures, to address global challenges, and to leverage the combined skills, data, and expertise of the world's leading scientists;
- foster the innovation potential of Research Infrastructures by increasing industry awareness of available opportunities, and by promoting the co-development of advanced technologies;

- employ Research Infrastructures as instruments of science diplomacy—using scientific collaboration to tackle shared challenges and build international partnerships.

The European Commission also provides the Charter for Access to Research Infrastructures, which outlines the principles and guidelines to be followed when defining access policies for Research Infrastructures (European Commission: Directorate-General for Research and Innovation, 2024). Specifically:

- Promoting Open Science and FAIR Principles: The revised Charter places strong emphasis on open science, advocating transparent sharing of knowledge, results, and tools. It underscores the importance of adhering to the FAIR principles—Findable, Accessible, Interoperable, and Reusable—to ensure that research data and outputs remain accessible, usable, and reproducible across scientific domains.
- Enhancing Research Security and Strategic Autonomy: In line with the EU's *Global Approach to Research and Innovation*, the updated Charter integrates considerations of economic and research security, as well as open strategic autonomy. This framework ensures that Research Infrastructures are equipped to respond to emerging opportunities and threats while maintaining the highest standards of integrity and security.
- Adapting to New User Communities: Acknowledging the expanding role of Research Infrastructures in supporting innovation and entrepreneurship, the revised Charter explicitly addresses the needs of new user groups, particularly industry stakeholders and small and medium-sized enterprises (SMEs). By doing so, it facilitates broader access to cutting-edge facilities, services, and expertise beyond traditional academic constituencies.
- Mitigating the Impact of Crises: The Charter highlights the importance of resilience, particularly in the context of crises such as global pandemics. It calls for strategies to mitigate disruptions affecting access to Research Infrastructures, as well as impacts on personnel and user communities, ensuring the continuity and robustness of scientific operations under adverse conditions.

Overall, the revised *Charter for Access to Research Infrastructures* reinforces the European Union's commitment to open science, research security, innovation, and resilience. It provides a comprehensive policy framework enabling Research Infrastructures to thrive, foster scientific discovery, and contribute to the advancement of the European Research Area and the EU's broader strategic objectives.

In line with the EU's and Member States' commitment to the European Research Area and with the shared values and principles set out in the *Pact for Research and Innovation in Europe*, the Charter establishes a set of non-regulatory principles and guidelines to be used as a reference when developing Access policies for Research Infrastructures and related services. Although not legally binding, Research Infrastructures are encouraged to adopt the Charter when revising existing access frameworks or designing new ones, and funding organisations are likewise invited to promote its provisions.

The Charter supports access to RIs to enable innovative research and development, enhance methodological capabilities and workforce skills, and foster scientific collaboration. It also emphasises the importance of engagement with a broad range of social and economic actors—including, where appropriate, businesses, industry stakeholders, and public services—in order to maximise returns on investments in Research Infrastructures and to drive innovation, competitiveness, resilience, and efficiency in the use of limited resources.

Intended as a concise and non-prescriptive reference, the Charter serves as a benchmark for those responsible for defining access policies within Research Infrastructures, their host institutions, and their respective funding bodies. It may also inform policies governing access for research activities, experimental development, education and training, and the provision of specialised services.

Within this policy landscape, the European Commission has adopted a long-term *European strategy on research and technology infrastructures* (European Commission, 2025a), a central component of the *Choose Europe* initiative. The strategy outlines how Europe intends to strengthen and invest in its unique infrastructure ecosystem, ensuring that it remains globally competitive, increasingly accessible, and better aligned with the needs of researchers, innovators, and industry.

At the core of this strategy are Europe's world-class Research Infrastructures, which provide the facilities, data, and services required to advance the frontiers of knowledge and deliver breakthrough innovations. These infrastructures constitute the backbone of the European research and innovation system, supporting activities that range from fundamental scientific discovery to solutions ready for societal deployment and market uptake.

European policies on Research Infrastructures (RIs) aim to ensure the openness, accessibility, and security of world-class, sustainable facilities for researchers and innovators across the European Research Area (ERA). They also seek to consolidate the role of RIs within the broader research and innovation ecosystem and strengthen their capacity to address EU priorities. A long-term strategy is therefore essential to streamline the RI landscape and identify the services and technologies needed to enhance Europe's scientific competitiveness, strategic autonomy, and ability to tackle societal challenges.

To develop an effective and sustainable strategy for European RIs—one that promotes their long-term viability while ensuring openness and broader use across research and innovation communities—it is necessary to:

- monitor RI performance through clear and consistent metrics;
- assess financial support mechanisms for RIs;
- conduct a strategic landscape analysis of RIs in Europe (Council of the European Union, 2025).

Europe's world-class ecosystem of research and technology infrastructures represents a unique asset for scientific progress, innovation, competitiveness, and talent mobility. It is a cornerstone of Europe's attractiveness as a destination for pioneering research. However, maintaining this position requires continuous reinforcement, deeper integration, and improved accessibility across borders.

Over the past 25 years, the EU has made significant investments in new capacities and cutting-edge research infrastructures to consolidate its leadership in science and innovation and attract top global talent. Today, strong investment in strategically important technology infrastructures is equally vital to support Europe's competitiveness, resilience, and technological sovereignty, particularly by accelerating the translation of research into market-ready innovation. This is especially crucial for deep-tech start-ups and scale-ups, which rely heavily on access to advanced infrastructures to test and validate emerging technologies.

The European strategy for research infrastructures sets out a long-term vision to expand and strengthen this ecosystem, maximising its contribution to Europe's scientific, technological, and industrial future. The strategy aligns with the ambition of the proposed Horizon Europe framework for the next Multiannual Financial Framework (2028–2034) and with the proposed European Competitiveness Fund, offering a comprehensive framework for guiding related research and technology infrastructure actions (Council of the European Union, 2025).

This strategy also supports the realisation of the EU's "fifth freedom"—the free circulation of researchers, scientific knowledge, and technology within the ERA—thereby promoting innovation and technological progress. It will help unlock the full potential of Europe's leadership across strategic domains such as artificial intelligence, life sciences, Earth observation, social sciences and humanities, quantum technologies, fusion energy, biotechnology, clean and renewable energy, and advanced materials, while complementing broader efforts to improve the framework conditions for start-ups and scale-ups.

As the EU seeks to strengthen its leadership in the clean transition and reinforce its competitiveness and strategic autonomy, bolstering research and innovation efforts becomes imperative. Fully leveraging the potential of research and technology infrastructures is essential to meeting Europe's longstanding objective of investing 3% of GDP in research and development.

Research and technology infrastructures are critical to closing Europe's innovation gap with other world regions, as highlighted in the Draghi Report and the Competitiveness Compass (Draghi, 2024). They provide the facilities where breakthrough ideas can be conceived, tested, and transformed into market-ready solutions. By leveraging their collective strengths, these infrastructures enable the pooling of resources, the sharing of knowledge, and coordinated action across the European research and innovation (R&I) ecosystem.

Because research and technology infrastructures complement one another, a more holistic and interconnected ecosystem approach is needed. Such an approach would exploit synergies in service provision, simplify user access, and ensure alignment with EU policy priorities. Strengthening this integration is essential for supporting frontier research, driving deep-tech innovation, and revitalising strategic value chains. Europe already offers advanced capacities that allow innovative firms—including start-ups and scale-ups—to access world-class facilities, validate emerging technologies, develop standards, and accelerate their market readiness. An ambitious and coordinated infrastructure strategy is therefore indispensable for reinforcing Europe's innovation fabric, economic security, and long-term technological competitiveness.

At a time when major global powers are withdrawing from international cooperation in R&I, Europe must reinforce its position as a hub of open, excellent science. With a research community of more than two million scientists, Europe is well placed to develop transformative solutions in areas such as public health and climate change. Strategic investment in research and technology infrastructures will further consolidate Europe's reputation as a centre of knowledge-driven progress and help attract global talent within the Choose Europe initiative. Expanding capacity also strengthens Europe's role as a trusted international partner while safeguarding key assets for the future.

Over several decades, Europe has built a constellation of world-class research infrastructures—from large single-site facilities to distributed organisations operating across borders—that form the backbone of the European R&I system. As major producers and stewards of scientific data, these infrastructures generate the high-quality datasets that underpin fundamental research and support responses to global challenges such as climate change, pandemic preparedness, and hybrid threats.

The primary mission of RIs is to enable scientific excellence by providing access to state-of-the-art equipment, laboratories, and digital resources that are too costly or complex for individual institutions to develop independently. These infrastructures include major instruments, collections, archives, and scientific data infrastructures, typically publicly owned and sustained.

Since the launch of the European Research Area (ERA) in 2000, more than 60 new pan-European research infrastructures have been established, ranging from large-scale facilities such as synchrotrons and high-intensity lasers to distributed platforms in life sciences, energy, the environment, and the social sciences and humanities. Many operate under the legal framework of the European Research Infrastructure Consortium (ERIC), which provides a unique legal framework for research infrastructures of pan-European relevance.

Since 2002, the European landscape has been guided by the European Strategy Forum on Research Infrastructures (ESFRI). Its roadmaps and landscape analyses inform strategic investment decisions: the current roadmap represents more than €25 billion in total investment and over €2 billion annually in operating costs. EU funding for 2021–2027 adds an additional €2.4 billion to support scientific instrumentation, transnational access, and the design of new infrastructures. ESFRI's analyses, which map existing capabilities and identify strategic gaps, increasingly shape national strategies. The European Regional Development Fund has also played a key role in strengthening regional R&I capacity through infrastructure investment.

Under Horizon Europe, the EU will continue to provide world-class sustainable research infrastructures that remain open and accessible to researchers from Europe and beyond. The programme also promotes the use of existing infrastructures, including those supported by EU Cohesion Policy funding.

In this context, strengthening the capacity of RIs to support scientific advancement and innovation is essential. This includes enabling open and excellent science in line with the FAIR principles, while contributing to EU policy objectives and international cooperation efforts.

As global competitors intensify their investment in large-scale research facilities, Europe must respond decisively. A renewed European strategy for research and technology infrastructures is therefore crucial to maintaining scientific leadership and technological competitiveness.

Research and technology infrastructures are indispensable for addressing complex, interdisciplinary scientific questions and for unlocking the potential of emerging technologies such as artificial intelligence, which have a significant impact on European social and economic development. The IRs must also serve an increasingly diverse user base, including innovative small and medium-sized enterprises (SMEs), start-ups, scale-ups, and heterogeneous research communities. Despite IRs strategic importance, Europe's ability to consolidate a robust infrastructure ecosystem continues to be constrained by several structural challenges:

- Fragmented policies and funding: while research infrastructures benefit from strategic guidance through ESFRI, technology infrastructures lack a coherent EU-level investment framework. Budget limitations, dispersed funding streams, and insufficient private investment slow the development and renewal of critical capacities;
- Limited collaboration across infrastructures: cross-sectoral and cross-border synergies remain underexploited. This reduces opportunities for shared access and coordinated services, while reinforcing territorial disparities across the ERA;
- Insufficient access opportunities and complex procedures: cumbersome administrative processes, high access costs, and limited visibility of available services hinder access for researchers and companies. These barriers are particularly acute for start-ups, as highlighted in the EU *Start-up and Scale-up Strategy;*
- Skills gaps: rapid technological evolution requires continuous upskilling of technical and scientific personnel to ensure that infrastructures remain at the cutting edge, attract top talent, and provide high-quality support to users;
- Underuse of digitalisation and AI: increased digitalisation, enhanced data-sharing capabilities, and broader adoption of AI tools are needed to reinforce the functionality, resilience, and efficiency of infrastructures and to reduce operational and access costs;
- Limited reuse of research data: the exponential growth of research data—especially in domains with high AI integration—is outpacing current capacities for effective use. Efficient and secure data storage and management, aligned with FAIR principles, is essential to ensure that data can be meaningfully reused for scientific and technological progress.

The European strategy's overarching objective is therefore to ensure that scientists, researchers, innovators, inventors, and industry in Europe have at their disposal easily accessible, cutting-edge facilities, high-quality data and tailored services that drive scientific and technological excellence, industrial competitiveness, and well-being of people. This entails:

(1) **strengthening the European ecosystem of research and technology infrastructures** through a holistic approach to capacity building and mobilising investments, improving the alignment of user needs and available facilities and services, while ensuring alignment with EU strategic priorities.
(2) **bolstering the accessibility of research and technology infrastructures as a continuum of complementary services** for researchers and innovative companies, including startups and scaleups, across the EU, in order to support scientific breakthroughs and boost technology development, testing and validation, accelerating their societal and market-readiness,
(3) **attracting and cultivating talent in Europe through** strong career pathways in research and technology infrastructures, from technicians to scientific leaders, developing new skills and competences, benefitting from the wider *Choose Europe*,
(4) **improving and simplifying the governance framework** for research and technology infrastructures to support long-term investment decisions and promote the alignment of priorities among the EU Member States and stakeholders, strengthening coordination across funding sources and increasing the impact of public investment.
(5) **improving the international dimension and resilience** of research and technology infrastructures through cooperation with strategic partners addressing global societal challenges, improving the integration of candidate and associated countries in the ERA, while at the same time supporting management of risks, in particular related to access to critical data and facilities, fostering EU's sovereignty in critical technologies.

In this context, the Draghi report on 'The Future of EU competitiveness' and the 'Align, Act Accelerate'—report by the Commission Expert Group on the Interim Evaluation of Horizon Europe—highlight the need for substantially increasing the investments in research and technology infrastructures capacities as the backbone of EU competitiveness.

Europe must heavily invest in the upgrading and construction of cutting-edge research infrastructures to ensure global leadership in frontier science and enable breakthrough technological development. These facilities are becoming increasingly complex and costly. The scale of financing required is beyond what any single country can manage alone, and the current pace of decision-making for pan-European investments risks leaving Europe trailing behind global competitors. Strategic, large-scale investment is needed to establish and maintain these cutting-edge infrastructures, ensuring Europe[1] remains the premier region for 'Big Science', which underpins deep-tech innovation (Draghi, 2024).

Research infrastructures need continuous technology development to upgrade equipment, improve services, and meet the evolving needs of R&I users. Co-creation with industry is essential to building and maintaining these capacities. As

[1] Including the EU outermost regions.

highlighted by the ESFRI report on energy and supply challenges (ESFRI, 2021), resilience and crisis preparedness require both short-term greening and long-term investment in technological upgrades.

The need to bridge the EU's innovation gap with its main global competitors requires swift action to identify the unmet needs of EU's innovative companies for research and technology infrastructures services in strategic industrial sectors and technology areas. Addressing these needs will strengthen the development of new technologies in areas of strategic interest for the EU, supporting climate and competitiveness objectives, defence capabilities, and the civil security of citizens.

Boosting the capacities of European technology infrastructures is essential for the development of critical technologies such as advanced materials, semiconductors, biotechnology, and quantum technologies, but also holds for energy, health, transport, connectivity and networks, metrology, agriculture and space or defence, as well as the transition to a circular economy. In such strategic areas, the EU would benefit from coordinated assessment of available facilities and services, their competitiveness in the global landscape, and identification of needs and gaps in the context of EU policy priorities. Establishing robust criteria to identify the infrastructures which can support companies beyond their local ecosystems would enable the identification of common European priorities and the development of joint investment roadmaps. These are necessary for better mobilisation and promotion of better alignment of funding at EU, national and regional levels.

Addressing the fragmentation of technology infrastructure services across the EU requires increased collaboration between research and technology organisations, universities, and other infrastructure operators to develop joint service offers addressed to innovative companies across the EU. Stronger connections between technology infrastructures and research infrastructures operated by industry as well as links with other experimental spaces such as regulatory sandboxes and living labs, should also be pursued.

Developing and sustaining research infrastructures as strategic assets for scientific excellence and industrial competitiveness requires major investment, as outlined in the Pact for R&I in Europe (Council of the European Union, 2021). However, slow decision-making on pan-European research infrastructure investments is weakening Europe's global position. The EU should play a stronger role in supporting cutting-edge infrastructures, alongside Member States and other funding bodies. Closer alignment of EU, national and regional funding is essential—building on existing guidance and best practices.

The ESFRI roadmap and the ERIC framework enable joint investments, but challenges remain distributed ERICs are not fully recognised in national funding systems, and international partner involvement is limited. These issues prevent the full potential of ERICs from being realised.

The ESFRI report on funding (ESFRI, 2024a, 2024b) highlights gaps in tracking funding streams and capturing the full cost of research infrastructure lifecycles—from construction and operation to upgrades and evolving needs. Distributed infrastructures face financing challenges. Many also contribute to broader EU priorities—such as feeding data into Copernicus—but rely solely on R&I funding, threatening their long-term sustainability. These contributions should be reflected in relevant EU programme funding.

To strengthen the research and technology infrastructure capacities, the Joint Research Centre is preparing a series of Flagship projects in view of offering scientists from academia and research institutions, as well as from small businesses, industry, start-ups and scale-ups, further opportunities to develop and test their innovations in a unique research and technology infrastructure continuum with a European perspective.

To increase capacities and investments in European research and technology infrastructures, the Commission is working jointly with Member States and stakeholders to:

- Develop criteria for identifying technological infrastructures of European interest, in synergy with the ESFRI roadmap for research infrastructures.
- Map and assess the research and technology infrastructures capacities in Europe in the context of global competition, policy priorities and user needs, and develop joint capacities investment roadmaps, identifying priority areas for targeted investments in a continuum from research infrastructures to technology infrastructures, including in EU-level sectoral initiatives.
- Invest in building and sustaining critical new capacities for world-class research and technology infrastructures in Europe, spearheaded by EU priorities, facilitating the implementation of strategic initiatives aimed at ensuring long-term global leadership.
- Increase funding opportunities for research and technology infrastructures at EU level and propose specific funding and financing models to encourage a more effective pooling of public and private funding for investments, leading to better exploitation of existing funding frameworks, while also addressing the need to reduce regional disparities.

To further strengthen pan-European research infrastructure capacities, the Commission will:

- Provide a **stable framework for maintaining and upgrading world-class research infrastructures** by providing the support to the **implementation of existing and new roadmaps** for research infrastructure technologies, responding to jointly identified needs and commonalities across research infrastructures and, where applicable, across domains; support the roadmapping for new technology needs, taking into account aspects of digitalisation of operation, standardisation, interoperability, resilience and sustainability of research infrastructures.
- **Support the mapping of research infrastructure funding sources at national, regional and EU level and promote synergies among complementary funding instruments** by promoting good practice and appropriate guidance; where applicable, explore adjusting the conditions and rules of EU funding instruments for combined and complementary funding, notably for research infrastructures regarded as essential infrastructures for EU operational or deployment programmes.

- **Propose a revision of the ERIC Regulation** on specific aspects that cannot be addressed by revised Practical Guidelines such as facilitating the participation of international partners, promoting this legal framework as a reliable vehicle for joint investments.

To improve and optimise the services of European research and technology infrastructure, the Commission will work with Member States and stakeholders to Support and implement measures facilitating transnational and multisite collaboration among technology infrastructures, developing coordinated service offers in strategic technologies, including for defence, and promoting their visibility and uptake.

Maximising the potential of digitalisation and AI in Europe's infrastructures Digitalisation is not only transforming the way research is conducted; it is also transforming infrastructures. Research infrastructures generate vast amounts of reliable research data. Efficient management, reuse and sharing of these data is essential to maximise their value for driving scientific progress, tackling global challenges, and fuelling innovation and AI. The European Open Science Cloud (EOSC), Europe's Data Space for R&I, is developing a federation of data repositories and digital services of research infrastructures and other scientific service providers to provide researchers and innovators with a trusted platform for sharing and reusing high quality, FAIR research data, tools and services across disciplines and borders in Europe. The production of high-volume and high-value data and the use of novel digital technologies, including AI, in service provision can significantly increase the efficiency and accessibility of infrastructures while lowering their operational costs and strengthening security and confidentiality. Building the digital capabilities of research and technology infrastructures includes computational modelling, digital twins and virtual/extended reality.

Research and technology infrastructures can also play an important role to achieve the goals of the European Strategy for AI in Science and in the Resource for AI Science in Europe (RAISE) contributing to the pooling of resources, data and computing capacity for accelerating the responsible use of AI in science (European Commission, 2025b).

Moreover, issues related to the accessibility of certain categories of data for R&I purposes will be explored in the context of the upcoming ERA Act. The Commission will work with Member States and stakeholders to:

Sustain and enhance the EOSC Federation as Europe's research and innovation data space, enabling sharing and reuse of high-quality, FAIR research data, scientific results and digital services; Support compliance with FAIR principles, increasing FAIR data productivity, and connections to EOSC and other relevant data spaces; Support the pooling and development of AI-ready research data as well as tools and services that enable the development of scientific AI models, and their technological applications, accelerating the use of AI in science and, through it, contributing to the pilot phase of RAISE.

For the European Commission, a strategic objective is represented by the need to strengthen accessibility to research and technological infrastructures, through the implementation of an integrated continuum of complementary and interconnected services with high added value for the communities of European researchers and innovators.

Implementing the 'fifth freedom' of the EU single market—regarding the free circulation of researchers, scientific knowledge and technology in the European Research Area (ERA), promoting innovation and technological progress—requires progress towards a single market for research and technology infrastructures services in the EU. From the user and services perspective, the two types of infrastructure form a continuum of complementary facilities and services, which need to be increasingly reflected in access policy. However, research and technology infrastructures have been developed to serve different needs and hence different primary user communities. Transnational access to research infrastructures, based on scientific excellence, has been a longstanding feature of successive EU R&I framework programmes. It enables researchers to use cutting-edge facilities beyond their home countries—a cornerstone of the ERA. These schemes benefit less research-intensive countries greatly and thus help close the innovation gap, as Figs. 2.1 and 2.2 shows. However, access remains fragmented and short-term. There is a need for more sustainable schemes, greater visibility—especially for distributed ERICs—and better outreach to new communities and industry. Consultations highlight the importance of expanding remote and virtual access, and of developing common access policies and user-friendly, interoperable service catalogues. A long-term, one-stop-shop European access scheme would be transformative.

To strengthen the European ecosystem of research and technology infrastructures, which allows us to identify and agree on European priorities, as well as to mobilise and align strategic investments accordingly, an appropriate governance framework is needed, steering a holistic approach while recognising the different missions of research infrastructures and technology infrastructures respectively. The framework must notably consider the need for stable and structural support to frontier and excellent research and a more challenge-driven approach for industrial competitiveness and deployment of strategic technologies.

Strategic planning for research infrastructures is supported by the EU-level governance of ESFRI, which should be further consolidated to address the areas with most fragmentation among Member States. The latest ESFRI Roadmap includes over 60 infrastructures representing over € 25 billion in investment, much of it expected in the coming years. The accompanying Landscape Analysis offers a detailed overview of the state, services, impact, and future outlook of European research infrastructures. ESFRI also shapes national research infrastructure planning, with many countries aligning their roadmaps with their methodologies.

As most ESFRI infrastructures are distributed, they help integrate and connect numerous national facilities and services. Building on this, the strategy aims to further consolidate and streamline the European landscape of research infrastructures, and strengthening their governance, by promoting a more strategic landscape analysis and monitoring to better address European priorities and economic security needs, and to link to the work on technology infrastructures. Beyond specific digital technologies such as *AI or Digital Twin for the innovation* for example,

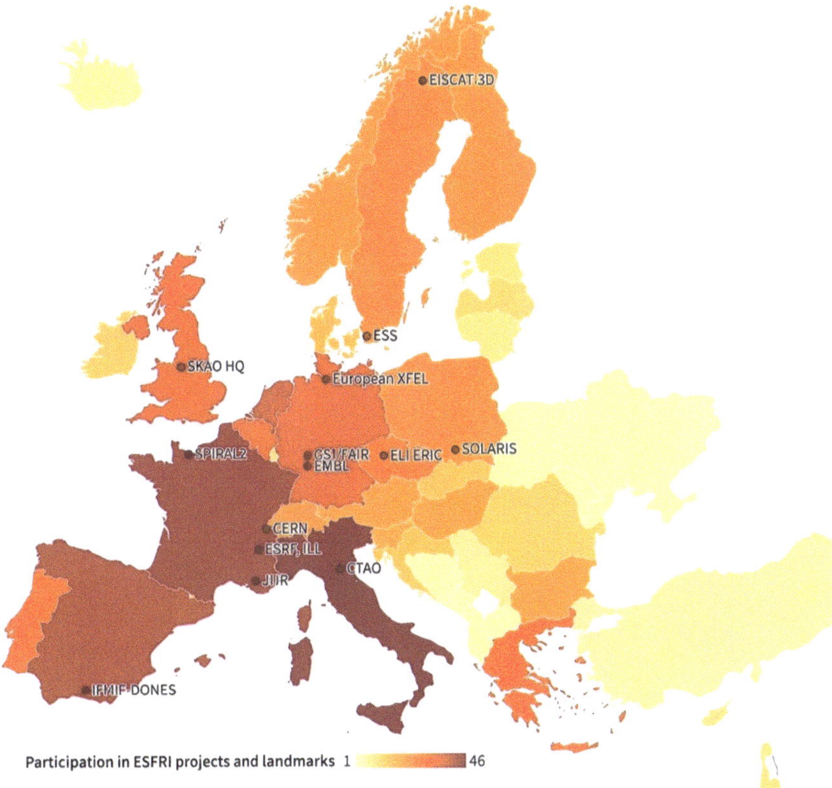


**Fig. 2.1** The figure 2.1 shows the commitment of national governments to supporting research infrastructures on the ESFRI Roadmap, while showing the location of major European research infrastructures—(Source: European Commission, 2025a. Communication from the Commission to the European Parliament, the Council, the European Economic and Social Committee and the Committee of the Regions. European Strategy on Research and Technology Infrastructures—COM(2025) 0497/final 2—https://eur-lex.europa.eu/legal-content/EN/TXT/?uri=COM:2025:497:REV1) (Creative Commons Attribution 4.0 International—CC BY 4.0 licence)

there is currently no coordination mechanism in the EU to facilitate cooperation and dialogue on research and technology infrastructures among Member States, regions and territories (policy makers/decision makers), research communities and institutions, and stakeholders. Setting up an effective and inclusive multi-actor governance framework is necessary to identify existing service gaps and new strategic priorities at EU level to meet industry needs and to facilitate coordinated investments in technology infrastructure, leveraging public and private funding for large-scale upgrades or new facilities. A robust coordination mechanism will provide a platform for strategic, forward-looking reflection, mutual learning, development of common standards and monitoring of the implementation and outcomes of agreed actions.

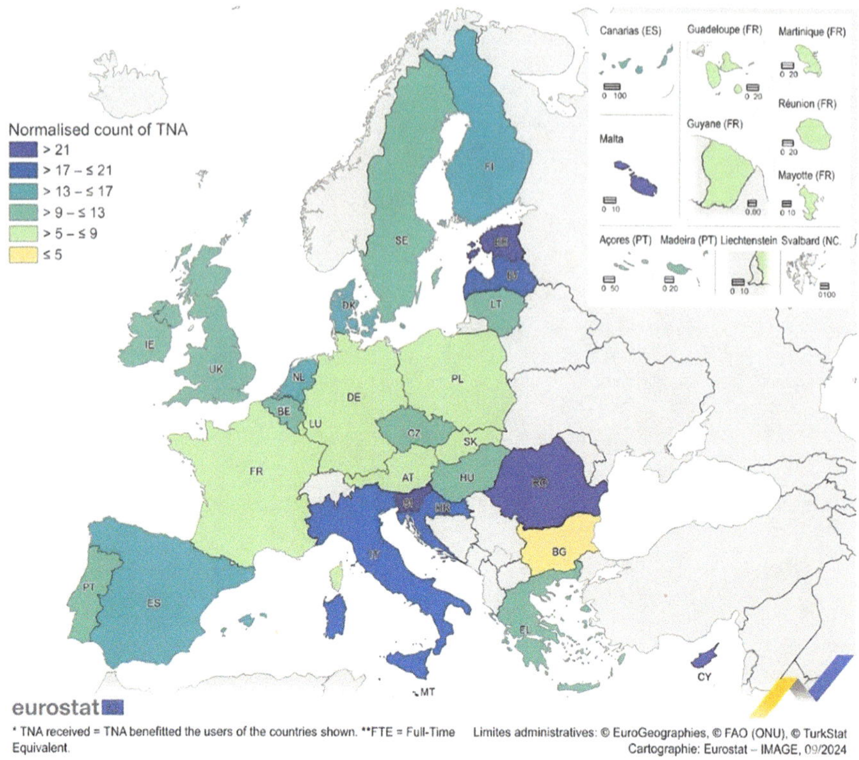


**Fig. 2.2** Transnational access to research infrastructures provided by Horizon 2020 projects normalised by the number of researchers in each country. (European Commission, 2025a) (Source: European Commission—European Research Executive Agency and FAO (ONU), 2025—https://eur-lex.europa.eu/legal-content/EN/TXT/?uri=COM:2025:497:REV1) (Creative Commons Attribution 4.0 International—CC BY 4.0 licence)

This work will be done in cooperation with the Research Infrastructures framework, including ESFRI (Reggiani et al., 2017).

The EU-level coordination mechanism for technology infrastructures needs to be supported by dedicated national strategies leading to the prioritisation of investments and robust funding programmes.

In the longer term, a light overarching EU coordination framework would help align research and technology infrastructures policies and streamlining investment and funding mechanisms, ensuring synergies across the entire European ecosystem of research and technology infrastructures while respecting their specific needs and objectives, and the specific domains and policy contexts they operate in. This framework should facilitate further convergence of the research and technology infrastructures governance. In parallel, coherence will be ensured with other European initiatives, with distinct governance frameworks, that provide capacity and infrastructure, supporting the development, uptake and deployment of digital technologies14 including beyond research and innovation.

To strengthen the governance framework for research and technology infrastructures, the European Commission will:

- Propose an overarching EU coordination framework for the research and technology infrastructures ecosystem steering a holistic, synergy-based approach, while recognising the different missions, objectives and policy contexts of these infrastructures;
- Implement a governance mechanism, in collaboration with Member States and stakeholders, that will provide a common framework for a European approach to technology infrastructures;
- Encourage ESFRI, to engage further with relevant stakeholders and review its landscape analysis methodology and long-term vision accordingly. Propose indicators to assess and raise awareness on the strategic relevance of ESFRI Landmarks and ERICs or of their services according to EU priorities, including economic security.

The appeal of European research and technology infrastructures lies not only in their excellence, but also in their role as global cooperation hubs. European research infrastructures are often engaged in international collaboration, especially in Big Science fields, where costs and expertise demand joint efforts. These include, among others, the European Digital Innovation Hubs, High Performance Computing capacities, AI Testing & Experimentation Facilities, as well as AI Factories and Gigafactories as presented in the AI Continent Action Plan.

Global cooperation is also vital for addressing challenges like environmental monitoring, where data gains value through global coverage, like in social innovation and sustainable development. These infrastructures act as tools of science diplomacy, building relationships of trust with regions such as Latin America, Africa, and the Association of Southeast Asian Nations (ASEAN). Supporting international cooperation activities in research and technology also creates opportunities for European researchers and innovators to access world-class instruments and services in other world regions.

At the same time, a rapidly changing geopolitical context calls for increasing the resilience of the European research and technology infrastructures ecosystem to ensure the EU's autonomy and control over its critical research and technology assets, including data and digital resources. In line with the Protect EU Strategy adopted in 2025, this requires actions to address threats related to research and technology infrastructures considered as critical infrastructures for EU economic security, for EU strategic interests, including in the critical technology areas of defence and space, and for key societal challenges such as global health, social innovation and sustainable development, the transition towards a circular economy, energy and food security, climate change, biodiversity loss, and natural or anthropogenic hazards. Such threats can be related to shrinking geographical coverage, loss, leakage or interruption of critical data, limited or expensive access to data, equipment or facilities, as well as to supply resources and instruments. Access to technology infrastructures dealing with critical technologies needs to be carefully managed. The integration of candidate countries and potential candidates as well as associated countries in the ERA is also a key element of the resilience of the research and technology infrastructures.

As pan-European research infrastructures contribute towards the aims and objectives of the European Ocean Commission Recommendation (EU) 2023/2113 of 3 October 2023 (European Commission, 2023) on critical technology areas for the EU's economic security for further risk assessment with Member States strengthen European research and technology infrastructures in the international arena, the Commission is working with Member States to:

- Strengthen the **international dimension of pan-European research infrastructures** and their role for science diplomacy notably through enlarging geographical coverage in high-priority scientific fields, promoting European standards and approaches to access, data management and open science globally, promoting reciprocal access for EU researchers, facilitating exchange of best practices, while ensuring the appropriate levels of security/confidentiality.
- Develop actions to support: (i) the implementation of **risk management, mitigation and contingency** measures for infrastructures, (ii) aligning and coordinating investments across Europe for **trusted and secure storage**, processing and sharing of critical data including through EOSC, and (iii) the development of **data sovereignty** frameworks for secure and efficient data sharing. These will also benefit by cooperating with the EU Observatory on Critical Technologies and relevant research security initiatives of the Protect EU strategy.
- Promote the **integration of candidate countries, potential candidate and associated countries, with a focus on Ukraine,** into the ERA, by supporting cooperation among research and technology infrastructures, and their host organisations, and by facilitating access to European research and technology infrastructures where appropriate.

In connection with the development and implementation of shared strategies and policies for Open Science and Open Innovation, the European Union aims to develop and implement, in collaboration with the Member States, an *European policy* capable of strengthening sustainability, accessibility and resilience of research infrastructures in the European Research Area (ERA) (Reggiani et al., 2017). For the European scientific, technological and social-economic development and for the implementation of the EU policies for Open Science, a central role is played by European research infrastructures and constitute therefore a priority area of intervention of new *ERA policy Agenda.*

This priority objective is broken down into specific, mutually interconnected objectives, as Table 2.1 shows:

- Strengthened Research Infrastructure (RI) services, better adapted to user needs, in the context of contemporary and emerging scientific, technological and innovation challenges and EU policy priorities;
- strengthened European RI ecosystem including through consolidation of existing RI and identification of new RI projects filling gaps;

**Table 2.1** Timeline for implementation of actions—EU Research and Technology Infrastructure. (European Commission, 2025a) (Source: European Commission, 2025—https://eur-lex.europa.eu/legal-content/EN/TXT/?uri=COM:2025:497:REV1) (Creative Commons Attribution 4.0 International—CC BY 4.0 licence)

| Action | Starting |
|---|---|
| **Increasing capacities and mobilising investment** | |
| 1. Develop criteria for identifying technological infrastructures of European interest, in synergy with the ESFRI roadmap for research infrastructures | 2025 |
| 2. Map and assess the research and technology infrastructures capacities in Europe in the context of global competition, policy priorities and user needs, and develop joint capacities investment roadmaps, identifying priority areas for targeted investments in a continuum from research infrastructures to technology infrastructures, including in EU-level sectoral initiatives. | 2026 |
| 3. Invest in building and sustaining critical new capacities for world-class research and technology infrastructures in Europe, spearheaded by EU priorities, facilitating the implementation of strategic initiatives aimed at ensuring long-term global leadership. | 2027 |
| 4. Increase funding opportunities for research and technology infrastructures at EU level and propose specific funding and financing models to encourage a more effective pooling of public and private funding for investments, leading to better exploitation of existing funding frameworks, while also addressing the need to reduce regional disparities. | 2026 |
| 5. Provide a stable framework for maintaining and upgrading world-class research infrastructures by providing the support to the implementation of existing and new roadmaps for research infrastructure technologies, responding to jointly identified needs and commonalities across research infrastructures and, where applicable, across domains; support the roadmapping for new technology needs, taking into account aspects of digitalisation of operation, standardisation, interoperability, resilience and sustainability of research infrastructures | 2025 |
| 6. Support the mapping of research infrastructure funding sources at national, regional and EU level and promote synergies among complementary funding instruments by promoting good practice and appropriate guidance; where applicable, explore adjusting the conditions and rules of EU funding instruments for combined and complementary funding, notably for research infrastructures regarded as essential infrastructures for EU operational or deployment programmes. | 2025 |
| 7. Propose a revision of the ERIC Regulation on specific aspects that cannot be addressed by revised Practical Guidelines such as facilitating the participation of international partners, promoting this legal framework as a reliable vehicle for joint investments. | 2026 |
| 8. Support and implement measures facilitating transnational and multisite collaboration among technology infrastructures, developing coordinated service offers in strategic technologies, including for defence, and promoting their visibility and uptake. | 2026 |

(continued)

**Table 2.1** (continued)

| Action | Starting |
|---|---|
| **Maximising the potential of digitalisation and AI** | |
| 9. Sustain and enhance the EOSC Federation as Europe's research and innovation data space, enabling sharing and reuse of high-quality, FAIR research data, scientific results and digital services. | 2025 |
| 10. Support compliance with FAIR principles, increasing FAIR data productivity, and connections to EOSC and other relevant data spaces. | 2025 |
| 11. Support the pooling and development of AI-ready research data as well as tools and services that enable the development of scientific AI models, and their technological applications, accelerating the use of AI in science and, through it, contributing to the pilot phase of RAISE. | 2025 |
| **Bolstering accessibility** | |
| 12. Support the development of an integrated and sustainable scheme for access to state-of-the-art research infrastructures of European interest, offering a 'one-stop-shop' for access to them, and to a single European portfolio of complementary and cross-domain R&I services of European interest, including AI assisted research infrastructure service navigation. | 2025 |
| 13. Implement pilot access schemes to technology infrastructures for startups and scale-ups, with the view to scaling-up future implementation. | 2026 |
| 14. Test joint research and technology infrastructures transnational access schemes addressing priority areas e.g. advanced materials, clean energy, quantum technologies, AI or health and biotechnology. | 2027 |
| **Attracting and growing talent** | |
| 15. Develop research and technology infrastructures strategies for attracting talent from outside Europe, in line with the Choose Europe approach. | 2026 |
| 16. Support the training of research infrastructure and technology infrastructure staff, while promoting the recognition of their diverse contributions in research assessment. | 2026 |
| **Improving and simplifying the governance framework** | |
| 17. Propose an overarching EU coordination framework for the research and technology infrastructures ecosystem steering a holistic, synergy-based approach, while recognising the different missions, objectives and policy contexts of these infrastructures. | 2026 |
| 18. Implement a governance mechanism, in collaboration with Member States and stakeholders, that will provide a common framework for a European approach to technology infrastructures | 2026 |
| 19. Encourage ESFRI to engage further with relevant stakeholders and review its landscape analysis methodology and long-term vision accordingly. Propose indicators to assess and raise awareness on the strategic relevance of ESFRI Landmarks and ERICs or of their services according to EU priorities, including economic security. | 2025 |

(continued)

**Table 2.1** (continued)

| Action | Starting |
|---|---|
| **Strengthening the international dimension and resilience** | |
| 20. Strengthen the international dimension of pan-European research infrastructures and their role for science diplomacy notably through enlarging geographical coverage in high-priority scientific fields, promoting European standards and approaches to access, data management and open science globally, and promoting reciprocal access for EU researchers, facilitating exchange of best practices, while ensuring the appropriate levels of security/confidentiality. | 2025 |
| 21. Develop actions to support: (i) the implementation of risk management, mitigation and contingency measures for infrastructures, (ii) aligning and coordinating investments across Europe for trusted and secure storage, processing and sharing of critical data including through EOSC, and (iii) the development of data sovereignty frameworks for secure and efficient data sharing. These will also benefit by cooperating with the EU Observatory on Critical Technologies and relevant research security initiatives of the Protect EU strategy. | 2025 |
| 22. Promote the integration of candidate countries potential candidate and associated countries, with a focus on Ukraine, into the ERA, by supporting cooperation among research and technology infrastructures, and their host organisations, and by facilitating access to European research and technology infrastructures where appropriate. | 2025 |

- create more integrated and sustainable schemes to strengthen access to RI and their services, notably for researchers and innovators from across the ERA;
- enhanced impact on research and society and strengthened engagement with industry;
- create better links and a common interoperability framework between different kinds of infrastructures (RIs, technology infrastructures, e-infrastructures, data infrastructures) (Motta et al., 2016);
- encourage greater involvement of stakeholders in RI activities.

## 2.3 European Research Infrastructures, Open Science and the European Open Science Cloud (EOSC)

The European Research Area (ERA) Policy Agenda 2025–2027, as Fig. 2.3 shows, identifies and defines the structural policies and actions of the ERA, which are organized into priority areas as established by the Pact for R&I in Europe (Council of the European Union, 2025).

The ERA has produced major achievements over the past 25 years in core policy areas including research infrastructures, open science, international cooperation,

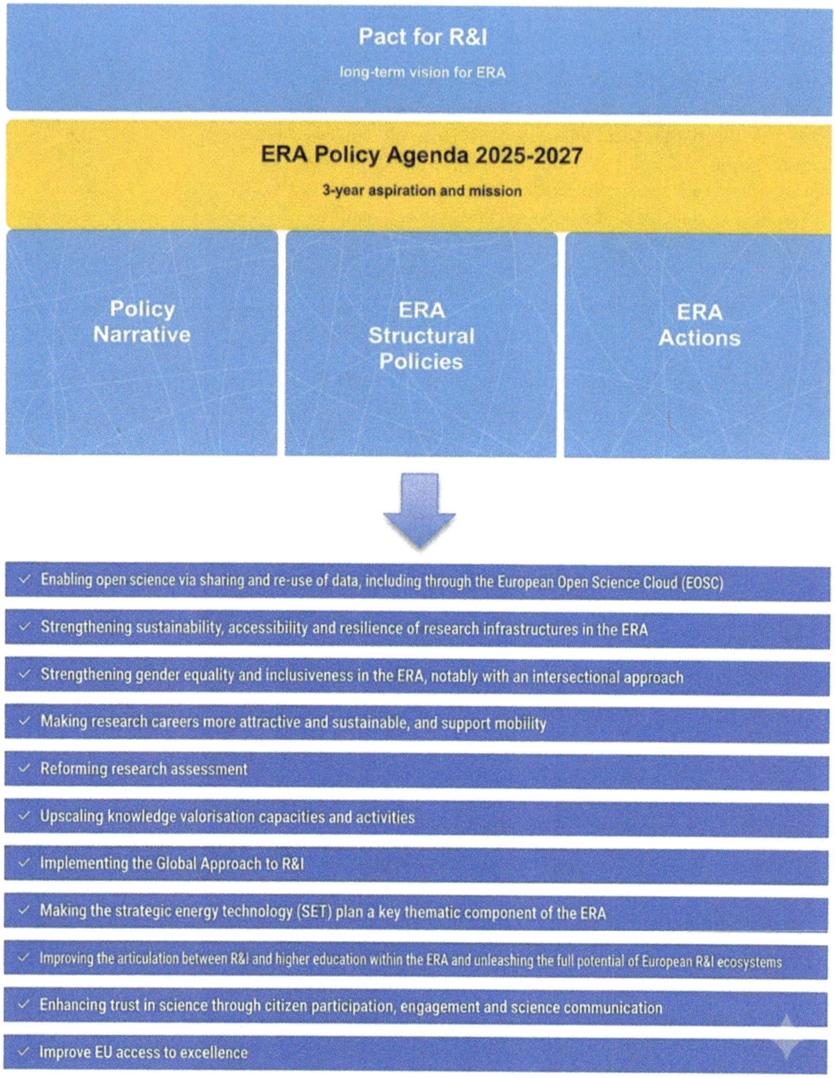


**Fig. 2.3** ERA policy Agenda 2025–2027. (Source: European Commission, 2025: https://european-research-area.ec.europa.eu/era-policy-agenda-2025-2027) (Creative Commons Attribution 4.0 International—CC BY 4.0 licence). Figure 2.3 shows the framework and structure of the ERA Policy Agenda 2025–2027,with a focus on the structural policies identified in the Agenda. (authors' reworking image starting from European Research Area web site, https://european-research-area.ec.europa.eu/era-policy-agenda-2025-2027, 23/06/2026)

gender equality and inclusiveness in R&I, joint programming, research careers and researcher mobility. Contributing to these achievements, among other European initiatives, the European Open Science Cloud (EOSC), which provides seamless access to quality data and digital services while supporting collaboration across borders and disciplines.

One of the key priority areas of ERA concerns the development of a truly functioning Internal Market for knowledge, capable of supporting the social, economic, industrial, and scientific development of Europe. An efficient, effective, and well-functioning internal market for knowledge, based on the free movement of researchers, knowledge, and data, as well as brain circulation, is essential for building a more efficient and inclusive European R&I system. It ensures that efforts and investments are used efficiently and creates the critical mass necessary for effectiveness. To strengthen the EU's competitiveness, it is essential to strengthen its international position and scientific leadership by conducting pioneering R&I across the entire value chain, including fundamental and applied sciences, and by increasing the EU's attractiveness to global talent, retaining talent within the EU, and overcoming the fragmentation of the ERA. The Commission and the Member States, in coordination, where appropriate, with associated countries and stakeholder organizations, will continue to work on this priority through the following ERA structural policies (Council of the European Union, 2025):

- Enabling open science via sharing and re-use of data, including through the European Open Science Cloud (EOSC);
- Strengthening sustainability, accessibility and resilience of research infrastructures in the ERA;
- Strengthening gender equality and inclusiveness in the ERA, notably with an intersectional approach;
- Making research careers more attractive and sustainable, and support mobility;
- Reforming research assessment;
- Upscaling knowledge valorisation capacities and activities;
- Implementing the Global Approach to R&I.

Over the next 3 years, the European Union, in agreement with its Member States, will implement the following mutually interconnected actions, to develop and strengthen the ERA:

- Enforce fairness in open science;
- Promote the European Science for Policy (S4P) ecosystem;
- Facilitate and accelerate the responsible use of AI in science in the EU;
- Improve the safety of research.

The first two structural policies that address the European Research Area—*Enabling open science via sharing and reuse of data, including through the European Open Science Cloud (EOSC)* and *Strengthening sustainability, accessibility, and resilience of research infrastructures in the ERA*—are closely and mutually interrelated and involve the implementation of specific objectives, expected outcomes, and actions developed in a coordinated manner by the EU and its member states.

The first ERA structural policies, which concerns the implementation of open science through the sharing and reuse of research data, services, advanced tools and resources—managed by European Research Infrastructures (RIs) and thematic RIs networks—through the implementation of the European Open Science Cloud (EOSC), which aims to:

- Europe is in the driving seat towards a web of Findable, Accessible, Interoperable, and Reusable (FAIR) research data with established links to other data spaces;
- researchers are provided with better legal conditions and resources to access and reuse publicly funded research results and use publications and data for scientific purposes.

EOSC is recognised by the Council of the European Union among the priority actions of the policy agenda of the European Research Area (ERA) with the objective to deepen open science practices in Europe. It is also recognised as the common European research and innovation data space, articulated with the other sectoral data spaces defined in the European strategy for data.

This ERA structural policy aims to achieve a step change across research communities and research infrastructures in Europe. It seeks to create a better EU legal framework for open sharing, seamless access and reliable re-use of research data and other digital research objects used and produced along the research life cycle (European Commission: Directorate-General for Research and Innovation, 2024). Among the actions envisaged by the are:

- Support the enlargement of the EOSC Federation with several nodes and ensure its scalability through common EOSC Federation standards and use policies, as of 2025;
- conducting further stakeholder consultations and collecting more evidence on identified policy options to make the EU copyright and data legislative and regulatory framework fit for research;
- develop a federation of European research infrastructures and their thematic networks within the EOSC, increasing their impact and adoption by Europe's research and innovation communities.

The EOSC objective is to provide researchers and innovators in Europe with an open and trusted multi-disciplinary environment where they can publish, find and reuse FAIR data, tools and services for research and innovation. Through this environment, EOSC aims to mobilise, align and scale resources across Europe to accelerate open science, higher productivity and increased reproducibility and trust in research.

EOSC should catalyse access for researchers and machines to high-value, machine-actionable research data and other digital objects produced along the research life cycle, such as software and publications. It should enable interoperability of data across and within disciplines, and (re-)use of data by linking them with related tools and services, in line with the 'FAIR' (Findability, Accessibility, Interoperability, Reusability) data principles. EOSC ultimately aims to contribute to a 'web of FAIR (Findable, Accessible, Interoperable and Reusable) data and services' for science in Europe, upon which a wide range of value-added services can be built.

The implementation of EOSC is currently taking place in the context of the EOSC European co-programmed partnership according to a Strategic Research and Innovation Agenda (SRIA), which is co-developed with the EOSC community. Steps are being taken to realise the objective to establish EOSC as a federated system of systems for sharing research data and digital resources across Europe.

The EOSC EU Node, procured by the European Commission, was launched in October 2024. It is the first node of the EOSC Federation, providing a set of data, tools and services to researchers across Europe. It also serves as reference node and facilitates the interconnection of other nodes in the EOSC Federation. It is implemented by federating data, tools and services by data repositories, research infrastructures, e-infrastructures and other scientific service providers across Europe into a network of nodes. Engagement and inclusion of other organisations, European Research Infrastructures (RIs) and thematic networks of IRs are currently being pursued to expand the EOSC Federation with additional nodes for the benefit of researchers (EOSC Federation, 2024).

The development of EOSC governance is steered by the EOSC tripartite governance involving the EU represented by the European Commission, the participating countries represented in the EOSC Steering Board and the research community represented by the EOSC Association. The EOSC Steering Board is composed of the EU member states and countries associated to Horizon Europe, with the aim to provide advice and expertise to the Commission in relation to the strategy for the implementation of EOSC as part of the ERA actions, to support coordination of and synergies with European and national policies and investments in EOSC and to help monitoring the overall EOSC strategic development and implementation.

The EOSC Association is an international non-profit organisation under Belgian law that aims to provide a single voice for advocacy and representation of the broader EOSC stakeholder community.

The EOSC tripartite governance ensures dialogue and strategic coordination towards achieving the EOSC policy objectives. It typically meets twice a year to discuss achievements of the implementation of EOSC and strategic orientations for its future development. See the published reports of past meetings and the EOSC tripartite policy narrative for EOSC. The EOSC Tripartite governance is also addressing options for the governance, operations and financing of EOSC after the end of the current funding framework to ensure the long-term sustainability and uptake of EOSC as the common European research and innovation data space.

The digital age, the most recent stage in an evolving continuum of ways in which technology has supported science and innovation, presents an opportunity to improve the conduct of research in multiple directions, including with regard to openness, speed of access to scientific results, reproducibility and multidisciplinarity. This should result in better science, increased trust in science, and an improved ability to meet global challenges. However, this potential will only be realised if research infrastructures evolve to allow scientists to exploit, in an easy-to-use and integrated environment, the (vast amounts of) relevant data being produced.

EOSC will help deliver Europe's contribution to the realisation of scientists', and science's, potential in the digital age, enhancing Europe's leadership position in exploiting digital capabilities at the service of science. It is an integral part of, and supports, the European Commission's strategy for realising and revitalising the European Research Area (ERA). In particular, it helps deliver the policy priorities of *Open Innovation, Open Science and Open to the World* (European Commission. Directorate-General for Research and Innovation, 2016) and the goal of findable, accessible, interoperable and reusable (FAIR) data. It also contributes to the six priorities driving the EC's work programme for 2019–2024, and to the specific objectives of the Horizon Europe framework programme. Three overarching objectives form the driving force in building EOSC and developing the EOSC ecosystem. These are laid out in a matrix, known as the EOSC Objectives Tree (Fig. 2.4), which also identifies the main problems, barriers and benefits (EOSC Association, 2024).

In addition, a set of guiding principles has been agreed upon with academic and research institutions and IRs involved in the EOSC community. These principles will help position EOSC within Horizon Europe and the next Framework Programme and shape its development:

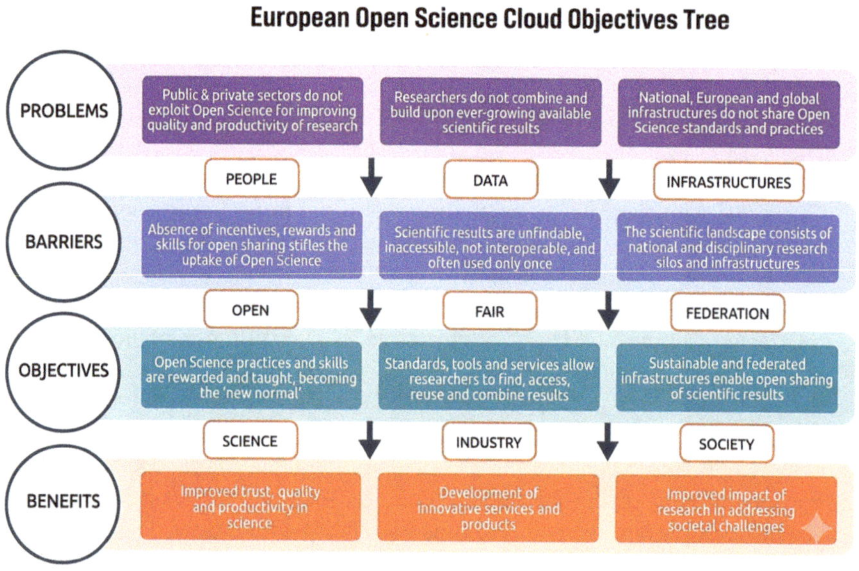


**Fig. 2.4** European Open Science Cloud Objectives Tree (Source: Horizon Europe Co-programmed Partnership for the European Open Science Cloud (EOSC), 2024. *Strategic Research and Innovation Agenda (SRIA) of the European Open Science Cloud (v1.3, 2024)*—https://doi.org/10.5281/zenodo.17582648*) (Creative Commons Attribution 4.0 International)*

- **Research-community centred**: EOSC will place research at the centre of the initiative and will thus prioritise engagement with research communities to understand their requirements, helping them and ensuring academic sovereignty of research data.
- **Multi-stakeholderism**: EOSC will succeed if and only if it follows a multi-stakeholder approach;
- **Openness**: EOSC will ensure that research artefacts are 'as open as possible, as closed as necessary';
- **FAIR principles**: EOSC will assemble research artefacts that are findable, accessible, interoperable and reusable;
- **Federation of infrastructures:** EOSC will federate existing and upcoming research infrastructures;
- **Machine-actionable**: EOSC will strike the right balance between machines and people in delivering the services that will serve the needs of European scientists.

Building on the guiding principles, a number of recommendations for research communities and policy makers have been identified, to help them progress towards an Open Science ecosystem that is based on, incentivises and facilitates Open Science principles and practices in performing and sharing science. Research communities should:

- Normalise their Open Science processes (standards);
- Regulate them (policies);
- Facilitate their implementation (guidelines and frameworks, e.g. information models that describe flows and elements);
- Make sure their thematic services embed Open Science aspects by design (roadmaps).

The EOSC recommendations have provided a basis for determining the action areas that will help deploy the EOSC ecosystem and be part of the EOSC programme over the Horizon Europe and next programme framework period. For each action areas the status has been assessed, gaps identified and priorities proposed; the priorities, in turn, have helped determine the roadmap and key performance indicators for the near future.

The seven action areas relating to social, financial, legal, educational, cultural challenges and prerequisites to implementing the EOSC ecosystem—referred to as the *boundary conditions*—focus on:

- **Rules of Participation.** A process of change in the research environment is required to adopt Open Science practices, make digital research objects FAIR and federate research data infrastructures. The Rules of Participation (RoP) provide transparent and consistent terms for involvement in EOSC, helping to build the trust and confidence required to support and deliver this process of change.
- **Landscape monitoring.** Sustainable long-term monitoring of EOSC landscape developments—the infrastructures, initiatives, investments, and policies at national and institutional levels—is required to allow informed decisions on EOSC.

- **Funding models.** Viable funding models are an essential element of ensuring an operational, scalable and sustainable EOSC ecosystem.
- **Skills and training.** In order to leverage the potential of EOSC for open and *data intensive* research, a key challenge for Europe is to ensure the availability of highly and appropriately skilled people. The vision of a strong EOSC ecosystem that exploits digital technologies and has data and software at its core necessitates comprehensive skills and education strategy.
- **Rewards and recognition.** Culture changes need to be realised in the way scientists are appraised, by looking at their broader contribution to education, research, impact and leadership. A responsible rewards and recognition system is a catalyst to foster good research practice and quality in terms of content, openness, scientific integrity and contribution to society.
- **Communication.** EOSC's diversity of stakeholders requires a communication policy that meets the different needs of each group, providing clarity on the why, how and what of EOSC, and sending out its messages in a consistent way.
- **Widening to public and private sectors and going global.** To successfully extend the EOSC ecosystem beyond the core research community, EOSC must demonstrate value and impact that is relevant and meaningful to the diverse groups belonging to the broader public sector and to the private sector. In parallel, there is clearly a global dimension to EOSC, a common vision that enables Europe to enhance scientific collaboration with other parts of the world and drive a cultural change towards Open Science, which EOSC must respect and exploit to maximise its potential impacts.

EOSC aims to be a major European vehicle for helping transform individual research efforts into collective efforts to face global challenges such as the climate crisis, clean energy, global poverty, and social and economic inequalities.

Referring to the Objectives Tree (Fig. 2.4), the anticipated benefits of EOSC in the areas of Science, Industry and Society are as follows:

- Opportunities to improve support for researchers, widening opportunities for collaboration by enabling pan-European access to data and services, facilitating rapid delivery and reuse of results at each stage of the research lifecycle, and fostering the development of value-added services.
- Opportunities to improve support for the private and public sector by extending the additional functionalities, services and open data EOSC provides beyond the research community, bringing more actors and investments into the research and innovation process.
- Opportunities to improve European leadership and collaboration in a global setting by positioning EOSC as the European component of a Global Open Research Commons.
- Increased awareness of and trust in scientific research in society, and a higher level of interdisciplinarity and scientific evidence in decision making, planning and strategy at societal level, increasing the return on public investment in science.

In order for the benefits deriving from the strengthening of Open Science and the wide opening of European research infrastructures within the EOSC to be effectively and sustainably achieved, it would be necessary to first promote the development of a common *socio-cultural environment* for the sharing of principles, rules, criteria, methodologies, languages and practices, defining (Reggiani et al., 2017):

- a conceptual framework and methodology shared by all stakeholders involved in the R&D system (Reference Framework);
- the fundamental values and processes of the R&D system to be addressed at multiple levels and in different areas of intervention;
- a common language among the various stakeholders and research and innovation communities, going beyond the specificities of individual entities (policymakers/institutions/companies/individuals) and groups of entities (EU, disciplinary and/or national communities, research and innovation groups and networks, national and European organizations, etc.).

The Reference Framework (Di Rosa & Saccone, 2019) for framing the policies and rules at play, is complex and heterogeneous and shows a variety of aspects:

- multidimensionality: it concerns different scenarios and sectors in which strategies, actions, and processes are defined and developed, at various levels (macro, meso, micro);
- interdisciplinary and multidisciplinary nature of the issues and problems;
- diachrony, which distinguishes the different phenomena and their mutual relationships.

The multidimensional, interdisciplinary, multidisciplinary, and diachronic approach that characterizes the method adopted within the *Reference Framework* is crucial both for correctly identifying all the actors and stakeholders involved/potentially involved (who), the actions (what), the contexts, rules and tools (how), and the temporal dynamics (when); and for acquiring a broad and comprehensive view of the phenomena implicated.

To this end, it therefore seems necessary to:

- define a holistic and adaptive methodology to be used in the analysis, definition, planning, organization and implementation of interventions for the *European Open Science* and the *Open Innovation ecosystems*;
- systematically analyse, identify, and map the various actors and stakeholders (research communities, policymakers and decision makers, public and private funding bodies, evaluation bodies, ICT and information specialists, institutions, organizations, businesses, trade associations, etc.), in order to have all the information needed to adequately assess needs, strategies, policies, skills, resources, relationships, etc. (landscape analysis);
- analyse and structure knowledge systems of different cultural and communication contexts, identifying their practices, norms, and behaviours (formal and informal), approaches, processes, information channels, and the various technical and scientific jargon;

- analyse, identify and structure *organizational models, regulatory frameworks and tools* for the promotion and optimal management of Open Science and Open Innovation processes, within technological and research infrastructures and the EOSC;
- define and develop multidimensional cultural, educational, and technical-technological interventions to make data and information management processes transparent, and to efficaciously implement and manage open, interoperable, secure, sustainable, and interconnected *web-based knowledge and information ecosystems* within the EOSC. These *web-based knowledge and information ecosystems* will thus be easily usable for monitoring, programming, planning, and management of research and innovation activities and initiatives, across different application areas and at various levels of *stakeholder engagement*;
- systematically monitor the implementation status of interventions and their effectiveness at various levels (macro, meso, micro), through *ex ante*, *in itinere*, and *ex post assessment and evaluation systems* (macro level: political, economic, cultural, social, scientometric and technological analysis; meso level: scientometric, organizational, economic, financial analysis, audit, process monitoring, knowledge transfer analysis, etc.; micro level: knowledge management, performance, soft skills, target and context indicators, etc.);
- optimize the various assessment and evaluation processes through their harmonized integration across the different phases of research and innovation (*ex-ante, in itinere, ex post*) and within research infrastructures;
- verify the stable and contextualized correlation of interventions and their degree of integration and sustainability in the medium and long term.

## 2.4 Research Infrastructures in Italy: The National Research Infrastructures Plan (PNIR) 2021–2027 and the National Plan for Open Science (PNSA)

In the social sciences, a research infrastructure represents a leap in both scale and organizational, scientific, technological and financial commitment compared to standard research efforts. In the European context, local projects can range from individual efforts to small collaborative groups, occasionally extending to EU-funded consortia. Infrastructure, in contrast, is a long-term undertaking that requires not only significantly higher levels of financing, but also Infrastructures, by contrast, are long-term undertakings that demand not only significantly higher levels of funding but also continuity in that funding—a characteristic that distinguishes them from the more episodic nature of conventional research projects. What makes social science infrastructures demanding is their hybrid nature: they are at once technical systems, organizational frameworks, and social contracts. Social science infrastructures must deal with and accommodate evolving legal norms, ethical standards, and shifting societal expectations (Taddei & Paolucci, 2025).

Research infrastructures in the social sciences are not only scientific ecosystems; they also serve as strategic assets for policymakers, supporting the analysis of socio-economic trends, the assessment of policy impacts, and the development of sectoral strategies at European, national, and regional levels. By design, European research infrastructures (RIs) foster transnational cooperation and institutional alignment. As highlighted in the Council Conclusions on Research Infrastructures (Council of the European Union, 2022), they are "cornerstones of the European Research Area" and instruments of "cohesion, resilience, and openness." At a time of internal and external pressures on European integration, the RIs embody long-term investments in interoperability, shared capacity, and unity.

Furthermore, they advance core EU priorities such as the free circulation of knowledge and the implementation of Open Science, as emphasized in the Horizon Europe legal framework, the European Research Area Policy Agenda 2025–2027 (Council of the European Union, 2025), and in the ESFRI Roadmaps. They also help bridge the digital and data divides between member states—especially important for the social sciences, which must contend with fragmented statistical systems and uneven regulatory practices.

The Research Infrastructures (RIs) respond to researchers' needs for advanced digital services—networking, computing, data management, and other essential tools—while contributing to the emergence of Open Science as a foundational component of the European Research Area. The 2021 ESFRI Roadmap underscores this role, noting that "most of the Research Infrastructures on the ESFRI Roadmap are at the forefront of the Open Science movement and make important contributions to the digital transformation by transforming the whole research process according to the Open Science paradigm" (ESFRI, 2021).

European, federated and national Infrastructures provide trusted, open environments for storing, sharing, and re-using scientific data, as well as for offering resources, tools, and services that support frontier research and the uptake of Open Science practices (ESFRI, 2024a, 2024b). Over the past decade, the European e-research infrastructure ecosystem has evolved through two major developments: the creation of a sustainable advanced computing infrastructure under EuroHPC, and the emergence of the European Open Science Cloud (EOSC), envisioned as a European Data Space for Science, and Innovation.

The EOSC provides researchers with a seamless virtual environment for the storage, management, analysis, and reuse of data across borders and disciplines by federating existing infrastructures. Its development is driven by projects funded by the European Commission (EC) alongside initiatives from Member States (MS) and Associated Countries (AC). EOSC is expected to further consolidate the European RI ecosystem by providing open access to advanced digital capabilities and expertise, enabling collaboration and supporting data- and computing-intensive science.

Over the past decade, Open Science has become a policy priority in Europe, establishing itself as the standard method within the European Commission's research and innovation funding programmes.

Digital transformation is reshaping research practices by introducing new tools for accessing, analysing, sharing, and preserving research data. As datasets expand in size and complexity, computational demands grow exponentially, driven by modelling, simulation, and AI-assisted analysis. This evolution requires the development of a common and interoperable European ecosystem of digital research infrastructures capable of supporting the secure and wide use of AI for research and innovation activities, through the EOSC and EuroHPC infrastructure.

In Italy, the National Research Programme (PNR 2021–2027) provides the strategic multi-level framework for national research policies (MUR, 2021). It encompasses the development of research infrastructures and Open Science under the coordination of the Ministry of Universities and Research and is linked to two strategic documents: the National Research Infrastructure Plan (PNIR) (MUR, 2021a) and the National Plan for Open Science (PNSA) (MUR, 2022).

As stated in the PNIR, "RIs are crucial to our ability to make scientific progress and promote open innovation." The PNIR aims to provide more detail on the technical and strategic Italian plan for Research Infrastructures (RIs), by defining and updating national priorities. The PNIR details national priorities by integrating both European and national perspectives, with explicit reference to Horizon Europe and the role of ESFRI in shaping the European RIs landscape (Di Donato, 2025).

According to the PNIR, RIs must be attractive, open physical or virtual environments that support cutting-edge research, experimentation, training, and innovation. Open access to data, equipment, services, and expertise is essential for advancing knowledge and addressing global societal challenges. RIs also offer valuable opportunities for the private sector to access state-of-the-art technologies and develop innovative products and services. Promoting open, secure, and sustainable access—whether virtual, remote, or physical—is therefore crucial.

To assess the strategic relevance and impact of RIs in Italy, the PNIR, in accordance with the criteria defined by ESFRI and the PNR priorities, has identified eight evaluation parameters:

- **Scientific excellence**
  The aspects related to the number of Italian and foreign researchers who have had access to the infrastructure, the publications produced and the European projects financed using the RIs are evaluated.
- **Socio-economic impact**
  This criterion is linked to the economic and social impact of the infrastructure, whether actual or potential. Aspects that consider the impact the RI has on the regions are considered, in terms of companies that have benefited from the RI, or that have directly or indirectly created jobs, and patents that explicitly reference the infrastructure;
- **Critical analysis of history and prospects**
  The criterion is primarily linked to the support already received at the national or regional level and, especially, with regard to prospective aspects, to its legal status, both at the national and European levels;

- **Completeness of access policies**
  This aspect is connected to the intrinsic nature of a Research Infrastructure, its access policies, which, by definition, must be "open access." That is, the RI must offer the opportunity, through evaluation procedures (calls for access), to conduct research activities to those who request it, charging, at most, costs strictly related to the out-of-pocket costs of use, if it does not have specific funds for "free" access. Furthermore, this criterion must also consider the fairness of the data produced, compliance with the European Open Science Cloud, currently in the criteria definition phase, as well as the number of Italian or foreign researchers who have had access;
- **International relations and pan-European relevance**
  Various elements are considered. The pan-European relevance of RIs is primarily attributable to the infrastructures included in the ESFRI Roadmap or those that have formally initiated the ERIC application process. Furthermore, value is also given to RIs that, although not ESFRI or have not chosen the legal status of a European consortium, have strong international standing, formalized by their own legal status that involves agreements between different countries. Finally, participation in European projects (Horizon) is also taken into consideration, as it implies recognized pan-European relevance and participation in international research networks;
- **Political commitment and financial support from participating countries**
  This criterion is linked to the participating countries' adoption of binding multi-year financial agreements. In this sense, being a formalized ERIC or in advanced negotiations guarantees the countries' formal commitment, both political and financial;
- **Governance, Management, and Human Resources Management**
  The governance system and management of IR are key aspects of its success. RIs with their own formalized governance and dedicated management staff were considered;
- **Financial Aspects**
  This criterion is closely linked to the IR's sustainability and its ability to attract investment, not only nationally, but also regionally, from structural funds, other regional funds, and even European funds.

In the Italian science and innovation policy landscape, the PNSA forms an integral component of the National Research Program (PNR). It complements the PNIR and aims to establish the conditions for Italy's full participation in European and international Open Science initiatives. The PNSA highlights that the exponential growth of research data requires an acquisition strategy that is "FAIR-by-design." Consequently, new technologies must support the automated acquisition of FAIR datasets, their processing, and the definition of appropriate access and usage rules, in line with developments within the EOSC.

The Plan focuses on open access to publicly funded publications, the FAIR data paradigm, research assessment reform, participation in European initiatives, and the opening of research data generated within research infrastructures. It stresses the need to develop advanced data acquisition strategies, strengthen research data management practices, and train and recruit qualified personnel, such as "data scientists" and "data stewards." Key challenges include metadata automation, sustained investments in infrastructure, specialised training, and the management of legal and ethical constraints. The PNSA also emphasises the importance of national and European coordination.

In this context, the Italian Computing and Data Infrastructure (ICDI) and the Competence Centre (CC-ICDI)—which involves Italian nodes of European Research Infrastructures—has been developed to support the implementation of the PNSA, by promoting the culture and knowledge of the FAIR principles of data stewardship and open science in Italian Research and Innovation system, through coordinated actions, including training and support initiatives, consultancy, and specific open tools and services. ICDI vision is to create a national coordination body that is representative of Italian research infrastructures and interact with national and European institutions on their behalf.

In 2025, the National Research Centre in High Performance Computing, Big Data and Quantum Computing (ICSC) formally joined the EOSC federation as the Italian national node of the EOSC. As the Italian EOSC Node, ICSC will amplify its impact by supporting the national scientific community in adopting FAIR practices and fostering collaborations between academic institutions, research entities, and industry partners for the management and valorisation of scientific data. The decision to apply as the Italian EOSC Node was backed by the Italian Computing and Data Infrastructure (ICDI), which has coordinated Italy's participation in EOSC since 2018. This initiative is fully aligned with ICSC's mission, established just 2 years ago to enable a data-driven value chain to support national growth.

Implementing the PNIR and PNSA is essential not only to accelerate research progress and increase the impact of national research, but also to allow Italy to align with the research and innovation policies of the European Research Area.

In the context of the evolving European strategy for Open Science and the expansion of the EOSC federation, a post-2027 policy framework is being defined. This framework is expected to increase the responsibility of Member States for sustaining and developing national EOSC nodes, consolidating EOSC as an ecosystem of national and thematic components. In this context, the coordinated implementation of the PNIR and PNSA is crucial for Italy's effective participation in the development and governance of the EOSC.

This new phase is conceived as a shared effort in which Member States operate locally while contributing to the definition of common European resources enabling the integration and exchange of data, services, and expertise. Several countries are already advanced in this process, having implemented national open science strategies and allocated dedicated funding. Those that have consolidated governance and financial structures at national level are better positioned within the European decision-making process on shared services and resources.

A timely, coherent, and multilevel implementation of the PNSA and PNIR will also allow Italy to play a leading role in decision-making processes regarding the substantial resources dedicated to open science and research infrastructures at the EU level. The development of the EOSC framework for its operation and development over the next decade has direct implications for the role the European Commission will play through the FP10 Framework Programme, which will be defined in 2026. The operational phase, initiated with the launch of the first EOSC node—EOSC EU Node—in 2025, requires an operational capacity of services that is not compatible with the management carried out in previous grant-funded preparatory EOSC projects. Therefore, at the level of the EOSC Tripartite governance, both solutions under Article 185 or Article 187 of the Treaty on the Functioning of the European Union (TFEU) are being discussed, and hybrid solutions that combine an operational body that will manage and govern the EOSC Federation with the shared services and resources (to be created). Their sustainability must also include the progressive commitment of member countries and the need to continue funding, supporting, and strengthening the various research infrastructures that support specific research and innovation sectors. These should continue to be funded through European, national, and regional framework programs with a view to progressive integration into the European EOSC ecosystem. All solutions impact both the current tripartite structure (the EOSC—Horizon Europe Strategic Partnership) and the national and institutional structure and roles within the EOSC Federation (MUR, 2023, 2024).

The 10-year financial outlook and the timeline for the federation's deployment will be decisive in shaping the EOSC governance model and the organisation of national hubs. The launch of EOSC's operations is a crucial step in the transition to open science as the norm, as its services will underpin, or at least be instrumental in, the implementation of the national research and innovation policies defined in the National Research Plan.

Rapid and coordinated implementation of the measures outlined by the PNSA and PNIR is therefore essential, not only to meet European Council recommendations but also to strengthen the competitiveness of Italian researchers and companies. Expected benefits include increased success rates in European funding programmes, as adherence to Open Science principles is now a positive evaluation criterion and grant agreements contain explicit Open Science requirements. To comply with these mandates, researchers need dedicated tools and services. Timely adaptation of the research system to Open Science standards will ensure that Italian research keeps pace with international developments, increases its global visibility, and enhances the country's attractiveness to foreign researchers. Effective implementation of the PNSA, combined with the strengthening of Italian nodes of European RIs, will also benefit the private sector, which will gain access to advanced resources, services, and research outputs essential for innovation. Italy's timely compliance with the PNSA will consolidate its role in shaping the EOSC ecosystem and ensure full participation in the monitoring and reporting requirements defined within the EOSC Partnership. It will also improve alignment between international reforms in research assessment and national tools supporting new evaluation practices.

Maintaining and enhancing the competitiveness of Italian research requires cultural, financial, and organisational investments across multiple dimensions,

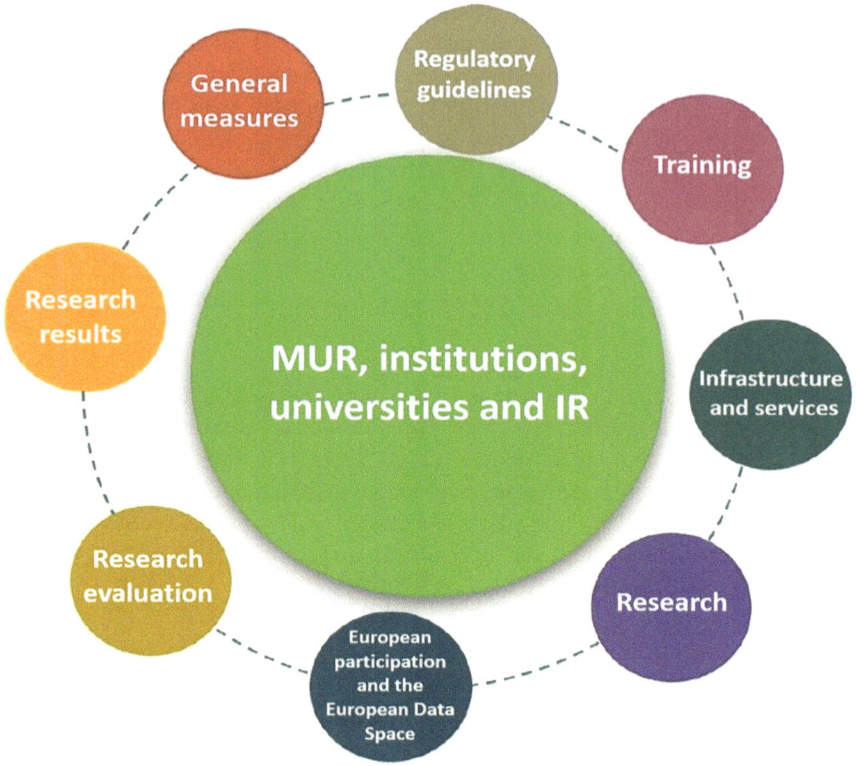


**Fig. 2.5** National Open Science Plan: Role and Priority Actions (authors' adaptation from MUR, 2024) (Source: MUR—Tavolo di lavoro per l'implementazione del Programma Nazionale per la Scienza Aperta, 2024—https://data.d4science.org/workspace-explorer-app/workspaceexplorerapp/DownloadServlet?ids=c67dbb87-d0bd-49ea-b333-54266d5a2555;&viewContent=true&redirectonerror=true) (Creative Commons Attribution 4.0 International)

including regulatory adaptations, skills development, technological upgrades, and innovative operational practices. The PNSA, as the next Fig. 2.5 shows, identifies eight axes of intervention (MUR, 2023):

1. General measures—political and regulatory measures;
2. Regulatory guidelines—actions to support the implementation of the plan and a cultural and organizational change towards open science;
3. Research results—development of targeted actions to strengthen the sharing and effective management of Italian research outcomes and outputs according to FAIR principles;
4. Research evaluation and assessment—actions to support the development of evaluation and assessment methodologies and practices, that enhance the open science approach;

5. Infrastructures and services—implementation and coordinated development of Italian nodes of European research and technology infrastructures, and their opening within the EOSC, to provide the country with advanced services and technological tools suitable for implementing the plan and to form the core of what will be the "National Node" according to the new EOSC governance model being developed for the years following 2027 and in any case for the next European Commission Framework Programme (FP10);
6. Training—actions aimed at developing the skills needed to implement Open Science practices and standards;
7. European Participation and the European Data Space—to connect with the European landscape and emerging initiatives focused on sharing research outputs;
8. Research—to identify new solutions that natively address the need to make research more effective and efficient, as it will be conducted in the next future when open science becomes the norm.

At national level, the Italian National Recovery and Resilience Plan (PNRR) also plays a strategic role by identifying research infrastructures as key assets for national development. Projects launched in 2022 and planned for completion in 2026 include five National Centres for Supply Chain Research, 11 Territorial Innovation Ecosystems, and 49 Research and Technology Innovation Infrastructures, for a total investment exceeding EUR 4.3 billion. Through Italian nodes of European RIs and new national thematic RI networks, a coordinated Italian research and innovation ecosystem is being established to share data, resources, tools, and services securely and openly—integrated within the EOSC—thus maximising the impact and visibility of Italian research outcomes (Antonini et al., 2022). Within the PNRR context, the knowledge assets of Italian and European research institutions are supported by a dedicated ecosystem of research infrastructures, ensuring the visibility, accessibility, and long-term preservation of scientific results through a national network of RI nodes, thematic networks, and national aggregator services forming the basis of the EOSC national node.

## 2.5 National Initiatives: Research Infrastructures in Italy and PNRR: The Case of Social Sciences and Humanities Research Infrastructures

Following the pandemic crisis that began in 2019, the European Union developed the Next Generation EU (NGEU), an extraordinary recovery instrument designed to support Member States in overcoming the socio-economic impact of COVID-19 and to foster a greener and more digital European economy. NGEU is a €750-billion package composed of grants and loans. Its main component is the Recovery and Resilience Facility (RRF), a 6-year programme (2021–2026) with a total budget of €672.5 billion, of which €312.5 billion are allocated as grants and the remaining €360 billion as low-interest loans. To access NGEU resources, each Member State is required to prepare a National Recovery and Resilience Plan (Piano Nazionale di Ripresa e Resilienza, PNRR), outlining reforms and investments aligned with the European policy framework. Italy's PNRR foresees total investments of €222.1 billion: €191.5 billion financed by the EU through the RRF and an additional €30.6 billion provided through a national Complementary Fund, approved by the Council of Ministers on 15 April and authorised by Parliament on 22 April. Overall, 25% of the resources in the Plan are dedicated to the digital transition, while 37.5% target actions to mitigate climate change. Notably, the Plan earmarks €82 billion for Southern Italy out of the €206 billion disposable according to territorial criteria, corresponding to approximately 40% of allocable resources (Antonini et al., 2022). For Italy, the PNRR represents a major opportunity to implement structural reforms and strategic investments, enabling the country to resume a trajectory of fair and sustainable socio-economic growth. The Plan is designed to address longstanding barriers that have constrained Italian development over recent decades, while positioning the national system to respond more effectively to future challenges.

The PNRR is structured around six missions:

1. Digitalisation, innovation, competitiveness, culture, and tourism;
2. Green revolution and ecological transition;
3. Infrastructure for sustainable mobility;
4. Education and research;
5. Inclusion and cohesion;
6. Health.

The Plan is fully consistent with the six pillars of NGEU framework and complies with the regulatory parameters concerning the required shares of "green" and "digital" investments. Within this structure, resources are allocated to ensure consistency with EU priorities and to maximise the transformative potential of the funded interventions (see Fig. 2.6).

Beyond the investment dimension, the PNRR also includes an extensive package of structural reforms. According to the Italian government, the Plan is intended to act as a genuine game changer, capable of breaking the inertia that has characterised the Italian economy over the past two decades. Italy has indeed experienced persistent economic stagnation, largely attributable to declining productivity, an outcome linked to a set of deep-rooted structural deficiencies affecting both the private and public sectors (Giordano & Zollino, 2021). In the short term, the PNRR aims to repair the economic and social damage caused by the pandemic; in the medium and long term, it seeks to tackle long-standing structural weaknesses that have weighed on the country's development, including persistent territorial disparities, gender inequalities, weak productivity growth, and chronically low investment in both human and physical capital. At the same time, the Plan is intended to drive a comprehensive ecological transition.

Within this framework, 'Mission 4—Education and Research', and specifically 'Component 2—From Research to Enterprise (M4C2)', plays a pivotal role in strengthening the country's scientific, technological, social, and economic foundations. The Component, supported by €11.44 billion in funding, aims to

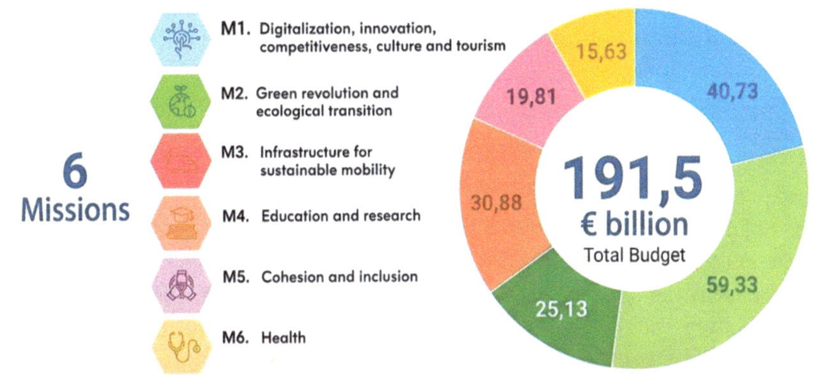


| M4. Education and research | Budget (billion €) |
|---|---|
| M4C1 - *Boosting educational services from kindergartens to universities* | *19.44* |
| M4C2 - *From research to firms* | *11.44* |
| 1. *M4C2.1 - Strengthening research and dissemination of innovative models for basic and applied research carried out in synergy between universities and businesses* | *6.91* |
| 2. *M4C2.2 - Support for innovation processes and technology transfer* | *2.05* |
| 3. *M4C2.3 - Strengthening the support conditions for research and innovation* | *2.48* |
| - Investment 3:1: Fund for the creation of an integrated system of research and innovation infrastructures | *(1.58)* |
| Mission 4 Total | 30.88 |

**Fig. 2.6** PNNR: missions, investments and sources of financing. The Fig. 2.6 shows the structure and related investments of the PNRR - the six PNRR missions, with a specific focus on mission 6 - component 2: From research to business

foster an environmentally sustainable, knowledge-based development model by promoting integrated, multi-level policies and tools to address complex cross-cutting challenges, including generational, gender and territorial disparities. M4C2 seeks to stimulate investment in research and development and promote both technological and social innovation, while strengthening human capital and supporting the transition towards a knowledge-intensive economy. Crucially, it encourages enhanced openness of the research and innovation system, benefiting not only research communities, but also key actors in the broader R&D ecosystem, including enterprises and SMEs, the third sector, public administrations, and civil society.

The three intervention lines under M4C2 cover the entire research and innovation value chain, from frontier research to technology transfer. The measures vary in terms of the heterogeneity of the networks they foster—comprising universities, research centres, enterprises and other institutions—as well as their Technology Readiness Levels (TRLs). All initiatives are implemented through competitive selection procedures, ensuring merit-based allocation of resources and alignment with national strategic priorities (MUR, 2021b).

The criteria guiding the selection of projects funded under M4C2 were shaped by several overarching objectives. First, the measures aimed to ensure that beneficiaries possess a sufficient critical mass, with particular attention to the valorisation and consolidation of existing capacities. Second, projects were required to demonstrate long-term impact, including the presence of co-financing—potentially involving private capital—reflecting their strategic relevance and sustainability. Third, the selected initiatives needed to guarantee significant and positive spillovers on the national economic and production system. Additionally, the feasibility of each project had to be compatible with the strict timelines imposed by the Plan. Finally, the interventions were expected to ensure medium and long-term sustainability.

These measures are also intended to strengthen and integrate the Italian research and innovation ecosystem, enhancing its capacity to contribute to the strategic objectives of Horizon Europe, the National Research Plan (PNR) 2021–2027, and the global challenges identified in the 2030 Agenda.

Within Component 4.2, four systemic and mutually interconnected lines of intervention have been defined:

1. Extended Partnerships—large-scale partnerships involving universities, research centres and enterprises, dedicated to funding basic research projects and promoting critical mass around key thematic areas.
2. National Centres—initiatives aimed at reinforcing research infrastructures to establish "national R&D champions" in major Key Enabling Technologies (KETs).
3. Innovation Ecosystems—the creation and consolidation of territorial "R&D leaders," designed to strengthen regional innovation trajectories in line with Smart Specialisation Strategies and to develop integrated interventions within specific technological domains.
4. Research and Innovation Infrastructure System—the establishment of an integrated network of research and innovation infrastructures serving research communities and key stakeholders (policy makers, SMEs, the third sector, citizens, etc.), in alignment with national and European Open Science and Open Innovation strategies.

Together, these intervention lines are designed to reinforce the entire research and innovation value chain, building a more coherent, competitive and internationally connected system capable of addressing complex scientific, technological and societal challenges.

Between 2021 and 2022, in the context of the PNRR and in close alignment with the interventions and projects implemented under Horizon Europe, the PNR 2021–2027 and the National Smart Specialisation Strategy (SNI), the National Research Council (CNR) launched a set of targeted monitoring, planning, coordination and organisational support activities (Antonini et al., 2022). These efforts were designed to pursue several key objectives:

- to integrate effectively the national and European project activities of the CNR within the institution's strategic and programmatic framework—including

the Ten-Year Strategic Vision Document 2024–2033, the Reorganization and Relaunch Plan, and the Triennial Activity Plan (PTA);
- to ensure the medium- and long-term sustainability of initiatives and projects;
- to prevent fragmentation or duplication in the participation of CNR scientific networks in calls for proposals or expressions of interest requiring systemic and coordinated action;
- to foster meaningful dialogue among CNR departments, academic and research institutions, and enterprises operating in relevant sectors;
- to promote and support effective participation of CNR institutes in the various systemic initiatives envisaged under PNRR Mission 4, Component 2 (M4C2), particularly those in which the organisation plays a leading role at national or European level.

Within PNRR Mission 4—Component 2 "From Research to Business"—as well as in Horizon Europe and the PNR 2021–2027, the Social Sciences and Humanities (SSH) also play a significant transversal role. Their contribution is essential for shaping system-level interventions and for embedding research and innovation policies within broader societal, economic and technological transformations. SSH integration within national initiatives is therefore expected to generate substantial impacts across scientific communities and key sectors of the Italian economy and society.

Social Sciences and Humanities (SSH) play a crucial and transversal role within several PNRR system initiatives, particularly in the Extended Partnerships (EP). Notably, EP5—Humanistic Culture and Cultural Heritage, which includes innovation and creativity laboratories, and EP9—Economic and Financial Sustainability of Systems and Territories, in which it is intended to consolidate and systematise, at national level, scientific expertise, methodological tools and knowledge. Their objectives include:

- addressing—through an integrated, mission-oriented and multi-level governance approach—the major challenges arising from climate change and socio-economic crises triggered by the pandemic, fostering synergies among culture, the arts, science, the economy and technology;
- promoting the creative transformation of public spaces, equitable territorial development and sustainability, and improving the quality of life and well-being of citizens.

In line with the objectives defined by *H*orizon Europe, the PNR 2021–2027 and the PNIR 2021–2027, the PNRR also places strong emphasis on strengthening RIs, supporting the development of systemic initiatives with national strategic relevance.

The PNRR, as Table 2.2 shows, allocates €1.08 billion to Research Infrastructures, with the aim of enhancing interaction between scientific knowledge—generated by high-quality RIs—and the productive fabric of the country. This investment is intended to stimulate systemic research, innovation and technology-transfer activities, generating significant scientific, technological

**Table 2.2** PNRR Funding for ESFRI Area of Research infrastructures (MUR. Direzione generale dell'internazionalizzazione e della comunicazione, 2021)

| ESFRI Area | Total funding (€) |
|---|---|
| DIGIT | 90.000.000,00 |
| Energy | 90.000.000,00 |
| Environment | 200.000.000,00 |
| Health and Food | 200.000.000,00 |
| Physical Sciences and Engineering | 400.000.000,00 |
| Social and Cultural Innovation | 100.000.000,00 |

and socio-economic impacts at both national and regional levels. The investment strategy for RIs under the PNRR focuses on three main priorities:

- Strengthening existing RIs identified as high-priority within the PNRR;
- Establishing new RIs with high or medium priority, responding to emerging scientific and technological needs;
- Creating thematic or multidisciplinary networks of existing RIs—also ranked as high or medium priority—promoting interconnection within and across the scientific domains defined by ESFRI (Digital, Energy, Environment, Health and Food, Physical Sciences and Engineering, Social and Cultural Innovation/Social Sciences and Humanities).

Together, these actions aim to reinforce Italy's research ecosystem by integrating infrastructures, promoting excellence, and aligning national capabilities with European strategic priorities in open science, open innovation, and interdisciplinary research.

In this context, Research Infrastructures (RIs) respond to the needs of the scientific community and of the country's broader production system, representing a key factor for competitiveness in both national and European research. RIs differ from laboratory networks, data collections, or libraries because they provide open access to the entire scientific community—public or private, academic or industrial—through a structured access system, without institutional or national affiliation constraints.

For the private sector, access to RIs represents a unique opportunity to exploit state-of-the-art technologies and expertise, develop and test new products and services for the market, and address technical challenges that might otherwise slow the development of innovative and highly competitive entrepreneurial activities.

With this in mind, the intervention funded by the PNRR aims to promote increasingly open and sustainable access to RIs, favouring the various existing types and methods of access. The *European Charter for Access to Research Infrastructures* (European Commission—Directorate-General for Research and Innovation, 2024) and the *ERA Policy Agenda* (Council of the European Union, 2025) identify three different types of access:

- Virtual access, enabling direct online use of data, tools, and digital resources;

- Physical access, allowing on-site use of laboratories, instrumentation, training, and specialized support;
- Remote access, which provides real-time operation of instruments and services without the need for physical presence.

These modalities are paired with access methods that determine how users are selected. Even within open frameworks, physical and remote access often require competitive evaluation due to finite resources and capacity constraints. Where competition is necessary, expert panels assess proposals according to three criteria:

- Excellence-driven: scientific quality, novelty, and socio-economic relevance at national and European levels;
- Need-driven: the technical requirements essential for robust analyses, high-performance measurements, and data reliability;
- Market-driven: the innovation potential of private-sector requests and the feasibility of tailoring access to user-specific needs.

Through these mechanisms, RIs not only uphold scientific excellence but also catalyze innovation ecosystems, strengthening the interface between research and industry across Europe.

Within the PNRR framework, the Department of Humanities and Social Sciences, Cultural Heritage of the National Research Council (CNR-DSU) has implemented a multi-level strategy aimed at defining, developing, and ensuring the long-term sustainability of systemic and interconnected research infrastructure projects in the ESFRI Social and Cultural Innovation (S&CI)—Social Sciences and Humanities (SSH) domain. The strategy pursues two overarching objectives:

- Integrating and systematizing European, national, and regional research infrastructure initiatives within a coherent and shared framework;
- Supporting the continuous improvement of the scientific, technological, and managerial quality of research infrastructures, while strengthening and expanding access to their innovative services for a wide range of beneficiaries, including scientific communities, policymakers, enterprises, trade associations, public administrations, and cultural/social institutions operating in the relevant sectors.

The RI enhancement plan is designed to foster and support:

- Excellence in SSH research;
- Broad openness of RIs, in line with Open Science (OS) and Open Innovation (OI), through the implementation of policies, collaborative platforms, and shared tools and services for OS and OI;
- Synergies between RIs and national innovation actors, including National Technology Clusters, technology districts, competence centres, and regional digital innovation hubs, across the thematic areas of the National Smart Specialisation Strategy—NSSS (SNSI—Strategia Nazionale di Specializzazione Intelligente) and Regional Smart Specialisation Strategies (RIS3): Tourism, Cultural Heritage and Creative Industries; Health, Nutrition and Quality of Life; Digital Agenda, Smart Communities, Intelligent Mobility Systems;

- Coordinated implementation of research training programmes and human-capital development initiatives, a key component of the emerging knowledge economy, through:
  - the creation of innovative PhD programmes in Digital Humanities, Social Sciences, and Heritage Science, emphasizing internationalisation, interdisciplinarity, and inter-sectorality;
  - effective incentives and enhanced capacity to attract scientific and managerial excellence, together with improved career-development opportunities for research fellows, PhD candidates, and researchers/technologists;
  - strengthened capacities for knowledge and skills transfer to the private sector, and the development of innovative start-ups, open innovation ecosystems, and collaborative platforms;
  - The consolidation of the clustering process of Italian SSH RI nodes (initiated under H2020), through shared policies, platforms, sustainability plans, and the integration of SSH RI marketplaces within the European Open Science Cloud (EOSC);
  - The implementation of a federated Italian Open Science Cloud—a distributed digital research infrastructure for the SSH (S&CI) domain—designed to provide broad, integrated access (via a unified marketplace) to facilities, tools, FAIR data, expertise, and advanced services for research communities and key stakeholders (policymakers, companies, trade associations, public administrations, etc.).

The coordinated implementation of research training programmes and human-capital development initiatives—an essential component of the emerging knowledge economy—includes:

- The development of innovative PhD programmes in Digital Humanities, Social Sciences, and Heritage Science, with a strong emphasis on internationalisation, interdisciplinarity, and inter-sectoral collaboration;
- Effective incentives and enhanced capacity to attract scientific and managerial excellence, together with improved opportunities for professional growth for research fellows, PhD candidates, and researchers/technologists;
- Strengthening knowledge-transfer and skills-transfer capacities towards the private sector, and supporting the creation of innovative start-ups, open-innovation ecosystems, and collaborative platforms;
- Advancing the clustering process of Italian SSH RI nodes (initiated under H2020) through shared policies, platforms, sustainability plans, and the integration of SSH RI marketplaces within the European Open Science Cloud (EOSC);
- Implementing a federated Italian Open Science Cloud, a distributed digital research infrastructure for the SSH (S&CI) domain, designed to provide broad and integrated access—via a unified marketplace—to facilities, tools, FAIR data, expertise, and advanced services for research communities and key stakeholders (policymakers, companies, trade associations, public administrations, etc.).

Within this action plan, the CNR-DSU, working in close collaboration with the national academic and research system, has launched an integrated and sustainable implementation of three PNRR research infrastructure projects in the ESFRI SSH sector:

- A project aimed to strengthen RESILIENCE (Religious Studies Infrastructure: tools, innovation, experts, connections and centers in Europe), a research infrastructure of high strategic relevance in the SSH domain, through the PNRR ITSERR—Italian Strengthening of the Resilience of ESFRI RIs initiative;
- Two thematic cluster projects involving major research infrastructures of high and medium strategic impact, as identified in the PNIR—National Plan of Research Infrastructures and the ESFRI Roadmap (ESFRI, 2021; MUR, 2021a):
  - H2IOSC—Humanities and Cultural Heritage Italian Open Science Cloud, aimed at developing a national thematic network of research infrastructures—a national Open Science Cloud for the Humanities and Heritage Science sector—with the participation of the Italian nodes of the European research infrastructures CLARIN-ERIC, DARIAH-ERIC, E-RIHS-ERIC and OPERAS;
  - FOSSR—Fostering Open Science in Social Science Research, aimed at implementing a national thematic infrastructural network—a national Open Science Cloud in the Social Sciences sector—with the participation of the Italian nodes of the European research infrastructures CESSDA-ERIC, RISIS, SHARE-ERIC, GUIDE and GGP.

The three projects coordinated by the CNR were funded under the PNRR with a total allocation of €90 million and constitute the backbone of the PNRR's infrastructure enhancement strategy in the field of Social and Cultural Innovation—Social Sciences and Humanities (SSH).

Mutually interconnected through a multidimensional and multilevel approach, the three projects aim to integrate and systematize the facilities, data, resources, services, and expertise managed by the Italian nodes of the main European research infrastructures in the SSH domain, as identified in the ESFRI Roadmap and the PNIR. Their objective is to expand the openness and usability of these infrastructures not only for researchers, but also for businesses, the third sector, public administrations, policymakers, and cultural and social institutions or associations.

In line with research infrastructure policies established at the European and national levels, the two RI networks will implement shared, multi-level methodologies, policies, systems, platforms, services, and tools to support the adoption of Open Science and Open Innovation principles and strategies within the SSH sector, promoting their federation within the European Open Science Cloud (EOSC).

Following this rationale, the facilities, expertise, resources, and services pooled by the two national RI networks will be made broadly accessible to research and innovation communities and to relevant stakeholders through the development of a national Social Sciences and Humanities Open Science Cloud.

The primary objective is therefore to develop open and integrated systems for research, innovation, and technology transfer, capable of enabling effective and widespread access to—and use of—SSH RIs by researchers, enterprises, policy-makers, and other actors operating in the relevant sectors. This coordinated effort will enhance and strengthen the collective capacity to share and access the data, knowledge, expertise, services, and tools provided by the research infrastructures.

## 2.6 Conclusions

In the context of European SSH Research Infrastructures and European Open Science Cloud (EOSC), the FOSSR Open Science Cloud aims to become the main national thematic network of research infrastructures for social research and social innovation—a national RI cluster capable of attracting researchers from around the world and serving as a key digital ecosystem for conducting cutting-edge research, experimentation, growth, and innovation.

Through its integrated FOSSR marketplace, FOSSR will provide open, trustworthy, and secure access to FAIR data, services, tools, and expertise, enabling high-quality scientific studies, experiments, and socio-economic-political analyses across multiple fields. This will support the production of new knowledge, technologies, and competencies necessary to address major global social, economic, health, environmental, and technological challenges, which exert significant impacts at European, national, and regional levels. These challenges increasingly require innovative, interdisciplinary, transdisciplinary, and inter-sectoral approaches. By ensuring open access to scientific and technological results, as well as to the facilities required for producing, refining, and transferring research outcomes, FOSSR aims to play a central role in implementing the European and national Open Science Strategy, promoted by the European Commission and, in Italy, by the Ministry of Universities and Research (MUR), to enhance the circulation of knowledge and innovation.

To this end, in line with recommendations from the European Commission and MUR, and consistent with the access policies of the European RIs participating in the thematic network, FOSSR is implementing a multi-stakeholder access programme designed to promote open, trustworthy, and secure access to the FOSSR marketplace:

- For national and international researchers, fostering multidisciplinary, interdisciplinary, and transdisciplinary approaches to social research. These approaches are increasingly essential to systematically address contemporary societal challenges that require complex knowledge extending beyond traditional disciplinary boundaries. Scientific and technical research must rely on close collaboration among diverse research groups and scientific communities—nationally and internationally—so that multiple perspectives can converge on shared topics of interest.

- For users and researchers in the private sector, particularly in enterprises, services, and the third sector, promoting the development of ad hoc services tailored to specific needs and requirements. This enables full exploitation of the innovation and knowledge-transfer opportunities offered by research infrastructures.
- For policymakers and public administrations, supporting the development, analysis, and evaluation of public and sectoral policies.
- For PhD students and research fellows in universities and research institutions, ensuring access to advanced scientific and technological equipment and high-level specialised support for their studies. This includes ad hoc PhD programmes and specialised training initiatives developed in collaboration with universities and businesses, with the aim of establishing a strategic hub connecting research, research training, and the business ecosystem.

Finally, in addition to access policies, the FOSSR access programme will include the implementation of specific guidelines to ensure:

- the adoption of user agreements;
- compliance with workplace safety regulations, particularly in relation to physical access;
- the protection of data and intellectual property;
- the safeguarding of research ethics and integrity;
- non-discrimination and gender balance;
- public engagement and the development of transversal, intersectoral, and interdisciplinary communities contributing to the co-development of the network and its services.

## References

Antonini, G., Dell'Orletta, F., Filippetti, A., Nuzzolese, A. G., Palaia, R., Reale, E., Saccone, M., Sfameni, C., Spinello, A. O., Trufelli, L., & Tuzi, F. (2022). *Le attività dipartimentali di monitoraggio e programmazione della ricerca nel settore delle scienze umane, sociali e del patrimonio culturale: metodologie, processi, risultati e soluzioni proposte per lo sviluppo di un sistema CNR integrato e multilivello per il monitoraggio e la programmazione della ricerca*. CNR. https://iris.cnr.it/handle/20.500.14243/445394.

Council of the European Union. (2021). Council recommendation (EU) 2021/2122 of 26 November 2021 on a pact for research and innovation in Europe. *Official Journal of the European Union*. https://eur-lex.europa.eu/legal-content/EN/TXT/?uri=CELEX%3A32021H2122

Council of the European Union. (2022). *Council conclusions on research infrastructures*. https://data.consilium.europa.eu/doc/document/ST-15429-2022-INIT/en/pdf

Council of the European Union. (2025). *Council recommendation of 24 June 2025 on the European Research Area Policy Agenda 2025–2027 (C/2025/3593)*. https://eur-lex.europa.eu/legal-content/EN/TXT/HTML/?uri=OJ:C_202503593

Di Donato, F. (2025). Open Science and the role of social sciences research infrastructures and data. In L. Taddei & M. Paolucci (Eds.), *Longitudinal data infrastructures in Europe: Tools for Open Science in social science research* (pp. 69–79). Springer.

Di Rosa, M., & Saccone, M. (2019). *Open Science. Ricerca e innovazione Responsabile in Italia* (pp. 24–32). AIRI—CNR.

Draghi, M. (2024). *The future of European competitiveness—Part B: In-depth analysis and recommendations*. European Commission. https://commission.europa.eu/document/download/ec1409c1-d4b4-4882-8bdd-3519f86bbb92_en?filename=The%20future%20of%20European%20competitiveness_%20In-depth%20analysis%20and%20recommendations_0.pdf

EOSC Association. (2024). *Strategic research and innovation agenda (SRIA) of the European Open Science Cloud (EOSC), (Version 1.3)—1 November 2024*. https://zenodo.org/records/17582648

ESFRI. (2021). *Roadmap 2021. Strategy report on research infrastructures*. Publications Office of the European Union. https://roadmap2021.esfri.eu/

ESFRI. (2024a). *ESFRI landscape analysis 2024*. ESFRI. https://landscape2024.esfri.eu/media/coqdoq0q/20240604_la2024.pdf

ESFRI. (2024b). *ESFRI report: Funding of research infrastructures*. ESFRI. https://doi.org/10.5281/zenodo.14770891

European Commission. (2023). *European Commission Recommendation (EU) 2023/2113 of 3 October 2023 on critical technology areas for the EU's economic security for further risk assessment with Member States*. https://eur-lex.europa.eu/legal-content/EN/TXT/HTML/?uri=OJ:L_202302113

European Commission. (2025a). *Communication from the Commission to the European Parliament, the Council, the European Economic and Social Committee of the Regions: A European strategy on Research and technology infrastructures*. COM(2025) 497 final 2. https://eur-lex.europa.eu/legal-content/EN/TXT/HTML/?uri=CELEX:52025DC0497R(01)

European Commission. (2025b). *Communication from the Commission to the European Parliament and the Council—A European Strategy for Artificial Intelligence in Science. Paving the way for the Resource for AI Science in Europe (RAISE)*. COM (2025) 724 final. https://eur-lex.europa.eu/legal-content/EN/TXT/HTML/?uri=CELEX:52025DC0724

European Commission—Directorate-General for Research and Innovation. (2016). *Open innovation, Open Science, open to the world. A vision for Europe*. Publications Office of the European Union. https://digital-strategy.ec.europa.eu/en/library/open-innovation-open-science-open-world

European Commission—Directorate-General for Research and Innovation. (2024). *European charter for access to research infrastructures: Principles and guidelines for access and related services*. Publications Office of the European Union. https://data.europa.eu/doi/10.2777/8299402

Giordano, C., & Zollino, F. (2021). Long run factor accumulation and productivity trends in Italy. *Journal of Economic Surveys, 35*(3), 741–803.

Motta, G., Puccinelli, R., Reggiani, L., & Saccone, M. (2016). Extracting value from grey literature: Processes and technologies for aggregating and analyzing the hidden "Big Data" treasure of organizations. *Grey Journal, 12*(1), 15–25. https://www.greynet.org/images/TGJ_V12_N1,_Spring_2016.pdf

MUR. (2021). *Programma nazionale per la ricerca 2021–2027*. https://www.mur.gov.it/sites/default/files/2021-01/Pnr2021-27.pdf

MUR. (2021a). *Piano Nazionale Infrastrutture di Ricerca (PNIR) 2021–2027*. https://www.mur.gov.it/sites/default/files/2021-10/Decreto%20Ministeriale%20n.1082%20del%2010-09-2021%20-%20PNIR%202021%20-%202027.pdf

MUR. (2021b). *PNRR MUR: linee guida per le iniziative di sistema della Missione 4: Istruzione e ricerca—Componente 2: dalla ricerca all'impresa*. https://www.mur.gov.it/sites/default/files/2021-10/Decreto%20Ministeriale%20n.1141%20del%2007-10-2021%20-%20Linee%20Guida_MUR_PNRR_M4C2.pdf; https://research-and-innovation.ec.europa.eu/news/all-research-and-innovation-news/revised-charter-access-research-infrastructures-foster-open-science-innovation-and-research-security-2024-11-27_en

MUR. (2022). *Piano nazionale per la scienza aperta. PNR 2021–2027.* https://www.mur.gov.it/sites/default/files/2022-06/Piano_Nazionale_per_la_Scienza_Aperta.pdf
MUR. (2023). *Piano Nazionale della Scienza Aperta: ruolo ed azioni prioritarie—Documento tecnico.* MUR. https://iris.cnr.it/retrieve/8fe65123-b1d7-4ab3-ad4a-027f884d1c82/Scienza%20Aperta%20in%20Italia.V2.2024.01.05.pdf
MUR. (2024). *Processi per individuare le attività in essere nel Paese riconducibili agli obiettivi del PNSA 2021–2027.* https://iris.cnr.it/retrieve/31cc2a42-2159-449a-88e4-20d598200273/Doc%202-%20Processi%20per%20individuare%20le%20attivita%CC%80%20gia%CC%80%20in%20essere%20V2%20-%202024.02.05.pdf
MUR. Direzione Generale dell'Internazionalizzazione e della Comunicazione. (2021). *Decreto MUR n. 3264 del 28 dicembre 2021. Avviso pubblico per la presentazione di proposte progettuali per "Rafforzamento e creazione di Infrastrutture di Ricerca" da finanziare nell'ambito del PNRR.* https://www.mur.gov.it/sites/default/files/2021-12/Avviso0n.032640del028-12-2021.pdf
Reggiani, L., Saccone, M., & Trufelli, L. (2017). *Open Science, verso un'apertura condivisa della scienza: analisi di contesto, approccio metodologico e iniziative CNR.* CNR. https://hdl.handle.net/20.500.14243/388140
Taddei, L., & Paolucci, M. (2025). *Longitudinal data infrastructures in Europe: Tools for Open Science in social science research.* Springer.

# Chapter 3
# From Principles to Practice: FAIR Data and the Infrastructural Turn in Social Science

**Sonia Stefanizzi and Domingo Scisci**

## 3.1 Introduction

The increasing digitization of research has fundamentally altered how scientific knowledge is produced, managed, and preserved. In the social sciences, the growing availability of digital data has expanded analytical possibilities while simultaneously exposing structural weaknesses in data governance, documentation, and long-term accessibility. Large volumes of research data coexist with fragmented infrastructures, heterogeneous standards, and limited mechanisms for discovery and reuse, constraining transparency and cumulative knowledge production.

In response to these challenges, the FAIR principles—Findable, Accessible, Interoperable, and Reusable—have become a central reference point for data management and open science policies. FAIR articulates a framework in which research data are treated as durable and intelligible components of the scientific record, requiring structured documentation, stable access conditions, and sustainable infrastructures. Rather than prescribing uniform technical solutions, the FAIR principles emphasize shared responsibility across researchers, institutions, and infrastructures, aligning data practices with broader goals of accountability and long-term reuse.

Within the social sciences, the adoption of FAIR raises domain-specific questions related to the contextual nature of data, ethical and legal constraints, and the diversity of methodological traditions. As a result, FAIR cannot be understood solely as a technical standard but must be examined as part of a broader transformation in research infrastructures and governance arrangements. This chapter

S. Stefanizzi · D. Scisci (✉)
Dept. of Sociology and Social Research, University of Milano-Bicocca, Milan, Italy

DASSI—Data Archive for Social Sciences in Italy, Milan-Rome, Italy
e-mail: sonia.stefanizzi@unimib.it; domingo.scisci@unimib.it



G. Cerulli, E. Reale (eds.), *Research Infrastructures for Open Science in Social Science Research*, https://doi.org/10.1007/978-3-032-29575-0_3

approaches FAIR from this perspective, focusing on the relationship between principles, infrastructures, and research practices in the social sciences.

Section 3.2 introduces the conceptual background of the FAIR framework and outlines its core dimensions. Section 3.3 examines key challenges associated with applying FAIR in social science research. Section 3.4 discusses the role of European research infrastructures and international initiatives in enabling FAIR implementation, including national experiences as illustrative cases. The chapter concludes by reflecting on the implications of FAIR for research practices and academic cultures in the social sciences.

## 3.2 The Origins of the FAIR Principles: Theoretical, Ethical, and Epistemological Foundations

### *3.2.1 Background and Rationale Behind the FAIR Principles*

Over the past two decades, the increasing digitization of scientific research has profoundly transformed the ways in which data are produced, managed, and shared. The amount of information generated by computational tools, sensors, social media, and digital infrastructures has reached such proportions that it requires a fundamental rethinking of how scientific data are preserved, connected, and reused (Borgman, 2017; Leonelli et al., 2021; Leonelli & Tempini, 2020). Within this context, the FAIR principles—an acronym for Findable, Accessible, Interoperable, and Reusable—have emerged as a cornerstone of responsible data management and open science. Introduced in 2016, FAIR was designed to address the growing "crisis of data accessibility", a paradox where the massive increase in data production was not matched by corresponding advances in discoverability or reuse (Wilkinson et al., 2016). Rather than a rigid standard, the FAIR framework constitutes an ethical and epistemological shift in how knowledge is conceived and managed. It aligns with the ideals of transparency, reproducibility, and interdisciplinarity that underpin the broader Open Science movement (Dunning et al., 2017). Since its publication, FAIR has been adopted globally by major research institutions, funders, and international organizations—including the European Commission, the OECD, and the Global Open FAIR Data Initiative—as a foundational policy for ensuring open, sustainable, and collaborative science (European Commission, 2021; OECD, 2020). FAIR's rise marks a pivotal moment in the cultural history of science: it shifts the locus of responsibility from individual researchers to collective infrastructures of knowledge stewardship (Leonelli & Tempini, 2020). By embedding ethical reflection within the architecture of data management, the FAIR paradigm redefines what it means to produce and share scientific knowledge in the digital age.

The emergence of the FAIR principles can be traced to the convergence of three key trends (Borgman, 2017; Fecher & Friesike, 2014):

1. the global expansion of Open Science and Open Data movements.
2. the proliferation of data-intensive research and computational methodologies.
3. a growing awareness of the reproducibility crisis affecting many scientific domains.

In the early 2000s, the explosion of digital data revealed an infrastructural paradox: while researchers produced more data than ever, the fragmentation of repositories, the lack of metadata standards, and the absence of shared governance systems rendered much of that information effectively inaccessible. Wilkinson et al. (2016) therefore articulated the FAIR principles as a systemic solution—a set of high-level guidelines for improving the discoverability, accessibility, and reusability of digital research outputs across disciplines. Mons et al. (2017) highlight the epistemological ambition of this project. FAIR was not designed merely to facilitate data exchange but to make data "machine-actionable", enabling computational systems to interpret, link, and integrate datasets automatically. In this sense, FAIR represents the infrastructural backbone of what Hey et al. (2009) describe as the Fourth Paradigm of science—data-intensive discovery.

At the policy level, the European Open Science Cloud (EOSC) institutionalized FAIR as the cornerstone of its digital research infrastructure in 2018. The OECD (2020) subsequently reinforced this approach, positioning FAIR within a global agenda that views data as a public good. This policy shift reflects an epistemic transition from a model of individual data ownership to one of relational stewardship, where sharing becomes a moral and professional obligation (Leonelli & Tempini, 2020). As Dunning et al. (2017) note, FAIR introduces an ethics of accountability: scientists are not merely responsible for generating data but for ensuring that their work remains interpretable and reusable by others. In doing so, the FAIR framework transforms the very concept of "scientific authorship"—from producing results to curating infrastructures of knowledge.

### 3.2.2 *The Four FAIR Dimensions: Definitions and Implications*

At the heart of the FAIR framework lies its most operationally distinctive feature: the articulation of four interrelated principles—Findability, Accessibility, Interoperability, and Reusability—that together establish a shared foundation for data stewardship in the digital age. These dimensions offer not only a normative orientation but also a functional roadmap for implementing open and responsible data practices across scientific domains.

**Findability** constitutes the first and most fundamental requirement for enabling data reuse. Data that cannot be discovered cannot be reused. To ensure findability, each dataset must be assigned a globally unique and persistent identifier (PID), such as a Digital Object Identifier (DOI), and be described with rich metadata using domain-relevant standards (Wilkinson et al., 2016). These metadata should be indexed in public or federated registries to ensure their visibility to both humans and machines. In the context of the social sciences, metadata standards such as the Data Documentation Initiative (DDI) are widely used to capture the complex provenance of datasets, including sampling designs, variable definitions, modes of data collection, and ethical safeguards.

This principle captures the epistemic value of visibility: data become part of the scientific record only when they can be located, cited, and traced. Borgman (2017) interprets this as a new ontology of the scientific object. A dataset acquires legitimacy not solely through its empirical content but through its integration into a searchable, networked infrastructure—a system of relations that confers transparency and reproducibility.

**Accessibility** builds on findability by ensuring that once discovered, data and metadata can be retrieved using open and universally implementable communication protocols. These typically include standard web-based services such as HTTP, FTP, or OAI-PMH, and must support appropriate authentication and authorization mechanisms where required. A key tenet of the FAIR approach is that metadata should remain accessible even if the underlying data are subject to usage restrictions, such as those imposed by informed consent agreements or data protection regulations like the GDPR (Beaulieu & Leonelli, 2022; Leonelli & Tempini, 2020). In this respect, FAIR does not mandate that data be fully open, but that the conditions of access be transparent, standardized, and machine-readable. Social science data infrastructures have operationalized this principle through tiered access models, where metadata are openly available and data access is granted based on clearly defined criteria, licenses, and user credentials.

**Interoperability** addresses the challenges of integrating and reusing data across different systems, disciplines, and analytical platforms. It requires that data and metadata use formal, accessible, shared, and broadly applicable vocabularies and ontologies that are themselves FAIR (EOSC Executive Board, 2021). In the social sciences, where concepts are often context-dependent and measured in diverse ways, semantic interoperability is particularly challenging. Nevertheless, controlled vocabularies such as the European Language Social Science Thesaurus (ELSST), classifications like NACE or ISCED, and community-driven metadata models like SDMX for statistical data provide important building blocks for harmonization. Moreover, linking variables and concepts to established ontologies enhances semantic precision, enabling automated discovery and machine reasoning.

However, Dunning et al. (2017) warn that interoperability is not merely technical: it has epistemic and political dimensions, determining whose data practices become legible within global infrastructures. As Leonelli and Tempini (2020) argue, ensuring interoperability without acknowledging epistemic diversity risks reproducing hierarchies of knowledge and excluding non-Western or community-based epistemologies.

**Reusability** represents the culmination of the FAIR principles and embodies the aim of responsible data management: enabling data to be reliably used in future research contexts. This depends not only on technical accessibility but also on legal clarity, contextual richness, and adherence to quality standards. Reusable data must be accompanied by clear usage licenses—preferably in standard, machine-readable formats such as Creative Commons—and include detailed provenance information that documents the origins, processing steps, and limitations of the data (Molloy et al., 2020). In the social sciences, reuse is often complicated by the need to understand historical and cultural contexts, methodological variations, and the subjective meanings embedded in qualitative or survey-based data. Therefore, documentation should cover aspects such as the wording of instruments, versions of datasets, variable derivations, and anonymization protocols.

Reusability transforms data into shared epistemic resources, extending their value beyond the original project (Leonelli & Tempini, 2020). This principle redefines the scientist's role as a data steward—a guardian of the research commons. It encapsulates the idea that scientific responsibility extends beyond production to include preservation, curation, and communication (Mons et al., 2017).

While FAIR originated as a technical framework, its broader impact lies in its ethical and epistemological implications. Leonelli and Tempini (2020) conceptualize FAIR as an infrastructure of responsibility: a socio-technical system that embeds values such as transparency, care, and accountability into the fabric of scientific practice. However, Dunning et al. (2017) caution that excessive standardization may obscure the local and interpretive dimensions of data. By privileging machine readability, FAIR can inadvertently marginalize forms of knowledge that resist codification—particularly qualitative, indigenous, or community-based data (Carroll et al., 2020).

## 3.3 Applying the FAIR Principles in the Social Sciences: Opportunities and Challenges

Applying the FAIR principles within the social sciences raises profound theoretical, methodological, and ethical challenges. While the FAIR framework emerged primarily from the natural and biomedical sciences, where data can often be standardized, decontextualized, and integrated computationally, social science research produces data that are deeply situated, interpretive, and relational (Borgman, 2017; Leonelli & Tempini, 2020). This fundamental difference reshapes how Findability, Accessibility, Interoperability, and Reusability can and should be understood in these disciplines. At the core of the tension between FAIR and the social sciences lies the epistemic nature of social data. In contrast to the instrumental logic of measurement typical of the natural sciences, social data are constructed through interaction—emerging from interviews, ethnographies, surveys, digital traces, and participatory observations that are embedded in cultural, political, and affective relations. They are not neutral "facts" but rather co-produced artefacts of social meaning (Beaulieu & Leonelli, 2022).

As Betancort Cabrera et al. (2020) observe, this situatedness challenges FAIR's emphasis on universality and machine-actionability. While FAIR promotes standardization to enhance interoperability, social science data often resist full standardization because their meaning depends on contextual interpretation—including the positionality of the researcher, the socio-political environment, and the participants' categories of experience. In sociological fieldwork or ethnography, the data are inseparable from the methodological and ethical frameworks that produced them. An interview transcript, a field diary, or a focus group summary contains interpretive layers—emotion, silence, gesture, irony—that cannot be captured through metadata alone (Bratt, 2023).

To make these data "FAIR" in any meaningful sense requires an expanded notion of metadata that includes not only descriptive elements but also reflexive documentation of research design, ethics, and theoretical framing (Leonelli & Tempini, 2020). This epistemic reframing implies that FAIR must be translated, not simply transferred, into the social sciences. The goal is not to impose the same degree of formal interoperability achieved in physics or genomics but to design contextual infrastructures that respect the interpretive integrity of social knowledge while fostering transparency and reusability.

### *3.3.1 Ethics and Responsibility in Handling Sensitive Data*

Ethical concerns occupy a central place in the adaptation of FAIR to the social sciences. Research in sociology, anthropology, and political science often involves sensitive and personal data collected through relationships of trust. As Bratt (2023) and Rainey et al. (2023) highlight, the imperative to make data findable and reusable can come into tension with the duty to protect the identities and privacy of participants. FAIR thus demands a shift from a procedural view of ethics toward a broader ethic of stewardship. Researchers become responsible not only for the data they collect but also for how that data might circulate, be recombined, or reinterpreted beyond their control (Leonelli & Tempini, 2020). This is especially pressing in the digital era, where open datasets can easily intersect with other public sources, potentially leading to re-identification of participants or the misuse of sensitive information.

To address this, social scientists are developing adaptive FAIR strategies, such as publishing metadata without releasing the full data corpus, creating controlled-access repositories that require ethical clearance for reuse, and designing consent procedures that explicitly inform participants about the potential reusability of their data. These practices embrace the idea of "responsible openness"—an approach that balances transparency with protection, in line with the ethical norms of relational research (Leonelli, 2022; Lvovs et al., 2025). The FAIR debate in social sciences also intersects with the CARE principles (Collective Benefit, Authority, Responsibility, Ethics) introduced by the Global Indigenous Data Alliance (2025). CARE complements FAIR by foregrounding equity and self-determination, insisting that data should serve collective benefit, respect community authority, and uphold ethical responsibility in their reuse (Carroll et al., 2020). When integrated, FAIR and CARE together define a dual ethical architecture: FAIR ensures that data are technically sound and discoverable, while CARE ensures that data practices remain socially and politically just.

Among the four FAIR principles, Interoperability poses perhaps the most complex challenge for social scientists because it touches directly upon issues of epistemic diversity and power. Interoperability requires that data conform to shared vocabularies and ontologies so that they can be combined across contexts. Yet, as Dunning et al. (2017) notes, the creation of these standards is not neutral: it reflects the priorities, languages, and epistemologies of dominant institutions, often located in the Global North. This becomes particularly evident in comparative or cross-national datasets, where the drive for standardization and comparability often erases local epistemologies or culturally specific understandings of social categories such as gender, ethnicity, or class. To counteract this, a growing number of initiatives advocate for inclusive interoperability. This approach promotes flexible metadata models that allow for multiple ontologies and locally defined categories to coexist. Rather than enforcing uniformity, these infrastructures should embrace an epistemic diversity (Leonelli, 2022). In this sense, FAIR in the social sciences is not simply a matter of technological alignment but a question of data justice: interoperability must serve both computational efficiency and the recognition of diverse epistemic communities.

### *3.3.2 Toward Contextual and Reflexive FAIRness: The Case for "Data Fairness"*

A distinctive contribution of recent scholarship is the proposal to extend FAIR into a framework of "data fairness" (Leonelli et al., 2021). This concept pushes the FAIR agenda beyond technical compliance toward a reflexive awareness of the social life of data—how data are produced, circulated, and interpreted within networks of power and meaning. In the social sciences, this means that datasets should not only be findable and reusable but also contextually intelligible. Metadata must capture the conditions of knowledge production—including who collected the data, under what assumptions, for which audiences, and with what implications. This reflexive approach transforms metadata from a descriptive tool into a critical and ethical medium that communicates the epistemic commitments of research (Leonelli & Tempini, 2020).

Moreover, "data fairness" underscores the need to consider the social consequences of openness. Opening data without adequate contextualization can reproduce inequalities: for example, communities that generate data may lack the resources to analyse or benefit from them, while better-funded institutions can capitalize on the same datasets. As OECD (2020) notes, achieving fairness requires redistributive practices—capacity-building, equitable collaboration, and shared authorship in data reuse—ensuring that FAIR infrastructures do not deepen epistemic asymmetries but help to reduce them.

Reflexivity, therefore, operates on two levels:

- Epistemic, by questioning how data infrastructures shape what can be known.
- Institutional, by examining how FAIR's implementation distributes visibility, authority, and credit across the global knowledge system.

Looking ahead, the success of FAIR in the social sciences depends on its capacity to remain adaptive, inclusive, and reflexive. FAIR cannot be achieved through technical compliance alone; it must evolve into a practice of care—a set of values guiding how data are created, shared, and reused in ways that respect human and social complexity (Leonelli & Tempini, 2020).

To achieve this transformation, several strategic directions are essential:

1. Develop discipline-specific guidelines for applying FAIR to qualitative, ethnographic, and mixed-methods data.
2. Integrate ethics and data literacy training into graduate education, fostering a culture of responsibility and reflexivity.
3. Encourage collaborative infrastructures that involve academic, community, and policy actors, ensuring that data governance reflects the needs of diverse users.
4. Revise FAIR evaluation metrics to include qualitative indicators of social impact, contextual integrity, and epistemic justice.

Ultimately, FAIR should not be understood as a static checklist but as a dialogical framework—one that invites ongoing negotiation between openness and protection, standardization and diversity, efficiency and fairness. The true measure of FAIR's success lies not in how many datasets it makes available, but in how it transforms our collective understanding of what it means to know, to share, and to care in the digital age.

## 3.4 European Research Infrastructures for FAIR Data in the Social Sciences

The implementation of the FAIR principles in research depends fundamentally on an ecosystem of research infrastructures (RIs) that turn abstract principles into practical, scalable solutions. Without robust RIs, FAIR guidelines would remain aspirational statements lacking concrete traction (European Commission Expert Group on FAIR Data, 2018). Research infrastructures provide the technical, semantic, organizational, and legal scaffolding that makes FAIR data management feasible across disciplines. Technically, RIs supply crucial services: for example, persistent identifier registries (e.g. DataCite DOIs for datasets, ORCID for researchers) ensure global findability of data and contributors, while metadata catalogues and discovery portals aggregate and index data descriptions for searchability. Likewise, federated identity and authorization frameworks (such as eduGAIN single sign-on) managed by RIs enable controlled yet streamlined data access across institutions (EOSC

Executive Board, 2021). Semantically, RIs develop and curate shared vocabularies, ontologies, and metadata standards that are prerequisites for interoperability and reuse—without common data languages and schemas, the FAIR principles “I” and “R” cannot be operationalized. Organizationally and legally, RIs establish community norms, governance, and trust: they often coordinate certification schemes (e.g. CoreTrustSeal for trustworthy data repositories) and promulgate best practices through training programs, thus fostering a culture of data stewardship. Importantly, RIs also ensure sustainability: they maintain services, standards, and repositories over time beyond individual projects, so that data remain accessible and reusable for years. In this sense, research infrastructures are not merely implementation tools but constitutive elements of FAIRness itself—their layered architecture of registries, protocols, semantic standards, and human expertise is what translates FAIR from principle into practice (European Commission Expert Group on FAIR Data, 2018).

Contemporary examples across disciplines illustrate how RIs enable FAIR at scale. In the environmental sciences, for instance, European RIs such as LifeWatch (biodiversity/ecosystems) and EPOS (earth science) have adopted common metadata standards and interoperability frameworks so that heterogeneous observational data can be integrated and reused beyond their original context (Zhao et al., 2019). In astronomy, open data infrastructure is well established: the European Southern Observatory (ESO) operates a pioneering open-access science archive through which all observations are freely accessible online under FAIR-aligned licenses (Romaniello et al., 2023). This archive contains millions of data files and adheres to common formats and rich metadata, exemplifying how findability and accessibility are built into the infrastructure. Looking ahead, the Square Kilometre Array (SKA), a next-generation radio telescope, is explicitly designing its data ecosystem such that the exabyte-scale data products will be FAIR by default, distributed via a federated network of regional data centres responsible for curation and user support under FAIR principles (Possenti, 2025). In the social sciences and humanities, domain-specific RIs have developed federated repositories and platforms that enable cross-border data discovery and reuse of complex, language-rich datasets (European Commission Expert Group on FAIR Data, 2018). For example, the consortium of European Social Science Data Archives (CESSDA), the Common Language Resources and Technology Infrastructure (CLARIN), and the Digital Research Infrastructure for the Arts and Humanities (DARIAH) each illustrate how FAIR practices are embedded in infrastructure design. These RIs, along with integrative initiatives like the European Open Science Cloud, demonstrate that FAIR data management at scale is fundamentally an infrastructural achievement: it requires connecting technical components with community standards and policies. The following discussion examines how four major European initiatives—CESSDA, CLARIN, DARIAH, and EOSC—operationalize the FAIR principles, focusing on their approaches to data discovery, metadata standards, interoperability, and reuse.

### 3.4.1 *CESSDA: Interoperability and Data Quality in Social Science Data Management*

CESSDA is a European Research Infrastructure Consortium (ERIC) uniting national social science data archives in over 20 countries. Its mission is to enable researchers to discover and access social science datasets across borders through a single federated platform. A centrepiece of CESSDA's FAIR implementation is its one-stop Data Catalogue, which aggregates the metadata of tens of thousands of data collections held by member archives into a unified, multilingual search portal (CESSDA, 2023). Through this catalogue, a researcher can, for example, find survey data from multiple countries via a single query interface, greatly enhancing data findability and accessibility. Common metadata standards are a priority: CESSDA adopts the Data Documentation Initiative (DDI) metadata schema to richly describe social science datasets (covering study design, variables, etc.), and it encourages all archives to assign DOIs (Digital Object Identifiers) to datasets for persistent identification and citation. These practices ensure that data are not only findable but also reliably citable and traceable over time, supporting reuse. To further support interoperability, CESSDA maintains a controlled Vocabulary Service and a Metadata Validator tool. The Vocabulary Service hosts multilingual controlled terminologies for key metadata fields (for example, standardized terms for survey topics, demographic variables, etc.), which helps align semantics across different archives. The Metadata Validator checks that dataset descriptions conform to the CESSDA Metadata Model (an application profile of DDI), enforcing consistent structure and content in metadata records. By using such tools, CESSDA ensures that metadata harvested from, say, the Norwegian or Polish data archive will include common core elements and vocabularies, making those records integrable into the central catalogue without loss of meaning. In terms of reuse, CESSDA puts strong emphasis on guidance and training. Notably, it has published the CESSDA Data Management Expert Guide, an extensive online guide that helps social scientists implement sound data management practices aligned with FAIR principles (CESSDA Training Team, 2022). This guide covers everything from planning for documentation and metadata to legal and ethical aspects of sharing data, thereby improving the reusability of data by promoting high-quality documentation and appropriate licensing. Many of CESSDA's member archives also carry CoreTrustSeal certification, reflecting a commitment to long-term preservation and data quality—an organizational assurance that archived data will remain accessible and meaningful in the future. By building shared technical infrastructure (catalogues, APIs, vocabularies) and fostering a trust network among national archives, CESSDA has created an interoperable ecosystem for social science data in Europe. Researchers can seamlessly find and obtain data from multiple countries, confident that the datasets are documented in a comparable way and can be readily combined or compared. Indeed, CESSDA has become a key pillar of open science in the social sciences, ensuring that valuable data—from opinion polls to longitudinal surveys—are properly curated and made FAIR to fuel new research across disciplines.

### 3.4.2 CLARIN: FAIR Language Resources for the Social Sciences and Humanities

CLARIN is a European RI that focuses on language-based data (linguistic corpora, textual datasets, speech and multimedia, language technology tools) and has been a leader in FAIR implementation in the humanities and social sciences (de Jong et al., 2018). A cornerstone of CLARIN's approach to interoperability is its Component Metadata Infrastructure (CMDI). CMDI is a flexible framework that allows CLARIN centers to define custom metadata schemas as "components" for their particular data collections while still adhering to a shared core ontology and structure (Broeder et al., 2012). In practice, this means that a given archive can extend metadata to capture specifics of, say, a medieval charter collection or a spoken dialect corpus, but fundamental elements (like Author, Language, Date, etc.) remain mapped to common concepts across CLARIN. This component-based design enables rich, domain-specific descriptions without sacrificing cross-portal interoperability. The benefit is evident in CLARIN's central discovery portal, the Virtual Language Observatory (VLO), which harvests metadata from all participating centers. Thanks to common protocols and semantic mappings, the VLO now indexes over one million language resource records from diverse sources (Haaf et al., 2014), making them findable through a single interface. A researcher can search the VLO for, say, "parliamentary debates," and retrieve results from many countries' collections at once, with the assurance that core metadata fields are harmonized for easy filtering and comparison. To further support semantic interoperability, CLARIN has developed services like CLAVAS (CLARIN Vocabulary Alignment Service), which provides centralized access to standard controlled vocabularies and thesauri used in language resource metadata (Brugman, 2017). For example, CLAVAS offers the complete ISO 639-3 language code list in a uniform format, so all CLARIN centers can use the same codes for language identifiers. Similarly, common data category registries (now managed through the CLARIN Concept Registry) ensure that terms like part-of-speech tags or annotation types carry consistent definitions across datasets. These efforts mean that when datasets are combined or compared, their metadata and annotations refer to the same conceptual universe. CLARIN also places a strong emphasis on data reuse. Resources deposited in CLARIN come with detailed documentation and standardized metadata, and CLARIN's guidelines highlight that extensive metadata is crucial for meaningful reuse of corpora—users must know how and why data were created to reuse them properly. Accordingly, CLARIN encourages depositors to include information on corpus collection methods, linguistic annotations, and processing history. Reusability is further enhanced by CLARIN's promotion of open licenses (whenever legal and ethical conditions allow) and by its setup of a federated identity system (EduGAIN integration) so that researchers from any member country can access protected resources via their home credentials. In sum, CLARIN's infrastructure makes a wealth of language data findable through centralized search, accessible via unified authentication and standards-compliant formats, interoperable through common metadata/ontology frameworks, and reusable thanks to rich metadata and documentation. Its close collaboration with DARIAH and other RIs also extends these benefits beyond linguistics.

### 3.4.3 DARIAH: Semantic Standards for Interoperability in Cultural and Digital Humanities

DARIAH supports digital scholarship across the humanities and qualitative social sciences, and it complements CLARIN by covering a broader variety of data types—from literary texts and historical records to music, cultural heritage artifacts, and beyond. Implementing FAIR in such a diverse domain requires a focus on community standards and semantic richness (Jander & Weimer, 2021). One of DARIAH's strategies for interoperability and reuse is to promote widely accepted formats for content and metadata. For textual resources, DARIAH encourages use of the Text Encoding Initiative (TEI) XML standard for encoding texts. TEI provides a structured, semantically enriched way to represent texts by marking up elements like persons, places, dates, and other entities in the content. A medieval manuscript encoded in TEI, for example, will have people and locations tagged in a standardized way, making it machine-readable and interlinkable. This practice greatly enhances interoperability: a TEI-encoded corpus from one project can be parsed and understood by tools and researchers elsewhere, and it facilitates linking texts to external data (like aligning a person mentioned in a text with an authority record in Wikidata or VIAF). Beyond TEI, DARIAH engages its community in developing ontologies and controlled vocabularies suited to humanities research. In collaboration with CLARIN and other partners, DARIAH has worked on multilingual conceptual models—a notable example being a multilingual Occupation Ontology created under the SSHOC project that aligns occupation classifications across languages and historical periods (Tijdens et al., 2022). By agreeing on, say, a concept for "school teacher" that maps English terms to equivalent terms in German (Schullehrer), French, etc., DARIAH enables datasets from different countries or eras to interoperate, supporting cross-cultural studies and longitudinal analyses. Such ontologies, when applied to metadata, make data more findable (through unified terminology) and more reusable (through clear semantics). DARIAH also invests in training and guidelines to ensure that researchers produce FAIR-ready data. Through initiatives like DARIAH-Campus, it offers tutorials on topics such as linking cultural heritage data to the semantic web, using persistent identifiers for artifacts, and annotating data with standardized vocabularies. By disseminating this know-how, DARIAH addresses the "softer" infrastructure of FAIR: the human practices needed alongside technical tools. Like CLARIN, DARIAH supports accessibility via federated login and encourages open access where possible. It has also been active in cross-infrastructure integrations; for example, DARIAH partners with CLARIN, CESSDA, and others in the SSH Open Marketplace, a platform emerging from SSHOC that allows researchers to discover not just data but also tools and services relevant to social sciences and humanities. The Marketplace aggregates resources with rich contextual metadata (including pointers to both CLARIN and DARIAH outputs), further breaking down silos between infrastructures. Through these efforts, DARIAH makes otherwise disparate humanities data discoverable and interoperable at a European scale. Researchers can, for instance, search a DARIAH registry or Marketplace and find datasets from multiple digital humanities centers, knowing that those resources adhere to shared standards (like TEI, Dublin Core, CIDOC-CRM, etc.) and can therefore be more easily combined or compared. The reusability of humanities data is markedly increased when sources come with thorough documentation—something DARIAH advocates as part of good data stewardship. Overall, DARIAH's contribution to FAIR lies in fostering a common layer of standards and documentation practices across a very heterogeneous field, enabling data to travel beyond local projects and be reused in unforeseen ways.

### *3.4.4 EOSC: A Federated European Infrastructure for FAIR and Open Science*

The European Open Science Cloud is a flagship initiative to connect and integrate RIs across Europe, effectively serving as a meta-infrastructure or "system of systems" for FAIR data and services (EOSC Executive Board, 2021). Unlike a single repository, EOSC is conceived as a federated cloud environment spanning disciplines—a virtual platform where research data, tools, and computing resources from many community RIs are made interoperable and accessible through common rules. EOSC's design has FAIR principles at its core: the EOSC Strategic Implementation Plan and Strategic Research and Innovation Agenda explicitly define FAIR compliance as a prerequisite for any service or data resource to be onboarded into EOSC (EOSC Executive Board, 2021; European Commission Expert Group on FAIR Data, 2018). In practice, this means that participating RIs (such as CESSDA, CLARIN, DARIAH, and numerous others in fields from physics to health) must expose their metadata in standard ways, use persistent identifiers, and adhere to agreed protocols so that their holdings can be discoverable and usable via the EOSC portal. One of EOSC's key contributions to FAIR is the development of an Interoperability Framework that provides guidelines on technical and semantic interoperability across domains (EOSC Executive Board, 2021). This framework addresses how metadata should be structured for cross-domain search, how to handle identity/authentication (for instance, leveraging eduGAIN for a seamless user login across services), and how to ensure that data objects are accessible in a consistent manner (through standard APIs and licenses). For the social science and humanities RIs specifically, EOSC offers an opportunity and a challenge. On one hand, by connecting SSH infrastructures into a broader cloud, EOSC greatly expands findability and accessibility: a social science researcher using EOSC could discover data not only from CESSDA archives but also, say, from a health study or environmental data repository that might be relevant to socio-economic questions. Indeed, CESSDA, CLARIN, and DARIAH participated in the SSHOC project (Social Sciences & Humanities Open Cloud) precisely to prepare their resources for EOSC integration, developing common services like the aforementioned Open Marketplace and aligning metadata so that their catalogues can be harvested into EOSC. The result is that previously siloed datasets become part of a wider open science mesh, enabling interdisciplinary research—for example, combining social survey data with climate data or genetic data to study complex societal challenges. On the other hand, EOSC integration requires resolving cross-cutting issues such as data privacy and copyright. Social science data often include personal or sensitive information protected under strict ethical and legal regimes. EOSC's policies and its federation of services need to accommodate such restrictions by supporting fine-grained access controls and "privacy-aware" metadata. This has led to ongoing efforts to develop standard solutions for controlled access within a FAIR context (so that even restricted data can be found and their conditions of access known, if not openly downloaded). Furthermore, harmonizing metadata across disciplines is non-trivial—EOSC must encourage use of broadly compatible schemas or crosswalks so that, for instance, the concept of "author" or "date" means the same in a physics dataset and a sociological dataset. Significant work by EOSC's FAIR Working Group and others has gone into defining these common metadata elements and ontologies for EOSC's registry of resources (EOSC Executive Board, 2021). Despite the challenges, the vision of EOSC as a Europe-wide platform for FAIR data has powerful implications for the social sciences and humanities. It creates incentives for data archives and researchers to improve the FAIRness of their outputs (since data that are not properly documented or not accessible via standard protocols simply will not be included in EOSC). It also provides the technological backbone for cross-disciplinary collaboration, allowing, for example, social scientists to easily find relevant data in environmental or biomedical repositories and vice versa. In effect, EOSC is making FAIR a structural component of European research: by embedding the requirement for findable, interoperable data into the funding and infrastructure landscape, it is driving cultural change towards openness. Early experiences show both the promise and the complexity of this integration. Projects under EOSC have demonstrated, for instance, how common authentication and authorization can let a researcher move between CLARIN's repository and CESSDA's catalogue with a single login, or how a common indexing service can list datasets from DARIAH alongside those from life sciences. At the same time, continuous policy work is needed to ensure that issues like sustainability and governance are addressed—EOSC must guarantee long-term support and coordination so that the federated services remain reliable. Nonetheless, as of mid-2025 EOSC has established itself as a "commons" for European research data, with hundreds of services and data resources onboarding under FAIR terms (Appleton et al., 2020). For the social sciences and humanities, this means an unprecedented level of exposure and integration of their data: sociolinguistic corpora, parliamentary records, ethnographic databases, and more are becoming visible and accessible to any researcher in Europe through the EOSC portal. In conclusion, EOSC amplifies the work of individual RIs like CESSDA, CLARIN, and DARIAH by situating them in a unified open science cloud, thus pushing the frontiers of what can be done with research data and underscoring that FAIR principles thrive on collective infrastructure efforts.

### 3.4.5 *European and Global Projects: Ecosystems for FAIR Implementation*

The European research landscape has witnessed a rapid consolidation of efforts to make scientific data and digital objects Findable, Accessible, Interoperable, and Reusable. Over the past decade, a constellation of interlinked projects—funded primarily through the Horizon 2020 and Horizon Europe programmes—has progressively transformed FAIR from a conceptual ideal into an operational framework underpinning European Open Science. Central to this transformation has been the cumulative work of SSHOC, GO FAIR and its EcoSoc Implementation Network, FAIRsFAIR, FAIR-IMPACT, and the globally oriented WorldFAIR project. Each of these initiatives, while differing in scope and governance, has contributed essential components to the shared architecture of FAIR research ecosystems.

The Social Sciences & Humanities Open Cloud (SSH Open Cloud, 2025) (SSHOC, 2019–2022) was the first large-scale European effort to embed FAIR principles directly within the social sciences and humanities. Building on existing research infrastructures such as CESSDA, CLARIN, and DARIAH, SSHOC developed a federated cloud environment that facilitated seamless access to data, tools, and training materials. Its flagship achievement—the SSH Open Marketplace—brought together data repositories, analytical software, and educational resources into a single discovery platform, thereby enhancing findability and reusability across disciplines. SSHOC also addressed the specific needs of social research, such as managing sensitive or personal data. By implementing secure "safe room" environments and privacy-preserving access mechanisms, it demonstrated how legal and ethical constraints could coexist with open science. Multilingualism, another challenge inherent to European research, was tackled through harmonized vocabularies and translation tools, making cross-border data interoperability feasible. These developments laid the groundwork for the social sciences and humanities node within the European Open Science Cloud, ensuring that FAIRness was adapted to domain-specific contexts rather than imposed through one-size-fits-all policies.

In parallel, the GO FAIR initiative (GO FAIR Initiative, 2025) provided a complementary, bottom-up mechanism for FAIR implementation. Launched as an international movement, GO FAIR organized its activities around self-governed Implementation Networks (INs), each focusing on applying FAIR principles within a specific disciplinary or institutional community. Among these, the EcoSoc-IN (Economic and Social Sciences Implementation Network), established in 2018 and coordinated by Germany's RatSWD, pioneered FAIR adoption for sensitive microdata such as surveys and administrative records. The network operationalized the "Five Safes" framework—ensuring that FAIR compliance coexists with privacy protection through safe data, people, projects, settings, and outputs. EcoSoc-IN's White Paper (Betancort Cabrera et al., 2020) articulated how persistent identifiers, standard metadata schemas like DDI, and legal interoperability mechanisms can make even restricted social data findable and reusable without compromising confidentiality. GO FAIR's decentralized approach—summarized in the triad "Go Change," "Go Train," and "Go Build"—empowered data stewards and researchers to cultivate FAIR awareness organically, emphasizing training and community engagement over prescriptive regulation. In this sense, EcoSoc-IN bridged the normative and technical dimensions of FAIR, demonstrating that openness can be responsibly extended to ethically sensitive data domains.

The FAIRsFAIR (FAIRsFAIR, 2025) project (2019–2022) marked a critical inflection point by translating FAIR ideals into practical, measurable tools and policies. It provided the European research community with standardized instruments for assessing FAIR compliance. The interactive tool FAIR-Aware helped researchers self-evaluate their understanding of FAIR principles, while the automated F-UJI tool allowed repositories to measure FAIRness programmatically using defined metrics drawn from the RDA FAIR Maturity Model. Beyond assessment, FAIRsFAIR built institutional capacity for FAIR-aligned repository certification. By aligning CoreTrustSeal criteria with FAIR standards, it created a Capability Maturity Model guiding repositories through incremental improvement pathways. Ten repositories—several in the social sciences—received direct mentoring to achieve certification, thus expanding the network of trustworthy archives. FAIRsFAIR also influenced policy and pedagogy: it published recommendations for embedding FAIR data management in university curricula and developed guidelines for national and institutional data policies. Its enduring impact lies in establishing FAIR evaluation as a routine institutional practice, moving FAIRness from rhetoric to measurable reality.

Building on these foundations, the FAIR-IMPACT (FAIR-IMPACT, 2025) project (2022–2025) extends the FAIR paradigm beyond datasets to encompass all digital research objects—software, workflows, protocols, and services—within the Horizon Europe framework. Its explicit goal is a "FAIR EOSC", an ecosystem in which every digital component of the research lifecycle adheres to FAIR principles. The project develops domain-sensitive interoperability frameworks, persistent identifier infrastructures, and certification schemes for both repositories and services. Within the social sciences, FAIR-IMPACT conducts pilot studies on FAIR+restricted data, developing strategies to make sensitive datasets discoverable and interoperable while respecting GDPR and ethical mandates. It also enhances tools inherited from FAIRsFAIR—such as extending F-UJI with domain-specific metrics reflecting DDI metadata and social survey standards. Through cascading grants, interdisciplinary workshops, and training activities, FAIR-IMPACT strengthens cross-domain learning: solutions for legal interoperability in social research are now informing data governance in health and environmental sciences. As a result, FAIR-IMPACT reinforces the vision of EOSC as a dynamic, FAIR-compliant ecosystem spanning all scientific domains.

Complementing these European initiatives, WorldFAIR (WorldFAIR, 2025) (2022–2024), led by CODATA (the Committee on Data of the International Science Council) and the Research Data Alliance, globalizes FAIR data implementation. Through 11 disciplinary case studies, WorldFAIR advances cross-domain interoperability and promotes convergence between regional and global FAIR practices. Its case study on Comparative Social Surveys—involving the European Social Survey (ESS) and Australia's AUSSI-ESS—demonstrates how the DDI metadata standard and controlled vocabularies can harmonize survey data across languages and national boundaries. The project's outputs include FAIR Implementation Profiles for diverse disciplines and a Cross-Domain Interoperability Framework that provides guidelines for linking datasets from disparate domains. For the social sciences, these activities have produced reusable workflows for integrating survey data globally and have informed high-level policy recommendations for data governance and capacity building. By situating FAIR within an international context, WorldFAIR ensures that European advancements inform—and are informed by—global open science efforts, emphasizing that addressing grand challenges such as climate change or pandemics requires seamless interoperability between social and natural science data.

Taken together, these initiatives form a coherent and evolving ecosystem that has progressively institutionalized FAIR principles in European—and increasingly global—research. From SSHOC's domain-focused infrastructures to FAIRsFAIR's metrics, from GO FAIR's community-driven networks to FAIR-IMPACT's cross-object integration, and culminating in WorldFAIR's international alignment, they collectively demonstrate that FAIRness is not a static compliance checklist but a dynamic, collaborative process. Their combined legacy is a European research environment where data stewardship, interoperability, and open access are integral to scientific culture rather than peripheral aspirations—a model that now informs global standards for responsible and FAIR research.

### 3.4.6 *Italian National Initiatives for FAIR Data: The Cases of DASSI and FOSSR*

At both European and national levels, open science and FAIR data principles have become central to research policy and infrastructure planning. In Italy, the Ministry of University and Research (MUR) has embedded a FAIR data mandate into its strategic planning instruments. The National Research Programme (PNR) 2021–2027 explicitly requires that publicly funded research outputs, including datasets, adhere to FAIR principles and be deposited in certified repositories (MUR, 2021b). This policy framework is further substantiated by the National Plan for Open Science (PNSA), introduced through Ministerial Decree no. 268/2022, which sets out guidelines for promoting open access to publications and for managing research data in accordance with international standards (MUR, 2021a). In parallel, the National Research Infrastructure Plan (PNIR) highlights the importance of sustained investment in data infrastructures and e-infrastructures, particularly those enabling interdisciplinary access and long-term data preservation (MUR, 2021c). These coordinated efforts place Italy in line with European strategies such as the European Open Science Cloud and reinforce its commitments under the European Research Area (ERA). Within this framework, dedicated initiatives in the social sciences are contributing to the broader national goal of establishing a robust and sustainable FAIR ecosystem.

A central actor in this ecosystem is DASSI–the Data Archive for Social Sciences in Italy– (DASSI, 2025) which operates as Italy's national service provider within CESSDA. Established in 2021 through a joint initiative of the University of Milano-Bicocca and the National Research Council (CNR), and funded by MUR, DASSI provides a full suite of services designed to ensure the curation, long-term preservation, and FAIR alignment of social science datasets. Its core mission is to support researchers in documenting and depositing data according to internationally recognized standards, notably the CESSDA Metadata Model (CMM) and the Data Documentation Initiative (DDI). Through this alignment, DASSI enables Italian data collections to be easily discoverable and interoperable with archives across Europe. To ensure persistent access and citability, the archive assigns Digital Object Identifiers (DOIs) to all curated datasets.

Beyond technical services, DASSI plays an essential role in supporting responsible data management and open science practices. It provides expert guidance on anonymization, licensing options, and multilingual metadata creation—tools that are especially valuable for dealing with context-specific social science data. Its metadata are integrated into the CESSDA Data Catalogue, significantly increasing the visibility and findability of Italian datasets within the European landscape. DASSI also contributes actively to training and capacity-building efforts, offering workshops and support materials that help social scientists acquire skills in data stewardship, data protection, and reuse planning.

By participating in working groups and implementation networks within CESSDA and EOSC-related projects, DASSI helps translate high-level FAIR policies into concrete, field-specific practices. Its role demonstrates how national-level infrastructures can serve both local research communities and broader European objectives. In this way, DASSI is not only a repository but also a strategic interface between Italian social science and the global open science movement, advancing the alignment of Italian research practices with the European FAIR data agenda.

Complementing DASSI's role, the **FOSSR project (Fostering Open Science in Social Science Research)** represents a new national-scale initiative to connect and enhance Italy's FAIR data infrastructure. Launched in 2022 under the National Recovery and Resilience Plan (PNRR) and coordinated by CNR, FOSSR functions as an "infrastructure of infrastructures". It integrates the Italian nodes of CESSDA, SHARE-ERIC, and RISIS into a unified open science platform for the social sciences, effectively building an Italian Open Science Cloud that provides a single point of access to diverse datasets and services in alignment with the European Open Science Cloud vision.

FOSSR is developing a cloud-based architecture linking a network of distributed data centers, expanding computing and storage capacity across Italy. On top of this infrastructure, a federated platform with common interfaces (including Virtual Research Environments) enables unified discovery and analysis of data from DASSI, SHARE, and RISIS. To facilitate such interoperability, FOSSR emphasizes the harmonization of metadata standards and FAIR-compliant data workflows across the participating archives. Innovative services are being implemented to standardize data documentation and harmonize variables, leveraging shared standards like DDI and controlled vocabularies. All datasets curated under FOSSR are assigned persistent identifiers and rich metadata, ensuring they remain findable and properly citable in accordance with FAIR principles.

Beyond technical innovations, FOSSR invests in capacity-building and promotes a FAIR data culture. It features training programmes—including workshops, new academic courses, and doctoral grants—to cultivate data management and stewardship skills among emerging social scientists. FOSSR also adopts a community-oriented approach that engages a broad range of stakeholders (researchers, data providers, and policymakers alike) in co-designing and utilizing its services. This inclusive strategy strengthens trust and co-responsibility in data sharing, embedding open science practices more deeply within the social science community. By aligning its efforts with broader European initiatives like EOSC, FOSSR amplifies Italy's efforts and helps drive a cultural shift toward openness and collaboration. Together, DASSI and FOSSR show how Italy is building a FAIR data ecosystem that links local data stewardship with European Open Science goals.

## 3.5 Conclusions

The adoption of the FAIR principles within the social sciences has triggered both technical and cultural transformations. Technically, researchers have improved how data are managed, documented, and shared, leading to higher-quality datasets and more transparent analytical practices. Culturally, FAIR has reshaped how scholars conceive data—no longer as by-products of research but as intellectual artifacts that embody the epistemic foundations of their disciplines. This shift has elevated expectations of transparency and reproducibility: every element of a study—from raw data to analytical code—is now increasingly expected to be accessible for scrutiny, validation, and reuse. In disciplines such as psychology and economics, the so-called replication crisis (Forbes et al., 2023) has revealed not only methodological fragility but also a crisis of trust within academic communities. FAIR-aligned practices, by making data findable and accessible, contribute to rebuilding that trust through transparency, accountability, and collective verification.

Another significant impact is the evolving understanding of data as first-class research outputs rather than mere ancillary materials. Historically, social science data might have been seen as a means to an end (the publication), but today there is growing recognition that datasets have standalone scholarly value. Initiatives like the Joint Declaration of Data Citation Principles explicitly states that *"data should be considered legitimate, citable products of research."* and provide guidelines for citing datasets just as one would cite literature (Data Citation Synthesis Group, 2014). As a result, researchers are now expected to formally cite and attribute data sources, and many data repositories issue DOIs (Digital Object Identifiers) for datasets to facilitate this practice. The reuse of data has become a mark of research productivity: a well-curated social science dataset can be reused in meta-analyses or comparative studies far beyond the original project. In fact, the impact of a study is no longer measured by its publications alone, but also by how discoverable and reusable its underlying data are. In the social sciences this has led to concrete changes such as journals requiring *data availability statements* and universities rewarding researchers for sharing data. Treating data as a genuine scholarly product encourages better documentation and long-term preservation, knowing that others may find and build upon these datasets in the future (with proper attribution to the original investigators). National initiatives like FOSSR further support this shift by providing researchers with the infrastructure and incentives necessary to treat data as enduring scholarly assets.

Implementing FAIR in the social sciences has also elevated the importance of professional data stewardship roles. Researchers often collaborate with dedicated experts—data stewards, data curators, and research data librarians—who specialize in managing and publishing data according to FAIR standards. These professionals guide investigators on everything from writing Data Management Plans and choosing standard formats, to handling ethical/legal issues (e.g. privacy regulations) for sensitive social data (Wendelborn et al., 2023). Data stewards serve as a bridge between technical data management and discipline-specific needs, helping ensure that, for example, a sociologist's dataset is properly annotated and archived in a trusted repository. The rise of data stewardship is part of a broader cultural change: universities and funding agencies have recognized that good data management and curation are integral to research excellence. These experts not only assist in making data FAIR, but also advocate for changes in academic incentives (so that sharing data and code is valued alongside publishing papers). In sum, FAIR adoption has professionalized the handling of research data in social science, embedding specialized skills into research teams to maintain data quality and usability. FOSSR plays a crucial role here, not only by formalizing data stewardship practices but by supporting the training and community-building activities needed to sustain them.

FAIR principles also bring attention to machine-actionability of data, which has both great potential and unique challenges in context-rich social science research. A key tenet of FAIR is that data and metadata should be structured in ways that computational systems can find, interpret, and reuse them with minimal human intervention (Wilkinson et al., 2016). Social science data—ranging from large quantitative surveys to qualitative interview transcripts—often carry complex context. Describing this context in metadata (so that a machine "understands" what a variable or concept means) is a non-trivial task. Metadata standards are evolving to address these issues: the Data Documentation Initiative (DDI) is one prominent standard in the social sciences that provides a detailed XML-based schema for documenting surveys, facilitating machine-readable descriptions of variables, methodology, and sampling. DDI and similar standards make it easier to integrate data from different studies or countries, since software can parse the metadata and harmonize variables where possible. However, truly context-rich data (such as ethnographic field notes, open-ended responses, or multimedia content) still pose challenges for machine-actionability. Such data require extensive contextual metadata and often cannot be fully understood without human insight. As a result, achieving interoperability for these datasets involves a mix of automation and human curation. The FAIR principles acknowledge that full machine-actionability is a continuum—rarely 100% attainable—but pushing data to be "as machine-actionable as possible" is beneficial. In social sciences this might involve, for example, using controlled vocabularies for key concepts, ensuring timestamps and locations are in standard formats, and linking qualitative data to quantitative codes. The discipline is gradually addressing these technical hurdles: projects are underway to develop ontologies for social science concepts and to improve text analysis tools so that even unstructured data can be more FAIR-compliant. Still, the rich context of social data means researchers must carefully balance formalizing information for machines with preserving nuance for human researchers. Ensuring machine-actionable social data is therefore an ongoing effort, requiring collaboration between domain experts and data scientists. Platforms like FOSSR, which promote metadata harmonization and ontology alignment, provide essential support in this process.

Finally, the FAIR movement in social sciences has significant implications for interdisciplinary and cross-border collaboration. When social science datasets are well-documented and openly shared, they become accessible to researchers from other disciplines and other countries, enabling novel collaborations. Grand challenges like climate change, public health, or global inequality demand insights from multiple fields—and FAIR data practices help by breaking down data silos. In the same vein, international efforts like the European Open Science Cloud (EOSC) aim to create a federated infrastructure where researchers can find, share, process, and reuse FAIR research outputs across borders and scientific disciplines. Social science data, when made FAIR, can thus travel far beyond their point of origin—a dataset collected in one country can be discovered and reused by a team on the other side of the world to ask new questions or perform cross-cultural comparisons. This global reuse is especially important for disciplines like development economics or political science, where comparing data across many countries enriches the analysis. Moreover, FAIR facilitates cross-border team science: multinational research projects can more easily pool data and ensure that all partners have equal access to well-annotated resources. Of course, achieving this level of collaboration also requires addressing legal and ethical issues (data governance, privacy, intellectual property) internationally, but FAIR provides the technical backbone (persistent identifiers, clear licenses, standard protocols) to support such agreements. Overall, by making social science data more universal and combinable, FAIR adoption accelerates interdisciplinary innovation and helps build a more connected global research community. In this landscape, FOSSR contributes as a national node strategically positioned to interface with European and global infrastructures, strengthening the social sciences' capacity to engage in international open science ecosystems.

In conclusion, the integration of FAIR principles into the social sciences represents a paradigm shift in both research practice and epistemic culture. It strengthens transparency and reproducibility, elevates data to the status of scholarly output, and institutionalizes professional stewardship. At the same time, it compels researchers to reflect on the social meaning of data sharing, the ethics of openness, and the boundaries of automation. Ultimately, FAIR represents more than a framework for managing information: it is a new social contract for knowledge production, aligning scientific rigor with democratic accessibility and collective responsibility.

## References

Appleton, O., Asmi, A., Bird, I., Dekker, R., Blomberg, N., Dimper, R., Ferrari, T., Grant, A., Jones, S., Manola, N., Petzold, A., Rettberg, N., Robertson, D., Tenhunen, V., Testi, D., & van de Sanden, M. (2020, September). *EOSC—A tool for enabling Open Science in Europe*. Zenodo. https://doi.org/10.5281/zenodo.4044010

Beaulieu, A., & Leonelli, S. (2022). *Data and society: A critical introduction*. SAGE Publications Ltd..

Betancort Cabrera, N., Bongartz, E. C., Dörrenbächer, N., Goebel, J., Kaluza, H., & Siegers, P. (2020). *White paper on implementing the FAIR principles for data in the social, Behavioural, and economic sciences*. RatSwD. https://doi.org/10.17620/02671.60

Borgman, C. L. (2017). *Big data, little data, no data: Scholarship in the networked world*. The MIT Press.

Bratt, S. (2023). 'Routine Infrastructuring': How social scientists appropriate resources to deposit qualitative data to ICPSR and implications for FAIR and CARE. *Proceedings of the Association for Information Science and Technology, 60*(1), 61–72. https://doi.org/10.1002/pra2.769

Broeder, D., Windhouwer, M., Van Uytvanck, D., Goosen, T., & Trippel, T. (2012). CMDI: a component metadata infrastructure. *Describing LRs with Metadata: Towards Flexibility and Interoperability in the Documentation of LR Workshop Programme, 1*, 47.

Brugman, H. (2017). CLAVAS: A clarin vocabulary and alignment service. In *CLARIN in the Low Countries*. Ubiquity Press.

Carroll, S. R., Garba, I., Figueroa-Rodríguez, O. L., Holbrook, J., Lovett, R., Materechera, S., Parsons, M., Raseroka, K., Rodriguez-Lonebear, D., Rowe, R., Sara, R., Walker, J. D., Anderson, J., & Hudson, M. (2020). The CARE principles for indigenous data governance. *Data Science Journal, 19*(1). https://doi.org/10.5334/dsj-2020-043

CESSDA. (2023). *CESSDA Data Catalogue*. https://datacatalogue.cessda.eu

CESSDA Training Team. (2022). *CESSDA Data Management Expert Guide*. CESSDA ERIC. https://doi.org/10.5281/zenodo.3820473

Data Citation Synthesis Group. (2014). *Joint declaration of data citation principles*. FORCE11. https://doi.org/10.25490/a97f-egyk

de Jong, F. M. G., Maegaard, B., De Smedt, K., Fišer, D., & Van Uytvanck, D. (2018). CLARIN: Towards FAIR and responsible data science using language resources. In *Proceedings of the eleventh international conference on language resources and evaluation (LREC 2018)* (pp. 3259–3264).

Dunning, A., de Smaele, M., & Böhmer, J. (2017). Are the FAIR data principles fair? *International Journal of Digital Curation, 12*(2), 177–195. https://doi.org/10.2218/ijdc.v12i2.567

EOSC Executive Board (Ed.). (2021). *EOSC interoperability framework—Report from the EOSC executive board working groups FAIR and architecture*. Publications Office. https://doi.org/10.2777/620649

European Commission. (2021). *European research area policy agenda—Overview of actions for the period 2022–2024*. European Commission.

European Commission Expert Group on FAIR Data. (2018). Turning FAIR into reality—Final report and action plan from the European Commission expert group on FAIR data. *Publications Office*. https://doi.org/10.2777/1524

Fecher, B., & Friesike, S. (2014). Open science: one term, five schools of thought. In S. Bartling & S. Friesike (Eds.), *Opening science: The evolving guide on how the internet is changing research, collaboration and scholarly publishing* (pp. 17–47). Springer International Publishing. https://doi.org/10.1007/978-3-319-00026-8_2

Forbes, H. J., Travers, J. C., & Johnson, J. V. (2023). Supporting the replication of your research. In D. J. Cox, N. Y. Syed, M. T. Brodhead, & S. P. Quigley (Eds.), *Research ethics in behavior analysis* (pp. 237–262). Academic. https://doi.org/10.1016/B978-0-323-90969-3.00003-7

Global Indigenous Data Alliance. (2025). *CARE principles*. Global Indigenous Data Alliance. https://www.gida-global.org/care

Haaf, S., Fankhauser, P., Trippel, T., Eckart, K., Hedeland, H., Herold, A., Knappen, J., Schiel, F., Stegmann, J., & Van Uytvanck, D. (2014). CLARIN's Virtual Language Observatory (VLO) under scrutiny – The VLO taskforce of the CLARIN-D centres. *CLARIN Annual Conference 2014 in Soesterberg*, The Netherlands.

Hey, T., Tansley, S., & Tolle, K. (Eds.). (2009). *The fourth paradigm: Data-intensive scientific discovery* (1st ed.). Microsoft Research.

Jander, M., & Weimer, L. (2021). The DARIAH-DE Data Federation Architecture as a highway to FAIR data. *DARIAH annual event 2021: Interfaces*, 29.

Leonelli, S. (2022). Open science and epistemic diversity: Friends or foes? *Philosophy of Science, 89*(5), 991–1001. https://doi.org/10.1017/psa.2022.45

Leonelli, S., Lovell, R., Wheeler, B. W., Fleming, L., & Williams, H. (2021). From FAIR data to fair data use: Methodological data fairness in health-related social media research. *Big Data & Society, 8*(1), 20539517211010310. https://doi.org/10.1177/20539517211010310

Leonelli, S., & Tempini, N. (Eds.). (2020). *Data journeys in the sciences*. Springer Nature. https://doi.org/10.1007/978-3-030-37177-7

Lvovs, D., Creason, A. L., Levine, S. S., Noble, M., Mahurkar, A., White, O., & Fertig, E. J. (2025). Balancing ethical data sharing and open science for reproducible research in biomedical data science. *Cell Reports Medicine, 6*(4), 102080. https://doi.org/10.1016/j.xcrm.2025.102080

Molloy, L., Nordling, J., Grootveld, M., van Horik, R., Whyte, A., Davidson, J., Herterich, P., Martin, I., Méndez, E., Principe, P., Vieira, A., & Asmi, A. (2020, June). *D3.4 recommendations on practice to support FAIR data principles (version 1.1)*. Zenodo. https://doi.org/10.5281/zenodo.5357329

Mons, B., Neylon, C., Velterop, J., Dumontier, M., da Silva Santos, L. O. B., & Wilkinson, M. D. (2017). Cloudy, increasingly FAIR; revisiting the FAIR data guiding principles for the European Open Science cloud. *Information Services and Use, 37*(1), 49–56. https://doi.org/10.3233/ISU-170824

MUR. (2021a). *Piano Nazionale per la Scienza Aperta 2021–2027.*

MUR. (2021b). *Programma Nazionale per la Ricerca 2021–2027.*

MUR. (2021c, September 10). *Programma Nazionale per le Infrastrutture di Ricerca (PNIR) 2021–2027.*

OECD. (2020). *The digitalisation of science, technology and innovation: Key developments and policies*. OECD Publishing. https://doi.org/10.1787/b9e4a2c0-en

Possenti, A. (2025). *The challenge of the data in the SRCnetwork* (No. https://arxiv.org/abs/2504.03103; Version 1). arXiv. https://doi.org/10.48550/arXiv.2504.03103

Rainey, L., Lutomski, J. E., & Broeders, M. J. (2023). FAIR data sharing: An international perspective on why medical researchers are lagging behind. *Big Data & Society, 10*(1), 20539517231171052. https://doi.org/10.1177/20539517231171052

Romaniello, M., Arnaboldi, M., Barbieri, M., Delmotte, N., Dobrzycki, A., Fourniol, N., Freudling, W., Grave, J., Mascetti, L., Micol, A., Retzlaff, J., Rosse, N., Tax, T., Vuong, M., Hainaut, O., Rejkuba, M., & Sterzik, M. (2023). *The ESO science archive facility: Status, impact, and prospects [Text]*. European Southern Observatory (ESO). https://doi.eso.org/10.18727/0722-6691/5338

Tijdens, K., Brugiavini, A., & BUIA, R. E. (2022). *D3.10 A 20th century version of the occupation multilingual ontology*. Zenodo. https://doi.org/10.5281/zenodo.6567239

Wendelborn, C., Anger, M., & Schickhardt, C. (2023). What is data stewardship? Towards a comprehensive understanding. *Journal of Biomedical Informatics, 140*, 104337. https://doi.org/10.1016/j.jbi.2023.104337

Wilkinson, M. D., Dumontier, M., Aalbersberg, I. J., Appleton, G., Axton, M., Baak, A., Blomberg, N., Boiten, J.-W., da Silva Santos, L. B., Bourne, P. E., Bouwman, J., Brookes, A. J., Clark, T., Crosas, M., Dillo, I., Dumon, O., Edmunds, S., Evelo, C. T., Finkers, R., et al. (2016). The FAIR guiding principles for scientific data management and stewardship. *Scientific Data, 3*, 160018.

Zhao, Z., Liao, X., Martin, P., Maduro, J., Thijsse, P., Schaap, D., Stocker, M., Goldfarb, D., & Magagna, B. (2019). Knowledge-as-a-Service: A community knowledge base for research infrastructures in environmental and earth sciences. *2019 IEEE World Congress on Services (SERVICES), 2642-939X*, 127–132. https://doi.org/10.1109/SERVICES.2019.00041

## Website Citations

DASSI—Data Archive for Social Sciences in Italy. (2025). *DASSI archive.*https://www.dassi-archive.it/

FAIR-IMPACT. (2025). *FAIR-IMPACT: Supporting FAIR implementation across domains.*https://fair-impact.eu/

FAIRsFAIR. (2025). *FAIRsFAIR: Fostering FAIR data practices in Europe.*https://www.fairsfair.eu/

GO FAIR Initiative. (2025). *GO FAIR initiative.*https://www.go-fair.org/go-fair-initiative/

SSH Open Cloud. (2025). *Social sciences & humanities open cloud (SSHOC).*https://sshopencloud.eu/

WorldFAIR Project. (2025). *WorldFAIR: Global cooperation on FAIR data.*https://worldfair-project.eu/

# Chapter 4
# Ethical Issues in a Research Infrastructure for Empirical Social Sciences

**Cinzia Caporale, Giulia Sciolli, and Roberta Martina Zagarella**

## 4.1 Introduction: Ethics by Design in a Research Infrastructure for Empirical Social Sciences

As clearly explained in Chap. 1 of this volume, open science fosters transparency, reproducibility and integrity in research, and the development and sustainability of so-called Research Infrastructures (RIs) is fundamental for its advancement (Duşa et al., 2014; Leonelli, 2023). Going well beyond the original meaning of "infrastructure" as a distribution system for electricity or public transportation (Jensen & Winthereik, 2013:1), Research Infrastructures are facilities that collect and standardize data to make them more reusable and accessible, and that therefore make research more transparent and diffusible (Lindstrøm & Kropp, 2017). RIs today provide free and open services including laboratories, data networks, panels, advanced technological tools and digital platforms for the collection, analysis, reuse and sharing of scientific data.

When it comes to the social sciences, RIs facilitate in-depth analysis of complex issues such as population aging, inequalities, migrations, reactions to catastrophic events, or the implementation and evaluation of social policies, giving researchers the opportunity to access comparable data, develop interdisciplinary collaborations and offer scientifically grounded solutions in support of data-driven institutional decisions (Maegaard et al., 2019). In this context, the goal of the PNRR funded

This work was supported by *FOSSR* (*Fostering Open Science in Social Science Research*), funded by the European Union—NextGenerationEU under PNRR Grant agreement n. MUR IR0000008.

C. Caporale · G. Sciolli · R. M. Zagarella (✉)
Interdepartmental Center for Research Ethics and Integrity, National Research Council, Rome, Italy
e-mail: cinzia.caporale@cnr.it; giulia.sciolli@cnr.it; roberta.zagarella@cnr.it



G. Cerulli, E. Reale (eds.), *Research Infrastructures for Open Science in Social Science Research*, https://doi.org/10.1007/978-3-032-29575-0_4

project *FOSSR—Fostering Open Science in Social Science Research*[1] (2022–2026) of the National Research Council of Italy (CNR) was to create an Italian Open Science Cloud dedicated to the social sciences, which could both strengthen the existing Italian nodes of established RIs on these topics and provide the national scientific community with innovative tools and services. The ambition was to create a long-term sustainable Infrastructure that would consolidate and harmonise the study of the country's economic and social changes and support evidence-based policies. On the one hand, a meta-infrastructure was thus developed to provide a single access point for the Italian nodes of existing Research Infrastructures that already collect data on health, aging, family dynamics, and working conditions (RISIS,[2] CESSDA,[3] SHARE,[4] GUIDE,[5] GGP[6]). On the other hand, the project developed new tools for data analysis, including AI, and data collection, such as: a non-probabilistic panel to conduct surveys on socio-economic changes, recruiting 10,000 adult participants; a probabilistic panel to collect longitudinal data on the behaviours and opinions of residents in Italy aged 18–74; and a platform that connects experimental behavioural research laboratories, enabling participant recruitment from a pool of 100,000 people.

The FOSSR Infrastructure has been developed following an *ethics by design* approach.[7] This approach conceives ethics not as an add-on or a simple bureaucratic requirement, but as an integral part of research and an essential component of scientific excellence that should shape all stages of a research project—from its initial design, with periodic reviews during its progress, to the publication of results. This proactive approach to ethics is the reference paradigm that has been applied to FOSSR through the establishment of a specific project Task dedicated to research on ethical issues (Activity 2.5 "FOSSR Ethical Issues"), entrusted to one of the partners of the project (i.e., the CNR Interdepartmental Center for Research Ethics and Integrity[8]). Within this task, an independent Ethics Committee (FOSSR-EC)[9] has also been appointed.

---

[1] See https://www.fossr.eu/en/

[2] Research Infrastructure on Science and Innovation policy Studies (www.risis2.eu)

[3] Consortium of European Social Science Data Archives (https://www.cessda.eu)

[4] Survey of Health, Ageing and Retirement in Europe (https://share-eric.eu)

[5] Growing Up in Digital Europe (https://www.guidecohort.eu)

[6] Generations and Gender Programme (https://www.ggp-i.org/)

[7] See Caporale & Mancini, 2023.

[8] https://www.ethics.cnr.it/

[9] The FOSSR Ethics Committee (FOSSR-EC) met two/three times per year and was composed by Cinzia Caporale (Chair of the FOSSR-EC), Giovanni Cerulli (FOSSR Scientific Coordinator of the project), Emanuela Reale (FOSSR Scientific Advisor), and the experts appointed by the FOSSR Scientific Coordinator, namely: Carlo Casonato, University of Trento; Alessia Melegaro, Bocconi University (Milan); Laura Palazzani, Lumsa University (Rome); Alberto Eugenio Ermenegildo Pirni, Sant'Anna School for Advanced Studies (Pisa); Federico Gustavo Pizzetti, University of Milan. See https://www.fossr.eu/en/governance/ethics-committee/. The authors Roberta Martina Zagarella and Giulia Sciolli hosted and took part in the meetings.

The FOSSR-EC had the role of monitoring the decisional aspects of the project with ethical implications. More specifically, the main contributions of the FOSSR-EC to the governance of the project included: i) ethical consultancy services to the project scientific network; ii) review and management of ethical and safety issues arising from the methodologies of participant recruitment, the construction of surveys and data analysis procedures; iii) ethical supervision of the conditions of use of the Infrastructure, including data access policies; iv) consultancy on ethical issues related to open science more in general, including issues around the use of the research data deposited, managed, and made accessible through the FOSSR Infrastructure; and v) contribution to the elaboration of ethics guidelines for the researchers that will use the Infrastructure.

At the same time, the Task 2.5 "FOSSR Ethical Issues" contributed to the governance of the project through the following activities: i) providing technical-scientific support to the FOSSR Ethics Committee through conducting research; ii) coordinating with the Scientific Director of the project and the Infrastructure Manager to plan and organise scientific and management activities; iii) regularly participating in project events and, as observers, in the meetings of the Executive Committee, the Strategic Management Committee, the Stakeholder Advisory Board, and the Scientific Advisory Board; iv) conducting semi-structured interviews to enquire about potential ethical issues emerging from the activities of the different Work Packages; v) providing scientific and organisational support to the FOSSR team (the Principal Investigator, the Infrastructure Manager, WP leaders and researchers) in the process of preparing the documents necessary to request and obtain ethics approval (so-called "ethical clearance")[10]; vi) assembling and submitting to the FOSSR-EC members the material prepared by the FOSSR researchers for the request of ethical clearance, and collecting the feedback of the FOSSR-EC members prior to the submission to the CNR Research Ethics and Integrity Committee[11];

[10] The ethical clearance is an official opinion from an Ethics Committee or independent board, such as an Institutional Review Board, whose ultimate purpose is to provide public assurance that the research project respects everyone involved and that, from the design stage of the project, potential ethical issues have been identified and measures have been planned to prevent or minimize possible risks. The ethical review process is usually carried out by independent, multidisciplinary and pluralistic bodies (committees or commissions), whose primary aim is to protect the dignity, rights, safety and well-being of research participants, as well as the researchers themselves. The European Commission has stressed that ethics is a key part of scientific quality and excellence since the Horizon 2020 Framework Programme for Research and Innovation, and even more so in the new Horizon Europe programme. As a consequence, although obtaining ethical clearance for studies in the social sciences is not legally mandatory in Italy, it has become essential for securing funding and for publishing research results in an increasing number of journals and with reputable publishers.

[11] The CNR Research Ethics and Integrity Committee is chaired by the President of the CNR. The Committee is an independent body with an advisory role on matters of research ethics, bioethics and biolaw. These include ethical, deontological and juridical issues that fall within the scope of research integrity, as it is described in the scientific literature and in the main international Charters and Conventions, as well as in the "Guidelines for Research Integrity" produced by the CNR. See: https://www.cnr.it/en/ethics

and finally vii) drafting, in collaboration with the FOSSR-EC members, ethics guidelines for the various stakeholders who will be involved in the FOSSR activities and make use of the FOSSR Infrastructure, its services, panels or datasets.

The first and preliminary activity among those just mentioned was a scoping literature review, necessary to identify critical ethical issues, existing practices, research gaps and implications for FOSSR while the Infrastructure was still being developed, with the final aim of drafting the ethics guidelines. The aim of this chapter is to summarize and communicate the findings of such review.

It is important to specify that this chapter does not examine legal and IT compliance in data protection, because a Data Protection Officer and a different Unit of the FOSSR project with specific expertise were in charge of privacy aspects. Nevertheless, the chapter offers some ethical considerations of privacy matters, especially on the important issues related to the risks of indirect identification of research participants.

After situating the FOSSR project in the context of the development of Research Infrastructures within the Open Science movement and having briefly explained the role of Task 2.5 "FOSSR Ethical Issues", Sect. 4.2 explains the methods employed to conduct the literature review; Sect. 4.3 reports and examines the findings of the scoping review, with a focus on the specific meanings and implications of "open data" in the Social Sciences; Sect. 4.4 discusses the fundamental issue that emerged from the analysis of the findings, i.e., how to balance between data openness and the protection of research participants; finally, Sect. 4.5 concludes by pausing on the implications of this review work both in terms of the ethics mentoring that has been done for the development of the FOSSR Infrastructure and in terms of the possible future developments of FOSSR and of other RIs that deal with data from empirical social sciences.

## 4.2 Methods

The authors decided to conduct a "scoping review", namely a type of literature review that aims to map the key concepts, evidence, and research gaps within a specific topic. Unlike a systematic review, which focuses on synthesizing the best available evidence to answer a specific research question, a scoping review is broader in scope and is used to: i) identify and categorize existing research on a topic; ii) clarify key concepts and definitions in the literature; iii) examine the extent, range, and nature of research activity; iv) highlight gaps in knowledge to guide future research; v) disseminate findings in an accessible way. This kind of review was chosen because scoping reviews are more flexible than systematic reviews, which makes them useful for exploring emerging or complex topics such as the one of interest. Existing literature on the ethical issues relevant to Research Infrastructures, especially for empirical social sciences, is in fact still poor and hard to find, as existing works tend to refer to Research Infrastructures but not necessarily for the social sciences—or the other way around, they address research ethics in the social sciences but without considering the added complications of Research Infrastructures.

A first exploratory search was conducted on the databases *Scopus* and *Web of Science* for papers which would contain the following combinations of keywords in the title and/or abstract: i) ethics, research infrastructures, social sciences; and ii) ethics, open data, social sciences. Starting from the results of these searches, additional cited or suggested resources were subsequently found to be relevant even if they did not necessarily include such keywords in the title and/or abstract, confirming the need for a flexible approach in a scoping review which targets a still emergent topic. In the end a total of 39 resources were collected, which were classified in three categories: scientific articles (21), grey literature (13) and books (5). Each resource was read and analyzed by one of the authors (GS; RMZ) using a shared file which, in addition to identificatory information, for every resource gathered abstract, keywords, useful extracts and a short comment. The contents were then discussed by the authors through regular meetings, which led to identify three particularly recurring and interconnected issues. Preliminary findings were presented in poster form at the First Italian Congress on Research Integrity, which was held in Rome on 27th–28th January 2025.[12] The poster was subsequently selected to be published in the Italian scientific journal *Bioetica.*[13]

## 4.3 Meanings and Implications of "Open Data" in the Social Sciences: Results from a Scoping Review

The limited literature on the ethical issues of Research Infrastructures for the social sciences tends to converge on the same topics and to be country-specific (e.g., Axelsson & Schroeder, 2009 for Sweden; Jacquemin et al., 2018 for France; Reiter-Pazmandy, 2021 for Austria). Moreover, it often does not offer constructive critique but only points out problems. The "upstream" of the process (data management, archiving, sharing) is particularly neglected in the literature compared to data reuse, for example, with the exception of some works in anthropology (Cliggett, 2015; Silverman & Parezo, 1995; Zeitlyn, 2000). These, in a context of increased standardization of scientific practices, point out the inevitably "tailor-made" nature of data management practices (Diaz, 2021:19). One thing that is clear from the existing literature is that addressing the ethical issues of Research Infrastructures should start from the design of the Infrastructure and continue through to its lifecycle, by integrating relevant ethical principles and practices into its development in order to encourage responsible use (Eke et al., 2020; Schöpfel et al., 2022).

Our analysis has identified three particularly recurring and interconnected issues, which we explore in detail in the next three sub-sections: i) although the social

[12] See: https://www.ethics.cnr.it/wp-content/uploads/2025/01/127-Sciolli-e-Zagarella-1.pdf.

[13] See Sciolli & Zagarella, 2024.

sciences use a wide variety of data, and different disciplines within the social sciences therefore generate different issues regarding the ethics and integrity of data, there is still little clarity on the concrete meaning of "open data" and "FAIR principles"[14] for the social sciences, especially for individual disciplines within the social sciences; ii) the variety and specificity of these data is not recognized, and they are often talked about and treated as if they were quantitative data; and iii) given their specificity, for these kinds of data it is more complex to balance ethical principles on the one hand (first of all, protecting research participants) and scientific needs on the other (e.g., ensuring that data are indeed reusable).

### 4.3.1 *Qualitative Data in the Social Sciences Differs Both from Quantitative Data and Within Social Science Disciplines*

As noted by the Open Qualitative Research Working Group at the University of Cambridge (Westbury et al., 2022), historically policy discussions of open research have tended to refer to the norms, workflows, methodological approaches and quality standards of STEMM subjects (Science, Technology, Engineering, Mathematics and Medicine), such as the "reproducibility" and the "portability" of data. When discussions of open research make distinctions in areas of study, it is generally between "the sciences" and "the humanities" (Knöchelmann, 2019). And, when the social sciences are mentioned, the many disciplines and diverse methodologies found in the social sciences are often conflated. But, as many scholars have noted, the notion of a unified field of "social sciences" is misleading, as there are many subfields with different methodological approaches (Gerring, 2001). The social sciences use a wide variety of data (images, text collections, data gathered from social media, surveys, etc.) and it is important to consider that the qualitative data that can be made open might also include, depending on the specific discipline: transcripts of unstructured, semi-structured, or structured interviews, or of focus groups; audio or video recordings; notes (including fieldnotes from participant observation in ethnographic research); maps and geographical data; official documents, reports and meeting minutes; autobiographies, diaries, letters, and photographs. Disciplinary differences within the social sciences can be as stark as those commonly identified between the "hard" sciences and the humanities, and they impact on what open research means for different social scientists. Different disciplines within the social sciences therefore generate different issues regarding the ethics and integrity of "open data" (Levain et al., 2023). Despite such complexity, there is still little clarity on the concrete meaning and implications of "open data" and "FAIR principles" for the social sciences, especially for individual

[14] The idea that to be really "open", data should be Findable, Accessible, Interoperable and Reusable. See Chap. 3 of this volume.

disciplines *within* the social sciences (Berkowitz & Delacour, 2022). Things become even more complicated in the case of multidisciplinary research projects, which combine different methods and epistemological stances.

For instance, a survey of open science practices and attitudes from a sample of authors published in the top-10 most cited journals and of PhD students in top-20 ranked North American departments from "four major social science disciplines" observed favourable personal attitudes toward open science practices: as of 2020, nearly 90% of scholars had used at least one such practice (Ferguson et al., 2023). Support for posting data online seems high (88%) and the reported lifetime prevalence of open science practices increased from 49% in 2010 to 87% a decade later. However, it is important to notice that the four disciplines considered in the survey (economics, political sciences, psychology and sociology) tend to use, as reported by the survey itself, mostly quantitative research methods. And it is not a chance that the authors also report the finding that sociology (which, among the four disciplines, is the one that most uses qualitative research methods) "has the lowest levels of lifetime usage for all open science practices" (ibid:6). This 'resistance' of sociologists to open science practices compared to other researchers points to something which has ethical significance, namely the fact that making open certain kinds of data, especially qualitative data, might be filled with problems. In fact, sharing data could pose significant safety, privacy, and confidentiality risks for participants of certain kinds of research projects, for instance for victims of sexual assault (see Campbell et al., 2019) or for those who attempted suicide (see Corriveau et al., 2021), or for exponents of extremist political movements (see Bizeul, 2021). For these kinds of research projects, and for many others, it may be more difficult to share data and protect participants' safety, privacy and confidentiality at the same time.

### 4.3.2 *Qualitative Data in the Social Sciences Are Treated Like Quantitative Data, and This Increases Resistance to Open Science Practices*

The variety and specificity of data in the social sciences is not recognized; instead, these data are often talked about as if they were quantitative data. The vast majority of the literature pushing towards data openness is indeed based on a positivist conception of data (Feldman & Shaw, 2019). From this perspective, data sharing is considered primarily a technical issue that can be managed through the implementation of appropriate data management tools and standard policies (Diaz, 2021). While some types of data, such as data collected through surveys with closed-ended questions, can be more easily shared and reused, other kinds of data, such as interview transcripts or field observations, are strongly tied to the context of collection and to the person collecting them, and suffer from too much decontextualization once archived and shared (ibid; Thabrew et al., 2022).

Researchers who use ethnographic methods to conduct in-depth case studies are therefore especially resistant to data sharing practices, on the grounds that it is not possible to understand and give meaning to the data without the context in which the material was observed and collected. More generally, these kinds of qualitative researchers express concerns about "the irreproducibility of the original interview, the face-to-face encounter with an interviewee; the insufficiency of a transcript against the ethnographic moment of the interview; and the impossibility of ever adequately archiving the context of data" (Geiger et al., 2010:8). Consequently, researchers accessing and reusing such archived data would not be able, for example, to anticipate and consider any undeclared biases, which are part of the 'baggage' of those data. Hosseini, Wieczorek and Gordijn (2022,11), for instance, point out that reusing data collected by others has a significant epistemic downside: if one has not been involved in the data collection processes, one necessarily has limited insight into how the data was collected and might be unable to account for undisclosed biases embedded in data sets, especially in cases where data sets are not linked with a published manuscript or lack supplementary information about the used methodology (Lazer et al., 2014), which poses a threat to the integrity of research.

Speaking of methodology, it is useful to remember that open science also includes so-called "open methodology", which implies sharing in repositories details about one's research methods and context of data collection. Sharing research instruments such as interview guides, informed consent forms and coding methods could enhance transparency, facilitate teaching, and also illuminate how research methods and ethics evolve over time (Westbury et al., 2022:6). Giving more space and value to this kind of data might be an important addition in Research Infrastructures to mitigate the problem just mentioned. Nevertheless, this practice, even if embraced and supported, would still have limitations and risks, unless it is accompanied by clear statements that remind those who will access the information of the inevitably partial and 'filtered' nature of those contextual data. Questions are in fact raised by some scholars, for instance, about the potential effects on the way field notes are written if researchers know that they will be made public, especially regarding the risk that they will shift from being a fundamental tool for oneself as a researcher (for instance as an aid to memory, reasoning, formulating arguments, etc.) to becoming something extremely polished, with only a remote relationship to how the research actually happened (Diaz, 2021:13).

### 4.3.3 The Specificity of Data and Methods in Empirical Social Sciences Makes It Difficult to Balance Ethics with Scientific Needs

Given their specificity, for these kinds of data it is more complex to balance ethical principles (first of all, protecting research participants) with scientific needs (e.g., ensuring that data are indeed reusable). In fact, data openness allows for the critical examination and evaluation of results and facilitates efficiency; but, at the same time, it also makes data vulnerable to unethical practices. The European Commission considers "privacy" the only justifiable ethical reason not to open data, in the same way as trade secrets, national security, legitimate commercial interests and intellectual property rights of third parties (see Jacquemin et al., 2018). In qualitative research, even if the details of some content can be modified or removed, there may be other elements that lead to the indirect identification of participants, especially in narrative data. The question thus arises about the extent to which it is necessary to modify data to make the transcript of an interview, for example, shareable without any risk to participants, and whether at that point, after such modifications and removals, the transcript will still be usable and useful to other researchers (Campbell et al., 2019).

As noted by Diaz (2021) in his introduction to a special issue on the ethics of archiving qualitative data, most data archives recommend that data are anonymized before they are deposited and shared, and many data protection regulations treat anonymity as a "taken-for-granted ethical necessity" (Moore, 2012:331). However, several authors point out that some kinds of data, especially qualitative data, is not only difficult to anonymize, but its integrity—and thus its scientific value—can be compromised by the process of anonymization (Parry & Mauthner, 2004), as anonymized data have lost their situatedness and this may prevent their (re)usability. Here it is also worth pointing out that a considerable amount of literature seems to conflate data "anonymization" (processing data with the aim of irreversibly preventing the identification of the individual to whom it relates) with data "pseudonymization" (replacing any identifying characteristics of data with a pseudonym or a value which does not allow the research participant to be directly identified, although the individual can still be identified through indirect or additional information). On the other hand, some authors also point to the potentially unethical implications of anonymization by way of its reinforcing power asymmetries between participants and researchers, with only the latter always being named and remembered (Moore, 2012).

Stewart and Shaffer (2021) for example, as a contribution to that special issue, describe and discuss the process of archiving interview transcripts from more than 100 refugees as part of the requirements of two Economic and Social Research Council (ESRC) funded projects in the UK, to highlight the practical and ethical challenges of depositing sensitive material. They raise how difficulties included the need to respect interviewees' confidentiality, the laborious and perhaps never complete process of anonymization, and having to choose the level of access for future users and conditions for release. Importantly, they notice the tensions encountered between what they call "procedural ethics" and "micro-ethics", namely the difference between decisions based on "abstract rules" and decision based on the evaluation of the concrete case one is confronted with, in which following the rules might not be the most ethical option. This is a reminder of the situatedness of ethical practice and of the importance of an *ethics by design* approach.

A further related aspect of this issue is that whereas, on the one hand, the openness of data enables critical scrutiny and assessment of results and facilitates transparency and efficiency, it also can make data accessible to abusive actors (Hosseini et al., 2022). The technological mediation through which researchers access data that were collected and deposited by others, moreover, inevitably 'detaches' researchers from participants, weakening the perception of research participants as human subjects with expectations, rights and vulnerabilities that should be respected and protected (ibid:14–15). Parallel to this kind of detachment is also the risk that, with such big amounts of data becoming available, there might be future interconnections between databases that could manage to go beyond current systems of identity protection.

Besides benefiting scholars, the push for making research data FAIR has also allowed non-academic entities to access free research data (Wilkinson et al., 2016), and these non-academic users might not necessarily adhere to norms and values that academic researchers are expected to uphold (Hosseini, Wieczorek, Gordij 2022:11). This is why it is fundamental that new Research Infrastructures are developed following a reflection on the criteria for allowing access to data, as it was done for FOSSR.

## 4.4 How to Balance Between Openness and the Protection of Research Participants?

From these three key points, a series of considerations can be made that are relevant to Research Infrastructures like FOSSR. The analysis of these considerations constituted the springboard to structure ethics guidelines for research carried out using the resources made available through the FOSSR Infrastructure.

As several authors note, open science carries an "ethical trap": data originally collected for a specific research objective, for which participants gave consent and an ethics committee provided approval, are exposed to a deviation from the originally defined framework (see Jacquemin et al., 2018). To protect data and the participants who provided those data, it seems necessary to subject open data to some sort of constraints, not only for those accessing data but also for the researchers depositing them.

Regarding data deposit, some scholars (Campbell et al., 2019; Meyer, 2018) recommend a "tiered consent approach": this approach allows research participants to choose how much and which parts of their data they consent to share (for example, all data, only some data, only quantitative data, only specific portions/themes of qualitative data) and how their data can be shared (for example, only in repositories with standardized security systems, or with access rules that allow data to be used for research purposes only). Once this is established, it remains important to define when to request consent for data sharing: participants are presumably more aware of the potential risks and benefits of sharing their data, and of how they might feel knowing that such data will become accessible to other researchers, *after* the data have been collected (ibid). Awareness and knowledge of these issues, and of their implications, are fundamental for researchers to ensure that their projects are conducted with attention to both ethics and integrity, and that they promote responsible open science.

In sum, for RIs in the social sciences the problem is how to ensure robust ethical frameworks that enable a balance between openness and the protection of research participants, including in the long term.

## 4.5 Conclusions

The FOSSR project received ethical clearance from the CNR Research Ethics and Integrity Committee on 18 December 2024 for the creation and launching of the FOSSR Infrastructure, and several of its specific sub-projects received ethics approval in the following months. In the ethical clearance, the Committee expressly requested that every new project making use of data, panels or laboratories of the FOSSR Infrastructure must be evaluated by the ethics committee of the research body/university to which the project's Principal Investigator belongs or, in the absence of such a committee, by the CNR Committee or by another competent body.[15] FOSSR has opted for the creation of several panels whose members are asked to give an initial informed consent, and then each research project that will recruit participants through those panels will itself provide a specific information sheet and consent form.

The ethical aspects identified in the FOSSR project can be grouped into the following macro-areas:

- the participant information sheet and consent form, particularly the information provided to participants regarding the objectives and methodologies of the research activity, the commitments undertaken by the participant, and the ways in which participants are involved, including methods for withdrawing consent;
- any specific condition or situation of vulnerability of the participants;
- the provision of incentives to research participants;
- the possibility that carrying out certain research activities may lead to unexpected findings (so-called "incidental findings"), including sensitive information;
- the need to inform users of the FOSSR Infrastructure about the use of artificial intelligence algorithms for which it is not possible to completely verify the relevance, adequacy and quality of the process and conclusions (the so-called "black box" issue), particularly when such data are used to develop data-driven policies;

[15] A dedicated group is in charge of the data access policy as one of the final products of the FOSSR project.

- potential ethical issues connected to open science and open data in the social sciences;
- the management of research in so-called "critical areas", meaning environments, contexts or circumstances that pose particular risks to the safety and wellbeing of researchers and research participants (for example, situations involving clandestinity, crime or terrorism).

These aspects have been examined by the project Task 2.5 "FOSSR Ethical Issues" in consultation with the FOSSR Ethics Committee, and have been addressed in depth in the form of ethics guidelines that constitute the final deliverable of the project.

A challenging ambition for FOSSR, as the future leading Research Infrastructure for the social sciences in Italy, would be to consider how to become attractive also to social science disciplines that privilege more qualitative methods and therefore produce more qualitative data, which inherently carry more ethical complexities. As we have seen in the previous sections, qualitative research in the social sciences involves topics and methods that result in data that are dialogic, emergent, abundant and relational—so-called "DEAR data" (Westbury et al., 2022)—and that, therefore, need to be treated not only following the FAIR principles (findable, accessible, interoperable, reusable) but also the "CARE principles"—collective benefit, authority to control, responsibility, ethics (Berkowitz & Delacour, 2022). Qualitative data are described as DEAR to emphasize their deep entanglement with context, researchers, instruments, and participants. Sharing qualitative data can be ethically problematic because such data often include sensitive or co-constructed material that researchers do not feel they 'own' (Westbury et al., 2022). Qualitative researchers' relationships with their data are diversely shaped by specific disciplinary traditions, methodological approaches and epistemological stances. Therefore, any policy or expectation regarding open qualitative data will have to embrace multiple, context-sensitive solutions that reflect the plurality and complexity of qualitative inquiry.

## References

Axelsson, A.-S., & Schroeder, R. (2009). Making it open and keeping it safe: E-enabled data-sharing in Sweden. *Acta Sociologica, 52*(3), 213–226. https://www.jstor.org/stable/25652127

Berkowitz, H., & Delacour, H. (2022). Opening research data: What does it mean for social sciences? *M@n@gement, 25*, 1–15. https://doi.org/10.37725/mgmt.v25.9123

Bizeul, D. (2021). Faut-il tout dévoiler d'une enquête au Front national ? Réflexions sur le partage des données et le devoir éthique en sociologie. *Bulletin of Sociological Methodology/Bulletin de Méthodologie Sociologique, 150*(1), 70–105. https://doi.org/10.1177/0759106320960887

Campbell, R., Goodman-Williams, R., & Javorka, M. (2019). A trauma-informed approach to sexual violence research ethics and open science. *Journal of Interpersonal Violence, 34*(23–24), 4765–4793. https://doi.org/10.1177/0886260519871530

Caporale, C., & Mancini, E. (2023). L'ethics by design nella ricerca scientifica. *Bioetica. Rivista Interdisciplinare, 1*, 177–193.

Cliggett, L. (2015). Preservation, sharing, and technological challenges of longitudinal research in the digital age. In R. Sanjek & S. W. Tratner (Eds.), *Fieldnotes: Makings of anthropology in a digital world* (pp. 231–250). Penn Press.

Corriveau, P., Cauchie, J.-F., Lyonnais, A., & Perreault, I. (2021). Créer et gérer une banque de données numérique: les défis méthodologiques et éthiques de la construction et de la pérennité de la Plateforme d'analyse de la régulation sociale du suicide au Québec (PARSSQ). *Bulletin of Sociological Methodology/Bulletin de Méthodologie Sociologique, 150*(1), 28–50. https://doi.org/10.1177/0759106321995706

Diaz, P. (2021). Introduction: Archiving qualitative data in practice: Ethical feedback. *Bulletin of Sociological Methodology/Bulletin de Méthodologie Sociologique, 150*(1), 7–27. https://doi.org/10.1177/0759106321995678

Duşa, A., Nelle, D., Stock, G., & Wagner, G. G. (Eds.). (2014). *Facing the future: European research infrastructures for the humanities and social sciences*. Scivero.

Eke, D., et al. (2020). Ethical issues of e-infrastructures: What are they and how can they be addressed? In M. Aras-Oliva et al. (Eds.), *Societal challenges in the smart society* (Ethicomp Book Series). Universidad de la Rioja.

Feldman, S., & Shaw, L. (2019). The epistemological and ethical challenges of archiving and sharing qualitative data. *American Behavioral Scientist, 63*(6), 699–721. https://doi.org/10.1177/0002764218796084

Ferguson, J., et al. (2023). Survey of open science practices and attitudes in the social sciences. *Nature Communications, 14*, 5401. https://doi.org/10.1038/s41467-023-41111-1

Geiger, T., Moore, N., & Savage, M. (2010). *The archive in question*. Discussion Paper. NCRM. https://eprints.ncrm.ac.uk/id/eprint/921

Gerring, J. (2001). *Social science methodology: A criterial framework*. Cambridge University Press.

Hosseini, M., Wieczorek, M., & Gordijn, B. (2022). Ethical issues in social science research employing big data. *Science and Engineering Ethics, 28*(3), 29. https://doi.org/10.1007/s11948-022-00380-7

Jacquemin, B., et al. (2018). L'éthique des données de la recherche en sciences humaines et sociales. Information-Communication: le recours à l'éthique en contexte numérique. 6e conférence "Document numérique & Société", GRESEC, Échirolles, France, Septembre 2018, pp. 71–86. https://doi.org/10.3917/dbu.balic.2018.01.0071

Jensen, C. B., & Winthereik, B. R. (2013). *Monitoring movements in development aid: Recursive partnerships and infrastructures*. MIT Press.

Knöchelmann, M. (2019). Open science in the humanities, or: Open humanities? *Publications, 7*(4), 65. https://doi.org/10.3390/publications7040065

Lazer, D., Kennedy, R., King, G., & Vespignani, A. (2014). The parable of Google flu: Traps in big data analysis. *Science, 343*(6176), 1203–1205. https://doi.org/10.1126/science.1248506

Leonelli, S. (2023). *Philosophy of open science*. Cambridge University Press.

Levain, A., et al. (2023). The credibility of ethnographic materials in the face of the open research data movement. *Revue d'Anthropologie des Connaissances, 17*(2). https://doi.org/10.4000/rac.30291

Lindstrøm, M. D., & Kropp, K. (2017). Understanding the infrastructure of European research infrastructures—The case of the European social survey (ESS-ERIC). *Science and Public Policy, 44*(6), 855–864. https://doi.org/10.1093/scipol/scx018

Maegaard, B., Pozzo, R., Melloni, A., & Woollard, M. (Eds.). (2019). *Stay tuned to the future: Impact of the research infrastructures for social sciences and humanities* (p. 128). Print. Lessico Intellettuale Europeo.

Meyer, M. N. (2018). Practical tips for ethical data sharing. *Advances in Methods and Practices in Psychological Science, 1*(1), 131–144. https://doi.org/10.1177/2515245917747656

Moore, N. (2012). The politics and ethics of naming: Questioning anonymisation in (archival) research. *International Journal of Social Research Methodology, 15*(4), 331–340. https://doi.org/10.1080/13645579.2012.688330

Parry, O., & Mauthner, N. S. (2004). Whose data are they anyway? Practical, legal and ethical issues in archiving qualitative research data. *Sociology, 38*(1), 139–152. https://doi.org/10.1177/0038038504039366

Reiter-Pazmandy, M. (2021). Data-access for the social sciences in Austria. Open data, closed data, research infrastructures and re-use. Austrian journal of. *Political Science, 50*(1), 15–20.

Schöpfel, J., Azeroual, O., & de Castro, P. (2022). Research information systems and ethics relating to open science. *CRIS2022: 15th International Conference on Current Research Information Systems*, Dubrovnik, Croatia, May 2022. ffhal-03695546.

Sciolli, G., & Zagarella, R. M. (2024). Etica e integrità nella scienza aperta. Implicazioni per le infrastrutture di ricerca nelle scienze sociali. *Bioetica. Rivista Interdisciplinare, 2*, 413–416.

Silverman, S., & Parezo, N. J. (1995). *Preserving the anthropological record.* Wenner-Gren Foundation for Anthropological Research.

Stewart, E., & Shaffer, M. (2021). The ethical and practical challenges of archiving refugee accounts: Reflections from two research projects in the UK. *Bulletin of Sociological Methodology/Bulletin de Méthodologie Sociologique, 150*(1), 51–69. https://doi.org/10.1177/0759106321995707

Thabrew, H., et al. (2022). 'As long as it's used for beneficial things': An investigation of non-Maori, Maori and young people's perceptions regarding the research use of the Aotearoa New Zealand integrated data infrastructure (IDI). *Journal of Empirical Research on Human Research Ethics, 17*(4), 471–482. https://doi.org/10.1177/15562646221111294

Westbury, M., et al. (2022). *Voice, representation, relationships: Report of the open qualitative research working group*. University of Cambridge Working Group on Open Qualitative Research. https://doi.org/10.17863/CAM.91979

Wilkinson, M. D., et al. (2016). The FAIR guiding principles for scientific data management and stewardship. *Scientific Data, 3*(1), 160018. https://doi.org/10.1038/sdata.2016.18

Zeitlyn, D. (2000). Archiving anthropology. *Forum: Qualitative Social Research, 1*(3), 17. https://www.qualitative-research.net/index.php/fqs/article/view/1034/2236

# Part II
# The FOSSR Contribution to Research Focus Areas

# Chapter 5
# FOSSR Project Background, Objectives and Impact

**Giovanni Cerulli and Emanuela Reale**

## 5.1 Introduction

Over the past two decades, social science research has undergone profound transformations driven by the increasing availability of data, the diffusion of digital technologies, and the growing demand for evidence-based policymaking. These transformations have progressively altered the ways in which social scientists collect, manage, analyse, and disseminate knowledge. At the same time, they have been exposed to structural weaknesses concerning national research systems, particularly in terms of data accessibility, methodological transparency, and long-term sustainability of research infrastructures (Reichmann & Wieser, 2022).

Within this evolving context, Open Science (hereafter OS) has emerged as a key paradigm shaping research policies at both European and national levels (Persic et al., 2021). OS promotes openness, transparency, reusability, and collaboration across all stages of the research process, from data collection to dissemination of results. For the social sciences, the OS transition is particularly challenging, as it involves sensitive data, complex ethical and legal considerations, and heterogeneous research traditions. Yet, it also represents a major opportunity to enhance the quality, relevance, and societal impact of research.

The Fostering Open Science in Social Science Research (FOSSR) project was conceived precisely at the intersection of these transformations. Funded under the Italian National Recovery and Resilience Plan (NRRP), Mission 4 "Education and Research", Component 2 "From Research to Business" (Investment 3.1), FOSSR aims to strengthen and integrate research infrastructures (RIs) in the social sciences by building a coordinated, open, and interoperable ecosystem of data, services,

G. Cerulli (✉) · E. Reale
CNR-IRCrES (Institute for Sustainable Economic Growth), National Research Council of Italy, Rome, Italy
e-mail: giovanni.cerulli@cnr.it; emanuela.reale@cnr.it



G. Cerulli, E. Reale (eds.), *Research Infrastructures for Open Science in Social Science Research*, https://doi.org/10.1007/978-3-032-29575-0_5

and tools. Its strategic ambition is to contribute to the creation of an Italian Open Science Cloud for the Social Sciences, aligned with the European Open Science Cloud (EOSC), and capable of supporting high-quality research on economic and societal "grand" challenges (European Commission, 2016).

The NRRP provides an unprecedented policy and financial framework for addressing long-standing structural gaps in the Italian research system. In particular, Mission 4 explicitly recognizes the central role of RIs in fostering scientific excellence, digital transformation, and innovation. Within this framework, social sciences are no longer viewed as ancillary disciplines, but as essential contributors to understanding and governing complex societal transitions, including demographic ageing, education dynamics, migration, inequalities, technological change, health dynamics, and sustainable development.

FOSSR responds to this policy vision by focusing on the infrastructural dimension of social science research. Rather than funding isolated research projects, it invests in the integration and enhancement of existing high-level Research Infrastructures coordinated by the National Research Council (CNR), namely CESSDA, SHARE, and RISIS. These infrastructures already play a key role at the European level, but their potential impact within the Italian research ecosystem has been constrained by fragmentation, uneven access, and limited interoperability.

By networking these infrastructures, developing new services, and embedding Open Science principles into their operation, FOSSR seeks to overcome these limitations generating an interoperable research digital eco-system. The project thus represents a strategic investment not only in digital capacities and advanced technologies, but also in new modes of knowledge production and dissemination, consistent with the broader objectives of the PNRR and the Next Generation EU programme.

The remainder of the chapter is structured as follows. Section 5.2 discusses the main societal and scientific challenges faced by social science research in Italy, highlighting the existing infrastructural gaps and the need for coordinated Research Infrastructures. Section 5.3 introduces the conceptual framework of FOSSR, situating the project within the broader paradigm of Open Science and the evolving role of Research Infrastructures in the social sciences. Section 5.4 presents the logic and strategic objectives of the FOSSR project, detailing its core dimensions and expected impacts. Section 5.5 describes the Work Package structure, illustrating the design logic, content, and complementarities across project activities. Section 5.6 addresses governance, ethics, sustainability, and long-term impact, while Sect. 5.7 concludes by summarizing the main contributions of FOSSR and outlining future perspectives.

## 5.2 Social Science Challenges and the Infrastructural Gap in Italy

The relevance of social sciences in contemporary societies has never been greater. Economic crises, pandemics, climate change, geopolitical instability, and technological disruptions have highlighted the need for robust empirical evidence to inform public debate and policy decisions. Social sciences provide essential analytical frameworks and empirical tools to study these phenomena, assess their distributional effects, and evaluate policy responses.

Despite this growing relevance, social science research has historically faced structural constraints, particularly in countries where investment in research infrastructures has been uneven, or not sufficiently promoted. In Italy, these constraints have manifested in several ways.

*First*, access to high-quality data has been fragmented. While numerous datasets exist, they are often dispersed across institutions, governed by heterogeneous standards, and difficult to combine. This fragmentation limits the ability of researchers to conduct longitudinal, comparative, and interdisciplinary analyses, which are increasingly necessary to address complex societal challenges.

*Second*, methodological innovation has been unevenly supported. Advanced methods such as causal inference, computational social science, agent-based modelling, and large-scale survey integration require not only individual expertise, but also shared infrastructures, computational resources, and standardized workflows. Without these, methodological advances risk remaining confined to small research groups, rather than becoming widely accessible.

*Third*, the connection between research and policymaking has often been weak. Although policymakers increasingly demand evidence-based analyses, the translation of research outputs into usable policy insights is hampered by barriers in data accessibility, reproducibility, and communication. This gap undermines the societal impact of social science research.

*Fourth*, ethical and legal challenges have become more prominent. The use of personal and sensitive data requires robust governance frameworks to ensure data protection, research integrity, and public trust. In the absence of coordinated infrastructures, ethical compliance risks being addressed in an ad hoc and inefficient manner.

These challenges are not unique to Italy, but they are particularly salient in a research system characterized by strong disciplinary traditions, institutional fragmentation, and limited long-term funding for infrastructures. In this context, RIs play a crucial role as enablers of cumulative, collaborative, and high-impact research (Cramer & Hallonsten, 2020).

RIs in the social sciences differ from those in the natural sciences. They are not primarily based on large physical facilities, but on data repositories, survey systems, digital platforms, and service ecosystems. Their value lies in their ability to curate data over time, ensure comparability and quality, and provide users with tools and support for analysis and reuse.

In recent years, Italy has significantly strengthened its participation in major European social science infrastructures, including CESSDA ERIC, SHARE ERIC, and RISIS. These infrastructures provide access to harmonized survey data, longitudinal studies, and integrated datasets on research and innovation systems. However, participation alone is not sufficient to maximize their impact. Without national-level coordination, integration, and service development, the benefits of these infrastructures may remain underexploited.

FOSSR was designed precisely to address this infrastructural gap. By creating linkages among existing infrastructures, enhancing their services, and embedding them within a coherent Open Science framework, FOSSR aims to transform fragmented resources into an integrated research ecosystem. This transformation is essential to enable Italian social scientists to fully participate in international research networks and to contribute effectively to national and European policy debates.

## 5.3 FOSSR Conceptual Framework

To fully understand the rationale and ambition of FOSSR, it is necessary to situate the project within the broader conceptual framework of Open Science and RIs.

Open Science is not a single policy instrument or technological solution, but a comprehensive transformation of the research system. It encompasses a set of principles and practices aimed at making scientific knowledge more accessible, transparent, and reusable. These principles include open access to publications, open data, open methodologies, open peer review, and citizen engagement in research processes.

In the social sciences, Open Science raises specific conceptual and operational challenges. Data often involve human subjects, personal information, and sensitive topics. Openness must therefore be balanced with ethical responsibility, data protection, and respect for participants' rights. This balance requires not only legal compliance, but also the development of shared norms, standards, and infrastructures.

RIs are central to operationalizing Open Science in the social sciences. They provide the organizational, technical, and governance frameworks necessary to implement Open Science principles in practice. Through standardized data curation, metadata, access protocols, and user support, RIs enable data to be FAIR, that is: findable, accessible, interoperable, and reusable (Wilkinson et al., 2016).

Beyond data management, RIs also play a crucial role in shaping research practices. They influence which questions can be asked, which methods are used, and which communities are formed. In this sense, infrastructures are not neutral: they actively structure the production of knowledge (Houghton, 2005).

The European research policy landscape has increasingly recognized this role. The inclusion of social science infrastructures in the ESFRI Roadmap and the development of the European Open Science Cloud reflect a strategic commitment to building sustainable, interoperable, and user-oriented infrastructures across disciplines.

Within this landscape, FOSSR adopts a *network-based* model of infrastructure development. Rather than creating a new, standalone infrastructure, it seeks to integrate and enhance existing ones, enhancing their complementary strengths. CESSDA provides expertise in social science data archiving and access; SHARE offers longitudinal survey data on ageing, health, and socio-economic conditions; RISIS delivers integrated datasets and analytical tools for studying science, technology, and innovation systems.

By connecting these infrastructures through shared services, interoperable platforms, and coordinated governance, FOSSR creates an added value that exceeds the sum of its parts. This integrative approach reflects a mature understanding of Research Infrastructures as evolving ecosystems rather than static facilities.

Importantly, FOSSR also emphasizes the social dimension of infrastructures. Open Science is not only about data and technology, but also about communities, skills, and trust. Training, capacity building, and stakeholder engagement are therefore integral components of the project. Through these activities, FOSSR aims to foster a broad and inclusive *research community* capable of using and contributing to Open Science infrastructures.

In this conceptual framework, FOSSR can be seen as a strategic experiment in infrastructural integration and Open Science implementation within the social sciences. Its outcomes are expected to extend beyond the immediate project horizon, providing a model for future investments and governance strategies for Research Infrastructures, both in Italy and across Europe.

## 5.4 Logic and Strategic Objectives of the FOSSR Project

The FOSSR project emerged from a long-standing strategic reflection within the Italian social science community on the role of Research Infrastructures in supporting scientific excellence, innovation, and societal relevance. This reflection was shaped by two converging processes: (i) the consolidation of major European Research Infrastructures in the social sciences, and (ii) the growing policy demand for evidence-based decision-making in the context of complex societal transitions.

At the European level, infrastructures such as CESSDA ERIC, SHARE ERIC, and RISIS have progressively demonstrated their capacity to generate scientific value by providing harmonized data, advanced services, and collaborative platforms. These infrastructures have enabled new forms of comparative, longitudinal, and interdisciplinary research, while also supporting policy-relevant analyses. However, their effectiveness depends critically on national-level engagement, coordination, and investment.

In Italy, the National Research Council (CNR) has played a central role in coordinating national participation in these infrastructures. Over time, it became increasingly clear that a further step was needed: moving beyond participation towards integration. The challenge was not merely to access European infrastructures, but to embed them within a coherent national *ecosystem* capable of amplifying their impact, fostering methodological innovation, and broadening their user base.

The opportunity to address this challenge was provided by the NRRP. Unlike previous funding schemes, the NRRP explicitly recognizes RIs as strategic assets for national development and allocates substantial resources to their creation, strengthening, and networking. Within Mission 4, Investment 3.1 specifically targets the development of integrated systems of research and innovation infrastructures, encouraging coordination, interoperability, and sustainability.

FOSSR was conceived as a response to this call, with a clear strategic positioning. Rather than proposing the creation of a new infrastructure from scratch, the project focuses on the networking and enhancement of existing infrastructures with high or medium priority in the National Research Infrastructure Programme. This choice reflects a mature understanding of infrastructural development as a cumulative and evolutionary process.

The strategic objectives of FOSSR can be grouped into the following interconnected dimensions:

*Infrastructural integration*. FOSSR aims to create a unified access framework for social science data and services by integrating CESSDA, SHARE, and RISIS. This integration is not limited to technical interoperability, but extends to governance, user support, and service design. The goal is to provide researchers with a seamless experience, reducing fragmentation and lowering entry barriers.

*Generation of new social data*. Through two brand-new socio-economic surveys, that is, the Internet Online Probability Panel (IOPP), based on probabilistic sampling, and the Online Research Panel (ORP), based on non-probabilistic sampling, FOSSR aims to produce new high-frequency longitudinal social data. These infrastructures will enable repeated interviews of a well-structured sample of the Italian population (approximately 10,000 individuals for both IOPP and ORP), significantly enhancing the understanding of both the static characteristics and the dynamic evolution of key socio-economic phenomena.

*Facilities for large-scale hardware infrastructure*. FOSSR will substantially enhance its computational and data management capabilities through the deployment of four new data centers strategically located at CNR sites in Turin, Naples, Catania, and Palermo, alongside a significant reinforcement of the existing node in Pisa. Together, these facilities will provide large-scale data storage and advanced computational power, supporting high-frequency data collection, complex analytical workflows, and secure data access. This constitutes a major investment in research hardware infrastructure, complementing software and service development, and is fully aligned with the NRRP objective of strengthening digital and computational capacities for research.

*Methodological and technological innovation*. By investing in new tools for data collection, curation, analysis, and visualization, FOSSR seeks to expand the methodological frontier of social science research. This includes support for advanced survey methods, innovative Machine Learning and AI toolboxes, semantic graph, causal inference, computational social science, and policy evaluation techniques. The project recognizes that infrastructures are key drivers of methodological change, as they shape what researchers can do in practice.

*Human capital development and training*. Through the recruitment of a significant number of young researchers and the implementation of high-level training activities, FOSSR aims to contribute to the construction of the next generation of social science researchers. By combining advanced methodological training, hands-on experience with working within a group building a new RI, the project invests in human capital development, fostering researchers who are both technically solid and fully aware of the methodological, ethical and societal dimensions of contemporary social science research.

*Open Science implementation*. FOSSR operationalizes Open Science principles by embedding FAIR data practices, ethical governance, and open access services into the daily functioning of infrastructures. Open Science is not treated as an abstract ideal, but as a concrete set of practices supported by dedicated services, training, and governance mechanisms.

*Scientific communication and community building*. FOSSR will make a substantial contribution to the advancement of scientific communication in the social sciences by developing dedicated dissemination and communication tools tailored both to non-technical external audiences and to the research community itself. Beyond outreach, these activities are explicitly designed to foster community building among social science researchers, strengthening networks, shared practices, and collective identities.

*Societal and policy impact*. FOSSR is explicitly designed to enhance the usability of social science research for policymakers, public administrations, and other stakeholders. By building dedicated tools, like the Policy Learning Platform (PLP), and by improving data accessibility, transparency, and reproducibility, the project strengthens the foundations for evidence-based policymaking and informed public debate.

These strategic objectives are mutually reinforcing, thus strengthening the legitimacy and sustainability of the entire RI.

## 5.5 Work Packages: Design Logic, Content, and Complementarities

The organizational backbone of FOSSR is its Work Package (WP) structure. The WPs are designed to reflect the project's strategic objectives and to ensure coherence between infrastructural development, scientific innovation, and societal impact. Each WP addresses a specific dimension of the infrastructure, while strong complementarities ensure integration across activities.

WP1 focuses on project coordination, governance, and management. Its role is to ensure strategic alignment with PNRR objectives, compliance with administrative and financial requirements, and effective coordination among partners. WP1 also addresses sustainability planning, monitoring progress, and managing risks. Given the complexity of FOSSR as a multi-institutional infrastructure project, robust governance and coordination are essential.

WP2 is dedicated to data integration and interoperability. This WP develops the technical and conceptual foundations for connecting datasets and services across infrastructures. Activities include the harmonization of metadata standards, the development of semantic tools, and the implementation of interoperability frameworks. WP2 is central to transforming fragmented data resources into an integrated research ecosystem.

WP3 addresses IT infrastructure and cloud services. It focuses on the deployment and management of computational resources, data centers, and secure access environments. WP3 ensures that researchers have access to scalable and reliable infrastructures capable of supporting advanced analytical workflows. It also addresses issues of cybersecurity, performance, and service continuity.

WP4 concentrates on innovative data collection and methodological tools. This WP supports the development of new survey methodologies, experimental designs, and data collection instruments. It builds on the strengths of existing infrastructures while exploring innovative approaches to capturing social and economic phenomena. WP4 is particularly relevant for addressing emerging research questions related to societal change.

WP5 focuses on data analysis, indicators, and advanced methodologies. This WP develops analytical tools and workflows for policy evaluation, causal inference, and computational social science. By integrating data from multiple infrastructures, WP5 enables new forms of analysis that were previously difficult or impossible. This WP plays a key role in enhancing the scientific value of the infrastructure.

WP6 addresses ethics, integrity, and legal compliance. Open Science in the social sciences requires careful attention to ethical and legal issues, particularly when dealing with personal and sensitive data. WP6 develops guidelines, tools, and support services to ensure responsible data sharing, research integrity, and compliance with data protection regulations. It embeds ethical considerations into the design and operation of the infrastructure.

WP7 focuses on training, capacity building, and education. This WP recognizes that infrastructures are socio-technical systems that depend on human skills and communities. Training activities target researchers at different career stages, as well as policymakers and practitioners. WP7 contributes to building a shared culture of Open Science and methodological innovation.

WP8 and WP9 are dedicated to dissemination, communication, and stakeholder engagement. These WPs ensure that FOSSR's services and results are visible and accessible to a broad audience. Activities include communication strategies, outreach events, and engagement with policymakers, public administrations, and civil society. WP8 and WP9 play a crucial role in maximizing the societal impact of the project.

The design logic of the WPs reflects a balance between specialization and integration. Each WP has a clear focus, but none operates in isolation. For example, methodological tools developed in WP4 are implemented on the infrastructures managed in WP3, integrated through WP2, governed ethically by WP6, and disseminated through WP8 and WP9. This interdependence is a defining feature of FOSSR.

Taken together, the Work Packages translate the project's strategic vision into concrete actions. They provide a structured pathway for achieving infrastructural integration, methodological innovation, Open Science implementation, and societal impact. Their complementarity ensures that FOSSR operates as a coherent and effective Research Infrastructure rather than as a collection of disconnected activities.

## 5.6 Governance, Ethics, Sustainability, and Long-Term Impact

The effectiveness and legitimacy of a Research Infrastructure depend not only on its technical capabilities, but also on its governance, ethical foundations, and sustainability. FOSSR explicitly addresses these dimensions, recognizing them as integral components of Open Science and responsible research.

Governance within FOSSR is designed to balance coordination and inclusiveness. Given the multi-institutional nature of the project, governance structures ensure strategic oversight, operational coordination, and stakeholder engagement. Clear roles and responsibilities support efficient decision-making, while mechanisms for consultation and feedback foster a sense of shared ownership among participating institutions and user communities.

Ethics and research integrity are central pillars of FOSSR. The social sciences often deal with sensitive data involving human subjects, making ethical oversight essential. FOSSR embeds ethical and legal expertise into its infrastructure, providing guidance on data protection, informed consent, responsible data sharing, and compliance with relevant regulations. Rather than treating ethics as an external constraint, the project integrates ethical considerations into the design of services and workflows, aligning Open Science practices with societal values and public trust.

Sustainability is a key concern for any infrastructure developed under time-limited funding schemes such as the NRRP. FOSSR addresses sustainability at multiple levels. Technically, it builds on existing infrastructures and institutional capacities, reducing the risk of obsolescence and duplication. Organizationally, it strengthens networks and competences that can be maintained beyond the project's duration. Strategically, it aligns its services with European initiatives such as the EOSC, increasing the likelihood of continued integration and support.

Financial sustainability is also addressed through the development of sustainability plans that explore diversified funding sources, including institutional support, competitive funding, and service-based models where appropriate. While maintaining openness and accessibility, FOSSR acknowledges the need for long-term resource planning to ensure continuity of services.

The long-term impact of FOSSR extends beyond the immediate research community. By improving access to high-quality data and analytical tools, the project enhances the capacity of policymakers and public administrations to design, implement, and evaluate policies based on robust evidence. This contribution is particularly relevant in areas such as social policy, health, innovation, and regional development, which are central to the NRRP agenda.

Moreover, FOSSR contributes to building a culture of Open Science in the social sciences. Through training, dissemination, and community-building activities, it promotes transparency, reproducibility, and collaboration. These cultural changes are essential for sustaining the benefits of infrastructural investments and for aligning research practices with societal expectations.

## 5.7 Conclusions

The FOSSR project represents a significant milestone in the development of social science RIs in Italy. By networking and strengthening existing infrastructures, embedding Open Science principles, and investing in methodological and organizational innovation, FOSSR addresses long-standing structural challenges and opens new opportunities for scientific and societal impact.

This chapter has outlined the background, objectives, and architecture of FOSSR, situating the project within the broader context of Open Science, European research policies, and the Italian National Recovery and Resilience Plan. FOSSR emerges as a strategic response to the need for integrated, sustainable, and user-oriented infrastructures capable of supporting high-quality research on economic and societal change.

Looking forward, the legacy of FOSSR will depend on its ability to evolve and adapt. RIs are not static entities: they must respond to emerging research questions, technological developments, and societal needs. By adopting a flexible and modular architecture, fostering strong governance and ethical foundations, and engaging diverse user communities, FOSSR is well positioned to continue playing a central role in the Italian and European social science ecosystem.

In a broader perspective, FOSSR offers a model for infrastructural development that emphasizes integration over fragmentation, openness over exclusivity, and long-term capacity building over short-term outputs. As such, it contributes not only to the advancement of social science research, but also to the broader goal of building a more knowledge-driven, inclusive, and sustainable society. Cerulli, G. (2022).

Econometric Evaluation of Socio-Economic Programs: Theory and Applications (second ed.). Springer.

## References

Cramer, K., & Hallonsten, O. (2020). *Big science and research infrastructures in Europe*. Edward Elgar.

European Commission. (2016). *European charter for access to research infrastructures*. Publications Office of the European Union.

Houghton, J. W. (2005). Changing research practices and research infrastructure development. *Higher Education Management and Policy, 17*(1), 63.

Persic, A., Beigel, F., Hodson, S., & Oti-Boateng, P. (2021). *The time for open science is now. UNESCO science report: The race against time for smarter development* (pp. 12–16). UNESCO Publishing.

Reichmann, S., & Wieser, B. (2022). Open science at the science–policy interface: Bringing in the evidence? *Health Research Policy and Systems, 20*(1), 70.

Wilkinson, M. D., et al. (2016). The FAIR guiding principles for scientific data management and stewardship. *Scientific Data, 3*, 160018.

# Chapter 6
# Probabilistic Surveys to Monitor Population and Societal Change

**Loredana Cerbara, Ferruccio Biolcati Rinaldi, Giulio Ecchia, Dario Germani, Letizia Mencarini, Claudia Pennacchiotti, Ilaria Primerano, Michele Santurro, Luciana Taddei, Cristiano Vezzoni, and Guglielmo Weber**

## 6.1 Introduction: Probabilistic Surveys in National and International Perspective

In the contemporary landscape of empirical social research, probability sampling remains the epistemological cornerstone of statistical inference and the methodological foundation upon which the entire edifice of survey-based evidence rests. Within a framework grounded in a probabilistic sampling design, inference derives not from assumptions about the distributional characteristics of the target variable but from the probabilistic mechanism by which sampling units are selected, in the specific case of inference from finite populations. Each element of the population has a known and non-zero probability of inclusion, and the probability of every possible

L. Cerbara · D. Germani · C. Pennacchiotti · I. Primerano · M. Santurro · L. Taddei (✉)
Institute for Research on Population and Social Policies, National Research Council (CNR-IRPPS), Rome, Italy
e-mail: loredana.cerbara@cnr.it; dario.germani@cnr.it; claudia.pennacchiotti@cnr.it; ilaria.primerano@cnr.it; michele.santurro@cnr.it; luciana.taddei@cnr.it

F. Biolcati Rinaldi · C. Vezzoni
Università degli Studi di Milano, Milan, Italy
e-mail: ferruccio.biolcati@unimi.it; cristiano.vezzoni@unimi.it

G. Ecchia
Alma Mater Studiorum—University of Bologna, Bologna, Italy
e-mail: giulio.ecchia@unibo.it

L. Mencarini
Bocconi University, Milan, Italy
e-mail: letizia.mencarini@unibocconi.it

G. Weber
University of Padua, Padua, Italy
e-mail: guglielmo.weber@unipd.it



G. Cerulli, E. Reale (eds.), *Research Infrastructures for Open Science in Social Science Research*, https://doi.org/10.1007/978-3-032-29575-0_6

sample can be theoretically deduced. Under this framework, the statistical behaviour of estimators—bias, variance, and mean square error—is evaluated with respect to these inclusion probabilities, not to any parametric model of the population itself (Hájek, 1981; Hansen et al., 1983). This principle ensures that inference is objective, in the sense that its validity depends solely on the properties of the random selection procedure. As Koch and Gillings (1984) noted, the assumption necessary for valid probability-sampling-based inference is that the sampling mechanism operates as intended.

The probabilistic sample, therefore, is not merely a technical artifact but a logical precondition for generalisation. Its essential role is to provide a defensible bridge between sample statistics and population parameters. Through stratified, clustered, or multistage sampling designs, it enables efficient representation of heterogeneous populations while maintaining calculable selection probabilities. This capability underpins the external validity of survey estimates and ensures that indicators derived from the sample can be generalised to the population with quantifiable precision. In contrast, non-probability designs—such as quota or convenience sampling—lack a stochastic selection mechanism and are consequently unable to support valid inferential statements, being prone to self-selection and coverage bias (Cornesse & Blom, 2023).

Yet, as Kruskal and Mosteller (1979) demonstrated, the concept of representativeness is multifaceted and often misused. A probability sample is "representative" only in a statistical sense—that is, in expectation over repeated samples—and not necessarily in any descriptive or substantive sense for a given draw. The validity of inference, therefore, relies not on the presumed similarity between sample and population but on the probabilistic properties of the sampling design. Still, as Särndal et al. (1992) observed, practical constraints often lead to purposive approximations—e.g. quota or balanced sampling—that attempt to mimic population structure while sacrificing probability-based objectivity. These methods, while operationally convenient, preclude the estimation of sampling error and therefore undermine the inferential transparency that defines scientific surveys. However, when the cognitive intent is not strictly inferential, but only qualitative insights or explorations of little-known phenomena are sought, this type of approach is widely used.

The probabilistic approach itself is not without criticism. Hájek (1981) questioned the epistemological legitimacy of basing inference on hypothetical samples that could have been drawn but were not. Nevertheless, an inference framework grounded in a probabilistic sampling design remains the only approach that yields inference independent of unverifiable assumptions about the underlying population model. Schreuder and Alegria (1995) empirically demonstrated the sensitivity of such inference to mis-specified or unknown inclusion probabilities: when unequal probabilities are mistakenly treated as equal, estimators become biased, sometimes severely so. The implication is clear—probabilistic inference is only as strong as the accuracy of its sampling frame and probability structure.

From a pragmatic standpoint, probabilistic designs face growing operational challenges. Declining response rates, frame imperfections, and escalating fieldwork costs threaten both their feasibility and statistical integrity (Groves et al., 2009). Non-response bias—particularly when correlated with key survey variables—introduces distortions that cannot be corrected through weighting alone, as post-stratification and calibration depend on auxiliary data that are often incomplete or lagged. Despite these challenges, probabilistic sampling remains the gold standard, its authority derived from the transparency of the inferential mechanism and its capacity for replication and cross-survey comparability.

The methodological power of probability sampling becomes even more evident in longitudinal and panel research designs, which extend the logic of the survey from static description to dynamic analysis. While cross-sectional surveys provide snapshots of populations at given points in time, longitudinal designs allow the study of change and causality, tracking the same or comparable units across multiple waves to reveal trajectories of individuals, households, and institutions (Lynn, 2012; Menard, 2002). In this context, the probabilistic basis of the initial sample ensures that the panel is representative at inception, while its longitudinal nature permits the modelling of temporal processes—life-course transitions, social mobility, or policy effects—within a coherent inferential framework.

However, maintaining representativeness over time introduces methodological complexities that transcend those of cross-sectional surveys. Chief among these is attrition, or sample mortality, the gradual loss of participants across successive waves. Attrition is rarely random: it tends to correlate with demographic, socioeconomic, or behavioural variables, leading to non-ignorable selection bias in longitudinal estimates (Maslovskaya & Lugtig, 2022). Differential attrition can distort observed trends and compromise causal inference, particularly when dropouts systematically differ from stayers in unobserved ways. To mitigate this, survey infrastructures employ a range of techniques—monetary or symbolic incentives, personalised contact strategies, adaptive fieldwork protocols, and, crucially, refreshment samples, i.e. the periodic recruitment of new respondents drawn probabilistically from the same target population. Refreshment sampling serves to restore representativeness, stabilise sample size, and adjust for demographic evolution, ensuring that the longitudinal database continues to reflect the living population structure.

Another issue, often underestimated, concerns time-dependent coverage error: as populations evolve, certain subgroups—especially migrants, young adults, or digitally marginalised individuals—may become underrepresented, gradually eroding the inclusiveness of the panel. This necessitates dynamic frame maintenance and, in online probability panels, the provisioning of digital access to offline households to prevent exclusion (Callegaro et al., 2014). In probabilistic panel infrastructures such as LISS (Netherlands), GESIS Panel (Germany), and ELIPSS (France), the mitigation of such bias has become a central operational concern. Each has adopted mechanisms for maintaining total coverage, including device provision, mixed-mode data collection, and continuous calibration of sampling weights.

To make probability operational for monitoring population and societal change, it is possible to adopt a broad quality framework that accounts for different sources of uncertainty in survey data. A consistent set of indicators can be used to assess and report data quality, including aspects such as coverage, response, precision, representativeness, and timeliness. Regularly publishing these indicators can promote transparency and enable comparisons over time and across domains.

The integration of probabilistic samples into a longitudinal design has yielded profound scientific dividends. First, it enables the estimation of individual-level change with known precision—a prerequisite for causal inference in non-experimental settings. Second, it supports the construction of synthetic cohorts and the analysis of intergenerational mobility. Third, it provides a robust empirical foundation for comparative research, a prerequisite to enable full comparability across nations and over time.

Within Europe, infrastructures such as the European Social Survey (ESS), the Generations and Gender Programme (GGP), and the Survey of Health, Ageing and Retirement in Europe (SHARE) exemplify this evolution. Their harmonised methodologies—based on probabilistic selection, standardised fieldwork, and longitudinal follow-up—have redefined the empirical foundations of comparative sociology and policy analysis (Callegaro et al., 2014; Groves et al., 2009). The emergence of CRONOS and CRONOS-2, developed under the Synergies for Europe's Research Infrastructures in the Social Sciences (SERISS) project, represents a decisive step towards the integration of probabilistic principles into the online environment, allowing for cross-national panel research with digital efficiency while maintaining probability-sampling integrity.

At the national level, probabilistic survey infrastructures have equally transformed the production of official and academic statistics. In Italy, the National Institute of Statistics (ISTAT) has institutionalised a family of probability-based instruments—e.g. Labour Force Survey, Multiscopo Surveys, and Family and Social Subjects Survey—which form the backbone of national evidence on social and economic life. These surveys are methodologically harmonised with international standards, ensuring both inferential validity and temporal comparability. Alongside institutional production, the academic community and the National Research Council has progressively embraced probabilistic principles in designing longitudinal and panel studies, culminating in the establishment of the Italian Online Probability Panel (IOPP)—a digital infrastructure explicitly modelled on the best European practices (e.g., LISS, GESIS, ELIPSS).

The cumulative impact of probabilistic longitudinal surveys extends beyond data quality to the epistemology of social inquiry itself. By embedding measurement within a stochastic framework, they provide the only means of quantifying uncertainty in the observation of social phenomena. Their probability-sampling logic, combined with longitudinal continuity, allows for the decomposition of variance into sampling, measurement, and temporal components, enabling fine-grained modelling of dynamic processes.

Moreover, adherence to FAIR principles—Findability, Accessibility, Interoperability, Reusability—ensures that data produced by probabilistic infrastructures are open, replicable, and amenable to computational integration (Florio & Sirtori, 2016). This alignment with the broader Open Science movement has transformed probabilistic surveys from isolated research tools into permanent research infrastructures, linking microdata to policy, science, and society.

Nonetheless, significant challenges remain. Sustaining probabilistic longitudinal infrastructures requires stable funding, methodological innovation, and institutional coordination. The long-time horizons necessary for panel data collection often exceed conventional research funding cycles, threatening continuity and data preservation (Huber et al., 2021). Heterogeneity in national legal and ethical standards further complicates data linkage and reuse, particularly when dealing with sensitive individual-level data across jurisdictions. Moreover, the technical integration of probabilistic datasets into computational environments remains uneven: as FAIR-IMPACT (2025) notes, the absence of interoperable APIs and machine-readable metadata limits automated analysis and federated learning applications. Addressing these issues demands not only technical solutions but also governance frameworks that reconcile scientific openness with data protection and sustainability.

Despite these constraints, probabilistic longitudinal surveys have established the methodological *gold standard* for studying social and economic change. Their combination of probabilistic sampling design, longitudinal continuity, and cross-national harmonisation enables both temporal comparability—the tracking of trends within populations—and cross-national comparability, the alignment of indicators across institutional contexts. They have fundamentally altered the scale and scope of social research, transforming it from isolated empirical exercises into an integrated, cumulative, and collaborative enterprise. In doing so, they have provided the empirical backbone for modern evidence-based policymaking and comparative social science, ensuring that the study of human societies remains anchored in principles of rigour, transparency, and representativeness.

## 6.2 The Life Course Observatory

The *Italian Life Course Observatory* represents a pioneering initiative within the European research landscape, designed to provide an integrated, interoperable, and sustainable infrastructure for the collection, harmonisation, and analysis of longitudinal and panel data on social, demographic, and economic change throughout the life course. It is conceived as a social science infrastructure shared digital ecosystem that enables researchers to access, interlink, and analyse datasets produced by major European and national survey programs within a coherent and FAIR-compliant framework.

At its core, the Observatory federates a set of complementary infrastructures included in the ESFRI Roadmap 2021—namely, Growing Up in Digital Europe (GUIDE), the Generations and Gender Programme (GGP), and the Survey of Health, Ageing and Retirement in Europe (SHARE-ERIC) together with the newly established Italian Online Probability Panel (IOPP) developed under the FOSSR project. Collectively, these four sources span the entire human life course, offering a unified empirical basis for analysing life trajectories from infancy to late adulthood.

*Growing Up in Digital Europe* (GUIDE) constitutes the first pan-European longitudinal birth and child cohort study aimed at documenting children's well-being in the context of the digital transition. Developed under the coordination of University College Dublin and Manchester Metropolitan University, GUIDE is structured around two overlapping cohorts: an infant cohort (children aged 6–18 months) and a child cohort (children aged 8 years old), followed longitudinally until early adulthood. It adopts a harmonised design across countries. The Italian pilot, coordinated by the University of Bologna and CNR-IRPPS, explores innovative multi-mode survey strategies (Computer-Assisted Personal Interview—CAPI and Computer-Assisted Web Interview—CAWI), privacy-compliant recruitment protocols, and sampling approaches across diverse territorial contexts. The Italian GUIDE pilot was implemented across four regions—Lombardy, Emilia-Romagna, Campania, and Apulia—selected to capture the socio-demographic and administrative diversity of the Italian context. The pilot tested the feasibility of a harmonised sampling and data collection design involving both an infant cohort and a child cohort. This regional distribution ensured variability in demographic structures, digital access, and institutional settings, thereby providing essential insights for the full national roll-out planned within the European GUIDE infrastructure. GUIDE thus fills a long-standing gap in European data infrastructures, creating a harmonised empirical base for analysing the multidimensional well-being of children and adolescents and their interaction with digital technologies.

The *Generations and Gender Programme* (GGP), whose core instrument is the Generations and Gender Survey (GGS), addresses the central transitions of adult and mid-life stages (18–59 years). Initiated in 2000 under the United Nations Economic Commission for Europe (UNECE) and currently coordinated by the Netherlands Interdisciplinary Demographic Institute (NIDI), it provides internationally comparable, high-quality panel data on family dynamics, fertility, partnership trajectories, gender roles, intergenerational support, and subjective well-being. The second round of data collection (GGS-II) adopts a redesigned methodology and expanded thematic scope, incorporating questions on new family arrangements, digitalisation, and gender identity. The Italian implementation of GGS-II—coordinated by the CNR and Bocconi University—represents a major national investment within the National Recovery and Resilience Plan (NRRP). Through the FOSSR and Age-It projects, it ensures full adherence to FAIR principles, long-term curation, and methodological harmonisation. The Italian questionnaire further enriches the baseline instrument with modules on late-life transitions, care expectations, and resilience, providing comprehensive coverage of adulthood and early old age.

The *Survey of Health, Ageing and Retirement in Europe* (SHARE-ERIC) extends the life-course continuum into the later stages of life. Established in 2004 and operating as a European Research Infrastructure Consortium (ERIC) since 2011, SHARE is a landmark of the European Strategy Forum on Research Infrastructures (ESFRI). It collects fully ex-ante harmonised longitudinal microdata from individuals aged 50 and over in 27 European countries and Israel, combining detailed information on health status, cognitive function, labour market participation, pensions, social networks, and subjective well-being (see Weber, 2018, for further details). Its methodological strengths lie in its multidisciplinary design, which integrates biomedical indicators (such as grip strength, cognitive tests, and biomarkers) with economic and social variables, and in its longitudinal continuity, achieved through biennial panel waves and retrospective "SHARELIFE" modules that reconstruct complete life histories. The Italian node—hosted by the University of Padua in collaboration with Ca′ Foscari University of Venice and CNR-IRPPS for the refreshment sample of the tenth wave—ensures national coordination, data quality, and scientific exploitation within the broader European framework.

Finally, the *Italian Online Probability Panel* (IOPP) aims to represent the national infrastructural backbone for probabilistic social research in Italy. Developed within the FOSSR initiative, coordinated by CNR-IRPPS and the University of Milan, IOPP provides a probability-based online panel of individuals aged 18–74 residing in Italy. Participants were recruited through mixed CAPI–CAWI modes and subsequently surveyed online, with offline individuals reached by postal mail. It supports modular survey deployment, rapid fieldwork, and high-quality metadata production, offering a flexible platform for integrating Italian social statistics with European-level infrastructures.

The Observatory's integration becomes tangible when mapped onto policy-relevant transitions. For education-to-work trajectories, GUIDE provides early competencies and educational context; the national panel tracks internships, contract sequences and regional labour demand; GGS adds household formation and care constraints; and SHARE contributes late-career exit and pension pathways. A similar logic applies to fertility and work–family reconciliation, intentions and norms (GGS), material constraints and local services (national panel, administrative enrichment), and intergenerational transfers (SHARE) and to healthy ageing, where SHARE's biomedical markers and care networks are complemented by mid-life risk factors from GGS and contextual exposures. The result is a continuous, probabilistic evidence line that preserves known error properties while supporting timely indicators.

The Observatory's process complies with all relevant Data Protection Impact Assessments (DPIAs) and, in the future, has the potential to enable not only the integration of data from the surveys currently involved, but also record linkage with other surveys, administrative databases, and additional data sources, where legally permitted and ethically approved.

While the four infrastructures differ in their temporal scope, disciplinary focus, and institutional governance, they are conceptually and methodologically interoperable within a shared life-course framework. Each addresses a distinct but contiguous segment of individual trajectories, ensuring analytical continuity from early childhood through youth, adulthood, and into old age. All four infrastructures adopt longitudinal or panel methodologies that allow for the dynamic study of social, demographic, and behavioural change. They are grounded in probability-based sampling designs and employ harmonised instruments compatible with European standards for cross-national comparability. Methodologically, they rely on CAPI, mixed with CAWI mode, and implement strict data quality protocols, metadata documentation, and FAIR-compliant curation procedures. From an institutional perspective, the CNR-IRPPS functions as the central coordinating hub for Italian participation in all four initiatives, supported by a network of university partners (Milan, Bologna, Padua, Venice, and Bocconi), thereby ensuring methodological alignment and efficient data integration. Moreover, the adoption of FAIR and Open Science principles across all infrastructures guarantees machine-actionable interoperability, metadata traceability, and the potential for automated data linkage.

The infrastructures diverge primarily along three analytical dimensions:

1. Life-course coverage and target populations. GUIDE focuses on children, observing the early determinants of well-being and digital inclusion; GGS centres on adults aged 18–59, documenting family formation, fertility, and intergenerational relationships; SHARE targets individuals aged 50 and over, analysing ageing processes, health trajectories, and retirement; while IOPP bridges these systems by covering the general population aged 18–74 through a probabilistic national panel. This staged design allows for a continuum of observation across successive cohorts.
2. Institutional configuration and governance. GUIDE and GGS are ESFRI Projects under development, whereas SHARE has consolidated into an ERIC legal entity, providing a stable governance framework and financial sustainability at the European level. IOPP, by contrast, operates as a national infrastructure aligned with ESFRI standards, functioning as Italy's domestic data backbone and entry point to European consortia.
3. Methodological and thematic focus. GUIDE adopts a child-centred, multidimensional well-being framework, including both subjective and objective indicators; GGS is grounded in demography and family sociology, focusing on life-course transitions, gender equity, and intergenerational support; SHARE is rooted in gerontology, health economics, and social epidemiology, integrating biomedical and socioeconomic indicators; while IOPP is a general-purpose social survey infrastructure, flexible enough to accommodate thematic modules from all domains.

Taken together, these lines of research form a methodologically continuous and conceptually integrated observatory system. GUIDE provides the empirical foundation for analysing early-life contexts and inequalities; GGS extends this perspective into adult life, exploring family, reproductive and labour-market trajectories; SHARE follows individuals into later life, tracing the cumulative consequences of earlier experiences; and IOPP provides the probabilistic sampling and technological framework that ensures representativeness and methodological coherence across all stages.

Although longitudinal data are indispensable for capturing dynamic social processes, individual life-course trajectories, and the cumulative effects of policy interventions, researchers still face substantial challenges in accessing, harmonising, preserving and analysing such data. The complexity of these datasets—often scattered across multiple repositories and heterogeneous in format—implies significant technical barriers, with data preparation, cleaning and harmonisation frequently absorbing up to 80% of total research effort (Huber et al., 2021; Press, 2016; Wickham, 2014).

Moreover, panel surveys face a significant challenge referred to as panel conditioning, in which repeated participation may influence respondents' behavior, cognition, or reported attitudes (Biolcati-Rinaldi & Vezzoni, 2012). Respondents may recall their previous answers and attempt to remain consistent, or conversely, become more reflective and thus modify their responses. Conditioning effects introduce measurement error that may either attenuate or inflate observed change, depending on their direction and persistence. Moreover, repeated measurement may foster social desirability biases, particularly in sensitive domains. Methodological remedies include rotating modules, randomising question order, lengthening inter-wave intervals, or introducing experimental manipulations to isolate conditioning effects. Despite these, panel conditioning remains an irreducible artefact of repeated-measure designs and must be accounted for analytically through appropriate model specifications and error structures.

The Life Course Observatory directly addresses these challenges by providing a unified, curated, probabilistic and FAIR-aligned environment for the management and integration of longitudinal and panel datasets. It thus acts as both a data infrastructure and an ecosystem enabling open access and interoperability between European and national data sources. Beyond the technical layer, the Observatory promotes the adoption of common ethical, legal, and governance frameworks—critical for data sharing and preservation—while enhancing the analytical capacity of social science research through machine-actionable workflows and semantic interoperability.

From an operational standpoint, the Observatory aims to facilitate the cross-integration of longitudinal surveys, maximising the informational value of each source while minimising redundancies, by enabling multi-cohort and multi-generational analyses that would otherwise be fragmented across distinct projects, fostering a holistic understanding of demographic, economic, and social transformations.

In this perspective, the Italian Life Course Observatory stands as a strategic national platform, aligning Italy's social science research infrastructures with European standards, strengthening cross-national comparability, and fostering synergies between complementary systems. By ensuring open, FAIR, and interoperable access to data and metadata, it bridges the gap between data repositories and computational research environments. Through a single-entry point to probabilistic and longitudinal data spanning the entire life cycle, it empowers researchers, institutions, and policymakers to conduct robust, timely, and policy-relevant analyses grounded in rich empirical evidence.

Ultimately, the Observatory is more than a federated collection of datasets: it constitutes the architectural backbone of a new generation of integrated social research, combining methodological rigour, technological innovation, and open collaboration to advance the understanding of the transformations shaping contemporary societies.

## 6.3 The Italian Online Probability Panel

The Italian Online Probability Panel (IOPP) represents a major step in the innovation of Italian social research, being the first national probability-based longitudinal infrastructure designed to collect high-quality data representative of the adult population.

It emerges in response to a long-standing gap within the Italian research landscape, which until now lacked a stable, methodologically rigorous, and digital-ready instrument comparable to the infrastructures already established in other European countries. The IOPP was conceived as part of a broader movement that, since the late 1980s, has transformed the methods of empirical social research through the progressive digitalization of survey processes and the introduction of computer-assisted and self-administered techniques (Callegaro et al., 2014). Building upon international experiences such as the Dutch LISS Panel, the German GESIS Panel, and the French ELIPSS Panel, the Italian initiative combines the solid tradition of national statistical surveys with the innovation of online probability panels, now considered a gold standard for producing reliable, timely, and longitudinal data in the social sciences (Kocar & Kaczmirek, 2023; Scherpenzeel, 2011).

The IOPP's primary goal is to produce representative and longitudinal data that can capture both short-term fluctuations and long-term trends in social, economic, and political domains. While traditional cross-sectional surveys have provided valuable snapshots of Italian society, they are limited in their ability to identify dynamic processes, causal mechanisms, and life-course trajectories. Longitudinal and panel data, on the other hand, make it possible to observe individuals over time, following their transitions across work, family, and political life, as well as their responses to policy changes and macro-level shocks. The IOPP was thus designed not only to generate new data but to make them immediately usable and interoperable, following the FAIR principles (Findable, Accessible, Interoperable, and Reusable) and the logic of Open Science, which promotes transparency, reusability, and collaboration within and beyond national boundaries.

Methodologically, the IOPP is built upon a probability-based sampling design grounded in the Italian National Population Register. The target population consists of individuals aged 18 to 74 residing in Italy, and the sample is drawn using a two-stage stratified random procedure. In the first stage, 550 municipalities are selected as Primary Sampling Units (PSUs), stratified by geographical area, municipality size, and level of urbanization. In the second stage, individuals are randomly selected within each municipality, with stratification by gender and five-year age groups to ensure proportionality and representativeness. The final sample aims to include approximately 10,000 individuals, allowing for robust estimates at both national and macro-regional levels. This design reflects best practices from established European probability panels and draws upon decades of methodological expertise developed within national statistical systems (Groves et al., 2009). Recruitment follows a push-to-web strategy, whereby selected individuals receive a personalized invitation letter containing a unique access code and QR link to an online platform. Those who do not respond online are contacted through multiple follow-ups, including postal reminders and face-to-face visits. Offliners are involved by paper questionnaires sent by postal mail (PAPI). This mixed-mode design ensures inclusiveness and mitigates the impact of Italy's persistent digital divide, which remains more pronounced than in many northern European countries. Such inclusiveness is essential for maintaining representativeness and avoiding bias in key population segments, particularly among older adults and those with lower levels of education or income.

The IOPP is structured as a longitudinal multi-wave panel, consisting of five annual survey waves. Three waves per year contain the Core Questionnaire, designed to measure stable and recurrent aspects of social life, while the remaining two are dedicated to Additional Questionnaires proposed through open calls to the research community. This modular structure—a hallmark of online probability panels—combines consistency and flexibility, allowing researchers to study temporal changes while incorporating new topics and experiments. The core component covers a wide array of themes including demographic and household composition, education, employment, income, health, social participation, political attitudes, values, and media use. These core variables ensure longitudinal continuity and comparability with international infrastructures such as the European Social Survey (ESS), the European Values Study (EVS), the Generations and Gender Programme (GGP), the Survey of Health, Ageing and Retirement in Europe (SHARE-ERIC), and ISTAT surveys.

To support timely monitoring, the panel implements model-assisted calibration with rich auxiliary frames and small-area estimation for subnational indicators, while continuous mode-effect audits maintain comparability in mixed-mode operations.

Beyond its core, the IOPP enables external researchers to propose thematic or experimental modules through competitive calls evaluated by a scientific committee. This participatory governance model democratizes access to high-quality data collection, transforming the panel into a collaborative infrastructure open to the entire scientific community. It reflects a broader cultural shift in data production, where infrastructures become shared laboratories for empirical inquiry rather than closed institutional projects (Florio & Sirtori, 2016). The ability to host embedded experiments and to link survey data with external sources, such as administrative registers or digital trace data, could further expand the analytical potential of the IOPP, enabling causal inference, evaluation of policy interventions, and hybrid designs that integrate subjective and objective information.

Participant engagement and retention are crucial in any longitudinal panel, and the IOPP adopts a comprehensive set of strategies to minimize attrition and ensure continuity. Recruitment materials emphasize the public value of participation and the confidentiality of responses. Incentives are offered conditionally for each completed wave, typically in the form of electronic vouchers. Communication with participants occurs through a dedicated online app that allows them to track their participation history, update contact information, and access summaries of results. This personalized relationship fosters a sense of involvement and belonging, which has proven essential in other long-running panels. The IOPP also plans to implement refreshment samples periodically, introducing new cohorts of participants to maintain representativeness across time and demographic renewal.

Data management within the IOPP follows a cyclical model of stewardship, in which planning, collection, documentation, and dissemination are integrated into a continuous process. Data are curated and documented according to CESSDA standards, using the Data Documentation Initiative (DDI) format to ensure both human and machine readability. The infrastructure adopts a model for digital preservation, ensuring the long-term stability and accessibility of data and metadata. Versioning, persistent identifiers (PIDs), and comprehensive metadata allow users to trace the provenance of variables and reproduce analyses, aligning the IOPP with the highest international standards of data transparency. All data are anonymized and released in accordance with GDPR regulations, with sensitive datasets available under secure access conditions for approved research projects.

A major ambition of the IOPP is to integrate traditional survey data with other forms of information. Its technical infrastructure allows linkage with administrative records, official statistics, and even sensor-based or digital data voluntarily provided by respondents—a practice known as data donation. These possibilities open new methodological frontiers, allowing the combination of subjective survey measures with objective behavioural traces. Moreover, the platform is designed to host in-survey experiments such as vignettes, randomized treatments, or adaptive designs, turning the panel into a dynamic laboratory for behavioural and methodological research.

While the scientific and operational benefits of such infrastructures are substantial, the IOPP also faces the classic challenges of longitudinal research. The long-time horizons required for panel data collection often exceed the lifespan of ordinary funding schemes, making institutional continuity a critical issue. Ensuring the IOPP's long-term sustainability requires stable financial support, technical maintenance, and human expertise. Yet the potential social value of these infrastructures is considerable, as they provide a foundation for informed decision-making, public policy evaluation, and social innovation.

The IOPP's contribution is not limited to the production of data but extends to the promotion of methodological literacy and scientific collaboration. By adhering to FAIR and Open Science principles, it encourages reproducibility, data sharing, and collective knowledge building. Harmonization with international standards ensures comparability with European data infrastructures, facilitating cross-country studies. The integration of metadata and APIs into computational environments further promotes the use of high-quality social data in automated workflows, as recommended by FAIR-IMPACT (2025). This not only reduces the burden of manual data cleaning but also enables advanced applications such as machine-assisted analysis, federated learning, and dynamic modelling across distributed datasets.

In addition to its scientific relevance, the IOPP has significant implications for policy and governance. By providing updated, representative, and longitudinal data, it offers a unique tool for evaluating the social impact of public interventions, monitoring inequality, and understanding the evolving relationship between citizens and institutions. The capacity to capture individual trajectories makes it possible to identify the long-term consequences of labour market reforms, welfare policies, or educational transitions, providing policymakers with evidence-based insights that traditional surveys cannot deliver.

The creation of the IOPP also represents an institutional innovation in itself. It contributes to building a national research infrastructure ecosystem aligned with the European Open Science Cloud (EOSC) and the ESFRI Roadmap 2021. By connecting to infrastructures such as GUIDE, GGP, and SHARE-ERIC, the IOPP forms part of a broader Italian Life Course Observatory, which integrates data from infancy to old age and allows multi-domain analysis across the entire life span. This vision reflects an emerging paradigm in the social sciences, where longitudinal infrastructures are interconnected to provide comprehensive and interoperable resources for research on demographic, economic, and cultural change.

Ultimately, the IOPP embodies a synthesis of tradition and innovation: it preserves the methodological principles of probabilistic sampling and rigorous fieldwork while embracing the efficiency, flexibility, and inclusiveness of digital data collection. It democratizes access to high-quality social data, fosters cooperation among researchers and institutions, and opens new pathways for interdisciplinary analysis. Although its development requires continuous investment and institutional coordination, the long-term benefits for Italian and European research are profound. In an era characterized by rapid technological, economic, and social transformations, infrastructures like the IOPP are indispensable for understanding how individuals and societies adapt and change. They make it possible to move beyond static snapshots toward a dynamic, process-oriented understanding of social life.

The Italian Online Probability Panel thus stands not merely as a survey project but as an open, living research infrastructure, capable of connecting data, people, and knowledge across time. It embodies the idea—central to the FAIR and Open Science ethos—that data are a public good to be shared, reused, and enriched collaboratively. By combining methodological excellence with institutional vision, it places Italy firmly within the European and global ecosystem of longitudinal social research, offering scholars, institutions, and citizens alike a transparent, sustainable, and inclusive platform for studying the complexities of contemporary life.

## 6.4 Conclusion: Complementarities and Future Developments

Seen as a whole, the added value of the Life Course Observatory lies in the fact that it is more than a juxtaposition of lines of research within a unique social research infrastructure; it has been designed to turn their different rhythms, populations and instruments into a single analytical continuum. GUIDE, GGS and SHARE articulate the life course across successive stages, while IOPP, acting as the national probabilistic backbone, provides the operational elasticity to respond to shocks, to trial methods and to fill temporal or thematic gaps. The complementarity is not only substantive—children and well-being, adults and families, older people and care systems—but also temporal (triennial versus biennial cadences; capacity for higher-frequency national modules) and methodological (from biomedical and cognitive indicators to attitudinal and behavioural measures). Another important aspect of this Observatory is its ability to orchestrate calendars, metadata and fieldwork so that evidence generated at one stage of life is interpretable in relation to evidence generated at another, with traceable provenance and known error properties.

Turning that vision into day-to-day practice, however, requires acknowledging a simple fact: integration is itself an infrastructure. The experience accumulated so far—access to population frames, changing procurement rules, start-up frictions in fieldwork—shows that the obstacles encountered by one research line are rarely idiosyncratic. They are, rather, the predictable by-products of bringing probabilistic designs and longitudinal follow-up into real legal, administrative and market contexts. For this reason, some of the most consequential development work in the years ahead is not statistical in the narrow sense; it is regulatory, organisational and procedural, and it sits "between" research lines.

The first area where this is evident is lawful access to sampling frames. Probability sampling is a methodological commitment, but it is also a legal and institutional arrangement: there must be a stable and auditable pathway—from registry custodianship and legal basis, through Data Protection Impact Assessments (DPIAs) and consent models, to secure extraction and documentation—that can be exercised reliably over time. The step change achieved with national registry access demonstrates that such pathways can be built; it also shows how much negotiation, documentation and institutional trust they require. A mature Observatory will treat these pathways as shared assets: maintained centrally, versioned, and reusable by GUIDE, GGS and SHARE national teams without re-inventing the wheel at each refreshment or top-up.

A second area concerns operational resilience. Procurement frameworks, interviewer capacity, postal logistics and mixed-mode costs are not neutral backdrops; they are determinants of coverage and non-response—and therefore of inferential quality. Regulatory changes to public contracting, stress on interviewer markets due to overlapping surveys, and the need to pivot from standard post to tracked services are not episodic nuisances; they are recurrent features of the ecosystem. The Observatory can absorb this volatility by moving from project-specific arrangements to shared instruments: umbrella contracts with option clauses for refreshment samples, pre-qualified vendors for mail and device provision, and a set of common fallback protocols—CAWI, CAPI, and adaptive incentives—that each research line can activate with minimal delay. What matters methodologically is that these operational choices are documented, their effects are reflected in paradata and weights, and their activation thresholds are coherent across surveys.

A third area is sustainability, understood not only as financing but as the preservation of institutional memory. Legal templates, registry negotiation trails, Translation–Review–Adjudication–Pretesting–Documentation decisions, metadata specifications under the Data Documentation Initiative (DDI), Application Programming Interface (API) security profiles, weighting code and diagnostics—all of this is capital that decays quickly when projects pause or teams turn over. If such knowledge is not curated, the cost of maintaining a probabilistic, longitudinal system is paid repeatedly. Here the Observatory's comparative advantage is to maintain a living knowledge base—methods blueprints, Standard Operating Procedures (SOPs) for registry access, versioned code libraries for calibration and variance estimation, risk registers with mitigation histories—and to mandate their use across research lines. The result is not uniformity for its own sake, but the ability to learn once and apply many times.

These considerations point to a broader tension that will shape future development. European integration rightly insists on standardisation and harmonisation to guarantee comparability and interoperability. National implementation, by contrast, often demands institutional creativity: translation and adaptation procedures tailored to specific linguistic contexts; metadata application profiles that reflect national conventions; consent language adjusted for minors and guardians; and API security patterns aligned with domestic regulations. There is no contradiction here if the Observatory treats these adaptations as first-class, documented profiles of common standards, and feeds them back into European governance. The apparent paradox—innovation constrained by standardisation—dissolves when local solutions are rendered visible, reviewable and reusable at scale.

Methodologically, the immediate horizon is clear. On the sample side, synchronising refreshment timing across research lines will make it easier to construct synthetic cohorts and to align weighting strategies when populations evolve. On the measurement side, stabilising a small set of cross-lines constructs—with shared definitions, translation memories and calibration targets—will improve the interpretability of transitions across life stages without freezing innovation in domain-specific modules. On the data side, consolidating Observatory-level stewardship under the Open Archival Information System (OAIS) reference model and documenting variables through DDI—together with harmonised APIs for discovery, access and provenance, and a public catalogue of cross-walks—will lower the fixed costs of re-use and enable federated analysis patterns without sacrificing confidentiality. Where identifiers are exposed, Persistent Identifiers (PIDs) such as Digital Object Identifiers (DOIs) should be used to guarantee citability and version traceability. Just as important are the quality chains that connect operations to inference. Paradata-based diagnostics of contact attempts, mode pathways and interviewer effects; longitudinal error decompositions that separate sampling, measurement and temporal components; and transparent documentation of deviations from planned designs are not ancillary deliverables. They are the means by which users reconstruct the uncertainty embedded in the data and by which the Observatory holds itself to account. Publishing research lines-level quality profiles, built from a shared template and released on a predictable schedule, will make this accountability routine.

The strategic bet, then, is straightforward. If the Observatory treats regulatory pathways, procurement resilience and knowledge stewardship as shared, versioned infrastructure—alongside the statistical designs themselves—it will convert the "hidden costs" of integration into durable capabilities. Complementarities will operate not only at the level of populations and measures, but at the level of institutions and processes. In doing so, the Observatory will remain what it set out to be: a platform where probabilistic, longitudinal evidence can be generated, linked and reused across the life course—methodologically transparent, legally robust, operationally resilient—and where national innovation strengthens, rather than fragments, the European research space.

## References


Biolcati-Rinaldi, F., & Vezzoni, C. (2012). *L'analisi secondaria nella ricerca sociale*. Il Mulino.

Callegaro, M., Baker, R., Bethlehem, J., Göritz, A. S., Krosnick, J. A., & Lavrakas, P. J. (2014). *Online panel research: A data quality perspective*. Wiley.

Cornesse, C., & Blom, A. G. (2023). Response quality in nonprobability and probability-based online panels. *Sociological Methods & Research, 52*(2), 879–908.

European Strategy Forum on Research Infrastructures (ESFRI). (2021). *Roadmap 2021. Strategy report on research infrastructures*. https://roadmap2021.esfri.eu/media/1295/esfri-roadmap-2021.pdf

FAIR-IMPACT. (2025). *Fair-impact use cases & stories: Real-world fair-enabling practices across scientific domains*. European Commission. https://fair-impact.eu/sites/default/files/2025-02/UseCasesStoriesA4February.pdf

Florio, M., & Sirtori, E. (2016). Social benefits and costs of largescale research infrastructures. *Technological Forecasting and Social Change, 112*, 65–78.

Groves, R. M., Fowler, F. J., Couper, M. P., Lepkowski, J. M., Singer, E., & Tourangeau, R. (2009). *Survey methodology* (2nd ed.). Wiley.

Hájek, J. (1981). *Sampling from a finite population*. Marcel Dekker, Inc.

Hansen, M. H., Madow, W. G., & Tepping, B. J. (1983). An evaluation of model-dependent and probability-sampling inferences in sample surveys. *Journal of the American Statistical Association, 78*(384), 776–793.

Huber, R., Schaeffer, B., Weigel, T., Ludwig, J., Vancauwenberghe, G., & Wubbe, M. (2021). Integrating data and analysis technologies within leading environmental research infrastructures: Challenges and approaches. *Ecological Informatics, 61*, 101245. https://doi.org/10.1016/j.ecoinf.2021.101245

Kocar, S., & Kaczmirek, L. (2023). A meta-analysis of worldwide recruitment rates in 23 probability-based online panels, between 2007 and 2019. *International Journal of Social Research Methodology, 27*(5), 589–604. https://doi.org/10.1080/13645579.2023.2242202

Koch, G. G., & Gillings, D. B. (1984). Inference, design based vs model based. In S. Kotz & N. L. Johnson (Eds.), *Encyclopedia of statistical sciences* (Vol. 4, pp. 84–88). Wiley.

Kruskal, W., & Mosteller, F. (1979). Representative sampling, III: The current statistical literature. *International Statistical Review, 47*, 245–265.

Lynn, P. (2012). *Longitudinal survey methods for the household finances and consumption survey*. Report prepared for the European Central Bank.

Maslovskaya, O., & Lugtig, P. (2022). Representativeness in six waves of cross-national online survey (CRONOS) panel. *Journal of the Royal Statistical Society Series A: Statistics in Society, 185*(3), 851–871. https://doi.org/10.1111/rssa.12801

Menard, S. (2002). *Longitudinal research. Quantitative applications in the social sciences*. SAGE Publications, Inc.

Press, G. (2016). *Cleaning big data: Most time-consuming, least enjoyable data science task, survey says*. (Forbes).https://www.forbes.com/sites/gilpress/2016/03/23/data-preparation-mosttime-consuming-least-enjoyable-data-science-task-survey-says

Särndal, C.-E., Swensson, B., & Wretman, J. (1992). *Model assisted survey sampling* (p. 694). Springer.

Scherpenzeel, A. (2011). Data collection in a probability-based internet panel: How the LISS panel was built and how it can be used. *Bulletin of Sociological Methodology, 109*, 56–61.

Schreuder, H. T., & Alegria, J. (1995). *Stratification and plot selection rules, misuses, and consequences*. USDA Forest Service RM Forest and Range Exp. Sta. Res Note RM-RN-536, 4 p.

Weber, G. (2018). SHARE: A data set for ageing research. *Journal of Public Health Research, 7*(1), 1397. https://doi.org/10.4081/jphr.2018.1397

Wickham, H. (2014). Tidy data. *Journal of Statistical Software, 59*(10), 1–23. https://doi.org/10.18637/jss.v059.i10

# Chapter 7
# Investigating the Transformation of Societal Ideas, Values and Civicness: The Contribution of Panel Data and CIVES Observatory

**Andrea Simone, Andrea Orazio Spinello, Emanuela Reale, and Salvatore Vassallo**

## 7.1 Introduction

This Chapter presents the potential of using representative research panels to obtain real-time longitudinal data on the opinions of the Italian population about issues affecting society and its development, such as political orientation and geopolitical risk, issues related to civicness, education and scientific research, climate change, economic growth, and inequalities.

The aim is to understand how scholars can improve the knowledge on the evolution of civicness, trust, and values matters, and how infrastructures such as the FOSSR Online Research Panel (ORP) and its flagship survey—the CIVES Observatory—can contribute to this overarching goal producing open and longitudinal data. The Chapter mainly addresses the following research questions: What is the added value of a representative online panel infrastructure for studying issues related to transformation of societal ideas and changing attitudes and values? What survey on civicness must include to delineate relevant connections between different societal aspects within specific groups of populations?

A. Simone
Department of Law, University of Palermo, Palermo, Italy
e-mail: andrea.simone01@unipa.it

A. O. Spinello (✉) · E. Reale
CNR-IRCrES-Research Institute on Sustainable Economic Growth, National Research Council of Italy, Rome, Italy
e-mail: andreaorazio.spinello@cnr.it; emanuela.reale@cnr.it

S. Vassallo
Department of the Arts, University of Bologna, Bologna, Italy

Carlo Cattaneo Institute Research Foundation, Bologna, Italy
e-mail: salvatore.vassallo@unibo.it



G. Cerulli, E. Reale (eds.), *Research Infrastructures for Open Science in Social Science Research*, https://doi.org/10.1007/978-3-032-29575-0_7

Societal attitudes and values of individuals are incorporated in collective beliefs, norms and principles, driven by technology, culture, economics, political choices and social movements, such as those for human civil rights. Changes affecting individual and collective beliefs produce an impact on society, with new ideas, behaviors and definition of well-being, changing priorities and policies towards sustainability and human rights. The mentioned changes reflect deeper transformations in what groups or population segments deem important, producing transformations that influence everything from institutions to daily personal interactions.

Understanding these transformations is a difficult task for several reasons. First, there are many items that can be relevant and many ways to investigate them. Second, items are interconnected, and the analysis often implies the need to deepen intersections between them, building frameworks of analysis to study how multiple social identities (race, class, gender, high-skilled occupation, etc.) overlap and interact, creating unique effects of privilege or marginalization, inequalities and exclusion, rather than viewing them in isolation. This is important to highlight the generative process of social phenomena and possibly try to foresee what changes will occur or how society might evolve. Third, the acceleration of changes due to concomitant events such as geopolitical instability, the normative turn of policies and the disrupting impact of the technological innovation (AI first and foremost) produce the need to have real-time data to monitor new social phenomena and the emergence of new ones.

The Chapter is organized as follows. Section 7.2 presents a broad overview of civicness as a key lens to read societal transformations, linking social trust, participation, and value change to democratic resilience and collective well-being. Section 7.3 demonstrates why both probability and opt-in panels are crucial for capturing real-time shifts in opinions and values, drawing insights from major international experiences. Section 7.4 introduces the structure, advantages and limitations of the Online Research Panel, developed within the FOSSR project, as an Open Science resource for research in the social sciences, emphasizing its openness, design, and methodological innovation. Section 7.5 presents the CIVES Observatory longitudinal survey and its main thematic areas—participation, trust, policy orientation, education and science—highlighting the analytical potential of longitudinal data and the added value of studying these dimensions jointly. Section 7.6 discusses how FOSSR data inform policies and foster collaboration between academia, institutions, and civil society. It also highlights the flexibility of the online panel, which allows the inclusion of new modules as emerging issues arise—an essential feature for investigating a constantly evolving social reality. Conclusions point out the evolution of ORP panel and CIVES Observatory in the light of the whole FOSSR research infrastructure and the need to build a network joining different panel experiences existing at European level to further improve our capability to understand societal change.

## 7.2 Civicness and Societal Change in Times of Uncertainty

Contemporaneity is increasingly defined by a condition of polycrisis, a convergence of ecological, economic, political, and social disruptions that amplify one another and undermine societies' capacity for coordinated response (Lawrence et al., 2024). Such overlapping crises affect the material structures of everyday life by destabilizing the systems that sustain basic social reproduction—such as housing, health, education, and mobility—and by deepening inequalities in access to these infrastructures (Fraser, 2022). The effects have been particularly severe for Europe. According to Eurostat (2024), 21% of the European population—more than 93.3 million people—are at risk of poverty or social exclusion. In Italy, 23.1% of the population, around 14 million individuals, is affected, a level that has remained consistently higher than the EU average for over a decade (*ibidem*).

Historically, crises have often acted as catalysts for collective renewal. They have mobilized civic energies and prompted cooperation, reciprocity, and mutual support within communities (Putnam, 2000). The early phase of the COVID-19 pandemic confirmed this dynamic. Across Europe, spontaneous networks of mutual aid and local solidarity emerged, sometimes involving individuals who had not previously participated in civic activities (Mould et al., 2022). These initiatives included neighborhood assistance, digital volunteering, and community-based support for vulnerable populations, reaffirming the social value of proximity and interdependence (Coletti & Simone, 2022). Public institutions also adopted cooperative strategies in policy design, as shown by the National Recovery and Resilience Plan (NRRP), which aimed to combine economic recovery with social inclusion and environmental transition.

This resurgence of solidarity, however, takes place within a longer-term trend of weakening civic engagement across many democracies. Erosion of trust, declining participation, and fragmented social ties have diminished the collective sense of belonging and confidence in institutions, while also undermining the ability to recognize oneself as part of a shared project and to act collectively toward common goals. Data from the *Living and Working in the EU* e-survey (Eurofound, 2025) show that the average level of trust in national governments across the EU fell from 4.8 to 3.8 on a 10-point scale between 2020 and 2024. In Italy, only 40.8% of citizens report sufficient confidence in Parliament, while participation in civic or voluntary organizations continues to decline, particularly among younger generations (ISTAT, 2025). Contemporary societies are thus facing not only material fragility but also a gradual erosion of civic cohesion and collective confidence. While this phase can be seen as part of a broader "story of ups and downs in civic engagement" (Putnam, 2000, p. 25, Italian Ed.), it also displays distinctive features that set it apart from earlier cycles of decline and renewal.

A first element of differentiation can be captured by the notion of "permacrisis" (Turnbull, 2022), a term adopted by the Collins English Dictionary as the word of the year for 2022. It describes a chronic state of instability in which crises are not isolated events but an ongoing condition that shapes public perception and erodes confidence in collective futures. Under prolonged uncertainty, the very mechanisms of social cooperation and institutional learning that enable recovery may erode, as collective responses become fragmented and oriented toward short-term survival rather than long-term transformation (Kornberger et al., 2025). In this environment, global challenges appear less as problems to be resolved than as pressures to be managed, since each measure adopted to mitigate one emergency can unintentionally accelerate another (Coletti, 2025).

A second factor concerns the ambiguous civic effects of recent crises. During the pandemic, civic initiatives proliferated as part of an extraordinary mobilization of civic energies, but many of them struggled to persist beyond the acute phase of the crisis (Simone & Coletti, 2023). At the same time, alongside this renewed informal engagement, levels of institutional trust declined, and perceptions of insecurity increased (Kritzinger et al., 2021). Indeed, crises such as the COVID-19 pandemic can produce a divergence between political and social trust: while confidence in institutions may fall due to dissatisfaction with crisis management, interpersonal trust can temporarily increase through mechanisms of group solidarity (Aassve et al., 2024). This pattern suggests that large-scale disruptions can fragment the structure of trust, weakening the relationship between citizens and institutions even when informal social ties remain intact or get stronger. The pandemic experience illustrates this duality: it temporarily stimulated solidarity and local activism while simultaneously reinforcing uncertainty and insecurity, which in the absence of sustained institutional trust led to renewed social disconnection and political disaffection (Kritzinger et al., 2021).

A third factor lies in the way declining trust has transformed individuals' relationships with information, the public sphere, and collective meaning. As confidence in public deliberation decreases, the communicative fabric that sustains shared understanding becomes fragile. This weakening of trust has been linked to the rise of disinformation and conspiratorial narratives that prosper in contexts of uncertainty, offering emotionally charged yet oversimplified explanations of complex realities (Trenz, 2024; Vezzoni et al., 2022). When citizens no longer perceive institutions or media as credible mediators of truth, the search for coherence and belonging often shifts toward alternative interpretive communities that provide symbolic reassurance but undermine shared standards of evidence (Sunstein, 2014). Over time, this dynamic contributes to the weakening of the communicative and affective infrastructures that sustain democratic coexistence. Eurobarometer data (2025) show that only 54% of EU citizens express confidence in the media, a figure that drops to 43% in the case of Italy (European Commission, 2025). This erosion of media credibility coincides with the growing influence of alternative information ecosystems on social media, which tend to reinforce polarization and skepticism toward collective knowledge (Barberá, 2020). Bauman (2017) described this condition as a retreat from a shared future, in which widespread uncertainty and insecurity undermine collective horizons and foster a turn toward regressive and nostalgic imaginaries.

These transformations make it necessary to reconsider *civicness* as a critical framework for understanding social change. The concept captures both the relational and normative dimensions of collective life: it refers to the density and quality of social bonds, and to the values that orient collective action and institutional cooperation. In this sense, civicness extends beyond a utilitarian understanding of social capital by embedding networks of reciprocity within systems of shared meaning and public responsibility (Putnam, 1993, 2000). The strength of civic life depends on a balance between cohesion within communities and openness toward difference. Where trust and collaboration are dense, institutions tend to operate more effectively and produce more equitable outcomes (Woolcock, 1998). Conversely, when distrust and indifference prevail, collective capacities for coordination and solidarity diminish. Patterns of trust and engagement are shaped by historical and cultural trajectories that influence how institutions evolve and how citizens perceive their credibility (Cartocci, 2007). Civicness is thus not an abstract virtue, but a situated capacity rooted in specific social and institutional contexts.

Studying these dynamics today is crucial for several reasons. First, despite its relevance, empirical knowledge about contemporary forms of civic engagement remains limited. Most large-scale surveys largely focus on formal political participation—voting, party membership, or union affiliation—while mostly neglecting informal and non-institutional practices such as digital activism, mutual aid, and neighborhood self-organization (della Porta, 2020). Such practices are redefining the boundaries of citizenship and reshaping the symbolic foundations of collective life, in an era of declining participation in traditional political entities (Bosi & Zamponi, 2019; Cellamare, 2019). Second, other dimensions of civic transformation remain underexplored, including public attitudes toward science, the diffusion of misinformation, and the appeal of conspiratorial narratives, all of which influence how individuals interpret social reality and relate to institutions (Lewandowsky et al., 2012). Finally, these phenomena must be examined together and over time, since their interdependence reveals how changes in one domain can reverberate across others. Understanding civicness means analyzing how its political, cultural, and epistemic dimensions interact and how they evolve under conditions of uncertainty. A longitudinal and multidimensional perspective is thus necessary to capture the transformations of trust, participation, and collective meaning that define democratic life in the twenty-first century.

## 7.3 The Value of Online Panel Research and Opt-In Designs in Capturing Social Change

Understanding the evolution of social trust, civic engagement, and value orientations requires high-frequency data that capture both individual and collective change. Supported by advances in digital data collection, research designs based on online panels have emerged as an effective solution for empirically monitoring these dynamics and are increasingly adopted in the social sciences and economics (Baker et al., 2010; ESOMAR, 2023). The meaning of "panel", when referring to the

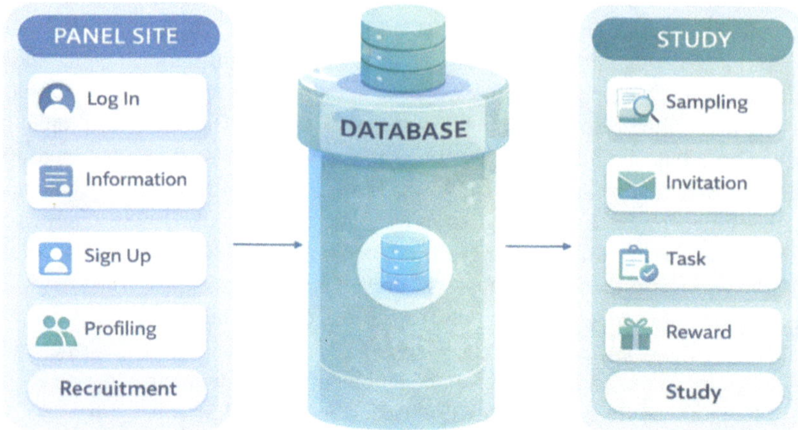


**Fig. 7.1** The operating structure of an online panel from recruitment to study implementation. Source: authors' adaptation from Göritz (2009)

theory on "online panel", diverges from the traditional meaning in survey research, where panels are groups of individuals who agree to participate in multi-stage studies, allowing for repeated measurements of the same respondents. As Callegaro et al. (2014) recall, an online panel is a form of *access panel*, defined by the International Organization for Standardization (2009) as "a sample database of potential respondents who declare they will cooperate in future data collection if selected". The process of creation involves a *recruitment process* using a website, where membership and profiling procedures are developed. This leads participants to be included into a database and then selected, from time to time, for participation in *specific studies* through invitations and sometimes rewarded for their participation with incentives (Fig. 7.1). While the enrolled individuals may participate in longitudinal designs that allow for the observation of phenomena over time through several waves, they may also participate in cross-sectional surveys, unrelated between each other.

A fundamental methodological distinction in online panel research design lies between *probability-based* and *non-probability-based* recruitment of the panelists. Probability panels recruit participants off-line through random sampling from population lists, so that every individual in the target population has a known and nonzero chance of selection. Non-probability (or opt-in) panels rely on participants enrolled on voluntary basis generally responding to online advertisements from social media. The former type is generally considered the gold standard for estimating valid population parameters when surveys are run, while the latter type, in which participants self-select into the sample, are more vulnerable to systematic bias in estimations (Cornesse et al., 2020; Lavrakas et al., 2022). Despite this, the distinction between these two designs, both in terms of potential for representativeness and data quality, is becoming increasingly blurred, and both are now considered valid options for conducting online surveys, each with its own trade-offs (Rivers, 2013; Schonlau & Couper, 2017). Surveys based on probability sampling are challenged by declining response rates and rising operational costs; meanwhile, methodological advances in post-survey adjustment techniques and model-based estimation have enhanced the inferential capacity of opt-in panel data (Kennedy et al., 2016; Kocar & Baffour, 2023; Pasek, 2016). Surveys based on a non-probability sampling can reduce or mitigate estimation biases when supported by rigorous methodological adjustments, such as quota sampling, post-stratification weighting, or propensity score correction, and they can be analytically robust in studies focused on association between variables, multivariate modeling or causal inference (Dassonneville et al., 2020; Kohler et al., 2019; Rohr et al., 2025). Furthermore, the features of non-probability designs make them "fit for purpose" for studying emerging social phenomena, building experimental indicators, responding to crisis contexts, and above all accessing specific subpopulations and groups that are difficult to reach through standard probability-based designs (Jerit & Barabas, 2023; Pyrooz et al., 2025).

Several research initiatives led by universities, research institutes, and international organizations rely on non-probability samples, whether drawn from access panels made up of volunteers or for the purpose of conducting cross-sectional surveys based on a non-probability approach. Fulop and Avvisati (2022) provide a review of 11 recent uses of non-probability samples in the context of cross-national surveys, covering a wide variety of topics and context. Some examples are the *Joint OECD-Harvard Graduate School of Education survey on the effects of COVID-19* (OECD, 2020), the *Eurofound Living, Working and COVID-19* e-survey, which captured the economic and social effects (i.e. impact on well-being, health and safety, work and telework, people's work-life balance and financial situation) of the COVID-19 pandemic in the European Union (Eurofound, 2021), the *European Union Agency for Fundamental Rights' 2019 LGBTI survey* (EULGBTI II Survey) which provided evidence on how lesbian, gay, bisexual, trans or intersex people experience their human and fundamental rights (European Union Agency for Fundamental Rights, 2020). At the national level, at least five notable cases of non-probability research panels for longitudinal investigations can be identified in the United Kingdom and other European countries.

In the United Kingdom, the *British Election Study Internet Panel* (BESIP), managed via a consortium of the University of Manchester and the University of Oxford, has become a valuable reference of political behavior research. Tracking around 30,000 opt-in participants per wave, it monitors public opinion, vote intention, and issue attitudes across major electoral events, including the 2016 Brexit referendum. Quota sampling and rigorous post-survey weighting ensure demographic balance, producing data of recognized analytical value. The BESIP has generated hundreds of scholarly publications,[1] providing evidence on electoral shocks, voter realignment, and polarization (Fieldhouse et al., 2019). The *COVID-*

[1] See https://www.britishelectionstudy.com/publications-using-bes-data/

*19 Social Study*, led by University College London and launched in March 2020, recruited more than 70,000 volunteers to examine the psychological and social effects of the pandemic (Fancourt et al., 2022). Weekly online surveys tracked trends in the fields of mental health, social relationships, and economic conditions, providing real-time evidence to inform policymaking. The use of advanced statistical weighting techniques enabled subgroup analyses, and its findings revealed inequalities in lockdown experiences—particularly among young people, ethnic minorities, and socioeconomically disadvantaged groups—and directly informed the United Kingdom's public health responses and communication strategies.

At a smaller scale, the *Spanish Political Attitudes Panel* (POLAT), managed by the Centro de Investigaciones Sociológicas in collaboration with the Universitat Autònoma de Barcelona, demonstrated how voluntary panels can reveal both social and political transformations. Active since 2010, the panel has completed 17 waves by 2025, tracking approximately 7,000 Spanish citizens (on average around 2,000 respondents per wave), during a period characterized by the global financial crisis, the Indignados movement, and the emergence of new political parties such as Podemos and Vox. The panel produced longitudinal evidence showing how personal experiences and major national events influenced political attitudes and voting behavior. Its findings significantly enhanced the understanding of polarization and party system realignment in Spain (Pannico et al., 2025).

Another notable example is the *Austrian National Election Study Online Panel* (AUTNES) managed by the University of Vienna. Designed to analyze public perceptions, political attitudes, and voting behavior among Austrian citizens, the panel involves approximately 3,000 respondents surveyed through repeated pre- and post-election waves since 2017. By integrating panel data with contextual information on political supply, media coverage, and campaign dynamics, AUTNES provides a multidimensional understanding of electoral behavior and opinion formation. Methodological evaluations have demonstrated that, when properly weighted, the panel achieves accuracy comparable to national probability surveys and effectively reaches underrepresented segments of the electorate, such as abstainers and politically disengaged citizens, traditionally difficult to capture through standard sampling techniques (Partheymüller et al., 2025).

Finally, a leading example of an important development towards hybridity of probability and opt-in approaches in panel research is the *Swedish Citizen Panel* (SCP), managed by the University of Gothenburg's SOM Institute (Bergström et al., 2024). With over 70,000 participants, the SCP merges a large set of self-recruited volunteers with respondents selected through probability sampling from the national population register.[2] This hybrid design enhances representativeness while preserving the rapid deployment of an online opt-in approach. The SCP provides a flexible infrastructure for both academic and policy-oriented research, supporting longitudinal and experimental analyses on issues such as climate change,

[2] Around 20% of the panel is recruited using a probability-based recruitment method, while remaining 80% of the panel is self-recruited.

immigration, and democratic trust. It also has functioned as a methodological testbed for innovations in questionnaire design and online survey techniques (such as testing question wording effects) in a controlled way.

## 7.4 The FOSSR Online Research Panel (ORP): A New Service for Social Sciences in Italy

Italy has long lacked a multi-purpose online research panel, managed by a research institution, that allows a systematic observation of social change over time. Most academic social research has relied on cross-sectional or ad hoc surveys that provide valuable snapshots but cannot capture dynamic processes, or on costly commercial panels with limited accessibility for research purposes. This constraint has hindered scholars' capacity to trace the evolution of individual attitudes and behaviors and to link these micro-level dynamics with broader social, political, and economic transformations. The FOSSR Online Research Panel (ORP), managed by the CNR-IRCrES,[3] was created as part of the FOSSR infrastructure, as an opt-in (non-probability) panel of adult residents in Italy recruited through voluntary participation, and aims to fill this gap offering a publicly managed infrastructure for social research in Italy. Although primarily designed to serve scholars and researchers, the ORP's potential extends beyond academia. In contexts characterized by rapid change—economic crises, political transformations, or public health emergencies—individual data collection can support the dialogue between empirical research and public policy, contributing to the production of knowledge useful for addressing complex social challenges.

From a methodological perspective, the FOSSR-ORP design takes into account strategies developed in recent studies to ensure the implementation of both longitudinal and cross-sectional research, leveraging the potential of opt-in panels (Bartoli & Tomaselli, 2023; Mercer et al., 2017). The panel, active since October 2025, consists of a core sample of 10,000 adults (aged 18 and over) residing in Italy, complemented by an additional reserve sample of 2,200 individuals to compensate for attrition. The core sample was selected through a *quota sampling procedure* based on age class, gender, education level, and geographic area (region and municipality size), with the goal of aligning the panel composition as closely as possible with that of the Italian population. Panel members accessed ORP through a double opt-in process, which included a confirmation phase following an initial invitation distributed via social media platforms such as Facebook. Once enrolled on ORP, participants may be invited to up to ten survey phases per year, and after five consecutive non-responses, they are considered inactive and may be replaced by the reserve pool. To each survey dataset, ORP applies *post-stratification procedures* for the recalibration of the collected data to fit the population distributions. While

[3] Research Institute on Sustainable Economic Growth of the National Research Council of Italy.

weighting procedures are used to mitigate bias in descriptive estimates, the panel is particularly effective for research aimed at uncovering patterns and relationships within evolving social dynamics (Freese & Jin, 2025; Jerit & Barabas, 2023). Another key strength of the ORP lies in its ability to reach subpopulations typically underrepresented in probability panels. Finally, as a non-probability panel, it is particularly well-suited for investigating emerging or rare phenomena and for providing timely empirical evidence in response to unexpected events or pressing policy issues.

What makes ORP unique at the European level is that it is designed as an "Open Science by design" service, in line with FOSSR's broader vision of creating an open, interoperable, and ethical data ecosystem. The panel is configured as an access panel and is made available to the scientific community upon request. Two main access methods are available. First, accredited researchers can propose surveys to be administered to panel members. These proposals undergo methodological and ethical review to ensure compatibility with the panel design and respect for participants. All collected data is anonymized and stored on the FOSSR Open Cloud, a secure digital environment that will serve as a national repository for social science data. Second, anonymized datasets drawn from ORP surveys will be made available for secondary analysis under controlled access conditions. These practices are in line with the FAIR (Findable, Accessible, Interoperable, and Reusable) principles and the requirements of the General Data Protection Regulation (GDPR) regarding privacy and data protection.

While the ORP is designed to host multiple surveys in response to requests from the scientific community, it runs a core longitudinal survey that ensures its continued operation over time—the *Observatory on Civicness and the Evolution of Society* (hereafter, CIVES Observatory)—which will be discussed in the following sections.

### Motivations and Expectations of the ORP Panelists

In opt-in panels, where recruitment relies entirely on self-selection, understanding who takes part and why is especially relevant. Factors such as trust in research institutions, interest in the topics covered, and the perceived value of the contribution determine who participates and how they engage. Psychographic studies show that motivations often go beyond financial incentives, including altruism and self-expression, which promote sustained participation and reduce dropout (Kocar & Lavrakas, 2025).

First evidence for the ORP panelists has come from the *ORP's activation questionnaire*, which shed light on participants' profiles, motivations, and expectations. ORP participants combine a relatively "new" profile with a strong willingness to engage repeatedly over time. Most respondents report no previous experience with research panels (51.6%), while a sizeable minority are already enrolled in one or more panels (26.8%) or have participated in the past (21.6%) (Fig. 7.2). This mix is relevant for panel governance and retention strategies. On the one hand, ORP is attracting many first-time panelists, potentially expanding participation beyond the "usual suspects"; on the other, it is intersecting with an existing ecology of survey

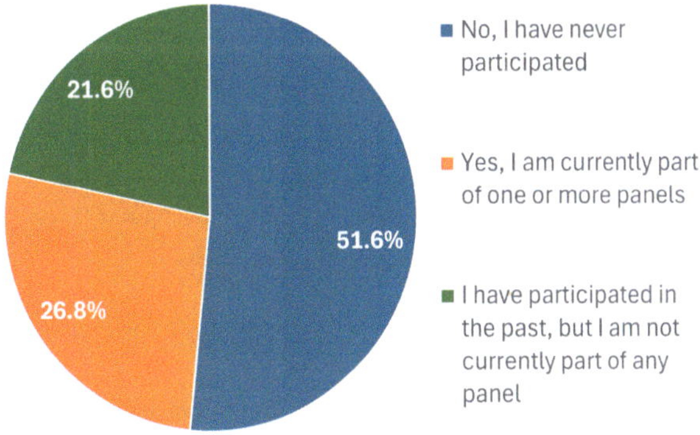


**Fig. 7.2** Participation in survey panels: previous and current involvement of ORP panelists. Source: ORP's activation questionnaire: "Participating in a panel: motivations and expectations". N = 5,464

participation in Italy, where respondents may already be familiar with panel logics and expectations.

Motivations to participate appear primarily substantive rather than purely transactional. The most frequently cited drivers are personal interest in the topic (51.8%) and the perceived social relevance of the issue (46.3%), followed by the reliability of the organizers (28.0%) (Fig. 7.3), in line with survey-participation research that highlights the role of the perceived value of the topic and personal interest as drivers of cooperation (Groves et al., 2004). At the same time, 24.3% of respondents identify financial incentives as a decisive factor, consistent with experimental evidence showing that even modest monetary rewards can improve participation and completion in both large-scale national surveys and panel settings, typically without substantial penalties for data quality (Stanley et al., 2020). Incentives must be framed transparently and proportionately as recognition of participants' time and contribution, rather than as a substitute for trust or as a mechanism that compromises voluntariness. This point is particularly salient in ethical discussions on when incentives risk becoming undue influence and when they remain an acceptable, fairness-oriented practice within research participation (Singer & Couper, 2008; Singer & Ye, 2012).

The panel is not only driven by interest in the topics proposed, but it also shows a marked willingness to be contacted frequently. A large majority (63.9%) would like to be contacted more than six times per year, and another 21.1% indicate a preference for 4–6 survey invitations (Fig. 7.4), broadly aligning with ORP's design (up to ten surveys per year) while underscoring the need for careful scheduling, topic rotation, and continuous monitoring of fatigue and attrition.

Finally, expectations regarding "returns" from participation emphasize reciprocity and public value (Fig. 7.5). Nearly half of respondents expects a summary and/or report of results (47%), and large shares seek further insights on the topics covered (42.2%) and useful information for everyday life (41.9%); over a third also expect the panel to contribute to public decision-making (35.9%) (Fig. 7.5). Only a small minority explicitly ask for access to data (9.5%) or report no expectations (3.6%). Taken together, these findings outline a panelist profile that

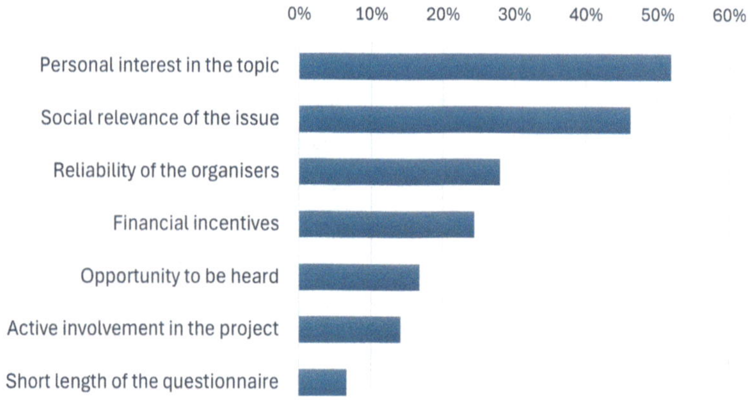


**Fig. 7.3** Factors influencing participation in panel surveys. Source: ORP's activation questionnaire: "Participating in a panel: motivations and expectations". N = 5,463

**Fig. 7.4** Desired annual frequency of participation in the panel to complete new surveys. Source: ORP's activation questionnaire: "Participating in a panel: motivations and expectations". N = 5,463

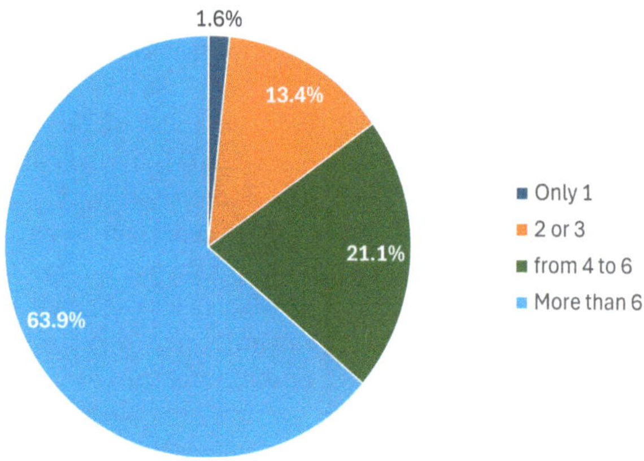


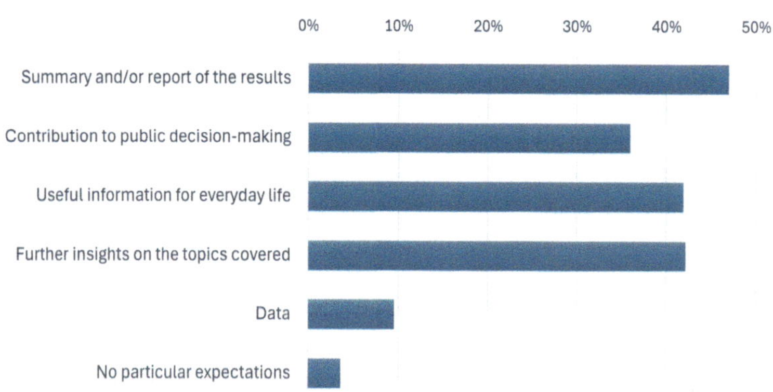


**Fig. 7.5** Expected feedback and results from participation in the ORP panel. Source: ORP activation questionnaire: "Participating in a panel: motivations and expectations". N = 5,463

values relevance, credibility, and feedback, but also recognizes participation as a repeated commitment that may warrant modest compensation. For ORP, this points to an integrated strategy that combines (i) accessible feedback loops to participants (short reports, themed briefs, and updates on societal relevance and policy uses), (ii) a transparent and proportionate incentive policy, and (iii) a contact plan that preserves engagement without overburden, elements fully consistent with ORP's "Open Science by design" philosophy within the wider FOSSR infrastructure.

## 7.5 Monitoring Values and Civic Attitudes through Panel Data: The CIVES Observatory

The CIVES Observatory surveys were designed to capture a range of individual attitudes and behaviors that are relevant for studying civic engagement and Italians' relationship with political institutions and with research. They measure, among other topics that will be presented in the following section, the modes, forms, intensity, and goals of political participation; interpersonal trust and trust in institutions; and a set of latent attitudes whose presence and impact in liberal democracies has long been studied in the scientific literature—such as a propensity to endorse conspiratorial narratives (Douglas et al., 2017; Mancosu & Vassallo, 2022; Uscinski & Parent, 2014) and a propensity to embrace populist views about the relationship between citizens and elites (Akkerman et al., 2014). They also measure attitudes toward salient issues that tend to polarize public opinion, such as those concerning Russia's military intervention in Ukraine and Israel's military intervention in Palestine, as well as issues that allow us to study the depth and structure of socio-political cleavages, with particular attention to the socioeconomic left–right dimension (state intervention in the economy and redistribution) and to the sociocultural progressive–conservative cleavage, also known as GAL–TAN (on crime, immigration, regulation of abortion, same-sex couples and euthanasia, climate change and environmental policies) (Hooghe et al., 2002; Kriesi et al., 2006). Political-electoral orientations are, of course, also recorded, with regard to past vote, vote intentions, and evaluations of the main national political leaders.

Taken together, these data enable numerous analyses, which can become progressively more in-depth and articulated once sufficiently long time series are available, allowing the stability and change of the observed dimensions to be studied. Here, purely by way of example, we show how they allow us to study political space in the Italian case—namely, the dimensions along which the electorates of the main parties appear closer to or farther from one another. In order to make the analysis understandable within a few pages, we therefore consider aggregations of the data that reflect the extent to which the attitudes in question are more or less prevalent among the voters of each party. The analyses are based on data collected during the first survey wave, conducted between the end of October and mid-December 2025, which yielded 6399 responses from the ORP panelists.

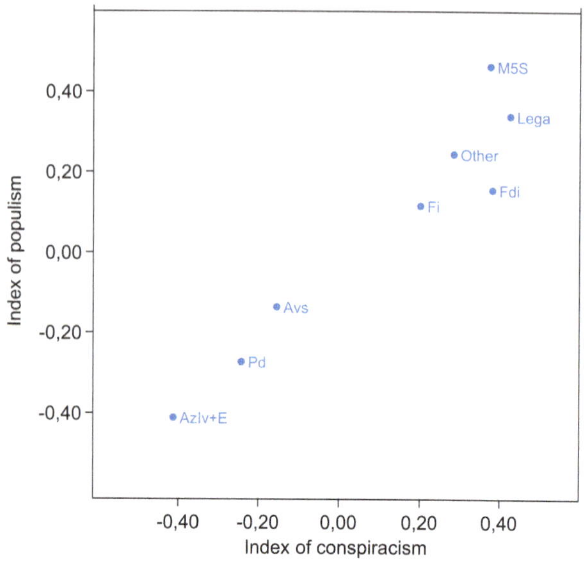


**Fig. 7.6** Index of conspiracism and populism

We exclude from the analysis the socioeconomic left–right dimension, which today is less salient (Hooghe & Marks, 2018; Kriesi et al., 2006), and focus instead on the sociocultural progressive–conservative dimension. Respondents' placement along this dimension is measured through a battery of questions capturing their attitudes regarding the four topics mentioned: crime, immigration, "civil rights", and climate change (see the questionnaire in the appendix). An exploratory factor analysis, in which other items had also been included, made it possible to verify that these topics and 11 items related to them do indeed reflect a latent dimension that can be identified with the progressive–conservative continuum. The confirmatory factor analysis, conducted including only the 11 items in question, shows that they are closely correlated with one another and can be taken as predictors of a unique progressive–conservative (prog-cons) dimension.

The placement of electorates along the continuum is estimated by calculating the mean value of the factor scores assigned to each party's voters. The placement that is attributed to parties in this way corresponds fairly closely to what can be inferred from Chapel Hill Expert Survey data on the axis they labelled GAL–TAN but referring to the same issues (Bakker et al., 2020).

A first aspect highlighted by our data concerns the relationship between attitudes toward elites and placement on the progressive–conservative axis. Attitudes toward elites are understood here along two dimensions: distrust mainly referred to the pursuit of interests, and distrust referred to the strategy of action. One is captured by what are defined as populist attitudes (the idea that political and economic elites pursue interests that conflict with those of the people), the other by conspiracist attitudes (the idea that particularly powerful and unscrupulous elites are able to influence relevant social phenomena in hidden ways). Figure 7.6 shows how these

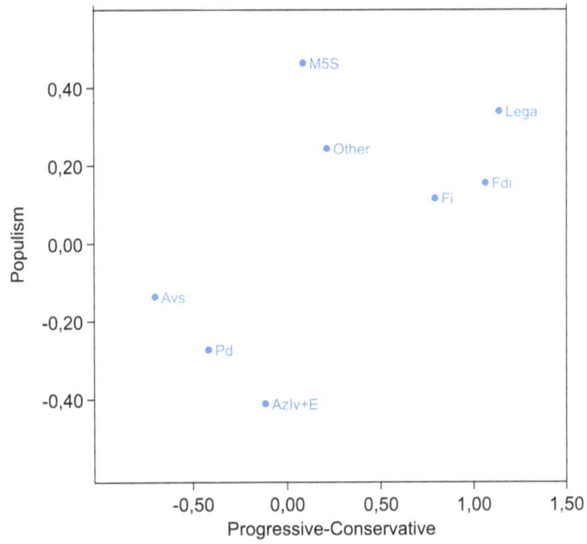


**Fig. 7.7** Populism and prog-cons dimension

two attitudes are correlated—or, more precisely, that party electorates are positioned more or less in the same way along the two continua. Above all, it shows how, with regard to this "cleavage", electorates are positioned in a way that differs quite markedly from political alliances, which are more clearly reflected in Fig. 7.7. In particular, Five Star Movement (M5S) voters appear much closer to voters of center-right parties, and even in an opposite position with respect to voters of center-left parties.

We now consider the two main international politics issues that have divided public opinion in recent years: support for the Ukrainian resistance in the face of Russia's military intervention; and support for the Palestinian civilian population in the face of Israel's military intervention (Figs. 7.8 and 7.9). In this regard, our data make it possible to show that while attitudes toward the Palestinian people separate party electorates in a way that is fairly similar to the progressive–conservative continuum—thus also coherently with the center-left and center-right camps—opinions regarding military support for the Ukrainian resistance mirror electorates' positioning with respect to conspiracism. In this case, Lega and M5S are far closer to one another than they are to the electorates of other parties within their own political area, with the Five Star electorate, once again, in a position opposite to that of the parties of the traditional center-left.

Our data, represented in a few graphs, thus make it possible to shed light on fundamental elements underlying the dynamics of alliances among political forces and components of the electorate. They explain, above all, the tensions immanent in the process of recomposition of the so-called *Campo largo* of the center-left, confirming—also at the level of individual attitudes within the electorate—the asymmetric character of the "new bipolarism" (Vassallo & Verzichelli, 2023).

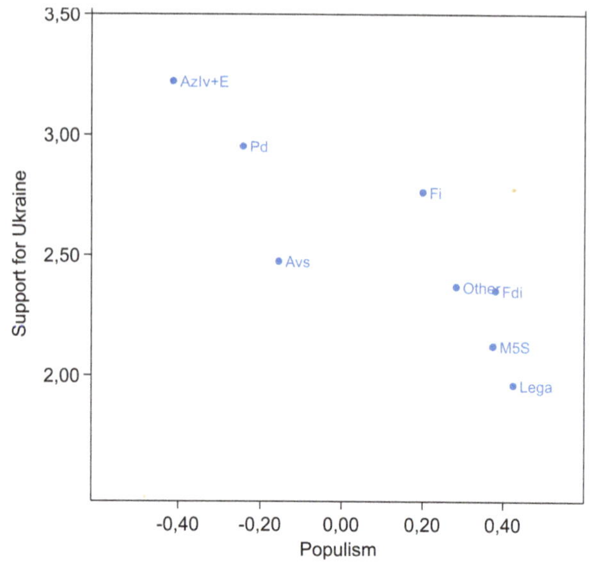


**Fig. 7.8** Support for Ukraine and populism

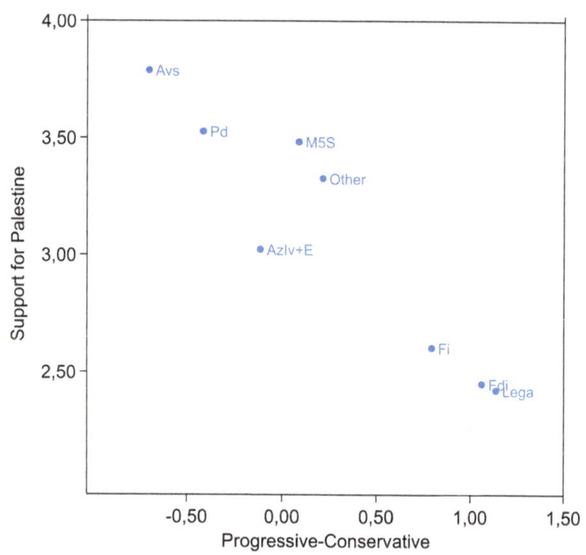


**Fig. 7.9** Support for Palestine and prog-cons dimension

A further cue to show the potential of the same data comes from the batteries of questions designed to measure the forms, modes, and intensity of political participation (cf. Norris, 2002; Verba et al., 1995). Respondents were asked whether, in the past 12 months, they have: supported associations, unions, or parties through donations or volunteer work; participated in solidarity purchasing groups, neigh-

**Fig. 7.10** Engagement index and prog-cons dimension

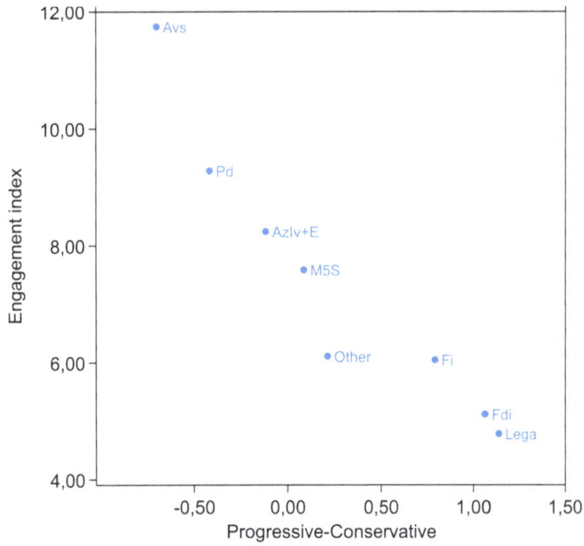


borhood cultural events, energy communities or communities of practice, religious or spiritual events, urban gardens or gardening, solidarity projects, initiatives for the elderly, volunteering associations, environmental associations, civil-rights associations, pacifist associations, religious associations, cultural associations, student associations, unions or professional associations, political parties; and whether they have participated in demonstrations on environment and climate, local issues, the conflict in Palestine, the conflict in Ukraine, femicides and patriarchy, workplace issues, and school issues. These are 27 dummy variables that can be treated in a more sophisticated way. For the purposes of this Chapter, we consider a simple additive indicator that measures the intensity of political participation by assigning a value of 1 to each participatory action that respondents say they undertake over the course of a year.

Finally, the most eloquent result—of greatest relevance and immediate intelligibility—from the analyses conducted to study the determinants of participation is presented in Fig. 7.10. This result is confirmed, like the previous ones, also in multivariate regressions conducted using individual respondents as the unit of analysis. Participation intensity is linearly correlated with the placement of respondents' reference parties on the progressive–conservative axis. This may reflect a deeper underlying orientation toward participation in social and political organizations, or it may also be connected to the government/opposition dynamic. Alternatively, it may be produced upstream by a biased selection of participatory items—i.e., one that tends to privilege forms, channels, and goals that are more consonant with people identified with the left. This is one of the questions that subsequent analyses, based on historical series, will be able to answer.

## 7.6 Implications for Research and Policy: Building Participation Beyond Academia

As a core activity, the CIVES Observatory survey, developed by the CNR-IRCrES and the Carlo Cattaneo Institute Research Foundation, is periodically administered through the ORP. The survey places particular emphasis on the evolution of relationships between individuals, communities, and institutions, offering a structured perspective on key dimensions of civic life and social change. As anticipated in the previous sections, the survey deals with different groups of topics that can be summarized as follows[4]:

- Civic and political participation, developed through traditional means (e.g. membership in parties or unions, voting, participation in demonstrations or strikes) and/or informal or emerging practices (e.g. engagement in solidarity networks, solidarity purchase groups, energy or practice communities).
- Trust in national and international public institutions (Parliament, local authorities, judicial system, law enforcement), as well as in the systems that are likely to impact deeply our everyday life, such as healthcare system, schools, science, and research. The survey also investigates dimensions often underexplored by major statistical surveys such as conspiracy beliefs and risk perceptions.
- Political opinions and orientations toward parties, leaders, or political blocs; perceived importance of major public issues; priorities assigned to the national and/or the European policy agenda.
- Values and cultural orientations, with particular attention to issues such as climate change and mitigation policies, social inequalities, civil rights, migration, and geopolitical conflicts.
- Attitudes toward science and research: support for public investment in research, perceptions of scientists, willingness to collaborate with researchers, opinion on alternative sources on scientific information. The section also incorporates a PhD-specific module: a battery administered to respondents holding a doctoral degree, collecting information on engagement in research activities, sector of employment, and international mobility.
- Technologies and innovation: evaluations of the impacts of AI and other technologies, expectations, regulatory preferences.

One element that can be added about the advantages of using a panel to investigate these topics is that panels are tools that can enable public participation of citizens to the public debates and to some extent to policy making in a new and innovative way.

Some authors have pointed out the usefulness of planners or policy analysts working closely with citizen panels, composed of a randomly selected sample of community members who have been stable in the panel for a long time, to seek

[4] See also: https://www.fossr.eu/en/online-research-panel-orp-2/ and Spinello and Reale (2026).

appropriate solutions to many of the shortcomings of traditional opinion-gathering techniques. The results of these experiments have demonstrated that panels can overcome many of the limitations to effective citizen participation (Baxter et al., 2016; Kathlene & Martin, 1991).

Further research has highlighted the importance of digital citizenship to increase public participation. Digital citizenship involves the responsible, safe, and ethical use of technology, including skills such as critical thinking and digital literacy. It combines with participatory practices to foster active civic engagement, enabling citizens to use digital tools to influence government, foster community collaboration, and access information, bridging the gap between online and offline participation.

Panels can contribute to this participatory process by allowing individuals to provide information, for a medium or long period of years, on how their opinions, values, attitudes, and ideas are changing, thus indirectly sending messages to decision makers and politicians about societal evolution. Furthermore, when panels are integrated into a public research infrastructure they operate within a broad ecosystem of services and resources for research and development, provided according to the principles of Open Science and data fairness (see Chap. 3 in this volume).

Panelists, therefore, are supposed to be timely informed on results deriving from their contributions and retain the right to control the documentation on the process of panel formation, which is in public domain, information on how data are collected, stored, treated, and used to maintain anonymity, and the scientific and methodological robustness of the results presented. This also means that panel members' participation is likely to produce new research results and new knowledge, thanks to the unique possibility of panels handled by public research organizations to generate public goods available to a broad community through the access to the panel and the data.

Given these characteristics—scientific soundness, representativeness of special populations in the national context, transparency of methods and practices, openness of results achieved—both the use of the panel and the data from the Observatory, can provide a valuable contribution to the knowledge on social and economic change. In this respect, it is also important to recall the flexibility and adaptability of the ORP panel and the CIVES Observatory to address new events observed or upcoming problems that can be anticipated. Anticipation by using evidence collected through high-frequency individual surveys is a big challenge, but at the same time an important objective to deal with. Anticipation allows us to proactively identify, analyze, and mitigate emerging social problems before they escalate, rather than react after they have caused harm. It serves as a key mechanism for building social resilience, improving strategic planning, and promoting faster and more effective interventions in critical areas.

## 7.7 Conclusions

In this Chapter we elaborate around the new service built by FOSSR: an online opt-in panel and an Observatory on ideas, values, trust and civicness.

We recall the main literature and studies that have documented pros and cons of non-probability sampling: non-probability panels are more efficient and cost-effective, especially because appropriate statistical techniques allow researchers to mitigate the selection biases associated with non-probability sampling. Furthermore, non-probability sampling increases the possibility of rapidly gaining in-depth knowledge of specific populations, such as those related to health, ethnic minorities, and professional or occupational groups.

Non-probability sampling is largely performed by commercial firms specializing in consumer surveys and is the most widely used method for studies conducted by social scientists, including inferential research. However, it is a method that can be easily replicated at very low cost by public research and statistical institutions for non-commercial purposes, especially if this effort is not limited to various niches created by individual research groups but is coordinated around a single infrastructure performing at national level and under Open Science principles, which means the possibility for all the scholars to access the panel. The important part of openness is not only the possibility for scholars to use the panel but also transparency of the process of recruitment of the panelists and the perfect compliance with the ethical principles and privacy rules thus large control that users such as social scientists can exert, as commercial firms are not always willing to disclose their panelist's recruitment and sample selection techniques.

We also highlight the importance of using the panel to build a permanent observatory to investigate issues related to the civic ideas, values and opinions, those that are supposed to signal how society is moving and evolving over time. In this respect, the creation of an open integrated public research infrastructure dealing with the collection of high-frequency social data can empower the possibility to find innovative solutions and results (Andrighetto et al., 2026).

Further work is needed to address problems related to the maintenance of the panel, its capability to interact with other ongoing initiatives operating in other European countries, thus creating a network of panels dealing with civicness issues in contemporary society. One further line of research will be to deepen innovative ways to investigate new topics of interest that can support with robust evidence and inspire more responsive policies and interventions on economy and society.

## References

Aassve, A., Capezzone, T., Cavalli, N., Conzo, P., & Peng, C. (2024). Social and political trust diverge during a crisis. *Scientific Reports, 14*(1), 331.

Akkerman, A., Mudde, C., & Zaslove, A. (2014). How populist are the people? Measuring populist attitudes in voters. *Comparative Political Studies, 47*(9), 1324–1353. https://doi.org/10.1177/0010414013512600

Andrighetto, G., Bigoni, M., Cerbara, L., Pennacchiotti, C., Simone, A., Spinello A. O., & Vriens, E. (2026). *High-quality, high-frequency individual data production in Italy: Innovation introduced by FOSSR-FOSSR policy brief series, issue 3*. Zenodo. doi:https://doi.org/10.5281/zenodo.18401450.

Baker, R., Blumberg, S. J., Brick, J. M., Couper, M. P., Courtright, M., et al. (2010). Research synthesis: AAPOR report on online panels. *Public Opinion Quarterly, 74*(4), 711–781.

Bakker, R., Hooghe, L., Jolly, S., Marks, G., Polk, J., Rovny, J., Steenbergen, M., & Vachudova, M. A. (2020). *2019 Chapel Hill expert survey* (Version 2019.3) [Dataset]. University of North Carolina at Chapel Hill. (Available on chesdata.eu)

Barberá, P. (2020). Social media, echo chambers, and political polarization. In N. Persily & J. A. Tucker (Eds.), *Social media and democracy* (pp. 34–55). Cambridge University Press.

Bartoli, B., & Tomaselli, V. (2023). *Costruire indagini statistiche su basi solide. Guida pratica alla rilevazione campionaria e alla gestione degli errori*. Loghìa.

Bauman, Z. (2017). *Retrotopia*. Polity.

Baxter, S., Clowes, M., Muir, D., Baird, W., Broadway-Parkinson, A., & Bennet, C. (2016). Supporting public involvement in interview and other panels: A systematic review. *Health Expectation*. https://doi.org/10.1111/hex.12491

Bergström, A., Cassel, S., Cassel, F., Ekström, T., & Garcia-Nilsson, A. (2024). *Technical report citizen panel 54–2024*. University of Gothenburg, The SOM Institute.

Bosi, L., & Zamponi, L. (2019). *Resistere alla crisi. I percorsi dell'azione sociale diretta*. Il Mulino.

Callegaro, M., Baker, R., Bethlehem, J., Göritz, A., Krosnick, J., & Lavrakas, P. (2014). Online panel research. History, concepts, applications and a look at the future. In M. Callegaro et al. (Eds.), *Online panel research: A data quality perspective* (pp. 1–22). Wiley.

Cartocci, R. (2007). *Mappe del tesoro. Atlante del capitale sociale in Italia*. Il Mulino.

Cellamare, C. (2019). *Città fai-da-te: tra antagonismo e cittadinanza. Storie di autorganizzazione urbana*. Donzelli.

Coletti, R. (2025). *Policrisi e governance transfrontaliera: prospettive ai confini italiani*, federalismi.it, n. 21/2025. ISSN 1826-3534.

Coletti, R., & Simone, A. (2022). Confini e ponti: Covid-19 e associazionismo a Roma Est. In *Catene/chains. Memorie Geografiche* (Vol. 21, pp. 509–514). Società di Studi Geografici.

Cornesse, C., Blom, A. G., Dutwin, D., Krosnick, J. A., De Leeuw, E. D., et al. (2020). A review of conceptual approaches and empirical evidence on probability and nonprobability sample survey research. *Journal of Survey Statistics and Methodology, 8*(1), 4–36.

Dassonneville, R., Blais, A., Hooghe, M., & Deschouwer, K. (2020). The effects of survey mode and sampling in Belgian election studies: A comparison of a national probability face-to-face survey and a nonprobability Internet survey. *Acta Politica, 55*(2), 175–198.

Della Porta, D. (2020). *How social movements can save democracy: Democratic innovations from below*. John Wiley & Sons.

Douglas, K. M., Sutton, R. M., & Cichocka, A. (2017). The psychology of conspiracy theories. *Current Directions in Psychological Science, 26*(6), 538–542. https://doi.org/10.1177/0963721417718261

ESOMAR. (2023). *Global market research 2022: An ESOMAR industry report*. ESOMAR.

Eurofound. (2021). *Living, working and COVID-19 (update April 2021): Mental health and trust decline across EU as pandemic enters another year, factsheet, no. EF/21/064/EN*. Publications Office of the European Union, Luxembourg.

Eurofound. (2025). *Living and working in Europe 2024*. Publications Office of the European Union.

European Commission. (2025). *Public opinion in the European Union: Standard Eurobarometer 103 (spring 2025)*. Publications Office of the European Union. https://europa.eu/eurobarometer/surveys/detail/3372

European Union Agency for Fundamental Rights. (2020). *A long way to go for LGBTI equality-EU-LGBTI II*. Publications Office of the European Union.

Eurostat. (2024). *People at risk of poverty or social exclusion by age and sex*. European Union, EUROSTAT database. Retrieved December 2025, from https://ec.europa.eu/eurostat/databrowser/view/ilc_peps01/default/table?lang=en

Fancourt, D., Steptoe, A., & Bradbury, A. (2022). *Tracking the psychological and social consequences of the COVID-19 pandemic across the UK population: Findings, impact, and recommendations from the COVID-19 social study (March 2020–April 2022)*. UCL.

Fieldhouse, E., Green, J., Evans, G., Mellon, J., Prosser, C., Schmitt, H., & van der Eijk, C. (2019). *Electoral shocks: The volatile voter in a turbulent world*. Oxford University Press.

Fraser, N. (2022). *Cannibal capitalism*. Verso.

Freese, J., & Jin, O. (2025). Online nonprobability samples. *Annual Review of Sociology, 51*, 109–128.

Fulop, G., & Avvisati, F. (2022). The analytical value of non-probability samples in the context of TALIS: A review of current practices in the use of non-probability samples in comparative, cross-national research. *OECD Education Working Papers, 272*, 1–42.

Göritz, A. S. (2009). Using online panels in psychological research. In A. Joinson et al. (Eds.), *Oxford handbook of Internet psychology* (Oxford library of psychology) (pp. 473–485). Oxford University Press.

Groves, R. M., Presser, S., & Dipko, S. (2004). The role of topic interest in survey participation decisions. *Public Opinion Quarterly, 68*(1), 2–31.

Hooghe, L., & Marks, G. (2018). Cleavage theory meets Europe's crises: Lipset, Rokkan, and the transnational cleavage. *Journal of European Public Policy, 25*(1), 109–135. https://doi.org/10.1080/13501763.2017.1310279

Hooghe, L., Marks, G., & Wilson, C. J. (2002). Does left/right structure party positions on European integration? *Comparative Political Studies, 35*(8), 965–989. https://doi.org/10.1177/001041402236310

International Organization for Standardization. (2009). *ISO 26362:2009, access panels in market, opinion, and social research–Vocabulary and service requirements, Geneva, ISO*.

ISTAT. (2025) *Rapporto Bes 2024: il benessere equo e sostenibile in Italia*.

Jerit, J., & Barabas, J. (2023). Are nonprobability surveys fit for purpose? *Public Opinion Quarterly, 87*(3), 816–840.

Kathlene, L., & Martin, J. (1991). Enhancing citizen participation: Panel design, perspectives and policy formation. *Journal of Policy Analysis and Management, 10*(1), 46–63.

Kennedy, C., Mercer, A. W., Keeter, S., Hatley, N., Mcgeeney, K., & Gimenez, A. (2016). *Evaluating online nonprobability surveys*. Pew Research Center. http://www.pewresearch.org/files/2016/04/Nonprobability-report-May-2016-FINAL.pdf

Kocar, S., & Baffour, B. (2023). Comparing and improving the accuracy of nonprobability samples: Profiling Australian surveys. *Methods, Data, Analyses, 17*(2), 171–206.

Kocar, S., & Lavrakas, P. J. (2025). Understanding nonprobability online panel members' psychographic profiles. *International Journal of Market Research, 67*(5), 560–588.

Kohler, U., Kreuter, F., & Stuart, E. A. (2019). Nonprobability sampling and causal analysis. *Annual Review of Statistics and Its Application, 6*, 149–172.

Kornberger, M., Meyer, R. E., Martí, I., Frey-Heger, C., Cornelissen, J., & Gatzweiler, M. (2025). Collective action in crisis? Introduction to the special issue. *Organization Studies, 46*(7), 919–939. https://doi.org/10.1177/01708406251336033

Kriesi, H., Grande, E., Lachat, R., Dolezal, M., Bornschier, S., & Frey, T. (2006). Globalization and the transformation of the national political space: Six European countries compared. *European Journal of Political Research, 45*(6), 921–956. https://doi.org/10.1111/j.1475-6765.2006.00644.x

Kritzinger, S., Foucault, M., Lachat, R., Partheymüller, J., Plescia, C., & Brouard, S. (2021). 'Rally round the flag': The COVID-19 crisis and trust in the national government. *West European Politics, 44*(5–6), 1205–1231. https://doi.org/10.1080/01402382.2021.1925017

Lavrakas, P. J., Pennay, D., Neiger, D., & Phillips, B. (2022). Comparing probability-based surveys and nonprobability online panel surveys in Australia: A total survey error perspective. *Survey Research Methods, 16*(2), 241–266.

Lawrence, M., Homer-Dixon, T., Janzwood, S., & Rockstöm, J. (2024). Global polycrisis: The causal mechanisms of crisis entanglement. *Global Sustainability, 7*(e6).

Lewandowsky, S., Ecker, U. K., Seifert, C. M., Schwarz, N., & Cook, J. (2012). Misinformation and its correction: Continued influence and successful debiasing. *Psychological Science in the Public Interest, 13*(3), 106–131. https://doi.org/10.1177/1529100612451018

Mancosu, M., & Vassallo, S. (2022). The life cycle of conspiracy theories: Evidence from a long-term panel survey on conspiracy beliefs in Italy. *Italian Political Science Review, 52*, 1–17.

Mercer, A. W., Kreuter, F., Keeter, S., & Stuart, E. A. (2017). Theory and practice in non-probability surveys: Parallels between causal inference and survey inference. *Public Opinion Quarterly, 81*(1), 250–271.

Mould, O., Cole, J., Badger, A., & Brown, P. (2022). Solidarity, not charity: Learning the lessons of the COVID-19 pandemic to reconceptualise the radicality of mutual aid. *Transactions of the Institute of British Geographers, 47*(4), 866–879.

Norris, P. (2002). Democratic phoenix: Reinventing political activism. *Cambridge University Press*. https://doi.org/10.1017/CBO9780511610073

OECD. (2020). *Schooling disrupted, schooling rethought: How the Covid-19 pandemic is changing education, OECD policy responses to coronavirus (COVID-19)*. OECD Publishing.

Pannico, R., Galais, C., Hernández, E., et al. (2025). The Spanish political attitudes panel (12 waves). *Scientific Data, 12*, 1565.

Partheymüller, J., Kritzinger, S., & Wagner, M. (2025). The AUTNES online panel study 2017–2024: A dataset of Austrian voter attitudes and behavior. *Scientific Data, 12*, 1487.

Pasek, J. (2016). When will nonprobability surveys mirror probability surveys? Considering types of inference and weighting strategies as criteria for correspondence. *International Journal of Public Opinion Research, 28*(2), 269–291.

Putnam, R. D. (1993). *Making democracy work*. Princeton University Press.

Putnam, R. D. (2000). *Bowling alone: The collapse and revival of American community*. Simon & Schuster.

Pyrooz, D. C., Densley, J. A., & Sanchez, J. A. (2025). Are online opt-in panels viable data sources on hard-to-reach populations? Population and relational inferences on gang membership in the United States. *International Criminology*. https://doi.org/10.1007/s43576-025-00174-4

Rivers, D. (2013). Comment. *Journal of Survey Statistics and Methodology, 1*(2), 111–117.

Rohr, B., Silber, H., & Felderer, B. (2025). Comparing the accuracy of univariate, bivariate, and multivariate estimates across probability and nonprobability surveys with population benchmarks. *Sociological Methodology, 55*(1), 121–154.

Schonlau, M., & Couper, M. P. (2017). Options for conducting web surveys. *Statistical Science, 32*(2), 279–292.

Simone, A., & Coletti, R. (2023). Roma città solidale: il Covid-19 e la trasformazione dell'azione collettiva. *Annali del Dipartimento di Metodi e Modelli per l'Economia, il Territorio e la Finanza, 1*, 1–19. https://doi.org/10.13133/2611-6634/1461

Spinello, A. O., & Reale, E. (2026, June 10–12). *Studying public attitudes toward STI through open panel data. The CIVES Observatory*. Paper presented at the Eu-SPRI Annual Conference 2026, Valencia.

Singer, E., & Couper, M. P. (2008). Do incentives exert undue influence on survey participation? Experimental evidence. *Journal of Empirical Research on Human Research Ethics, 3*(3), 49–56.

Singer, E., & Ye, C. (2012). The use and effects of incentives in surveys. *The Annals of the American Academy of Political and Social Science, 645*(1), 112–141.

Stanley, M., Roycroft, J., Amaya, A., Dever, J. A., & Srivastav, A. (2020). The effectiveness of incentives on completion rates, data quality, and nonresponse bias in a probability-based internet panel survey. *Field Methods, 32*(2), 159–179.

Sunstein, C. R. (2014). *Conspiracy theories and other dangerous ideas*. Simon & Schuster.

Trenz, H. J. (2024). *Democracy and the public sphere: From dystopia back to utopia*. Bristol University Press.

Turnbull. (2022). *Permacrisis: What it means and why it's word of the year for 2022*. The Conversation. Retrieved December 2025, from https://theconversation.com/permacrisis-what-it-means-and-why-its-word-of-the-year-for-2022-194306

Uscinski, J. E., & Parent, J. M. (2014). *American conspiracy theories*. Oxford University Press.

Vassallo, S., & Verzichelli, L. (Eds.). (2023). *Il bipolarismo asimmetrico. L'Italia al voto dopo il decennio populista*. Il Mulino. https://doi.org/10.978.8815/374868

Verba, S., Schlozman, K. L., & Brady, H. E. (1995). *Voice and equality: Civic voluntarism in American politics*. Harvard University Press.

Vezzoni, C., Dotti Sani, G. M., Chiesi, A. M., Ladini, R., Biolcati, F., Guglielmi, S., et al. (2022). Where does the coronavirus come from? On the mechanisms underlying the endorsement of conspiracy theories on the origin of SARS-CoV-2. *Italian Political Science Review/Rivista Italiana Di Scienza Politica, 52*(1), 51–65. https://doi.org/10.1017/ipo.2021.19

Woolcock, M. (1998). Social capital and economic development: Toward a theoretical synthesis and policy framework. *Theory and Society, 27*(2), 151–208.

# Chapter 8
# Poolpo: An Online Platform for Large-Scale and Long-Term Behavioral Experiments to Study the Causal Mechanisms of Individual and Social Behavior

**Giulia Andrighetto, Maria Bigoni, and Eva Vriens**

## 8.1 Introduction

Experimental research has had a profound impact on psychology, economics, and sociology, leading to fundamental findings in these domains. In psychology, it has shown, among other things, how heuristics and biases guide judgment under uncertainty (e.g., anchoring, availability, representativeness) and, through prospect theory, it has highlighted loss aversion and reference dependence (Kahneman & Tversky, 1979). In economics, experiments using classic games, such as the ultimatum, dictator, trust, and public-goods games, have revealed social preferences and behaviors such as fairness, cooperation, reciprocity, and altruistic punishment, in contrast with the assumption of purely self-interested utility maximization (Fehr & Gächter, 2000; Güth et al., 1982). In sociology, experiments have shed light on why people trust, cooperate (Cook et al., 2005; Willer et al., 2009), and how social norms emerge (Diekmann & Przepiorka, 2016; Przepiorka et al., 2022; Szekely et al., 2021).

Despite their long history in the social sciences, experiments remained a niche methodology for many years. However, since the early Nineties, they have gained

M. Bigoni gratefully acknowledges funding by the European Union—NextGenerationEU—GRINS project (GRINS PE00000018—CUP J33C22002910001).

G. Andrighetto (✉) · E. Vriens
CNR-ISTC (Institute of Cognitive Sciences and Technologies), National Research Council of Italy, Rome, Italy
e-mail: giulia.andrighetto@cnr.it; eva.vriens@cnr.it

M. Bigoni
University of Bologna, Bologna, Italy
e-mail: maria.bigoni@unibo.it



G. Cerulli, E. Reale (eds.), *Research Infrastructures for Open Science in Social Science Research*, https://doi.org/10.1007/978-3-032-29575-0_8

prominence for their ability to identify causal effects, distinguishing them from observational and qualitative approaches (Isaac et al., 2011). Experiments are a powerful methodological tool for testing hypotheses and demonstrating causality. Unlike correlational studies, which describe associations between variables but do not allow to confidently establish cause-and-effect relationships, experiments introduce controlled variations in treatment conditions, thereby enabling more reliable estimation of causal effects. In an experiment, one or more independent variables are altered, and the resulting changes in the dependent variable are measured, revealing the causal effect of the intervention. Experiments, especially laboratory experiments, make it possible to work in controlled environments, where researchers manipulate variables systematically, keeping other factors that could confound the investigation constant, in order to rigorously assess causal effects.

## 8.2 Origins and Evolution of Experimental Laboratories for the Social Sciences

At the end of the 1990's dedicated laboratories emerged to standardize experimental protocols, and recruitment, enabling synchronous interaction among participants, precise timing, and replication across sessions. In economics and social sciences, lab infrastructure allowed researchers to implement incentive-compatible designs, minimize experimenter demand effects, and test strategic interaction in real time (e.g., markets, bargaining, cooperation). Over time, laboratories complemented lab studies with online and field experiments, creating an iterative pipeline: theory → lab test → field validation → policy evaluation. This institutionalization increased the reliability of findings but also made recruitment and coordination the bottleneck for larger, more representative studies.

Today, experimental research in social sciences pays far greater attention than before to reproducibility and methodological rigor. The replication crisis in psychology and behavioral social science has prompted collective reflection on the risks of *p*-hacking, publication bias, and low statistical power. In response, the Open Science movement promotes preregistration of hypotheses and analysis plans, the sharing of materials, code, and data (Open Science Collaboration, 2015). FAIR principles (Findable, Accessible, Interoperable, Reusable) set data-management standards that facilitate verification and reproducibility (Wilkinson et al., 2016). These practices, together with multi-lab collaborations and transparent reporting, have shifted the focus from singular, underpowered studies to cumulative evidence and robust inference.

Experiments provide causal evidence on behavioral and institutional dynamics, such as cooperation in collective contexts, sensitivity to incentives and social norms, and responses to information and nudges, thereby strengthening theory and guiding the development, implementation, and evaluation of public policy. However, translating experimental evidence into policy requires a rigorous evaluative process before any field testing. It is crucial to confirm their robustness and assess risks of unintended effects, and the ethical implications, taking into account heterogeneity across groups, cultural context, and institutional constraints. For example, interventions that harness social norms to improve public-goods provision may succeed in one setting but backfire in another if baseline norms, enforcement, or reputational dynamics differ.

## 8.3 Why Online Platforms for Experiments

Historically, experimental laboratories in the social sciences have operated as largely independent units. This has imposed significant limitations on large-scale recruitment, coordinated study design, systematic replication, and cumulative knowledge building. This decentralization raises coordination costs, introduces heterogeneity in protocols and data standards, and often yields small, homogeneous, and geographically bounded samples. These constraints pose challenges for external validity, statistical power, and the replicability of experimental findings.

In Italy, these constraints are exacerbated by a pronounced regional imbalance: most experimental infrastructure is concentrated in central and northern regions, leaving the south comparatively underrepresented. This geographic concentration reduces diversity in participant demographics, socio-economic backgrounds, and local context, and lengthens recruitment timelines for studies that require heterogeneity or larger samples. The absence of shared, integrated infrastructure also complicates coordinated multi-site data collection, which hinders reproducibility and cross-lab collaboration.

Online recruitment platforms can provide a response to these challenges and reduce fragmentation, improve reliability and replicability, and foster cumulative, multi-lab, and regional social science research. By centralizing access to participants, standardizing recruitment procedures, and increasing the total size of the participants pool, such platforms can drastically increase the efficiency, speed, volume, and geographic reach of participant recruitment. At the same time, the centralization of the administrative process of recruitment reduces cost and time associated with maintenance of the participants pool, scheduling, and compensation of participants. Crucially, online platforms can track participants' histories and characteristics, enforce screening rules (e.g., prior exposure to a task), and enable coordinated rollouts of identical protocols across sites and time slots, capabilities that directly strengthen reproducibility and power.

Beyond scalability and efficiency, online recruitment platforms can support a high degree of methodological flexibility. A single platform could support the recruitment of participants for online, laboratory, and field experiments. By reaching populations that are difficult to access through the recruitment procedures of traditional laboratories, online platforms can also improve the heterogeneity and representativeness of experimental samples. In addition, such platforms facilitate follow-up studies and longitudinal studies, since participants can be re-contacted.

Several (smaller and bigger) online platforms exist for experimental research, but none of these address all the challenges outlined above. ORSEE, for instance, is widely used internationally to manage subject pools at the local level, for specific experimental laboratories, but its use is restricted to single institutions. Platforms such as SONA Systems or Playstudies offer the infrastructure for experiment management, scheduling, and payment, but they do not themselves supply a participant pool. Platforms like Prolific and Amazon Mechanical Turk provide large-scale participant pools and the infrastructure for managing data collection and compensation of participants, but they were primarily designed for survey research, not for interactive behavioral experiments. In particular, they do not easily support the publication of experiments with predefined time slots to which participants can register and do not allow recruitment of participants for in-person laboratory and field experiments. In addition, service costs are relatively high, especially for large samples or longer experiments. Finally, researchers have limited control over the underlying subject pool, both in terms of its composition and participants' prior experience with experimental research. In practice, this means that multi-player games with synchronous interaction or longitudinal recontacts are either impossible or prohibitively costly to implement end-to-end on a single platform.

## 8.4 Poolpo

Poolpo is a national online platform designed to integrate and enhance experimental research in economics and social sciences across Italy. It has been developed and it is managed by the Institute of Cognitive Sciences and Technologies (ISTC) of the National Research Council of Italy (Consiglio Nazionale delle Ricerche, CNR) and by Alma Mater Studiorum, University of Bologna (UniBo). It is promoted within the framework of two projects, FOSSR (Fostering Open Science in Social Science Research) and GRINS (Growing Resilient, Inclusive, and Sustainable), both funded by the European Union through the NextGenerationEU programme. Technical development is managed by Indici Opponibili.

Poolpo is intended exclusively for scientific research and cannot be used for commercial or marketing research. Its primary goal is to connect academic researchers with a broad and diverse base of participants, facilitating the recruitment process for experiments and surveys while ensuring high-quality, reliable data collection. Every study conducted on Poolpo will adhere to high ethical standards, ensured by approval from the relevant institutional ethics committees or from the platform's own scientific committee.

Compared to existing online platforms that enable recruiting participants (e.g., Prolific), Poolpo is unique in that it applies a multi-modal approach. Researchers can recruit participants for on-site laboratory experiments, online experiments, or surveys. By integrating these multiple modalities into a single platform, Poolpo not only provides the opportunity to run large-scale experiments (with access to many more participants than the average subject pool of local laboratories), but also to connect to and run on-site experiments at laboratories all over Italy that become part of Poolpo.

Poolpo coordinates a federated network of participating laboratories, university and research centers across regions, so that identical protocols can be scheduled concurrently in multiple sites or sequentially for cross-regional comparisons. The network provides shared standards for consent, instructions, timing, and incentives, while allowing local teams to implement context-specific variations when scientifically justified.

The main attraction of Poolpo is its large-scale participant base. Poolpo aims to engage, in the first years, over 50,000 participants nationwide, recruited from diverse regions, educational backgrounds, and demographics. This extensive pool enables researchers to conduct studies on a scale previously unattainable in Italy, including multi-lab collaborations, longitudinal experiments following the same participants over time, follow-up experiments with "fresh" participants that have no experience with this particular experimental task, and multi-region studies exploring behavioral differences across populations. For instance, a series of public-goods games can be run in parallel in Sicily, Lombardy, and Lazio to estimate how baseline norms and local institutional trust shape cooperation, or a longitudinal trust game can recontact the same participants after major policy changes to measure dynamic responses.

In addition to facilitating recruitment, Poolpo offers efficient administrative tools for managing participant data, scheduling studies, and providing incentives. Researchers can filter participants based on socio-demographic characteristics or prior study participation, monitor enrollment and attendance in real-time, and promote or demote participants based on their reliability and presence on the platform. This combination of features ensures that both the logistical and scientific aspects of experimental research are optimized, allowing researchers to focus on study design and analysis rather than recruitment challenges.

All in all, by providing a centralized, secure, and user-friendly infrastructure, PoolPo represents a major step forward for experimental social science in Italy. It not only enhances the capacity for rigorous, large-scale experiments but also fosters collaboration among researchers, promotes methodological standardization, and strengthens the national research infrastructure. In doing so, Poolpo aligns with broader Open Science principles, supporting transparency, reproducibility, and accessibility in behavioral research. Looking ahead, Poolpo is expected to: (i) expand the evidence base with larger, more heterogeneous samples; (ii) accelerate multi-lab replications that adjudicate contested findings; (iii) enable lab-to-field pipelines that improve external validity and policy relevance; and (iv) cultivate a coordinated community of practice around shared protocols, data standards, and ethical governance. By addressing Italy's historical fragmentation, regional imbalance, small subject pools, and limited cross-site coordination, Poolpo positions the national community to contribute decisively to cumulative, credible, and policy-useful social science.

## 8.5 Implementing Poolpo

Poolpo was designed to provide a single, comprehensive, secure, and flexible infrastructure for experimental social science research across Italy. Its main functionality is to connect researchers with participants for their experimental studies while guaranteeing high usability for both users and strict standards of privacy and data integrity. The platform recognizes four user types: participants, researchers, managers (of a group of researchers), and administrators. Moreover, it relies on two complementary access points. Participants access Poolpo through a dedicated mobile application, which is available for desktops, smartphones and tablets and is optimised for frequent, simple interactions and user engagement. Researchers instead access the platform through a web interface, which is better suited to complex tasks such as planning studies, filtering participants, and managing recruitment and payment.

Participants eligible to register to the platform are all adults with an Italian taxpayer code. As part of the registration process, they provide informed consent for the collection and processing of their data according to GDPR regulations. Registration captures basic sociodemographic information, which participants have to update regularly, and allows them to indicate their availability for online studies or in-person experiments within specific provinces. By offering this level of customization, Poolpo ensures that participants are matched with studies that fit both their sociodemographic profile and logistical constraints.

Once registered, participants enter an interactive environment designed to be engaging and easy to navigate. They receive notifications of studies for which they are eligible, can review the purpose and duration of each study, and register to participate with a few clicks. Participants are reminded of upcoming sessions through automated notifications, ensuring higher attendance rates and engagement. During participation, their responses are linked to a unique person identifier. Researchers have no access to any personal information that can be traced back to the participant's identity (e.g., name, surname, address). This way, participants' unique ID preserves their anonymity while allowing data to be associated across multiple studies. Participants accumulate money for completing studies, which can later be redeemed as vouchers. Besides the monetary compensation of single studies, Poolpo integrates gamified elements on the platform (rewards for registration, participation, and completion of different studies) to encourage continued involvement. This combination of monetary incentives and gamification should foster both engagement and satisfaction, making Poolpo an attractive avenue for sustained participation in scientific research.

From the researcher's perspective, Poolpo offers many functionalities that streamline the planning and management of experiments and the recruitment and payment of participants. Researchers can create single, independent studies or longitudinal studies with multiple trials. They can select and filter participants for their study based on advanced sampling strategies, allowing, for example, for stratified recruitment based on several sociodemographic characteristics, including age, gender, education, marital status, or prior study participation. Recruitment of participants is monitored in real time, with researchers being able to track the number of participants registering and attending, adjust the number of invitations, and cancel or add experimental sessions as needed. Researchers also assign participation labels to participants to credit them for study completion and discredit them for no-show. On the platform, they can access aggregated, pseudonymized data about their subject sample. Importantly, researchers never have access to personal identifiers, preserving participant confidentiality while enabling longitudinal studies or cross-study comparisons by researcher(s) or when multiple researchers agree to share their data.

Poolpo's architecture incorporates two additional layers: the layer of managers and that of administrators and developers. Managers oversee researchers affiliated with a particular institution, by creating accounts for researchers within their department, coordinating (access to) the on-site laboratory (if they have any), and overseeing the calendar of programmed experiments. Administrators, a small and restricted group of users, are the only ones with access to personal data of participants. They maintain the platform's integrity, oversee service capacity, supervise data management, and enforce privacy and security standards. Developers handle technical maintenance, address platform issues, and implement upgrades to enhance usability, security, and scalability. Together, these roles create an environment in which all users can interact clearly and safely.

In practice, Poolpo transforms both participant and researcher experiences compared to existing recruitment platforms. Participants receive clear guidance, reminders, and rewards from registration to study completion, which stimulates continued involvement. Researchers gain access to a rich, nation-wide participant pool, advanced sampling and monitoring tools, administrative workflows designed specifically for experimental research, and no longer have to manage participant compensation themselves.

## 8.6 Conclusion

Poolpo represents an important addition to experimental social science in Italy. By bringing together a large and diverse participant pool, a user-friendly and attractive interface for both participants and research, and a robust administrative infrastructure, the platform overcomes many structural limitations of experimental research. For participants, Poolpo offers an engaging user experience, the opportunity to participate in scientific research, and to receive monetary incentives. For researchers, it offers access to a large participant pool, an infrastructure to conduct experiments more efficiently, and a single, nation-wide platform that may facilitate new and existing collaborations. Beyond its immediate benefits for individual studies, Poolpo is of national and international relevance as it strengthens the Italian research infrastructure and serves as a model for centralized experimental platforms aligned with Open Science principles.

Importantly, Poolpo can increase the policy relevance of experimental research by building a close link between researchers and decision-makers. For example, once Poolpo is adopted at scale, it can support a network through which policy-makers can easily access studies with high implementation potential, and select those with the greatest likelihood of being translated into policy interventions. This network can also facilitate proposals for policy-relevant scenarios and interventions to test on the platform, enabling iterative, co-designed experiments that strengthen external validity and practical impact. By aligning research timelines with policy cycles and incorporating practitioner input early, Poolpo can turn experimental insights into timely, actionable guidance for national and local policymakers.

## Glossary

**Experimenter demand effects** Changes in participant behavior due to perceived expectations from researchers rather than the treatment itself.

**External validity** The extent to which findings generalize beyond the study context, samples, and settings.

**FAIR principles** Data management standards, Findable, Accessible, Interoperable, Reusable, facilitating reuse and verification.

**Field experiment** An intervention tested in naturalistic settings, trading some control for greater external validity.

**Internal validity** The credibility of causal estimates within the study, given control of confounds and proper randomization.

**Laboratory/online experiment** A study conducted in a controlled setting (physical or virtual) allowing precise timing, synchronous interaction, and incentive-compatible designs.

**Longitudinal study** Research tracking the same participants over time to observe dynamics and persistence of effects.

**p-hacking** Data-dependent analysis practices that inflate false positives, such as selective reporting or multiple testing without correction.

**Pre-registration** Process of formally documenting and openly publishing the research design, methodology, and analysis plan of a study before data collection begins. This practice is intended to increase the transparency and credibility of research by sharing planned methods, analyses and hypotheses prior to data collection.

**Pseudonymization** Replacing direct identifiers with codes to protect privacy while enabling data linkage.

**Publication bias** The tendency for journals to favor significant results, skewing the published evidence base.

**Subject pool** The database of potential participants available for recruitment, with associated profiles and participation histories.

## References

Cook, K. S., Yamagishi, T., Cheshire, C., Cooper, R., Matsuda, M., & Mashima, R. (2005). Trust building via risk taking: A cross-societal experiment. *Social Psychology Quarterly, 68*(2), 121–142.

Diekmann, A., & Przepiorka, W. (2016). Take one for the team! Individual heterogeneity and the emergence of latent norms in a volunteer's dilemma. *Social Forces, 94*(3), 1309–1333. https://doi.org/10.1093/sf/sov107

Fehr, E., & Gächter, S. (2000). Cooperation and punishment in public goods experiments. *American Economic Review, 90*, 980–994. https://doi.org/10.2139/ssrn.203194

Güth, W., Schmittberger, R., & Schwarze, B. (1982). An experimental analysis of ultimatum bargaining. *Journal of Economic Behavior & Organization, 3*(4), 367–388.

Isaac, R. M. R., Morton, B., & Williams, K. C. (2011). Experimental political science and the study of causality: From nature to the lab. *Public Choice, 148*, 263–264. https://doi.org/10.1007/s11127-011-9782-2

Kahneman, D., & Tversky, A. (1979). Prospect theory: An analysis of decision under risk. *Econometrica, 47*(2), 263–291.

Open Science Collaboration. (2015). Estimating the reproducibility of psychological science. *Science, 349*(6251), aac4716.

Przepiorka, W., Szekely, A., Andrighetto, G., Diekmann, A., & Tummolini, L. (2022). How norms emerge from conventions (and change). *Socius: Sociological Research for a Dynamic World*, 8.

Szekely, A., Lipari, F., Antonioni, A., Paolucci, M., Sánchez, A., Tummolini, L., & Andrighetto, G. (2021). Evidence from a long-term experiment that collective risks change social norms and promote cooperation. *Nature Communications, 12*, 5452. https://doi.org/10.1038/s41467-021-25734-w

Wilkinson, M. D., Dumontier, M., Aalbersberg, I. J., Appleton, G., Axton, M., Baak, A., et al. (2016). The FAIR guiding principles for scientific data management and stewardship. *Scientific Data, 3*, 160018.

Willer, R., Kuwabara, K., & Macy, M. W. (2009). The false enforcement of unpopular norms. *American Journal of Sociology, 115*(2), 451–490. https://doi.org/10.1086/5992

# Chapter 9
# Supporting Evidence-Based Policy Making via the FOSSR's Policy Learning Platform (PLP)

**Giovanni Cerulli, Federico Brogi, Fabrizio De Fausti, Barbara Guardabascio, and Salvatore Riegler**

## 9.1 Introduction

The design and implementation of effective public policies increasingly demand that policymakers navigate complex, interdependent, and rapidly evolving socio-economic environments. Economic transformations, demographic shifts, technological disruptions, and global shocks contribute to an unprecedented level of uncertainty and diversity in policy outcomes. In this context, traditional approaches to policy-making, largely grounded in historical analogies and expert judgment (Sutherland & Burgman, 2015), often prove insufficient to address the scale and complexity of contemporary challenges. Recent scholarship has highlighted the necessity of complementing qualitative reasoning with systematic, data-driven analysis to inform decisions in a forward-looking manner (Athey & Wager, 2021; Manski, 2004).

G. Cerulli (✉)
CNR-IRCrES (Research Institute on Sustainable Economic Growth), National Research Council of Italy, Rome, Italy
e-mail: giovanni.cerulli@cnr.it

F. Brogi · F. De Fausti
ISTAT, National Statistical Institute of Italy, Rome, Italy
e-mail: fedebrogi@istat.it; defausti@istat.it

B. Guardabascio
Department of Economics, University of Perugia, Perugia, Italy
e-mail: barbara.guardabascio@unipg.it

S. Riegler
Independent Researcher, Naples, Italy
e-mail: salvatore.riegler@netengine.it



G. Cerulli, E. Reale (eds.), *Research Infrastructures for Open Science in Social Science Research*, https://doi.org/10.1007/978-3-032-29575-0_9

Against this backdrop, data-driven policy learning has emerged as a promising paradigm for enhancing evidence based policy design. Advances in econometrics, causal inference, and machine learning now make it possible to extract counterfactual information from observational data and to anticipate the likely consequences of different policy options before implementation. These tools allow analysts to move beyond average, ex-post assessments of policy performance and toward a more granular understanding of for whom, under what conditions, and to what extent policies are effective or ineffective (Hastie et al., 2001; Cerulli, 2022). Crucially, they also enable the formulation of explicit, empirically grounded rules for targeting and allocating policy interventions, thereby supporting more efficient and equitable resource use.

In this chapter, we adopt a quantitative, data-driven understanding of policy learning. Although the wider public policy literature treats policy learning as a broad and multifaceted process, encompassing everything from stakeholder coordination to institutional adaptation, organizational learning, and governance reform (May, 1992), our analysis centers on a narrower, econometric, and machine-learning-oriented perspective. Here, policy learning is framed as an iterative analytical cycle that moves between looking backward and looking forward. On the one hand, ex-post causal evaluation uses observational or administrative data to assess the effects of past policy interventions, often focusing on how impacts vary across individuals or groups, typically captured through Conditional Average Treatment Effects (CATE). On the other hand, ex-ante policy optimization takes these estimated impacts and applies them to a future or potential target population, allowing policymakers to design or adjust policy rules in ways that maximize social welfare while respecting practical constraints such as budgets, institutional capacity, and fairness considerations.

Taken together, these two components constitute an integrated evaluation learning cycle, in which ex-post evidence on what worked, for whom, and under which circumstances is translated into prescriptive, ex-ante decision rules for new beneficiaries. This shift, from retrospective assessment to proactive counterfactual design, represents a significant methodological and conceptual development in the practice of evidence-based policymaking, aligning closely with emerging literature on empirical welfare maximization, optimal treatment assignment, and offline policy learning (Kitagawa & Tetenov, 2018; Zhou et al., 2023; Atan et al., 2018).

Within this evolving landscape, the Policy Learning Platform (PLP)—developed as part of the FOSSR project—offers an advanced environment for operationalising this evaluation—learning cycle. By integrating causal estimators, CATE-learning algorithms, and transparent policy-search tools, it enables policymakers to simulate alternative scenarios, evaluate potential impacts, and optimise intervention rules prior to implementation. Leveraging its predictive and scenario-building capabilities, the PLP enables decision-makers to anticipate potential risks and evaluate associated trade-offs, thereby enhancing the overall robustness of policy design and implementation. By anchoring decisions in empirical evidence, it further promotes transparency, accountability, and reproducibility throughout the policy process.

The integration of advanced computational tools thus allows policymakers to compare the prospective impacts of alternative actions across economic, social, and environmental dimensions. This transition from reactive to proactive, ex-ante evidence-based design represents a major conceptual and methodological step forward, one with the potential to reshape decision-making and the formulation of public policies. By enabling the simulation of policy scenarios and the assessment of their likely consequences within a controlled analytical environment, data-driven policy learning helps reduce uncertainty, mitigate unintended effects, and improve the coherence and quality of policy design (Cerulli, 2023a).

Although the notion of policy learning varies across disciplines, it generally refers to the process through which policymakers draw lessons from past experiences to improve future interventions. This broad definition encompasses a variety of activities, including coordination, policy management, and monitoring. In this chapter, however, we confine the term to its quantitative, counterfactual meaning, rooted in statistical and econometric approaches to causal inference and policy optimisation. Nonetheless, qualitative and quantitative dimensions should be viewed as complementary: while data-driven tools provide empirical foundations for policy design, qualitative insights continue to shape the conceptual and procedural bases of policymaking (May, 1992). Together, they constitute a more comprehensive and coherent learning process.

The remainder of the chapter is structured as follows. Section 9.2 introduces the policy evaluation cycle that links ex-post and ex-ante analysis. Section 9.3 presents the theoretical foundations of quantitative policy learning. Section 9.4 details the architecture and functionalities of the PLP. Section 9.5 discusses software implementations in Stata, R, and Python. Section 9.6 introduces the PLP webapp developed within FOSSR. Section 9.7 addresses methodological and practical challenges, and Sect. 9.8 concludes.

## 9.2 Learning Within the Policy Evaluation Cycle

Within the perimeter of quantitative (or data-driven) policy learning, Fig. 9.1 shows a project funding policy evaluation cycle where ex-post and ex-ante quantitative policy evaluation are properly integrated (Cerulli, 2022). Let's describe this scheme. Given the policy eligibility rules, a unit can or cannot be eligible for the policy in question (step 1). If eligible, she can decide whether or not to apply for receiving the policy benefit (step 2). If she decides to apply (self-selection), then she can or cannot be selected by a technical committee (step 3). If the candidate passes also this step, she will be finally selected for support (step 4), thus receiving the treatment and exhibiting a certain behavior (step 5). At step 6, the policy maker can quantitatively assess—in an ex-post manner—the effect of the policy by contrasting—in a counterfactual way—the performance of treated and untreated

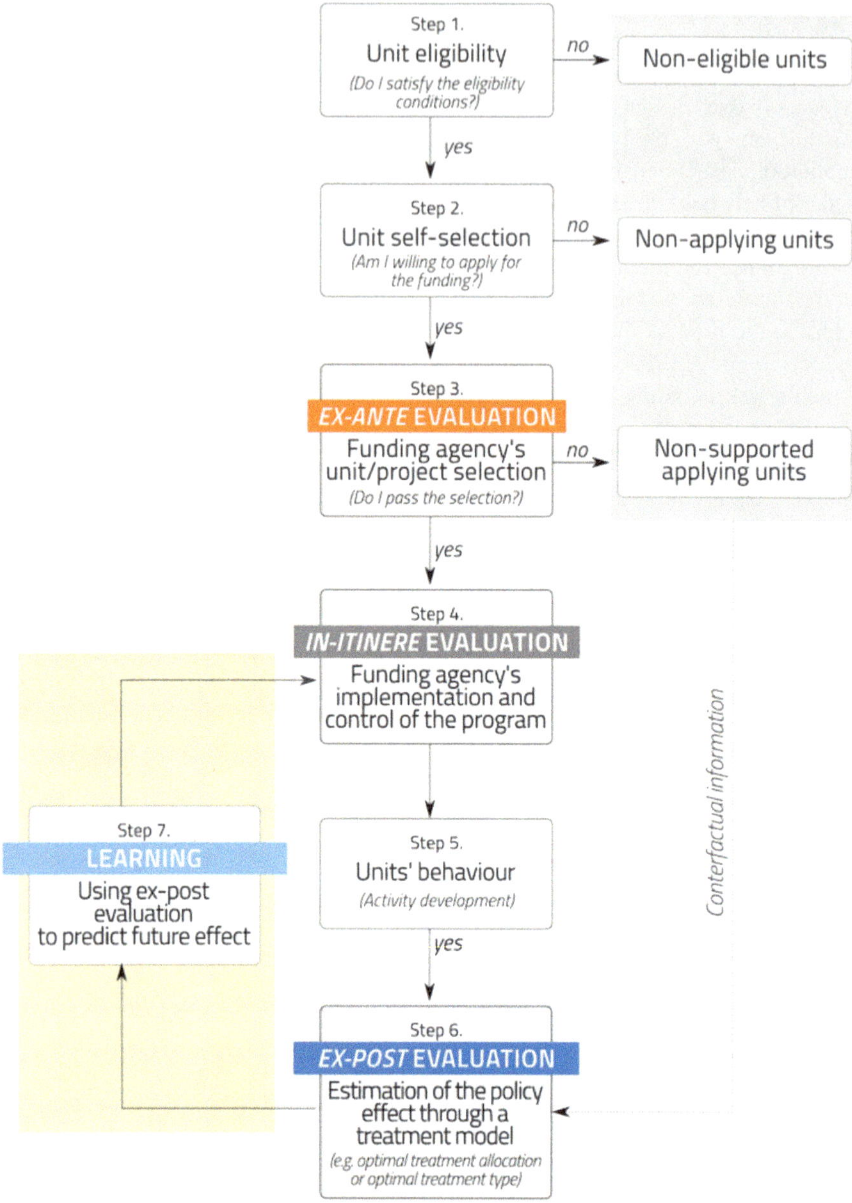


**Fig. 9.1** Policy evaluation and learning cycle. (Source: Cerulli, 2022)

individuals. This is the so-called ex-post evaluation process. In this framework, policy learning comes up at step 7, where the policy maker can use results from ex-post evaluation for bettering the selection process (step 3) with the purpose of increasing policy's welfare effects.

## 9.3 The Basics of Policy Learning

Suppose we have a setting where a policy maker has to decide who should be assigned a specific benefit (such as a grant). Given a certain monetary budget $C$ and some eligibility constraints, the policy maker has to decide the subset of the population who should be treated. This selection process can be carried out randomly, but the policy maker usually prefers an allocation that maximizes policy impact and/or welfare. If there exists an allocation providing larger social benefits than random assignment, she will be willing to implement it.

In this setting, a policy can be defined as a mapping between individual characteristics $X_i$ and a treatment variable $\pi_i$ indicating whether the individual should be treated:

$$\text{Policy: } X_i \rightarrow \pi_i(X_i)$$

Each individual $i$ has a potential policy effect on a target variable $Y$, defined as $\tau(X_i)$ which is defined as the Conditional Average Treatment Effect (CATE):

$$\tau(X_i) = E[Y_i(1) - Y_i(0) \mid X_i]$$

where $Y_i(1)$ and $Y_i(0)$ are the two potential outcome of unit $i$ respectively when treated ($Y_i(1)$) and when untreated ($Y_0(1)$). Estimating $\tau(X_i)$ requires counterfactual reasoning using causal inference techniques (Cerulli, 2022). Under assumptions such as selection-on-observables, the policy maker can estimate the mapping between $X_i$ and $\tau(X_i)$ using, for example, the T-learner based of various machine learning regressions/classifications (for example, Random Forests, or XGBoost) (Hastie et al., 2001; Cerulli, 2023b). The impact, measured through the Average Treatment Effect on the Treated (ATET), is defined as the average of the idiosyncratic effects across treated units. Unconstrained maximization of the impact typically yields a degenerate solution that selects for treatment only a single individual, specifically, the unit with the highest $\tau(X)$. To avoid this outcome, we consider constrained impact maximization, whereby optimization is performed within a predefined policy class (for example, a threshold-based policy). Under such constraints, the optimal treatment assignment $\pi^*$ selects a broader set of individuals, making the policy operationally feasible.

If the number of beneficiaries implied by the optimal solution does not match the policy maker's objectives, she can explore a menu strategy by varying the relevant policy parameters to obtain a treatment allocation that better aligns with her preferences. This necessarily requires renouncing the policy that yields the absolute maximum impact, thereby introducing a potential trade-off between policy optimality and policy feasibility. By systematically exploring these trade-offs, the policymaker can identify the policy specification that best aligns with her broader policy objectives.

## 9.4 The PLP Architecture and Features

Within the FOSSR project, the Policy Learning Platform (PLP) will bridge the gap between policy learning theory and practice through the construction of an open-source *web* that allows users to develop their own policy learning analysis. Moreover, for users with higher coding skills, we have also provided OPL platforms in Python, R, and Stata. Overall, the PLP will enable users to simulate and anticipate policy impacts across domains such as immigration, aging, employment, innovation, and education. Specifically, the FOSSR PLP will:

- Offer open access for policymakers to construct policy impact scenarios.
- Include a web-based data repository and online analysis tools.
- Provide an intuitive interface for policy simulation and visualization.
- Include tutorials and training sessions accessible to non-technical users.
- Support dissemination through events, workshops, and institutional channels.

Figure 9.2 summarizes the operational logic and the workflow of the PLP, from ex-post evaluation to ex-ante policy optimization, combining causal inference, machine learning, and welfare/impact maximization. The workflow shows how past data (i.e, the old population) informs better policies for *new* populations of potential beneficiaries.

*Data from an Old Population (Training Policy)* User data include an identifier, with the triplet $\{T, X, Y\}$ representing a past policy round data. This is the empirical basis for ex post causal evaluation, under the assumption of selection-on-observables.

*Learning Individual Effects* The block labelled "MAKE CATE" estimates the Conditional Average Treatment Effect (CATE), that is $\hat{\tau}(x) = \mathbb{E}[Y(1) - Y(0) \mid X = x]$, using as causal estimator the T-learner, and providing out-of-sample goodness-of-fit measures. Various machine learning methods can be used in this phase. The result of this stage is both a set of individual predictions and a model mapping $X \to \hat{\tau}(X)$.

*Projection to a New Population* The workflow applies the learned model to new covariates, $X'$, thus enabling ex-ante projection of CATE onto the new population of future possible beneficiaries.

*Policy Classes and Selection Variables* The user can define admissible and interpretable policy rules: (1) threshold-based, (2) linear-combination (or linear-score), (3) decision-tree with fixed 2-layer depth. To make it operative, the user must choose two *selection variables*, $Z_1$ and $Z_2$, over which the policy rules are implemented.

*Optimal Policy Learning and Constrained Search* Each selected policy rules select beneficiaries according to specific parameters. Within the chosen policy class, the proposed workflow searches the optimal parameters within a grid to maximize expected impact (i.e., the Average Treatment Effect on Treated, or ATET):

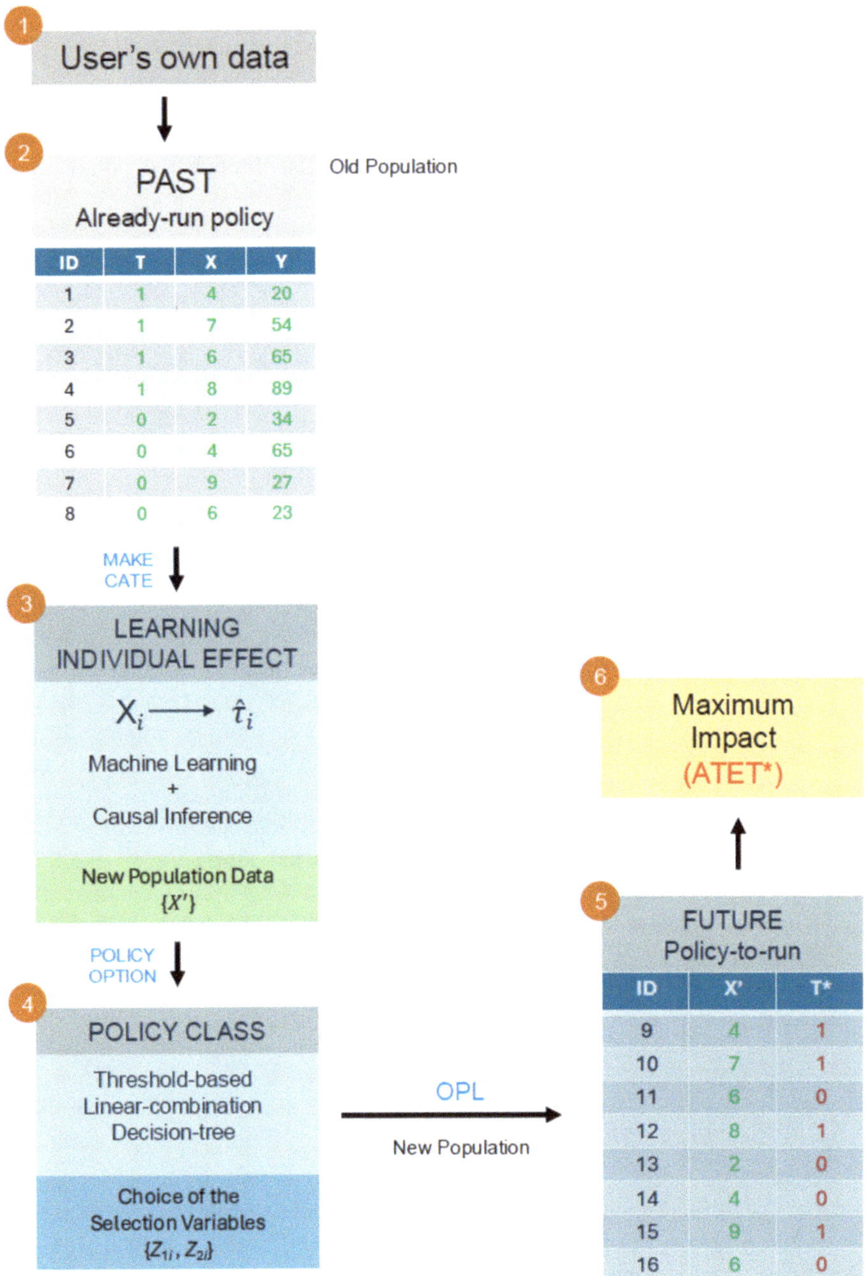


**Fig. 9.2** Policy Learning Platform workflow; from ex post evaluation to ex ante optimal policy design

$$\widehat{\text{ATET}}(\pi^*) = \frac{1}{\sum_{i=1}^{N} \pi^*(X_i)} \sum_{i=1}^{N} \hat{\tau}(X_i) \cdot \pi^*(X_i)$$

where $\pi^*(X_i) = \mathbf{1}\{\text{rule}(c^*, Z_1, Z_2) = 1\}$ is the optimal policy assignment rule corresponding to the optimal parameters $c^*$ specified through the policy class selected by the user.

*Final Outputs* The final step produces the policy-to-run, $T^*$, for the new population, and its related (maximal) impact. This closes the learning loop and turns empirical evaluation into prescriptive guidance.

## 9.5 Policy Learning in Stata, R and Python

### *9.5.1 Stata Implementation*

OPL is a Stata package for learning optimal policies from data for empirical welfare and impact maximization. Specifically, OPL allows to find *treatment assignment rules* that maximize the welfare, defined as the mean of individual potential outcomes (the so called, *value-function*), as well as the impact defined as the mean policy effect estimated over all the policy beneficiaries (the so-called, *average treatment effect on treated*, or ATET). OPL learns the optimal policy empirically, i.e. based on observations obtained from previous (same or similar) implemented policies. OPL carries out empirical welfare and impact maximization within three policy classes: (i) Threshold-based; (ii) Linear-combination; and (iii) Decision-tree.

Empirical welfare/impact maximization requires the estimation of the Conditional Average Treatment Effect (CATE) of the past policy. Currently, OPL estimates CATE in two ways: (i) by Regression Adjustment (or T-Learner), and (ii) by Cross-Fitting Augmented Inverse Probability Weighting (CF-AIPW), which has the double-robust property. CF-AIPW always assumes a continuous outcome. Parameters identification requires both unconfoundedness and overlapping.

### *9.5.2 R Implementation*

Similarly to its Stata counterpart, the **OPL package in R** provides a comprehensive set of functions for learning optimal policy assignment rules from data, with the objective of maximizing *empirical welfare* and *policy impact*. The R version is freely available on the Official R CRAN page, ensuring easy installation and accessibility for researchers and practitioners.

OPL for R carries out empirical welfare and impact maximization within the three policy classes: (i) **Threshold-based**, (ii) **Linear-combination**, and (iii) **Decision-tree**.

Empirical welfare maximization starts from the estimation of the Conditional Average Treatment Effect (CATE) from past or existing policy data. The package currently implements the `make_cate()` function, which estimates CATE using flexible machine learning learners such as generalized linear models (GLM)—with various family specifications (e.g., *binomial*, *gaussian*, etc.)—and random forests. Once CATEs are estimated, the user can proceed with policy learning using one of the three core functions:

- **Threshold-based policies**: implemented via `opl_tb_c()`, which estimates and evaluates threshold rules.
- **Linear-combination policies**: implemented via `opl_lc_c()`, which optimizes for a linear combination of parameters.
- **Decision-tree policies**: implemented via `opl_dt_c()`, which applies 2-layer fixed-depth decision-tree rules. Notably, this function also includes a feature for managing multiple optimal solutions: allowing the user to examine and select the preferred policy among several equally optimal alternatives.

All three functions share a fundamental feature: they allow the user either to let the algorithm automatically search for the optimal set of parameters that maximizes empirical welfare, or to manually specify parameters of interest. This second option is particularly useful when policymakers or analysts wish to explore *suboptimal* but *policy-relevant* scenarios, evaluating alternative rules, constraints, or feasibility conditions.

In addition, the package includes auxiliary functions such as `overlapping()`, which compares the covariates distribution between training and test samples, helping users verify the overlap assumption required for causal identification. This function applies Principal Component Analysis to the covariates of both datasets and then generates density plots for the first principal component to allow a clear visual comparison. Furthermore, the function performs a Kolmogorov-Smirnov test, adding a formal criteria to evaluate this crucial assumption.

Overall, the R version of OPL offers a flexible and extensible framework for empirical welfare optimization, enabling both researchers and policymakers to simulate alternative policy scenarios, assess their potential impacts, and identify the most effective strategies directly from data.

### 9.5.3 *Python Implementation*

The Python version, called `pyOPL`, is the backend engine of the Policy Learning Platform (PLP). The library provides a set of flexible and intuitive functions for designing optimal policies from data, with the goal of maximizing impact, in line with the other implementations (Stata and R). Similar to the Stata version, `pyOPL` also allows users to define treatment assignment rules that maximize the ATET, starting from the analysis of past policies.

The library is based on a single main OPL object that guides the entire analytical process, from estimating individual effects to defining the optimal policy. The user provides a historical training dataset—a population on which the policy has already been implemented—and a "new" dataset of potential future beneficiaries. Through the individual effects estimation function, pyOPL estimates the expected contribution of each individual using different statistical learning methods, each characterized by different levels of accuracy and training times. Among the main methods available are:

- linear regression,
- LASSO regression,
- random forests,
- gradient boosting,
- XGBoost.

These methods provide a range of solutions that allow balancing predictive accuracy, interpretability, and computational costs, depending on the needs of the policymaker.

In addition to effect estimation, the library includes tools for assessing the quality of forecasts. The user can activate an *out-of-sample* (OOS) procedure that measures estimation quality on data not used during training, providing useful indicators to verify model reliability. Furthermore, pyOPL offers a specific function for assessing the similarity between the historical population and the target population to which the new policy will be applied. This check—based on synthetic measures of the distributions—helps determine whether inferences derived from past data are transferable to the new population, a crucial requirement for an ex-ante policy grounded in robust evidence.

Once the potential effects are estimated, the library enables learning the optimal policy within three interpretable classes: (i) threshold-based rules, (ii) linear score-based rules, and (iii) decision trees. For each class, pyOPL identifies the configuration that maximizes the expected impact, taking into account the constraints specified by the user.

## 9.6 The FOSSR's Web-Based PLP

The Policy Learning Platform is a web platform operationalizing the Optimal Policy Learning methodology developed within the FOSSR project into an accessible web application. Rather than focusing solely on the statistical algorithm, our contribution lies in identifying and resolving three fundamental usability challenges that impede the adoption of computationally intensive causal inference methods in practice: data preparation opacity, black-box execution, and optimization rigidity. This chapter describes the design principles and architectural patterns we developed to transform a research-oriented statistical engine into a tool that researchers and policy analysts can operate independently.

### 9.6.1 A Transparency-by-Design Approach

Traditional statistical software treats data ingestion as a preliminary step external to the analysis workflow, requiring users to manually prepare datasets according to undocumented format expectations. When format mismatches or data quality issues exist, failures surface only after initiating computationally expensive procedures, forcing iterative debugging cycles that can span hours or days. For causal inference methods requiring careful specification of treatment indicators, outcomes and covariates, this opacity is particularly problematic because column role misassignments can produce statistically valid but substantively meaningless results.

We adopt a transparency-by-design principle wherein the platform performs comprehensive validation and profiling immediately upon data upload, surfacing potential issues before any statistical computation occurs. Our database-first ingestion architecture materializes uploaded datasets into a structured analytical database with inferred schemas, enabling the system to compute and display statistical profiles for every column including completeness percentages, cardinality estimates, value distributions, and type classifications. These profiles are presented through an interactive interface that guides users through variable role assignment decisions, displaying statistical properties that inform automated suggestions while allowing domain experts to override recommendations. This design transforms data preparation from an opaque prerequisite into a transparent collaborative process between user expertise and algorithmic inference.

The ingestion pipeline implements automatic dialect detection for diverse CSV formats, robust type inference balancing accuracy against processing time, and atomic materialization that ensures partially loaded datasets never corrupt the analysis environment. By validating data structure and quality before computation, we reduce iteration cycles from hours to minutes and prevent entire classes of user errors that would otherwise produce misleading results.

### 9.6.2 Progressive Disclosure Pattern

Causal inference analyses on realistic datasets frequently require substantial computation time, particularly when employing machine learning methods with cross-validated hyperparameter tuning. Existing implementations typically execute as batch scripts that provide no visibility into progress or intermediate results, leaving users uncertain whether computation is proceeding correctly or has stalled. When failures occur, cryptic error messages referencing internal implementation details offer little guidance for resolution. This black-box execution model undermines user confidence and creates dependency on technical support personnel for routine operations.

We address this challenge through a progressive disclosure pattern that decomposes the analysis pipeline into discrete stages with real-time progress feedback. The platform implements an asynchronous execution architecture where analyses run as background tasks while the user interface displays current status, progress percentages, and stage descriptors such as "Fitting causal forest models" or "Computing treatment effect estimates". This design enables users to monitor lengthy computations and make informed decisions about whether to wait for completion or cancel and adjust parameters. When failures occur, the system captures exceptions from the statistical engine and translates them into actionable diagnostic messages that explain what went wrong and suggest corrections, such as "Insufficient treated observations in evaluation dataset—consider selecting a larger sample or combining with training data".

The asynchronous architecture also supports graceful cancellation of running analyses, releasing computational resources cleanly rather than leaving orphaned processes. Results from completed analyses persist in the database, enabling efficient retrieval during exploration without recomputing expensive procedures. To ensure that this wrapper layer introduces no statistical artifacts, we developed comprehensive parity testing comparing outputs from our service against direct invocation of the standalone OPL engine across diverse scenarios, verifying numerical equivalence within tolerance bounds.

### *9.6.3 Interactive Exploration Framework*

The OPL methodology produces optimal treatment assignment rules by maximizing expected welfare or impact subject to specific policy constraints (that is, policy classes). However, in operational policy contexts, the theoretically optimal solution is often infeasible due to external factors not captured in the optimization formulation such as legal requirements, political considerations, administrative capabilities, or fairness criteria. Existing implementations output a single optimal policy as a final answer, providing no mechanism for policy makers to explore alternative scenarios, assess sensitivity to constraint specifications, or evaluate pre-existing policies against the computed optimum.

We introduce an interactive exploration framework that treats OPL outputs not as terminal results but as starting points for iterative refinement. The platform allows users to manually specify constraint parameters and immediately visualize the resulting policy performance, enabling what-if analysis where analysts can assess welfare and impact implications of alternative eligibility thresholds or budget allocations. A multi-run comparison interface supports side-by-side evaluation of analyses differing in model choice, hyperparameter configuration, or constraint specification, facilitating systematic sensitivity analysis and robustness checking.

Most critically, we implement a customized policy evaluation feature where users can upload datasets containing binary treatment indicators for up to ten predefined policies—-representing current practice, proposed alternatives, or politically negotiated compromises—and compute performance metrics including average treatment effect on the treated, total welfare, and coverage rates. These metrics are displayed alongside the OPL-optimized policies, enabling quantitative assessment of welfare and impact losses from deviations from optimality and supporting evidence-based negotiation between technical recommendations and operational constraints. This design acknowledges that policy making is fundamentally an iterative, human-centered process where optimization provides guidance rather than dictates final decisions.

**Architectural Foundations and Implementation**
The platform employs a three-tier architecture with a web frontend providing wizard-driven workflows, a computational backend orchestrating analysis execution, and a dual-database persistence layer using a relational database for metadata and a columnar analytical database for high-performance queries on tabular datasets. All components are containerized to ensure reproducibility across deployment environments. The frontend implements progressive disclosure patterns that expose advanced options only when needed, preventing novice users from being overwhelmed while preserving flexibility for expert users. Results visualizations prioritize actionable policy insights over raw statistical output, employing visual hierarchies and color-coding to highlight key metrics and facilitate rapid pattern identification.

### 9.6.4 Contributions and Broader Implications

Our work demonstrates that the deployment gap for advanced statistical methodologies can be addressed through principled user experience design and careful engineering architecture. The three design patterns we introduce—transparency-by-design for data preparation, progressive disclosure for execution visibility, and interactive exploration for optimization flexibility—are generalizable to other computationally intensive statistical methods beyond optimal policy learning. By reducing the barrier to entry from proficient statistical programmer to policy analyst with domain expertise, we enable a broader community to benefit from methodological advances that would otherwise remain confined to academic research. Future work will extend these patterns to collaborative environments where teams of analysts can jointly explore policy scenarios and integrate real-time stakeholder feedback into iterative refinement workflows.

## 9.7 Challenges, Limitations, and Future Development

**Data Availability** Comprehensive datasets are necessary for effective learning. Missing or sparse data (e.g., absence of a treatment type) can undermine optimal policy computation.

**Data Quality** Predictions depend on data accuracy. Real-world systems often include spillovers and unobserved interactions, complicating inference.

**Ethical Considerations** Privacy, data security, and transparency of analytical methods are vital to maintain trust and protect individual rights.

## 9.8 Conclusions

While data-driven policy learning is still emerging, it holds great potential for both methodological and practical expansion. Initiatives like FOSSR can accelerate this evolution by fostering methodological innovation, software development, and real-world application in policy analysis.

## References

Atan, O., Zame, W. R., & van der Schaar, M. (2018). Learning optimal policies from observational data. In *Proceedings of the 35th International Conference on Machine Learning*, Stockholm.

Athey, S., & Wager, S. (2021). Policy learning with observational data. *Econometrica, 89*(1), 133–161.

Cerulli, G. (2022). *Econometric evaluation of socio-economic programs; Theory and applications* (2nd ed.). Springer.

Cerulli, G. (2023a). Optimal treatment assignment of a threshold-based policy; empirical protocol and related issues. *Applied Economics Letters, 30*(8), 1010–1017.

Cerulli, G. (2023b). *Fundamentals of supervised machine learning; With applications in Python; R; and Stata*. Springer Series in Statistics and Computation. Springer.

Hastie, T., Tibshirani, R., & Friedman, J. (2001). *The elements of statistical learning*. Springer Series in Statistics. Springer.

Kitagawa, T., & Tetenov, A. (2018). Who should be treated; empirical welfare maximization methods for treatment choice. *Econometrica, 86*(2), 591–616.

Manski, C. F. (2004). Statistical treatment rules for heterogeneous populations. *Econometrica, 72*(4), 1221–1246.

May, P. J. (1992). Policy learning and failure. *Journal of Public Policy, 12*(4), 331–354.

Sutherland, W., & Burgman, M. (2015). Policy advice; use experts wisely. *Nature, 526*, 317–318.

Zhou, Z., Athey, S., & Wager, S. (2023). Offline multi-action policy learning; generalization and optimization. *Operations Research, 71*(1), 148–183.

# Chapter 10
# New Modes of Knowledge Production to Address Societal Challenges

**Antonio Zinilli, Emanuela Varinetti, Lorenzo Giammei, Andrea Orazio Spinello, Andrea Simone, and Emanuela Reale**

## 10.1 Introduction

The growing complexity of knowledge production in contemporary science is increasingly challenging social researchers to reconsider the organization, coordination, and governance of research. Over the past years, research infrastructures in the social sciences have undergone substantial transformations, driven not only by the expansion of data availability and computational methods, but also by the recent diffusion of generative artificial intelligence (Bail, 2024). Together, these developments have reshaped the ways in which scientific knowledge is produced, analysed, and validated. In response, researchers have progressively adopted alternative modes of knowledge production that are more open, networked, and participatory, moving beyond traditional scientific work (Turek, 2025). A driver of this shift is the rapid growth of computational social science, which relies on large-scale data, advanced analytical tools, and distributed expertise. These developments require new platforms for data management, interoperability, and collaboration, as well as novel forms of interdisciplinary teamwork that conventional organisational arrangements often struggle to support. The traditional methods of research, which usually focus on small, relatively uniform teams and fragmented data sources, are

A. Zinilli (✉) · E. Varinetti · A. O. Spinello · E. Reale
CNR-IRCrES—Research Institute on Sustainable Economic Growth, National Research Council of Italy, Rome, Italy
e-mail: antonio.zinilli@cnr.it; emanuela.varinetti@cnr.it; andreaorazio.spinello@cnr.it; emanuela.reale@cnr.it

L. Giammei
INAPP—National Institute for Public Policy Analysis, Rome, Italy

A. Simone
Department of Law, University of Palermo, Palermo, Italy
e-mail: andrea.simone01@unipa.it



G. Cerulli, E. Reale (eds.), *Research Infrastructures for Open Science in Social Science Research*, https://doi.org/10.1007/978-3-032-29575-0_10

becoming increasingly insufficient to keep up with the scale, complexity, and speed of modern research issues. As a result, social scientists are increasingly turning towards large-scale collaborative models (Franzoni & Sauermann, 2014) and deeper interdisciplinarity (D'Este & Robinson-García, 2023) as essential strategies for addressing today's grand societal challenges, including sustainability transitions, social inequalities, and rapid technological change. Against this background, research infrastructures in social science play a pivotal role. By structuring access to data, enabling comparability across contexts, and supporting collaborative research practices, they provide the backbone for these emerging modes of knowledge production. In this evolving landscape, the systematic study of research funding instruments, research projects, scientific publications, and collaboration structures has become central for understanding how knowledge is produced and circulated. These dimensions also constitute some of the key strands of work currently being developed within the FOSSR project. Within FOSSR, particular attention has been devoted to identifying gaps in the literature on knowledge production that can be addressed by exploiting advanced analytical techniques (as discussed in greater depth in Chap. 17).

Thanks to FOSSR, we have been able to construct and integrate new, large-scale datasets and to process them through advanced models for data cleaning, matching, and linkage. Combined modelling approaches have, for example, enabled the disambiguation of PhD holders' names by linking information from bibliometric databases such as Scopus and Web of Science with data on academic careers. Similarly, the use of text-mining and semantic analysis has allowed us to extract information on the orientation of research funding towards the Sustainable Development Goals (SDGs), and to explore in a systematic way the relationships between scientific production and the collaboration structures embedded in European research projects and programmes and co-authored publications. In this sense, FOSSR does not simply provide access to existing data; it actively extends the empirical basis for studying how programmes, projects, and publications jointly shape contemporary modes of knowledge production.

The following sections of this chapter illustrate how such infrastructures contribute to advancing social science research (Sect. 10.2), focusing respectively on the role of data on R&D programmes (Sect. 10.3), collaboration structures in scientific production (Sect. 10.4), and high skills resources in research (10.5). The chapter ends with some concluding remarks.

## 10.2 Theoretical Background

Contemporary scholarship on the organization of scientific research highlights a shift from traditional, discipline-bound knowledge production toward more hybrid, reflexive, and socially embedded systems of knowledge generation, as required to address complex societal challenges such as climate change, public health, equity, and sustainable development (Beck et al., 2022; Hessels & Van Lente, 2008).

In this process we can identify three main transitions that particularly affected the social science research and are strictly interconnected: a) from disciplinary to transdisciplinary knowledge production, b) from isolated and fragmented data and computational resources to integrated research infrastructures open to the use of multiple scholars; c) from the dominance of the government steering to different configurations of multi-level and multi-actors research and innovation systems.

In the nineties Gibbons and colleagues (Gibbons et al., 1994) introduced the idea that knowledge production was evolving beyond narrowly disciplinary practices (often referred to as Mode 1), to a new Mode 2 characterized by transdisciplinarity, context-of-application orientation, and heterogeneous actors. This concept received several critiques and was confronted with other competing concepts aimed at representing the transformative change occurring in the way in which scholars work, and scientific knowledge is generated. More recent research emphasises that the transformation of research systems continues to unfold along multiple, overlapping dimensions that cannot be fully captured by a single conceptual model. Although the original Mode 2 formulation offered a useful heuristic for understanding shifts toward interdisciplinary and application-focused research, subsequent literatures caution that these shifts are not linear or uniform across fields, regions, or institutional contexts (Hessels & Van Lente, 2008). Contemporary scholars stress pluralistic models of knowledge production that capture the coexistence of multiple epistemic logics and forms of scientific creativity.

Together with the emergence of these pluralistic perspectives, new values related to the generation of the scientific knowledge were drawn based on quality and integrity, collective benefit, equity and fairness, diversity and inclusiveness, which form the core of the Open Science paradigm redefining how knowledge is produced and shared (Armeni et al., 2021). Open Science emphasizes transparency, collaboration, and broad societal engagement in research, advocating that all aspects of scientific knowledge—from publications to data and methods—be openly accessible for scrutiny and reuse (Lilja, 2025; UNESCO, 2023). This involves adopting new ways of conducting and evaluating research (e.g. open peer review, collaborative platforms) and including non-academic stakeholders (industry, policymakers, civil society) in knowledge creation (Franzoni et al., 2025). In many ways, the Open Science ethos aligns with the Mode 2 ideals of reflexivity and context-driven research, but it pushes further by explicitly "democratizing" science through openness and participatory practices (Chtena et al., 2025).

Open Science drove a new way to produce, disseminate and use data, which are now supposed to be open, meaning that they must address the FAIR principles—being Findable, Accessible, Interoperable, and Reusable. These principles guide how data should be shared and used across scientific communities (Wilkinson et al., 2016) using open research infrastructures. Examples like the European Open Science Cloud (EOSC) aim to create shared, cross-disciplinary environments where data, tools, and services are available to researchers across borders and fields. Open data and research infrastructures help break down silos by linking datasets, analytical tools, and expert communities that would otherwise stay separate (https://research-and-innovation.ec.europa.eu/strategy/strategy-research-

and-innovation/our-digital-future/open-science/european-open-science-cloud-eosc_en?). However, large-scale open data infrastructures do not merely increase data availability; they actively reconfigure how knowledge is produced, enabling integration across disciplines, sectors, and territorial contexts. When combined with recent advances in generative artificial intelligence and machine learning, these infrastructures make it possible to explore, link, and interpret complex datasets at a scale and speed that were previously unattainable, opening new avenues for discovery and hypothesis generation.

In more recent times, the AI-intensive turn is raising important epistemic and ethical challenges. Thanks to advances in AI, the cost of producing scientific work has dropped sharply, leading to a dramatic increase in the number of papers being published. Large commercial publishers, driven by profit and shareholder expectations, are incentivized to maximize volume, impact metrics, and revenue, while shifting costs onto authors and publicly funded institutions. The pressure to "publish or perish," reinforced by rigid performance-based evaluation systems, has created a perverse incentive for scholars, exacerbating the trend toward increased productivity, with the negative consequence that quantity is often valued more than quality and speed more than reflection. Conformity and metric-chasing can outweigh critical thinking and genuine innovation.

The original goal of the open access movement to democratize access to knowledge, has been largely distorted in favor of fraudulent or otherwise unfair behaviours, fueling practices of pay-to-publish (Shu & Larivière, 2024). The increasing reliance on automated pattern recognition, opaque models, and pre-structured data can reinforce existing biases, obscure causal mechanisms, and shift epistemic authority away from human judgement toward algorithmic systems. Thus, the contemporary modes of knowledge production must balance the analytical power of infrastructures and the use of AI with reflexivity, transparency, and accountability, ensuring that openness and computational capacity enhance, rather than undermine, the robustness, interpretability, and social legitimacy of scientific knowledge. These developments point to a new and currently ongoing reconfiguration of knowledge production in which scientific outputs increasingly emerge from infrastructure-mediated, data-intensive and collaborative processes, rather than from isolated projects or individual research units. In this sense, open data infrastructures and AI-enabled analytics do not simply support research activities but constitute core elements of a new mode of knowledge production, shaping how problems are formulated, evidence is generated, and results are validated (Desai et al., 2022).

From an institutional perspective, contemporary science knowledge production emerges from the interaction of factors operating at policy, institutional, and individual levels, and it is carried out by multi-actor systems where government, intermediaries, scholars and stakeholders interact producing different national and transnational configurations. Recent work in the science of science shows that research dynamics are shaped simultaneously by micro-level mechanisms—such as scientists' problem choice, collaboration strategies, and career trajectories—and by meso and macro-level structures including teams, universities, research infrastructures, funding organizations, and regulatory regimes (Fortunato et al., 2018;

Lilja, 2025). These interactions are further complicated by evolving governance arrangements and responsibility framings that span individual ethics, institutional practices, and collective norms for socially responsible research (Abrams et al., 2025; Lilja, 2025). Empirical studies alike highlight how universities and research funders are reconfiguring assessment systems, incentive structures, and support measures to align Open Science practices with broader research culture and evaluation reforms. At the same time, scientific creativity increasingly depends on how openness and collaboration are organized across organizational boundaries and sectors, linking individual researchers' strategies with institutional logics and policy priorities (Beck et al., 2022). These contributions suggest that contemporary knowledge production can only be adequately described through integrative frameworks that connect policy and governance arrangements, organizational structures, and individual-level practices, rather than by focusing on any single level in isolation. From a systemic perspective, scientific knowledge production in different epistemic domains emerges as the outcome of interactions across policy, institutional and individual levels, where funding strategies, institutional cultures, and researcher choices jointly influence collaborative patterns and research outputs.

Research funding programs play a major role in this reconfiguration. Competitive funding can increase collaboration and shape networks of co-authorship, indicating that funding not only supports research but influences how science is done. Mobility grants, for example, tend to expand international collaborations and connect researchers with high-quality partners, enhancing diversity and integration across scientific networks (Baruffaldi et al., 2020). Major programs like Horizon Europe explicitly aim to stimulate cross-border cooperation and impactful research outcomes, reinforcing environments where collaboration and mobility are integral to productivity and scientific impact. In this view, research funding policies are structuring mechanisms in the new mode of knowledge production. They reinforce infrastructure-led, collaborative, and impact-oriented dynamics, shaping and reconfiguring the research systems at all levels.

## 10.3 Building Evidence in Research Policy Studies Through Data on R&D Programs

R&D programs constitute a valuable heuristic lens for enhancing research policy learning and investigating the evolving dynamics of research system governance (Reale et al., 2023a, 2023b). R&D programs serve as mechanisms through which funding is competitively allocated to individual researchers or teams for projects defined in time and scope, designed and managed by Research Funding Organizations (RFOs) (Lepori et al., 2007). Literature interprets them as research policy instruments that are far from neutral channels of resource distribution; rather, they embody embedded rationales that reflect strategies, goals and values, shaping the relationship between governments and the scientific community (Howlett,

2005; Lascoumes & Le Galès, 2007). They evolve in response to changing institutional environments, actor configurations, and implementation practices. Theoretical frameworks such as principal-agent theory (van der Meulen, 2003) help explain how RFOs mediate between governmental priorities and the autonomy of researchers. This mediation becomes evident in how programs define access criteria, evaluation procedures, and eligibility rules—elements operationalized through official documentation, calls for proposals, and peer review protocols, which may also be designed to promote, for instance, equal opportunities in access to leadership positions and in the allocation of research resources (Varinetti et al., 2025).

R&D programs may embody a variety of policy logics—ranging from scientific excellence and innovation to inclusion (e.g., gender equality) and competitiveness—which, when articulated within a broader portfolio, contribute to the formation of peculiar policy mixes (Cocos & Lepori, 2020). Increasingly, they are expected to not only promote scientific excellence but also achieve political and societal goals, addressing Societal Grand Challenges, supporting Key Enabling Technologies, and contributing to the achievement of the Sustainable Development Goals (SDGs) (Schneider et al., 2019). Nonetheless, the translation of policy objectives into outcomes is not always straightforward, and gaps between stated objectives and outcomes can arise due to implementation constraints or institutional inertia (Reale et al., 2014).

Efforts to analyse RFOs' funding portfolios across national research systems have long been hindered by fragmented and dispersed data. Information is typically scattered across RFO websites, call documents, and reports, with inconsistent labelling and categorization (OECD, 2018). While international initiatives such as the OECD's STIP Compass offer useful thematic overviews, they rely heavily on expert surveys and generally lack the granularity required for detailed analysis (https://stip.oecd.org/stip/). Constructing a reliable and analytically useful dataset on funding instruments entails a series of methodological and practical challenges, particularly when the goal is to enable meaningful cross-country comparisons. Similar difficulties were observed in earlier initiatives, such as the EC PREF project, which sought to reconstruct national public research funding portfolios for the European Commission (Lepori, 2017; Reale, 2017). That experience highlighted obstacles, including heterogeneity in data structures, inconsistent terminology, and limited accessibility of documentation, underscoring the need for robust, harmonized approaches to data collection and classification.

Building on the EC PREF experience, RISIS-EFIL—*European dataset of public R&D funding instruments* (Spinello et al., 2023), developed within the RISIS infrastructure[1] accessible from the FOSSR Open Cloud, was developed to fill this gap. RISIS-EFIL collects standardized empirical data on project-based public funding schemes, drawn from official documents and web sites obtained through systematic web search. It includes a wide range of instruments managed by the major European RFOs, from grants for research conducted by researchers

[1] Website: https://www.risis2.eu/

to thematic programs, fellowships, career development programs, infrastructure funding, and dissemination initiatives. Each instrument is described within the reference portfolio using qualitative and quantitative descriptors, including mission, aim, beneficiaries, evaluation criteria, budgetary appropriations. As of May 2023, RISIS-EFIL included data on 700 instruments managed by 55 RFOs across 11 countries, initially focusing on European countries, with preparations to expand its geographical scope to include the United States. Importantly, RISIS-EFIL is openly accessible upon submission of a research proposal; the availability of RISIS-EFIL under these conditions reflects the broader commitment of the FOSSR meta-infrastructure to open science.

A distinctive feature of RISIS-EFIL is its extensive archive, complementary to the dataset, composed of documents related to each instrument, such as calls for proposals, guidelines, and evaluation guidelines. Through text mining of this corpus, RISIS-EFIL identifies the degree to which funding instruments align with strategic agendas such as the KETs, SGCs, and the SDGs, thus providing an empirical basis for assessing policy orientation. Another key strength of RISIS-EFIL lies in its interoperability with other datasets on Science and Technology topics within RISIS, enabling multidimensional research policy analyses. RISIS-EFIL connects to OrgReg (a registry of research organizations), NATPRO (data on projects funded by national R&D programs), and SIPER (policy evaluation reports) via unique instrument and organization identifiers (Heller-Schuh et al., 2022). This integration allows researchers to link each funding instrument to funded projects and their evaluations, thus enhancing the capability to assess how policy objectives are implemented and translated into research outcomes.

Reale et al. (2023b) describe how the EFIL team addressed the main challenges in collecting data on R&D programs. To ensure cross-country comparability and account for the heterogeneity in how RFOs report their instruments, RISIS-EFIL introduced "funding routes" as aggregate categories within a hierarchical meso-micro model that preserves data integrity across institutional contexts. A major challenge concerned financial data reporting, as RFOs use diverse accounting conventions—from annual budgets to multi-year commitments. EFIL aligned with the OECD's GBARD methodology, prioritizing annual approved figures and flagging cumulative or estimated values accordingly. Data availability was another constraint, given the reliance on publicly accessible online sources prone to removal or fragmentation. To address this, the team tracked missing content via third-party aggregators and used the Internet Archive (Wayback Machine) to recover documents. To guarantee data quality, all entries underwent manual review and consistency checks, with preliminary records validated by national experts.

Building on these validation efforts, RISIS-EFIL supports detailed studies, both cross-national and longitudinal, promoting evidence-based policy learning on how public research funding reflects political and societal priorities.

For example, RISIS-EFIL has become a key source for assessing the alignment of funding instruments with inclusion and sustainability agendas. In Spinello et al. (2021), RISIS-EFIL supported the classification and benchmarking of R&D instruments across Europe, using descriptors and document-based analysis to map

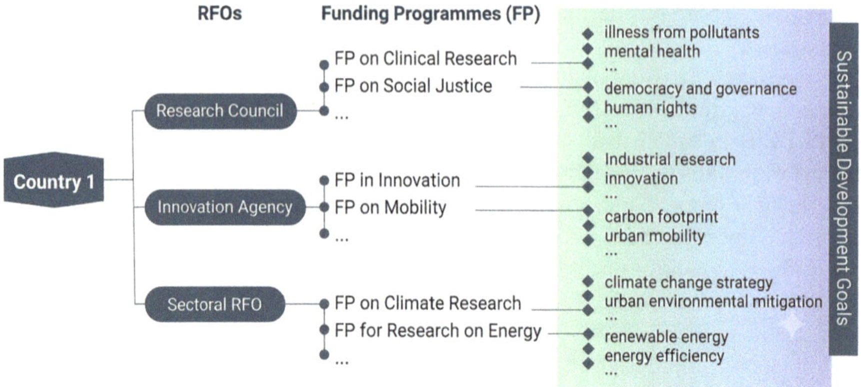


**Fig. 10.1** Process of SDGs identification in the RFOs' instruments portfolio from RISIS-EFIL

thematic orientations such as economic innovation, knowledge advancement, and social relevance. Keyword and word cloud analyses revealed how evaluation criteria integrate or omit social dimensions. In Zinilli et al. (2023), RISIS-EFIL data enabled a new mapping of national R&D portfolios against the SDGs. By applying text mining and semantic analysis to program documents, the study highlighted country-specific patterns of specialization or diversification in aligning with the SDGs, offering a method for monitoring the evolution of public research priorities over time (Fig. 10.1).

RISIS-EFIL was also central to study on gender equality in R&D funding (Varinetti et al., 2025). Using RISIS-EFIL, the study compared how RFOs in Austria, Germany, France, and Italy integrated gender provisions into competitive R&D instruments. Through automated document analysis, the researchers observed a clear increase in gender references between the two time periods. In the Italian case, RISIS-EFIL revealed a transition from the absence of gender considerations to the explicit criteria introduced after the pandemic period, showing a growing alignment with EU-level mandates. To further explore the practical application of gender equality principles, the study relied on PRINWINNERS, a spin-off dataset created to collect micro-level data on projects funded between 2017 and 2022 by a specific Italian scheme (i.e. PRIN project). This dataset allowed researchers to connect the instrument level to the project level. The combined use of RISIS-EFIL and PRINWINNERS thus enabled a multi-level analysis, from program design to actual resource allocation and researcher composition and confirmed that the recently introduced measures are positively steering the system towards greater equity.

These applications demonstrate how a newly established dataset, when embedded within a research infrastructure, can foster a more integrated and evidence-based approach to science policy analysis, in line with the overarching goals of the FOSSR meta-infrastructure.

## 10.4 Collaboration Structures and Scientific Production

Collaboration has become a defining feature of contemporary scientific knowledge production (Ductor, 2015; Landry et al., 1996; Lee & Bozeman, 2005; Resce et al., 2022; Yadav et al., 2023). Increasingly, research outputs emerge from inter-institutional partnerships and cross-sector collaborations that exploit complementary expertise. This transformation reflects the broader shift toward network and infrastructure-based knowledge production discussed earlier in this chapter. In such a context, collaboration structures are not merely ancillary to research activity but constitute a central mechanism through which scientific productivity and impact are generated (Defazio et al., 2009; He et al., 2009). Understanding how collaboration relates to scientific production is therefore essential for both advancing research policy studies and informing evidence-based policy.

A substantial body of literature documents a positive association between collaboration and research performance. Collaborative research can enhance productivity by enabling knowledge exchange, division of labour, and access to diverse skills and resources (Adams, 2013; Dusdal & Powell, 2021; Gazni et al., 2012; Glänzel & Schubert, 2001). At the same time, high-performing researchers and institutions are often more attractive collaborators, suggesting that productivity itself may foster further collaboration (Abramo et al., 2017; He et al., 2009; Zinilli, 2016). As a result, the relationship between collaboration and productivity is potentially bidirectional and shaped by cumulative advantage dynamics, where early success reinforces future opportunities. Disentangling these mechanisms poses significant empirical challenges, as collaboration and productivity are deeply intertwined and influenced by institutional, disciplinary, and contextual factors.

Scientific collaboration takes place both through co-authorship networks, reflecting joint knowledge production, and through formal project-based partnerships, often structured by competitive funding programmes. Each mode of collaboration follows distinct logics and incentives, and each may relate differently to scientific productivity. Capturing this complexity requires integrated data and analytical approaches capable of jointly examining multiple collaboration dimensions over time. In this respect, research infrastructures play a crucial enabling role. Historically, analyses of collaboration have been constrained by fragmented data sources: bibliometric databases provide information on co-authorship but limited insight into organizational contexts, while project databases document funded collaborations but are rarely linked systematically to scientific outputs. A key contribution of FOSSR lies in its capacity to support the integration of heterogeneous datasets on publications, projects, and organizations, thereby enabling a more comprehensive analysis of collaboration and its relationship with scientific production.

An empirical study has been conducted on FOSSR data, to investigate the mentioned multidimensional relation between collaboration and research productivity (Zinilli et al., 2026). The analysis explores three core datasets developed within the RISIS ecosystem and made accessible through the FOSSR Open Cloud: EUPRO (data on European-funded research projects), CWTS bibliometric data derived from Web of Science, and ETER (the European Tertiary Education Register). EUPRO enables the reconstruction of project-based collaboration networks among universities and firms; CWTS data supports the analysis of co-publication networks and research productivity; and ETER provides harmonized organizational identifiers and institutional characteristics. The linkage across these datasets, achieved through shared university identifiers, allows universities to be positioned consistently across publication and project networks and enables the joint analysis of collaboration structures, institutional features, and research performance.

Building on this integrated database, collaboration is investigated through network centrality measures that capture different dimensions of actors' positions within collaboration networks (Freeman, 1977). Degree centrality reflects the number of direct collaborative ties and serves as a proxy for collaboration intensity (Abbasi et al., 2011; Badar et al., 2013, 2015; Bornmann et al., 2013; Lee & Bozeman, 2005). Closeness centrality captures how near an actor is to others in the network, reflecting access to knowledge flows and institutional visibility (Katz & Martin, 1997; Kwiek, 2020; Zinilli & Cerulli, 2023). Betweenness centrality identifies brokerage positions that connect otherwise disconnected actors, potentially granting access to non-redundant information (Burt, 1992; Freeman, 1977). Importantly, the dataset allows further differentiation between university–university and university–firm collaborations, highlighting the growing relevance of partnerships between academia and industry in contemporary research systems.

The analysis focuses on European universities over the period 2016–2021 and distinguishes between two broad scientific domains defined by the European Research Council: Physical Sciences and Engineering (PE) and Life Sciences (LS). This distinction is analytically important, as collaboration practices, team structures, and funding environments vary substantially across domains. Research productivity is measured using a bibliometric indicator, the number of publications in the top 5% most cited in each field.

To address the endogeneity and potential bidirectionality between collaboration and productivity, the study employs Bayesian networks (Pearl, 1995). This probabilistic graphical approach allows the modelling of complex dependency structures among multiple variables and supports the identification of direct and indirect relationships without imposing strong assumptions. Bayesian networks are particularly well suited for analysing research systems, where collaboration, performance, institutional characteristics, and contextual conditions mutually influence one another. Further methodological details on Bayesian networks and their application within research infrastructures are discussed in Chap. 17.

Empirically, the findings reveal both persistent patterns and important domain-specific differences. In Physics and Engineering, degree centrality in publication networks consistently emerges as the most stable predictor of research productivity throughout the period considered. This indicates that, in PE, broad and sustained academic collaboration, as reflected in co-authorship links, is a structural condition for high scientific performance. The stability of this relationship underscores the centrality of collaboration in domains characterized by cumulative, team-based knowledge production.

In the Life Sciences, the relationship between collaboration and productivity is more nuanced and temporally variable. In the early years of the period (2016–2017), closeness centrality in publication networks plays a more prominent role, suggesting that central positioning and rapid access to circulating knowledge temporarily amplify research performance. From 2018 onward, degree centrality becomes the dominant factor also in LS, indicating a shift toward the importance of direct collaborative intensity.

A further contribution of the study lies in distinguishing between publication-based and project-based collaboration dynamics. The results suggest that collaboration within publication networks tends to play a leading role in shaping research productivity, while productivity more strongly influences collaboration patterns in project-based networks. In Physics and Engineering, higher research productivity is associated, in specific years, with an increased ability to attract firm partners in EU-funded projects, indicating that performance plays an important role in cross-sector collaboration. On the other hand, in the Life Sciences, productivity appears to reinforce academic collaborations in projects more than industry partnerships.

From an infrastructure perspective, these findings demonstrate the analytical gains enabled by integrated, multi-layer data. Analyses limited to publications or projects alone would capture only part of the collaboration–productivity relationship and risk misinterpreting causal dynamics. By linking project participation, co-authorship networks, and institutional characteristics, FOSSR-enabled analyses provide a more comprehensive view of how scientific production is embedded in multiple, interacting collaboration structures.

The policy implications are substantial. First, the consistent association between degree centrality in publication networks and research productivity suggests that policies fostering direct academic collaboration, such as support for mobility, networking, and collaborative platforms, can contribute to higher scientific performance. Second, the observed domain-specific patterns indicate that collaboration policies should be tailored to disciplinary contexts rather than applied uniformly. Third, evidence that high productivity enhances access to project-based and industry collaborations implies that capability-building is an important action to foster networking. Overall, the findings deepen understanding of the structural links between collaboration and research productivity and illustrate how integrated data can support more robust research policy analysis.

## 10.5 Human Resources in Research: The Case of PhD Holders

PhD holders are becoming an increasingly central component of contemporary research systems, contributing to the creation and dissemination of ideas that drive technological and social progress (Auriol, 2010; Reale et al., 2019). Between 2014 and 2019, the number of doctoral degrees awarded across OECD countries grew by about 25 per cent, reflecting a strategic commitment by governments and higher education systems to expanding the highly skilled research workforce (Sarrico, 2022). In Europe, the expansion of doctoral education has been part of a broader policy agenda aimed at reinforcing the research base of universities and aligning academic training more closely with regional development and innovation strategies (Hasgall et al., 2019).

As doctoral education has become an integral part of the broader architecture of innovation, PhD holders have emerged as key agents connecting the pursuit of new knowledge frontiers with its application across scientific, technological, and social fields. A well-established body of literature shows that engagement with peripheral or emerging research domains is vital for the diversification of regional and sectoral knowledge bases (Asheim & Coenen, 2005; Frenken et al., 2007). Such diversification is associated with lasting competitive advantages for both regions and firms (Boschma & Frenken, 2015; Simone, 2023), since it often underpins breakthrough innovations that are difficult to replicate elsewhere (Castaldi et al., 2015). This form of knowledge production typically characterises doctoral research, which involves bridging disciplinary boundaries and addressing questions that established programmes or industrial laboratories cannot easily pursue (Frenken, 2017), thereby extending the frontier of scientific and technological knowledge into new and uncertain territories (Enders, 2005). The involvement of doctoral researchers has been shown to strengthen both the intensity and diversity of innovation. Evidence from Gruber et al. (2013), based on more than 30,000 European patents, demonstrates that inventors with a PhD tend to produce inventions spanning a wider range of technological classes than those without doctoral training. Evidence from the German laser industry shows that PhD-trained inventors, who make up about 15 per cent of all inventors, account for nearly 45 per cent of firm patents, underscoring their disproportionate contribution to technological innovation (Buenstorf & Heinisch, 2020), while firm-level evidence from Denmark indicates that hiring former university researchers is associated with higher patenting activity, about 0.09 additional patent applications for each PhD holder hired, rising to around 0.20–0.35 extra patents among already patent-active firms (Ejsing et al., 2013).

Given their role as catalysts of economic dynamism and innovation (Corcoran & Faggian, 2017), the ability to attract and retain talent has become a key priority in local development strategies. PhD holders are among the most mobile segments of the research workforce (OECD, 2022), both nationally and internationally. While individual factors such as socio-economic background, family conditions, and career aspirations play an important role in shaping mobility decisions (Ackers, 2008; Netz & Jaksztat, 2017), institutional factors including universities' resources, networks, and international visibility also exert a strong influence (Horta & Santos, 2016; Mathies & Cantwell, 2022). At the structural level, broader labour market conditions, funding mechanisms, and academic career systems define the opportunities and constraints under which mobility occurs (Auriol, 2010; Bozzon et al., 2017). These multi-level factors jointly shape mobility dynamics, offering important levers for firms, research centres, and regional innovation systems to design policies that foster talent circulation and knowledge exchange.

These interacting dynamics generate an uneven geography of opportunity, reflecting broader disparities in innovation capacity and research investment (Crescenzi et al., 2017). Competitive, performance-based funding regimes have often amplified these inequalities, favouring already resource-rich institutions and regions (Capano et al., 2016). By contrast, territories that combine academic excellence with inclusive and well-funded research environments are better positioned to transform mobility into a channel for sustainable development and long-term resilience (Martin & Moodysson, 2013; Varinetti, 2020).

To gain a deeper understanding of the complex interplay between individual characteristics, institutional conditions, and regional contexts, we exploited data provided by the FOSSR project on the mobility of PhD holders in Italy. The project includes data from 1984 onwards on a very large sample of PhD holders, including detailed information on universities, dissertation titles and abstracts, year of completion, and other relevant variables (for further details, see Zinilli et al., 2025). The evidence suggests that early-career mobility does not follow a uniform centre–periphery logic: while persistence rates are highest in the Northern macroregion, the South and Islands also retain a substantial share of their doctoral graduates, whereas the Centre emerges as the most fluid area, characterised by pronounced bidirectional flows, particularly toward the North. These patterns point to differences in universities' recruitment capacity, their integration into research collaboration networks, and the availability of early-career academic positions within regional labour markets. Mobility decisions further reflect the interaction between individual and institutional factors. Gender differences remain significant, with women less likely to relocate across macro-regions, consistent with broader social and structural barriers in academic careers. At the institutional level, universities that are more strongly embedded in European research networks appear better positioned to retain doctoral talent, while universities with a high number of senior faculty may have lower absorptive capacity for early-career researchers, encouraging relocation as a response to constrained internal career opportunities.

These findings support the idea that regional differences in research capacity are tightly linked to how institutional conditions, career structures, and network embeddedness interact over time. More broadly, the analysis illustrates how the integration of individual career data with institutional and network indicators, made possible within the FOSSR research infrastructure, can inform a more nuanced understanding of mobility mechanisms relevant for research and regional development policies.

## 10.6 Conclusions

This chapter has argued that contemporary modes of knowledge production in the social sciences are increasingly organised around research infrastructures, integrated datasets, and AI-enabled analytics, rather than around isolated projects or individual scholars. In this sense, knowledge is less the outcome of discrete, laboratory-like endeavours and more the emergent property of infrastructure-mediated, multi-actor systems, where policy instruments, collaboration structures, and human resources are tightly linked. Across the three empirical strands discussed here, a common picture emerges.

First, R&D programmes and their funding instruments are not neutral channels through which resources flow, but structuring mechanisms that encode policy priorities, evaluation criteria, and normative expectations about what counts as valuable knowledge. Through RISIS-EFIL, these instruments can be systematically described and compared across countries, revealing how agendas such as sustainability, inclusion, and gender equality are translated (or fail to be translated) into funding logics and concrete schemes. When linked to project-level and organisational data, these instruments become key levers for evidence-based policy learning, enabling analyses of whether and how stated objectives, for instance related to the SDGs or gender equality, are reflected in actual resource allocation patterns.

Second, the analysis of collaboration structures and scientific production shows that research outputs are deeply embedded in multi-layer networks of co-authorship and project-based partnerships. Degree and closeness centrality in publication networks, together with brokerage positions, systematically shape universities' research performance, albeit with domain-specific nuances between Physical Sciences and Engineering and the Life Sciences. The FOSSR meta-infrastructure allows these patterns to be studied jointly in publication and project networks, revealing that the relationship between collaboration and performance is bidirectional and contingent on institutional and disciplinary environments. The use of Bayesian networks further highlights that collaboration, productivity, and organisational characteristics form dense webs of mutual dependence, rather than simple linear cause–effect relationships.

Third, the focus on PhD holders underscores that new modes of knowledge production are also fundamentally labour-intensive. Doctoral graduates act as carriers of expertise, bridging emerging and established domains, and contributing disproportionately to both technological and scientific innovation. At the same time, their mobility patterns reflect and reproduce regional inequalities in research capacity, as opportunities concentrate in institutions and territories that can combine excellence with favourable career structures and funding environments. Integrating individual career trajectories with information on universities and networks, as enabled by FOSSR, makes it possible to trace how systemic asymmetries in opportunities translate into uneven geographies of knowledge production.

These themes illustrate that new modes of knowledge production are multi-level: they are shaped simultaneously by policy instruments (funding programmes and their portfolios), organisational structures (universities, firms, research infrastructures), and individual trajectories (careers and mobility of researchers). The chapter shows that infrastructures such as FOSSR can make these levels analytically commensurable, by linking datasets on programmes, projects, publications, organisations, and people within a common framework. This integration is not merely technical: it creates the conditions for more reflexive, empirically grounded debates on how research systems address societal challenges. At the same time, the chapter has highlighted that the data- and AI-intensive turn in science is ambivalent. On the one hand, large-scale infrastructures and generative AI tools dramatically expand the capacity to explore, match, and interpret complex datasets, opening new possibilities for discovery, policy evaluation, and strategic intelligence on research systems. On the other hand, this turn is likely to amplify epistemic and institutional tensions: publication systems increasingly reward volume and speed over depth and critical scrutiny; opaque models and pre-structured data risk biases; and the rapid proliferation of AI-generated or fraudulent work strains peer review and erodes trust in formal certification mechanisms.

The first agenda is analytical: expand and interconnect data and infrastructures (e.g., RISIS-EFIL, patents, societal impact, Open Science practices) to better map how funding, collaboration, and human resources co-evolve. The second is normative: embed infrastructures and AI into evaluation and governance frameworks that prioritise quality, openness, and epistemic equity over mere output.

## References


Abbasi, A., Altmann, J., & Hossain, L. (2011). Identifying the effects of co-authorship networks on the performance of scholars: A correlation and regression analysis of performance measures and social network analysis measures. *Journal of Informetrics, 5*(4), 594–607.

Abramo, G., D'Angelo, C. A., & Murgia, G. (2017). The relationship among research productivity, research collaboration, and their determinants. *Journal of Informetrics, 11*(4), 1016–1030. https://doi.org/10.1016/j.joi.2017.09.007

Abrams, E., Leone, P. V., Cambrosio, A., & Faraj, S. (2025). The governance of open science: A comparative analysis of two open science consortia. *Research Policy, 54*(3), 105195.

Ackers, L. (2008). Internationalisation, mobility and metrics: A new form of indirect discrimination? *Minerva, 46*(4), 411–435.

Adams, J. (2013). The fourth age of research. *Nature, 497*(7451), 557–560.

Armeni, K., Brinkman, L., Carlsson, R., Eerland, A., Fijten, R., Fondberg, R., et al. (2021). Towards wide-scale adoption of open science practices: The role of open science communities. *Science and Public Policy, 48*(5), 605–611.

Asheim, B. T., & Coenen, L. (2005). Knowledge bases and regional innovation systems: Comparing Nordic clusters. *Research Policy, 34*(8), 1173–1190.

Auriol, L. (2010). *Careers of doctorate holders: Employment and mobility patterns, OECD science, technology and industry working papers, no. 2010/04*. OECD Publishing, Paris. https://doi.org/10.1787/5kmh8phxvvf5-en.

Badar, K., Hite, J. M., & Ashraf, N. (2015). Knowledge network centrality, formal rank and research performance: Evidence for curvilinear and interaction effects. *Scientometrics, 105*, 1553–1576.

Badar, K., Hite, J. M., & Badir, Y. F. (2013). Examining the relationship of co-authorship network centrality and gender on academic research performance: The case of chemistry researchers in Pakistan. *Scientometrics, 94*, 755–775.

Bail, C. A. (2024). Can generative AI improve social science? *Proceedings of the National Academy of Sciences, 121*(21), e2314021121.

Baruffaldi, S. H., Marino, M., & Visentin, F. (2020). Money to move: The effect on researchers of an international mobility grant. *Research Policy, 49*(8), 104077.

Beck, S., Bergenholtz, C., Bogers, M., Brasseur, T. M., Conradsen, M. L., Di Marco, D., ... & Xu, S. M. (2022). The open innovation in science research field: a collaborative conceptualisation approach. Industry and Innovation, 29(2), 136–185. B.

Bornmann, L., Leydesdorff, L., & Mutz, R. (2013). The use of percentile rank classes in the analysis of bibliometric data: Opportunities and limits. *Journal of Informetrics, 7*(1), 158–165.

Boschma, R., & Frenken, K. (2015). Evolutionary economic geography. In *Papers in evolutionary economic geography, #15.18*. Utrecht University, Department of Human Geography and Spatial Planning, Group Economic Geography.

Bozzon, R., Murgia, A., Poggio, B., & Rapetti, E. (2017). Work–life interferences in the early stages of academic careers: The case of precarious researchers in Italy. *European Educational Research Journal, 16*(2–3), 332–351.

Buenstorf, G., & Heinisch, D. P. (2020). When do firms get ideas from hiring PhDs? *Research Policy, 49*(3), 103913.

Burt, R. S. (1992). *Structural holes: The social structure of competition*. Harvard University Press.

Capano, G., Regini, M., & Turri, M. (2016). *Changing governance in universities*. Springer.

Castaldi, C., Frenken, K., & Los, B. (2015). Related variety, unrelated variety and technological breakthroughs: An analysis of US state-level patenting. *Regional Studies, 49*(5), 767–781. https://doi.org/10.1080/00343404.2014.940305

Chtena, N., Alperin, J. P., Morales, E., Fleerackers, A., Dorsch, I., Pinfield, S., & Simard, M. A. (2025). Towards an inclusive open science: Examining EDI and public participation in policy documents across Europe and the Americas. *Royal Society Open Science, 12*(4), 240857.

Cocos, M., & Lepori, B. (2020). What we know about research policy mix. *Science and Public Policy, 47*, 235–245.

Corcoran, J., & Faggian, A. (2017). Graduate migration and regional development: An international perspective. In *Graduate migration and regional development*. Edward Elgar Publishing.

Crescenzi, R., Holman, N., & Orru', E. (2017). Why do they return? Beyond the economic drivers of graduate return migration. *The Annals of Regional Science, 59*, 603–627.

D'Este, P., & Robinson-García, N. (2023). Interdisciplinary research and the societal visibility of science: The advantages of spanning multiple and distant scientific fields. *Research Policy, 52*(2), 104609.

Defazio, D., Lockett, A., & Wright, M. (2009). Funding incentives, collaborative dynamics and scientific productivity: Evidence from the EU framework program. *Research Policy, 38*(2), 293–305.

Desai, J., Watson, D., Wang, V., Taddeo, M., & Floridi, L. (2022). The epistemological foundations of data science: A critical review. *Synthese, 200*, 469. https://doi.org/10.1007/s11229-022-03933-2

Ductor, L. (2015). Does co-authorship lead to higher academic productivity? *Oxford Bulletin of Economics and Statistics, 77*(3), 385–407. https://doi.org/10.1111/obes.12070

Dusdal, J., & Powell, J. J. (2021). Benefits, motivations, and challenges of international collaborative research: A sociology of science case study. *Science and Public Policy, 48*(2), 235–245.

Ejsing, A.-K., Kaiser, U., Kongsted, H. C., & Laursen, K. (2013). *The role of university scientist mobility for industrial innovation*. IZA. IZA discussion paper no. 7470. http://ftp.iza.org/dp7470.pdf

Enders, J. (2005). Border crossings: Research training, knowledge dissemination and the transformation of academic work. *Higher Education, 49*(1), 119–133.

Fortunato, S., Bergstrom, C. T., Börner, K., Evans, J. A., Helbing, D., Milojević, S., et al. (2018). Science of science. *Science, 359*(6379), eaao0185.

Franzoni, C., & Sauermann, H. (2014). Crowd science: The organization of scientific research in open collaborative projects. *Research Policy, 43*(1), 1–20.

Franzoni, C., Sauermann, H., & Di Marco, D. (2025). When citizens judge science: Crowd evaluations in mode 2 knowledge production. *Research Policy, 54*(5), 105214.

Freeman, L. C. (1977). A set of measures of centrality based on betweenness. *Sociometry, 40*(1), 35–41.

Frenken, K. (2017). A complexity-theoretic perspective on innovation policy. *Complexity, Innovation and Policy, 3*(1), 35–47.

Frenken, K., Van Oort, F., & Verburg, T. (2007). Related variety, unrelated variety and regional economic growth. *Regional Studies, 41*(5), 685–697.

Gazni, A., Sugimoto, C. R., & Didegah, F. (2012). Mapping world scientific collaboration: Authors, institutions, and countries. *Journal of the American Society for Information Science and Technology, 63*(2), 323–335.

Gibbons, M., Limoges, C., Scott, P., Schwartzman, S., & Nowotny, H. (1994). *The new production of knowledge: The dynamics of science and research in contemporary societies*.

Glänzel, W., & Schubert, A. (2001). Double effort = double impact? A critical view at international co-authorship in chemistry. *Scientometrics, 50*(2), 199–214.

Gruber, M., Harhoff, D., & Hoisl, K. (2013). Knowledge recombination across technological boundaries: Scientists vs. engineers. *Management Science, 59*(4), 837–851.

Hasgall, A., Saenen, B., Borrell-Damian, L., Van Deynze, F., Seeber, M., & Huisman, J. (2019). *Doctoral education in Europe today: Approaches and institutional structures*. European University Association.

He, Z.-L., Geng, X.-S., & Campbell-Hunt, C. (2009). Research collaboration and research output: A longitudinal study of 65 biomedical scientists in a New Zealand University. *Research Policy, 38*(2), 306–317.

Heller-Schuh, B., Reale, E., Scherngell, T., Spinello, A. O., Varinetti, E., Zahradnik, G., & Zinilli, A. (2022). *New insights into project-based R&D funding from RISIS datasets: Some evidence from EFIL and NATPRO*. RISIS policy brief series, issue #10, May 2022. Zenodo. https://doi.org/10.5281/zenodo.6549168.

Hessels, L. K., & Van Lente, H. (2008). Re-thinking new knowledge production: A literature review and a research agenda. *Research Policy, 37*(4), 740–760.

Horta, H., & Santos, J. M. (2016). The impact of publishing during PhD studies on career research publication, visibility, and collaborations. *Research in Higher Education, 57*(1), 28–50.

Howlett, M. (2005). What is a policy instrument? Tools, mixes, and implementation styles. In M. Howlett, M. M. Hill, & F. P. Eliadis (Eds.), *Designing government: From instruments to governance* (pp. 31–50). McGill-Queen's University.

Katz, J. S., & Martin, B. R. (1997). What is research collaboration? *Research Policy, 26*(1), 1–18.

Kwiek, M. (2020). Internationalists and locals: International research collaboration in a resource-poor system. *Scientometrics, 124*(1), 57–105.

Landry, R., Traore, N. A., & Godin, B. (1996). An econometric analysis of the effect of collaboration on academic research productivity. *Higher Education, 32*(3), 283–301. https://doi.org/10.1007/BF00138868

Lascoumes, P., & Le Galès, P. (2007). Introduction: Understanding public policy through its instruments? From the nature of instruments to the sociology of public policy instrumentation. *Governance, 20*(1), 1–21.

Lee, S., & Bozeman, B. (2005). The impact of research collaboration on scientific productivity. *Social Studies of Science, 35*(5), 673–702. https://doi.org/10.1177/0306312705052359

Lepori, B. (2017). *Analysis of national public research funding PREF. Handbook for data collection and indicators production*. Publications Office of the European Union. ISBN: 978-92-79-71308-8.

Lepori, B., van den Besselaar, P., Dinges, M., Potì, B., Reale, E., Slipersæter, S., Thèves, J., & van der Meulen, B. (2007). Comparing the evolution of national research policies: What patterns of change? *Science and Public Policy, 34*, 372–388.

Lilja, E. (2025). Responsibility dynamics in open science: Exploring researchers' framing of ethical considerations in policy implementation. *Science and Public Policy, 52*(6), 852–864.

Martin, R., & Moodysson, J. (2013). Comparing knowledge bases: On the geography and organization of knowledge sourcing in the regional innovation system of Scania, Sweden. *European Urban and Regional Studies, 20*(2), 170–187.

Mathies, C., & Cantwell, B. (2022). Intra-regional mobility of PhD students in the European Union: The outcomes of region-making policy? *Policy Reviews in Higher Education, 6*(2), 230–251.

Netz, N., & Jaksztat, S. (2017). Explaining scientists' plans for international mobility from a life course perspective. *Research in Higher Education, 58*, 497–519.

OECD. (2018). *Effective operation of competitive research funding systems*. OECD Science, Technology and Industry Policy Papers No. 57, 16 October.

OECD. (2022). *International migration outlook 2022*. OECD Publishing. https://doi.org/10.1787/30fe16d2-en

Pearl, J. (1995). From Bayesian networks to causal networks. In *Mathematical models for handling partial knowledge in artificial intelligence* (pp. 157–182). Springer.

Reale, E. (2017). *Analysis of national public research funding (PREF)—Final report*. Publications Office of the European Union. ISBN: 978-92-79-73407-6.

Reale, E., Gulbrandsen, M., & Scherngell, T. (2023a). R&D programs as instruments for governmental R&D funding policy. In B. Lepori et al. (Eds.), *Handbook of public funding of research* (pp. 107–122). Edward Elgar Publishing.

Reale, E., Morettini, L., & Zinilli, A. (2019). Moving, remaining, and returning: International mobility of doctorate holders in the social sciences and humanities. *Higher Education, 78*(1), 17–32.

Reale, E., Nedeva, M., Thomas, D., & Primeri, E. (2014). Evaluation through impact: A different viewpoint. *Fteval Journal for Research and Technology Policy Evaluation, 39*, 36–41.

Reale, E., Spinello, A. O., Varinetti, E., & Zinilli, A. (2023b). *Documentation of RISIS datasets: EFIL*. Version 2.0. RISIS 2-European research infrastructure for science, technology and innovation policy studies 2, grant agreement 824091. Zenodo. https://zenodo.org/record/7938134#.ZGtopnZByUl

Resce, G., Zinilli, A., & Cerulli, G. (2022). Machine learning prediction of academic collaboration networks. *Scientific Reports, 12*(1), 21993.

Sarrico, C. S. (2022). The expansion of doctoral education and the changing nature and purpose of the doctorate. *Higher Education, 84*(6), 1299–1315. https://doi.org/10.1007/s10734-022-00946-1

Schneider, F., Buser, T., Keller, R., Tribaldos, T., & Rist, S. (2019). Research funding programmes aiming for societal transformations: Ten key stages. *Science and Public Policy, 46*(3), 463–478.

Shu, F., & Larivière, V. (2024). The oligopoly of open access publishing. *Scientometrics, 129*, 519–536. https://doi.org/10.1007/s11192-023-04876-2

Simone, A. (2023). The sources of unrelated diversification and its implications for lagging regions. *GeoJournal, 88*(2), 2139–2152.

Spinello, A. O., Reale, E., & Zinilli, A. (2021). Outlining the orientation toward socially relevant issues in competitive R&D funding instruments. *Frontiers in Research Metrics and Analytics, 6*, 712839.

Spinello, A. O., Varinetti, E., Zinilli, A., & Reale, E. (2023). *EFIL-European dataset of public R&D funding instruments* (Version 2) [Data set]. Research Institute on Sustainable Economic Growth. Dataset included in RISIS Research Infrastructure for Science and Innovation Policy Studies. https://doi.org/10.71835/WTDX-2G24.

Turek, K. (2025). Accelerating social science knowledge production with the coordinated open-source model. *Quality & Quantity, 59*(Suppl 2), 767–795.

UNESCO. (2023). *Development of the UNESCO recommendation on open science*. https://www.unesco.org/en/open-science/development?hub=686

van der Meulen, B. (2003). New roles and strategies of a research council: Intermediation of the principal-agent relationship. *Science and Public Policy, 30*(5), 323–336.

Varinetti, E. (2020). Fattori di spinta e attrazione per i ricercatori stranieri in Italia e in Spagna. *WELFARE E ERGONOMIA 1*, 139–150. https://doi.org/10.3280/WE2019-001012

Varinetti, E., Reale, E., Spinello, A. O., & Zinilli, A. (2025). Valorizzazione degli aspetti di genere nel finanziamento competitivo per la Ricerca e Sviluppo, in Consiglio Nazionale delle Ricerche, Relazione sulla ricerca e l'innovazione in Italia. In *Analisi e dati di politica della scienza e della tecnologia* (5th ed., pp. 183–218). CNR Edizioni.

Wilkinson, M. D., Dumontier, M., Aalbersberg, I. J., Appleton, G., Axton, M., Baak, A., et al. (2016). The FAIR guiding principles for scientific data management and stewardship. *Scientific Data, 3*(1), 1–9.

Yadav, P., Tam, D., Choshen, L., Raffel, C. A., & Bansal, M. (2023). Ties-merging: Resolving interference when merging models. *Advances in Neural Information Processing Systems, 36*, 7093–7115.

Zinilli, A. (2016). Competitive project funding and dynamic complex networks: Evidence from projects of national interest (PRIN). *Scientometrics, 108*(2), 633–652.

Zinilli, A., & Cerulli, G. (2023). Link prediction and feature relevance in knowledge networks: A machine learning approach. *PLoS One, 18*(11), e0290018.

Zinilli, A., Giammei, L., & Varinetti, E. (2026). Collaborative structures and research productivity: An empirical analysis with Bayesian networks. *Scientometrics*. https://doi.org/10.1007/s11192-026-05556-7

Zinilli, A., Reale, E., Spinello, A. O., & Varinetti, E. (2023). Diversification vs. specialization from the perspective of research programmes: A complexity approach. In *Atlanta conference on science and innovation policy 2023 abstract book*, p. 24. https://bpb-us-e1.wpmucdn.com/sites.gatech.edu/dist/4/4684/files/2024/09/2023_atlc_abstract_book.pdf

Zinilli, A., Tuccari, G. G., Poggi, F., Nuzzolese, A. G., Mongiovì, M., Giammei, L., et al. (2025). Anatomy of climate change research in Italian doctoral dissertations using a machine learning approach. *Scientific Reports, 15*(1), 38095.

# Chapter 11
# Deepening the Structure of the National Industrial System

**Massimiliano Guerini and Massimo Gaetano Colombo**

## 11.1 Introduction

The deepening of national industrial systems has increasingly been recognized as a key determinant of long-term economic growth, technological upgrading, and economic resilience. Beyond changes in sectoral composition, industrial deepening refers to the development of complex productive structures characterized by dense inter-firm linkages, cumulative learning processes, and the emergence of innovation-driven firms embedded within coherent entrepreneurial ecosystems (Spigel, 2017; Stam & Van de Ven, 2021). In this perspective, growth and structural transformation depend not only on the presence of innovative firms, but also on the quality of interactions among firms, investors, institutions, and supporting organizations that collectively shape ecosystem dynamics over time (Isenberg, 2010).

In this context, entrepreneurial finance, and venture capital (VC) in particular, plays a critical role as both a financial catalyst and a structural element that shapes the development of industrial and entrepreneurial ecosystems. Despite the disproportionate contribution of innovative startups to job creation and economic growth (Shane, 2009), these ventures often face severe financing constraints due to information asymmetries, limited track records, and their inherently high-risk profiles (Berger & Udell, 1998). A large body of early literature, largely grounded in the US experience, identifies VC firms as key actors in alleviating these constraints. VC firms are specialized financial intermediaries that provide equity financing to innovative, high-growth startups and actively support their development (Gompers & Lerner, 2001). Beyond the provision of capital, VC firms contribute strategic guidance, introduce advanced governance practices, and facilitate access to professional, technological, and market networks (Sapienza et al., 1996; Hellmann &

M. Guerini (✉) · M. G. Colombo
Politecnico di Milano School of Management, Milan, Italy
e-mail: massimiliano.guerini@polimi.it; massimo.colombo@polimi.it



G. Cerulli, E. Reale (eds.), *Research Infrastructures for Open Science in Social Science Research*, https://doi.org/10.1007/978-3-032-29575-0_11

Puri, 2002). Through the selective allocation of resources to high-potential startups, VC activity not only supports their growth but also shapes broader industrial and entrepreneurial ecosystems, influencing the direction of technological change, the spatial organization of innovation, and, ultimately, the long-term economic growth of regions and countries (Samila & Sorenson, 2011). In this sense, VC should be understood not as a neutral source of finance, but as a structural force contributing to ecosystem deepening and path-dependent development.

Extending this line of inquiry beyond its originally US-centric focus has long been constrained by data limitations. In Europe, fragmented VC markets, institutional heterogeneity, and the lack of harmonized firm- and investor-level data have historically hindered systematic empirical analysis. Recent advances in research infrastructures have substantially improved this situation. Building on this perspective, this chapter examines the data and analytical tools that enable the study of how VC and entrepreneurial activity shape the structure and dynamics of industrial and entrepreneurial ecosystems. The analysis focuses on resources provided by FOSSR (Fostering Open Science in Social Science Research; https://www.fossr.eu), which develops an innovative Open Science Cloud for the collection, management, and analysis of economic and social data. By integrating and building upon major Italian and European research infrastructures, FOSSR supports systematic, data-driven studies of science, technology, and innovation systems. Among these infrastructures, RISIS (Research Infrastructure for Science, Technology and Innovation Studies; https://www.risis2.eu) plays a central role by integrating microdata and analytical services for the study of knowledge dynamics, innovation processes, and policy-relevant outcomes.

More specifically, this chapter draws on empirical evidence derived from the VICO dataset, a core firm-level resource within the RISIS infrastructure. The development of VICO has been instrumental in extending the analysis of VC markets and outcomes to the European context by providing harmonized, longitudinal micro-level information on VC-backed startups, investors, and investment transactions across multiple countries. By reviewing and synthesizing contributions that exploit VICO data, the chapter examines the multifaceted role of VC along five interrelated dimensions. First, it analyzes the impact of VC on startup performance and value creation by disentangling selection effects from post-investment value-added, while also highlighting investor heterogeneity and showing how different types of VC investors (independent, corporate, and bank-affiliated) affect startup outcomes through distinct mechanisms. Second, it examines the interaction between VC and public policy, with particular attention to the complementary roles of public and private VC investors in entrepreneurial finance. Third, it explores the contribution of VC to internationalization and exit dynamics, including cross-border VC investment and foreign market entry. Fourth, it investigates how VC influences network formation with key partners (such as other investors, corporations, universities, and public research organizations) shaping startups' access to resources, legitimacy, and knowledge flows. Finally, it analyzes the spatial dimension of VC activity, showing how investment patterns shape the structure, geography, and path-dependent evolution of entrepreneurial ecosystems.

Overall, the analysis shows that VC influences not only firm-level outcomes but also the structure, depth, and long-term evolution of entrepreneurial and industrial ecosystems, with important implications for the design of industrial and innovation policies aimed at fostering sustainable and economic growth.

The remainder of the chapter is organized as follows. Section 11.2 describes the data infrastructure underlying the analysis, with a focus on RISIS and the VICO dataset. Section 11.3 reviews the empirical evidence on the role of VC in the deepening of industrial and entrepreneurial ecosystems, covering startup performance, public policy interventions, internationalization, network dynamics, and geography. Section 11.4 concludes the chapter by summarizing the main insights and discussing implications for research and policy.

## 11.2 Data and Research Infrastructure Within FOSSR: RISIS and VICO

The FOSSR Open Cloud enables the integration of heterogeneous data sources and provides advanced tools for their efficient use. Within FOSSR, RISIS constitutes a core component. RISIS is a pan-European research infrastructure devoted to systematizing and integrating high-quality data and analytical services for the study of science, technology, and innovation (STI) dynamics and policy. It supports a new generation of quantitative and qualitative indicators that go beyond traditional measures of scientific performance by capturing different dimensions of knowledge dynamics that are critical for evidence-based policy analysis and comparative research. RISIS also plays an active role in positioning STI analysis within the open science movement, closely aligned with initiatives such as OpenAIRE (https://www.openaire.eu), and encourages reproducible and transparent research through accessible documentation and community support.

RISIS originated in 2014 under the Seventh Framework Programme (FP7) of the European Union and was subsequently consolidated and expanded through the RISIS2 project within the Horizon 2020 programme. With funding from the European Commission, RISIS was developed into a robust and integrated e-infrastructure designed to provide harmonized and interoperable datasets, advanced analytical tools, and tailored services for researchers, policymakers, and innovation stakeholders. The infrastructure is designed to be open and accessible to European researchers following a registration and charter agreement, and it actively combines data integration with training, dissemination, and community building activities to broaden its user base and foster methodological innovation.

RISIS integrates and standardizes a diverse family of datasets (www.risis2.eu/risis-datasets) covering multiple aspects of research and innovation systems, including bibliometrics, patents, trademarks, R&D investments, public and private research organizations, firm innovation, and collaborative networks. Among the complimentary resources and tools developed within the infrastructure are registers of public and private research actors, geospatial annotation systems, semantic classifiers (e.g., for Sustainable Development Goals), and visualization platforms that facilitate multi-level analysis from local to regional and national scales.

A central firm-level resource within the RISIS infrastructure is the VICO dataset, maintained and updated by Politecnico di Milano as part of the RISIS portfolio. The VICO dataset is designed to provide comprehensive coverage of VC investment activity in Europe by integrating multiple proprietary and commercial sources, including Refinitiv Eikon, Zephyr, and Crunchbase, together with firm accounting information from Orbis.

The most recent version of the VICO dataset provides detailed information on VC-backed startups founded from 1988 onwards that received at least one VC investment between 1998 and 2024. It includes comprehensive firm-level data on geographical location, industry classification, financial accounts, and innovation activity, as well as deal-level information on investment timing, amounts, and VC syndication structures. In addition, it contains rich investor-level information, including investor type, experience, organizational affiliation, and country of origin. One of VICO dataset's defining strengths is its extensive coverage in both scale and geographic scope, encompassing tens of thousands of VC-backed startups and investment transactions across the European Union (EU-27), the UK, and Israel. Over time, the dataset has evolved into a unique research infrastructure for the empirical analysis of European VC markets. By combining longitudinal firm histories with detailed investor and deal characteristics, VICO enables researchers to investigate investment patterns, investor heterogeneity, syndication dynamics, and the role of VC in shaping firm performance, innovation outcomes, and the broader deepening of entrepreneurial and industrial ecosystems.

VICO has been extensively used by the academic community and policymakers alike, appearing in several scientific publications that investigate VC market structure, performance effects of different investor types, geographic and sectoral patterns of investment, and the effectiveness of policy incentives for entrepreneurial finance. Through RISIS and FOSSR, VICO data can be accessed together with other datasets and analytical services and is complemented by training and documentation that facilitate robust research design and reproducibility.

## 11.3 Venture Capital and the Deepening of Industrial and Entrepreneurial Ecosystems: Evidence from VICO

### *11.3.1 Venture Capital, Startup Performance, and Value-Added*

In the European context, the VICO dataset has played a pivotal role in advancing research on VC and startup performance by providing harmonized longitudinal firm-level data on investment events, investor characteristics, syndication structures, and startup outcomes. The availability of such data has enabled researchers to disentangle ex-ante selection effects from post-investment value-added and to track startup dynamics over time. Leveraging these data, a large body of empirical work documents that VC-backed firms outperform their non-VC-backed counterparts, particularly in high-technology and knowledge-intensive sectors, while also highlighting substantial heterogeneity in VC effects across investor types and institutional contexts.

Within this literature, a central question concerns whether the observed performance differentials reflect superior ex ante screening by VC investors or the causal impact of post-investment value-added activities. This distinction is directly addressed by Croce et al. (2013). Using a matched sample of European startups from VICO, the authors compare productivity growth before and after the receipt of a first VC round. Their findings reveal no significant differences in productivity growth prior to investment, while substantial and persistent divergences emerge in the post-investment period. This evidence strongly supports the value-added view of VC and highlights the presence of VC-induced "imprinting" effects on startups' organizational practices.

More recent sector-specific analyses based on VICO further reinforce this interpretation. Ambrois et al. (2025), focusing on VC investments in European cleantech startups, show that once selection effects are properly controlled for, VC financing significantly boosts startup growth, particularly in the short run. These results underscore the relevance of VC in mission-oriented and policy-sensitive sectors characterized by high uncertainty, capital intensity, and long development cycles.

Related work exploits VICO to examine the role of VC in alleviating financial constraints. Bertoni et al. (2015) analyze the investment behavior of young high-tech startups using an error-correction framework that allows for non-linear investment dynamics arising from capital market imperfections. Their results show that VC investment leads to a flattening of the investment curve, signaling a relaxation of financial constraints. Importantly, this effect becomes both economically and statistically significant only after follow-on rounds of VC financing. These findings underscore the importance of VC certification in improving startups' access to additional external sources of finance, including bank credit.

A fundamental contribution of VICO lies in enabling a systematic analysis of VC investor heterogeneity. Building on this perspective, Colombo and Murtinu (2017) explicitly leverage the investor-level granularity of VICO to distinguish between independent VC (IVC) and corporate VC (CVC). IVC refers to stand-alone, professionally managed VC funds whose primary objective is financial return, whereas CVC denotes venture investments made by established corporations, typically pursuing both strategic and financial objectives (Dushnitsky & Lenox, 2005). Their analysis shows that both forms of VC positively affect the economic performance of European high-tech startups, primarily through increases in real sales. However, the timing and channels of impact differ markedly: IVC investments are associated with more immediate performance improvements, consistent with growth-oriented strategies, whereas CVC effects materialize more gradually through access to complementary assets, technological knowledge, and industrial networks. Importantly, the authors find no systematic performance premium associated with IVC–CVC syndication per se, suggesting that complementarities depend on governance structures rather than joint investment alone, an insight made possible by VICO's detailed VC syndication data.

Recent work further exploits the richness of VICO to uncover organizational heterogeneity within CVC investors. Balz et al. (2023) distinguish between endoisomorphistic and exoisomorphistic CVC units, showing that the average underperformance of CVC-backed startups relative to IVC-backed startups is entirely driven by endoisomorphistic CVC units, which replicate the organizational structures and incentive schemes of their parent corporations. In contrast, startups backed by exoisomorphistic CVC units with governance structures resembling those of IVC funds exhibit no significant productivity disadvantage. These findings highlight the importance of organizational design in shaping CVC effectiveness and further illustrate the analytical leverage provided by VICO.

Finally, VICO has also been instrumental in analyzing the role of bank-affiliated venture capital (BVC), namely VC funds owned or managed by banking institutions that pursue complementarities between equity investments and traditional lending activities (Hellmann et al., 2008). Croce et al. (2015) document that BVC-backed starups exhibit lower ex ante financial distress, pointing to strong screening capabilities, but experience higher leverage following investment. Murtinu (2024) extends this analysis by showing that, while BVC-backed firms display weaker improvements in sales growth and operating efficiency, syndicated investments involving heterogeneous types of BVC investors significantly enhance exit outcomes.

### *11.3.2 Public Policies and the Role of Government Venture Capital*

A further stream of research based on the VICO dataset examines the role of public policy in entrepreneurial finance and VC through a comparison between private and governmental VC (GVC). GVC refers to government-owned or government-managed VC funds that directly invest public capital in startups, often combining financial objectives with broader policy goals such as innovation support, regional development, and the correction of financing gaps (Brander et al., 2015).

Grilli and Murtinu (2014, 2015) provide systematic evidence on the differential effects of IVC and GVC in Europe. Using large-scale longitudinal firm-level data from VICO, they show that IVC generates a robust and economically meaningful positive impact on startup performance, particularly sales growth, whereas GVC acting alone has no significant effect. Startups backed exclusively by GVC underperform relative to IVC-backed startups and do not grow more than non-VC-backed startups. The only context in which GVC has a positive and statistically significant impact is when it co-invests with IVC in syndicates targeting younger startups, especially when these syndicates are led by IVC investors. Overall, the evidence suggests that GVC is ineffective as a stand-alone instrument and that its contribution is primarily complementary to IVC-led investments. Extending the analysis to exit outcomes, Cumming et al. (2017) show that startups backed by IVC achieve significantly better exit performance than those financed by GVC. Mixed syndicates display a higher, though not statistically different, likelihood of successful exits relative to IVC-only backing. Taken together, this body of evidence indicates that IVC is the primary driver of firm-level value creation, while GVC plays a more limited but potentially complementary role when embedded in investment structures led by private investors.

Turning to innovation-related firm outcomes, Bertoni and Tykvová (2015) examine whether and how GVC affects invention and innovation in European biotech startups. Measuring invention through patent stocks and innovation through citation-weighted patent stocks, they find that GVC acting as a stand-alone investor has no significant impact on either outcome. By contrast, GVC significantly amplifies the effect of IVC on both invention and innovation, confirming that GVC is an ineffective substitute but an effective complement to IVC. Leveraging the investor classifications available in VICO, the authors further distinguish between technology-oriented GVCs (TVCs) and development-oriented GVCs (DVCs), showing that DVCs are more effective in stimulating startup inventive activity, while TVCs, when co-investing with IVC, play a stronger role in fostering startup innovation.

At the same time, other VICO-based studies show that the primary contribution of GVC lies not in directly enhancing firm-level performance, but in its screening, certification, and ecosystem-coordination functions. Guerini and Quas (2016) explicitly test the certification hypothesis (Lerner, 2000) using longitudinal firm-level data from VICO. Exploiting propensity score matching and event-history models, they show that startups receiving GVC are more than three times as likely to subsequently attract VC from private investors compared to observationally similar non-GVC-backed startups. Importantly, this effect is not driven by the amount of public funding received, but by the mere presence of GVC, which acts as a credible signal of startup quality. Moreover, GVC-backed startups are at least as likely as other VC-backed firms to receive follow-on rounds or achieve successful exits, indicating that GVC effectively screens and certifies startups with genuine growth potential rather than distorting private selection. Building on this firm-level evidence, Bertoni et al. (2019) adopt an organizational ecology perspective to analyze how the density of GVC investors shapes the behavior of private VC investors within national VC ecosystems. Using VICO data, they show that a higher presence of GVC systematically alters the investment niche of private VC, making private VC investors more likely to fund startups that they would otherwise neglect, namely younger and smaller firms located in less-developed regions. These effects persist even in deals where GVC does not directly co-invest, indicating that GVC generates ecosystem-wide certification and legitimacy effects that reduce information asymmetries and screening costs for private investors. The results support the existence of a mutualistic relationship between GVC and private VC, whereby GVC crowds in private capital and facilitate investor coordination. Taken together, these studies demonstrate that GVC can contribute to startup growth and innovation indirectly by improving access to private finance and strengthening the functioning of VC markets, reinforcing the view that GVC is most effective when designed as a complement to private VC rather than as a stand-alone investment vehicle.

### *11.3.3 Venture Capital and Internationalization*

One of the key features of the VICO dataset is its extensive cross-country coverage, spanning the EU-27, the UK, and Israel. This characteristic has made VICO central to research on VC internationalization. Bertoni and Groh (2014) exploit VICO's cross-country dimension to show that cross-border VC investors expand exit opportunities by transferring capital market conditions from their home countries, thereby increasing the likelihood of trade sales and, to a lesser extent, initial public offerings (IPOs). More broadly, their findings suggest that cross-border VC investment can, at least partially, compensate for inadequate local exit conditions. By spilling over the capital market activity and exit expertise of their home countries, cross-border VC investors enhance the set of exit options available to startups. In addition, international VC syndicates are shown to be quicker in writing off non-performing investments, contributing to a more efficient reallocation of capital within entrepreneurial ecosystems.

Hong et al. (2025) further deepen the analysis of VC internationalization by examining how the international syndication experience of domestic VC firms affects their subsequent investment outcomes in local markets. The authors argue that domestic VC firms can improve their future investment performance by accumulating syndication experience with highly reputable foreign VC firms. The authors identify two main mechanisms through which international VC syndication enhances domestic VC performance. First, domestic VC firms benefit from certification effects by co-investing with reputable foreign VC firms. Such certification improves their visibility and credibility, facilitating access to higher-quality investment opportunities and more valuable co-investment partners in subsequent deals. Second, domestic VC firms benefit from learning effects, as they can observe and internalize more advanced investment practices adopted by foreign VC partners, including due diligence procedures, post-investment nurturing activities, and exit preparation strategies. Through these channels, international syndication experience translates into improved exit outcomes for domestic VC portfolio companies. Empirical evidence from European VC investments supports these mechanisms, highlighting how cross-border VC syndication contributes not only to firm-level exit performance but also to the diffusion of capabilities and reputational capital within local VC ecosystems. In addition, the accumulation of syndication experience with reputable foreign VC firms allows domestic VC investors to build international networks that expand the set of available exit options. These international connections provide access to alternative foreign exit routes, increasing the likelihood that startups achieve successful exits in international markets rather than relying solely on domestic exit opportunities.

Foreign market entry has become a central challenge for startups seeking to scale and compete globally, yet many of them face severe resource constraints and a liability of outsidership (Johanson & Vahlne, 2009) in foreign markets. In this context, Guerini and Tenca (2026) examine the role of VC status in shaping startups' foreign market entry decisions and subsequent performance. They theorize that high-status VC firms enhance internationalization by providing access to high-quality complementary resources and by offering certification in foreign markets, thereby mitigating information asymmetries and legitimacy deficits. Using a dataset of 5471 private European startups that received VC funding between 2005 and 2018, and leveraging EU trademark registrations as a novel indicator of foreign market entry, the authors demonstrate that high-status VC firms significantly enhance the probability of startups expanding into foreign markets. This effect is particularly strong for startups with weaker pre-entry technological capabilities, which benefit more from the network access and endorsement provided by high-status VC firms. However, the study also finds that VC status does not translate into superior post-entry exit performance, suggesting that high-status VC firms primarily facilitate market entry rather than shaping long-term outcomes after internationalization. These results highlight the enabling, rather than performance-enhancing, role of VC status in the international expansion of startups.

### *11.3.4 Tie Formation and Network Dynamics of Startups*

The formation of interorganizational ties is a central process in the development and scaling of startups. For startups operating under conditions of high uncertainty and information asymmetry, ties with external actors are not only sources of financial and knowledge resources, but also mechanisms for legitimacy, protection, and risk sharing. A network-based perspective emphasizes that these relationships are neither random nor neutral: they emerge through selective processes shaped by signals, trust, institutional environments, and cumulative network dynamics, and they play a key role in the deepening of entrepreneurial and innovation ecosystems.

The VICO dataset has enabled a growing body of research on the broader ecosystem effects of VC, particularly in relation to innovation networks and policy-driven collaborations. Colombo et al. (2016) combine VICO data with information from EU Framework Programmes to show that VC-backed startups are significantly more likely to participate in publicly funded R&D partnerships than their non-VC-backed counterparts. Moreover, the strength of this effect varies systematically across investor types, indicating that VC not only affects firm-level performance but also shapes startups' integration into broader innovation systems and collaborative networks.

A key mechanism underlying tie formation between startups and VC investors is signaling (Spence, 1974). Startups rely on observable signals to convey unobserved quality to potential partners. However, recent evidence based on VICO data shows that signals can be ambivalent and influence network formation in non-linear ways. Colombo et al. (2023) demonstrate that patents protecting radical inventions constitute strong signals with a “dark side”, as they simultaneously convey high growth potential and elevated risk of failure. This duality affects which VC investors are willing and able to form ties with such startups. Highly reputable VC investors are more likely to initiate ties with startups holding radical patents, particularly in early financing rounds when information asymmetries are highest. Importantly, these investors mitigate the downside risk associated with radical innovation by forming syndicated ties, thereby sharing risk and pooling expertise. As startups mature and uncertainty declines, the signaling value of radical patents weakens and tie formation becomes less sensitive to such signals. These findings highlight that network formation depends not only on startup characteristics, but also on the capabilities, reputations, and network positions of potential investors.

Tie formation with CVC investors introduces additional opportunities and risks, particularly due to concerns over knowledge misappropriation. Colombo and Shafi (2016) show that startups strategically manage the timing and conditions under which they form CVC ties by deploying legal, social, and timing-based defensive strategies. In the European context, legal protections, most notably patents, play a particularly important role in facilitating CVC ties by reducing fears of misappropriation, although their effectiveness varies across institutional settings. The authors also show that affiliation with prominent IVC investors strengthens startups’ defensive positions, making them more attractive and less vulnerable partners in CVC relationships. Compared to the US, however, European startups benefit less from delaying CVC entry or relying on social defenses alone, underscoring how institutional environments shape both the structure and evolution of entrepreneurial networks.

Beyond signals and defensive strategies, trust plays a fundamental role in the formation of initial ties, especially when startups interact with unfamiliar and powerful partners. Colombo et al. (2024) develop a hybrid model of initial trust formation that combines institutional trust, social categorization, and individuating information. Using VICO data on European CVC investments, they show that startups are more likely to form initial ties with CVC investors whose parent companies are located in countries perceived as more trustworthy. This effect persists even when startups employ social defenses or are indirectly connected through shared IVC investors, indicating that country-level trust heuristics function as powerful shortcuts in early-stage network formation. At the same time, existing social ties and reputational endorsements partially substitute for institutional trust, illustrating how different layers of trust interact in shaping network entry decisions.

Finally, recent research adopts a multilayer network perspective to capture the complexity and path dependence of startups’ relational environments. Camerani et al. (2026) conceptualize university–industry collaborations as a multilayer network encompassing EU-funded projects, academic publications, and patents. Their findings reveal strong within-layer persistence and weak cross-layer transitions, suggesting that actors tend to reinforce existing types of ties rather than diversify across modes of collaboration. Network evolution is driven by cumulative advantage mechanisms, with preferential attachment being strongest in patent-based collaborations and weakest in project-based ones. For startups, these dynamics imply that early ties strongly condition future network positions, and that access to one layer of collaboration does not automatically translate into access to others. Such path dependence reinforces specialization and contributes to persistent inequalities in network centrality and access to opportunities, with important implications for ecosystem deepening and long-term innovation dynamics.

### *11.3.5 Geography of Venture Capital Entrepreneurial Ecosystems*

The deepening of entrepreneurial and industrial ecosystems is inherently a spatial process, shaped by the geographic concentration of knowledge, skills, institutions, and financial intermediaries. VC plays a central role in this process by allocating financial resources to high-potential startups and by fostering dense networks of interaction among firms, investors, and supporting organizations. Despite increasing globalization and digitalization, entrepreneurial finance remains strongly localized, reflecting the importance of spatial proximity for information exchange, monitoring, trust formation, and access to complementary resources. Leveraging the harmonized firm- and investor-level information provided by the VICO dataset, a growing body of European research shows that both the supply of VC and the demand for external equity by startups are deeply embedded in regional contexts characterized by heterogeneous knowledge bases, institutional environments, and agglomeration dynamics.

Early evidence based on VICO documents a pronounced spatial concentration of VC investments and VC-backed startups across Europe. Guerini and Tenca (2018) show that VC activity is unevenly distributed across European regions, with investments clustering in a limited number of areas characterized by high knowledge intensity, abundant human capital, and a dense local supply of VC investors. Favorable national legal and institutional frameworks further reinforce these agglomeration patterns. As a result, VC ecosystems tend to emerge where technological opportunities, skilled labor, and financial intermediaries co-locate, generating cumulative processes of regional specialization rather than an even spatial diffusion of VC-backed entrepreneurship.

More recent research exploits the investor-level granularity of VICO to highlight heterogeneity in the geography of VC activity across investor types. Colombo et al. (2026) show that while VC investments overall are highly concentrated in major metropolitan hubs such as London, Paris, and Berlin, CVC investments are significantly less geographically concentrated than those of IVC firms. Regional characteristics such as population density and income levels are strongly associated with IVC investment intensity, whereas their influence is weaker for CVC activity.

This pattern suggests that CVC investors, driven by strategic objectives and supported by corporate resources, are less dependent on agglomeration economies and can operate more effectively outside traditional VC hubs. The presence of top universities plays a limited role for VC activity overall, except in science-based sectors such as life sciences and R&D-intensive industries, where localized knowledge spillovers remain critical.

Geography also shapes startups' demand for VC. Using VICO, Colombo et al. (2019) show that European high-tech startups are significantly more likely to seek VC financing when local VC availability is high, while local competition among VC investors has a negligible effect. Importantly, the influence of VC availability exhibits a strong distance-decay pattern: it declines rapidly with geographic distance and effectively disappears beyond approximately 250 km. National borders further amplify this effect, as the positive impact of VC availability vanishes when borders are crossed, except between countries with strong cultural and institutional proximity. These spatial frictions persist even within the integrated European market. Finally, the strength of spatial constraints varies systematically across VC investor types. The demand-side effect of local VC availability is stronger for reputable and private VC investors, while GVC and less reputable VC investors face weaker spatial constraints. This heterogeneity implies that different categories of investors contribute differently to ecosystem deepening, with IVC reinforcing dense regional hubs and other investor types supporting more geographically dispersed, but often less intensive, patterns of entrepreneurial development.

Table 11.1 summarizes the core empirical findings from studies based on the VICO dataset.

## 11.4 Conclusions

The empirical evidence reviewed in this chapter provides a coherent picture of VC as a key driver of the deepening of industrial and entrepreneurial ecosystems in Europe, made possible by the availability of harmonized longitudinal microdata from the VICO dataset and its integration within the FOSSR research infrastructure. The main findings emerging from this literature review can be summarized as follows:

1. Overall, VC-backed startups exhibit superior performance compared to non-VC-backed startups, particularly in terms of growth, productivity, innovation, and exit outcomes, with especially strong effects in high-technology and knowledge-intensive sectors. Crucially, these performance differentials emerge primarily after VC entry, providing robust support for the value-added view of VC. VC investors actively shape startups' organizational practices, governance structures, and strategic trajectories, generating persistent effects over time. In addition, VC plays an important role in alleviating financial constraints, not so much through the size of investments, but through certification effects that improve startups access to external finance.

**Table 11.1** Core findings from VICO evidence

| Theme | Key study | VC type(s) | Main outcome(s) | Core findings |
|---|---|---|---|---|
| Startup performance and value added | Croce et al. (2013) | IVC | Productivity growth | Causal evidence of VC value-added |
| | Ambrois et al. (2025) | IVC | Firm growth (cleantech) | VC supports growth in mission-oriented, capital-intensive sectors |
| | Bertoni et al. (2015) | IVC | Investment dynamics | VC certification channel relaxes financial constraints |
| | Colombo and Murtinu (2017) | IVC vs. CVC | Sales growth | IVC effects immediate; CVC effects gradual via complementarities |
| | Balz et al. (2023) | CVC | Productivity | Underperformance driven by "corporate-like" CVCs only |
| | Croce et al. (2015) | BVC | Leverage, distress | BVC shapes financial structure rather than grow |
| | Murtinu (2024) | BVC (syndicates) | Exits | Heterogeneous BVC syndicates improve exits |
| Public policy and GVC | Grilli and Murtinu (2014) | IVC vs. GVC | Sales and employment growth | IVC positive; GVC ineffective alone |
| | Grilli and Murtinu (2015) | IVC vs. GVC | Sales growth | IVC positive in the early stage; GVC ineffective |
| | Cumming et al. (2017) | IVC, GVC | Exits | IVC superior; mixed syndicates not significantly better |
| | Bertoni and Tykvová (2015) | GVC, IVC | Invention & innovation | GVC ineffective alone; amplifies IVC impact |

(continued)

**Table 11.1** (continued)

| Theme | Key study | VC type(s) | Main outcome(s) | Core findings |
|---|---|---|---|---|
| | Guerini and Quas (2016) | GVC, IVC | IVC attraction | Positive certification effect of GVC in attracting IVC |
| | Bertoni et al. (2019) | GVC, IVC | Startup characteristics at IVC investment | Positive effect of GVC on IVC investments in young, small and peripheral startups |
| Internationalization and exits | Bertoni and Groh (2014) | Cross-border VC | Exit type & timing | Cross-border VC expands exits; faster write-offs |
| | Hong et al. (2025) | International syndicates | Exit success | Certification and learning effects from reputable foreign VCs |
| | Guerini and Tenca (2026) | High-status VC | Foreign market entry | VC status enables entry, not post-entry exits |
| Networks and tie formation | Colombo et al. (2016) | IVC | R&D collaborations | VC-backed firms more likely in EU R&D networks |
| | Colombo et al. (2023) | Reputable VC | Tie formation | Radical patents signal potential and risk |
| | Colombo and Shafi (2016) | CVC | Tie timing & defenses | Patents + IVC affiliation protect startups |
| | Colombo et al. (2024) | CVC | Initial ties | Country-level trust drives early ties |
| Geography of VC | Guerini and Tenca (2018) | IVC | Spatial concentration | VC clusters in knowledge-intensive regions |
| | Colombo et al. (2026) | IVC vs. CVC | Metro-level investment | CVC less spatially concentrated than IVC |
| | Colombo et al. (2019) | VC availability | VC demand | Strong distance decay; borders matter |

2. A central contribution of the VICO-based literature is the systematic documentation of VC investor heterogeneity. IVC consistently emerges as the main driver of direct value creation, with rapid and robust effects on firm growth and exit performance. CVC generates more gradual benefits, primarily through access to complementary assets, technological knowledge, and industrial networks, with outcomes that depend critically on organizational design and incentive structures. BVC investors display limited direct performance effects when acting in isolation.
3. Evidence on public policy interventions indicates that GVC is largely ineffective as a stand-alone instrument to foster firm growth or innovation. However, when embedded in co-investment structures with IVC, it can play a meaningful complementary role by crowding in private capital. These findings highlight the conditional nature of GVC effectiveness and the importance of complementarities between investor types.
4. The chapter further shows that VC contributes to ecosystem deepening through internationalization and network dynamics. Cross-border VC expands exit opportunities by transferring capital market expertise across countries and compensating for underdeveloped local exit markets. International syndication facilitates learning, reputation building, and the diffusion of advanced investment practices within domestic VC ecosystems. High-status VC investors lower barriers to foreign market entry for startups, especially those with weaker technological capabilities. At the same time, the formation of ties within entrepreneurial ecosystems is shown to be selective and path-dependent: early relationships, signaling mechanisms, trust, and institutional context strongly condition subsequent network positions, reinforcing cumulative advantage and specialization over time.
5. Finally, the evidence underscores that ecosystem deepening is inherently spatial. VC activity remains highly concentrated in a small number of regional hubs characterized by strong knowledge bases, human capital, and institutional quality. While heterogeneous investors such as CVC and GVC may partially mitigate this concentration, strong spatial and institutional frictions persist, shaping both the supply of VC and startups' demand for external equity.

Taken together, these findings suggest that VC policy should be understood as an integral component of industrial and innovation policy, rather than as a narrowly defined financial intervention. Policies aimed at strengthening VC markets are most effective when embedded in broader strategies that address complementarities between finance, research infrastructure, human capital, and demand conditions. Furthermore, recognizing investor heterogeneity is essential. GVC should focus on complementary roles (such as certification, coordination, and risk sharing) rather than attempting to substitute for IVC. A prominent example is provided by the European Investment Fund (https://www.eif.org), whose co-investment and fund-of-funds activities are explicitly designed to crowd in private capital and strengthen VC ecosystems by leveraging, rather than replacing, private investors. Similarly, policies supporting CVC should take into account organizational design and governance structures to ensure alignment between strategic objectives and startup development. At the regional level, the strong spatial concentration of VC calls for place-based policy approaches. Strengthening local knowledge ecosystems, improving institutional quality, and anchoring private investors to regional strengths are key to fostering sustainable ecosystem deepening outside established hubs. Finally, the fragmentation of the European market into distinct national segments is widely recognized as a major barrier to the provision of early-stage capital to innovative entrepreneurial firms (Asdrubali, 2023). Reducing cross-border institutional and regulatory frictions would therefore be critical to further enhancing the integration, scale, and effectiveness of entrepreneurial ecosystems across Europe.

The evidence reviewed in this chapter also points to several promising avenues for future research. First, future research could explore the interaction between VC and labor market dynamics. Combining VICO with employee data would enable the analysis of how VC-backed startups affect skill formation, occupational mobility, and the diffusion of managerial and technological capabilities across regions and sectors. This perspective would shed light on the human capital channel through which VC contributes to ecosystem and industrial deepening. Second, greater attention should be devoted to the long-term and dynamic effects of VC investor heterogeneity. While existing studies document heterogeneous short- and medium-term impacts across investor types, much less is known about how different governance models shape startups' strategic trajectories, resilience, and adaptation to shocks over longer horizons, as well as their broader effects at the ecosystem level. Longitudinal analyses exploiting the extended time coverage of VICO could address this gap. Third, the spatial dimension of entrepreneurial ecosystems warrants further investigation, particularly with respect to the interaction between local and cross-border dynamics. Future research could examine how VC interacts with regional industrial policies, and whether certain policy mixes are more effective in fostering ecosystem deepening in peripheral or less-developed regions. Continued investment in research infrastructures such as RISIS and FOSSR will be essential to support this research agenda and to inform evidence-based policies aimed at fostering sustainable, inclusive, and innovation-driven growth.

## References

Ambrois, M., Croce, A., & Ughetto, E. (2025). Greening the future: How venture capital nurtures cleantech companies' growth in Europe. *Small Business Economics, 65*, 1–39.

Asdrubali, P. (2023). *Patterns of cross-border venture capital flows in Europe* (No. 195). Directorate General Economic and Financial Affairs (DG ECFIN), European Commission.

Balz, F. P., Brinkmann, F., & Kanbach, D. K. (2023). The impact of independent and heterogeneous corporate venture capital on firm efficiency. *Journal of Business Venturing Insights, 19*, e00384.

Berger, A. N., & Udell, G. F. (1998). The economics of small business finance: The roles of private equity and debt markets in the financial growth cycle. *Journal of Banking & Finance, 22*(6), 613–673.

Bertoni, F., & Groh, A. P. (2014). Cross-border investments and venture capital exits in Europe. *Corporate Governance: An International Review, 22*(2), 84–99.

Bertoni, F., & Tykvová, T. (2015). Does governmental venture capital spur invention and innovation? Evidence from young European biotech companies. *Research Policy, 44*(4), 925–935.

Bertoni, F., Croce, A., & Guerini, M. (2015). Venture capital and the investment curve of young high-tech companies. *Journal of Corporate Finance, 35*, 159–176.

Bertoni, F., Colombo, M. G., & Quas, A. (2019). The role of governmental venture capital in the venture capital ecosystem: An organizational ecology perspective. *Entrepreneurship Theory and Practice, 43*(3), 611–628.

Brander, J. A., Du, Q., & Hellmann, T. (2015). The effects of government-sponsored venture capital: International evidence. *Review of Finance, 19*(2), 571–618.

Camerani, R., Guerini, M., & Zinilli, A. (2026). *Persistence, specialization, and coupling in university–industry multilevel networks*. Working paper.

Colombo, M. G., & Murtinu, S. (2017). Venture capital investments in Europe and portfolio firms' economic performance: Independent versus corporate investors. *Journal of Economics and Management Strategy, 26*(1), 35–66.

Colombo, M. G., & Shafi, K. (2016). Swimming with sharks in Europe: When are they dangerous and what can new ventures do to defend themselves? *Strategic Management Journal, 37*(11), 2307–2322.

Colombo, M. G., D'Adda, D., & Pirelli, L. H. (2016). The participation of new technology-based firms in EU-funded R&D partnerships: The role of venture capital. *Research Policy, 45*(2), 361–375.

Colombo, M. G., d'Adda, D., & Quas, A. (2019). The geography of venture capital and entrepreneurial ventures' demand for external equity. *Research Policy, 48*(5), 1150–1170.

Colombo, M. G., Guerini, M., Hoisl, K., & Zeiner, N. M. (2023). The dark side of signals: Patents protecting radical inventions and venture capital investments. *Research Policy, 52*(5), 104741.

Colombo, M. G., Montanaro, B., & Shafi, K. (2024). Dancing with strangers? Initial trust and the formation of initial ties between new ventures and corporate venture capitalists. *Entrepreneurship Theory and Practice, 48*(5), 1223–1265.

Colombo, M. G., Guerini, M., Montanaro, B., & Tenca, F. (2026). Mapping venture capital: Exploring regional differences among independent and corporate venture capital investors in Europe. In *Raising finance: From traditional to new forms of entrepreneurial finance* (pp. 347–381). World Scientific.

Croce, A., Martí, J., & Murtinu, S. (2013). The impact of venture capital on the productivity growth of European entrepreneurial firms: 'Screening' or 'value added' effect? *Journal of Business Venturing, 28*(4), 489–510.

Croce, A., D'Adda, D., & Ughetto, E. (2015). Venture capital financing and the financial distress risk of portfolio firms: How independent and bank-affiliated investors differ. *Small Business Economics, 44*(1), 189–206.

Cumming, D. J., Grilli, L., & Murtinu, S. (2017). Governmental and independent venture capital investments in Europe: A firm-level performance analysis. *Journal of Corporate Finance, 42*, 439–459.

Dushnitsky, G., & Lenox, M. J. (2005). When do incumbents learn from entrepreneurial ventures? Corporate venture capital and investing firm innovation rates. *Research Policy, 34*(5), 615–639.

Gompers, P., & Lerner, J. (2001). The venture capital revolution. *Journal of Economic Perspectives, 15*(2), 145–168.

Grilli, L., & Murtinu, S. (2014). Government, venture capital and the growth of European high-tech entrepreneurial firms. *Research Policy, 43*(9), 1523–1543.

Grilli, L., & Murtinu, S. (2015). New technology-based firms in Europe: Market penetration, public venture capital, and timing of investment. *Industrial and Corporate Change, 24*(5), 1109–1148.

Guerini, M., & Quas, A. (2016). Governmental venture capital in Europe: Screening and certification. *Journal of Business Venturing, 31*(2), 175–195.

Guerini, M., & Tenca, F. (2018). The geography of technology-intensive start-ups and venture capital: European evidence. *Economia e Politica Industriale, 45*(3), 361–386.
Guerini, M., & Tenca, F. (2026). *High-status venture capital and foreign market entry: Evidence from European new ventures*. Working paper.
Hellmann, T., & Puri, M. (2002). Venture capital and the professionalization of start-up firms: Empirical evidence. *The Journal of Finance, 57*(1), 169–197.
Hellmann, T., Lindsey, L., & Puri, M. (2008). Building relationships early: Banks in venture capital. *The Review of Financial Studies, 21*(2), 513–541.
Hong, S., Guerini, M., & Park, H. D. (2025). Global connections, local impacts: The enduring effects of international syndication experience on venture capital investments. *Entrepreneurship Theory and Practice, 49*(6), 1710–1740.
Isenberg, D. J. (2010). How to start an entrepreneurial revolution. *Harvard Business Review, 88*(6), 40–50.
Johanson, J., & Vahlne, J.-E. (2009). The Uppsala internationalization process model revisited: From liability of foreignness to liability of outsidership. *Journal of International Business Studies, 40*(9), 1411–1431.
Lerner, J. (2000). The government as venture capitalist: The long-run impact of the SBIR program. *The Journal of Private Equity, 32*, 55–78.
Murtinu, S. (2024). Bank-affiliated venture capital funds: Portfolio selection, strategic objectives, performance and exit. *Review of Corporate Finance, 4*(3), 375–416.
Samila, S., & Sorenson, O. (2011). Venture capital, entrepreneurship, and economic growth. *The Review of Economics and Statistics, 93*(1), 338–349.
Sapienza, H. J., Manigart, S., & Vermeir, W. (1996). Venture capitalist governance and value added in four countries. *Journal of Business Venturing, 11*(6), 439–469.
Shane, S. (2009). Why encouraging more people to become entrepreneurs is bad public policy. *Small Business Economics, 33*(2), 141–149.
Spence, M. (1974). Competitive and optimal responses to signals: An analysis of efficiency and distribution. *Journal of Economic Theory, 7*(3), 296–332.
Spigel, B. (2017). The relational organization of entrepreneurial ecosystems. *Entrepreneurship Theory and Practice, 41*(1), 49–72.
Stam, E., & Van de Ven, A. (2021). Entrepreneurial ecosystem elements. *Small Business Economics, 56*(2), 809–832.

# Chapter 12
# Building the RIs Facility for Open Science

**Mario Ciampi, Emanuele Damiano, Pier Giuseppe Meo, and Mario Sicuranza**

## 12.1 Introduction

### *12.1.1 Origins, Definition and Importance of Research Infrastructures*

From the outset, it is important to recognize that social sciences have specific needs in terms of managing, interpreting, and sharing contextual and heterogeneous data. Addressing these needs early helps frame *Research Infrastructures (RIs)* as not only technological systems, but also epistemic tools.

The scientific evolution of the last two centuries is inextricably linked to the transformation of RIs. Since the origins of the first European academies and Universities in the seventeenth and eighteenth centuries, the infrastructural element has progressively articulated itself from simple laboratories and manuscript archives to the large networks of data centers, digital repositories and integrated cloud platforms that we know today. Every significant advance in science—from Linnaeus' botanical classification, to the Industrial Revolution, via the discovery of DNA, to the era of big data and artificial intelligence—has been made possible by an underlying infrastructure that has enabled the systematic organization, storage, processing, and sharing of knowledge, data, tools, and practices (Burnard et al., 2012; Mortara & Scramaglia, 2023; Salvatori, 2021).

In the contemporary context, RIs are complex, multi-level systems intended to serve national and international scientific communities. They include not only buildings and physical tools, but—even more—digital networks, cloud platforms,

M. Ciampi (✉) · E. Damiano · P. G. Meo · M. Sicuranza
National Research Council of Italy, Institute for High Performance Computing and Networking (CNR ICAR), Naples, Italy
e-mail: mario.ciampi@icar.cnr.it; emanuele.damiano@icar.cnr.it; piergiuseppe.meo@icar.cnr.it; mario.sicuranza@icar.cnr.it



G. Cerulli, E. Reale (eds.), *Research Infrastructures for Open Science in Social Science Research*, https://doi.org/10.1007/978-3-032-29575-0_12

**Table 12.1** Evolution of research infrastructures

| Epoch | Main infrastructural characteristics | Historical examples |
|---|---|---|
| Seventeenth to nineteenth century (birth of "laboratories") | Physical spaces, manuscript collections, analogue instruments | Academies, University libraries |
| Twentieth century | Multi-sector labs, centralized computing | CERN, ENIAC, Bell Laboratories |
| Twentieth to twenty-first century | Data centers, digitalization, international networks | GARR, GEANT, Grid computing |
| Twenty-first century (Open Science era) | Cloud, collaborative platforms, digital repositories, AI, IoT, blockchain | EOSC, FOSSR, Genomics England |

semantic architectures and shared procedures, capable of integrating advanced computational resources (HPC, GPU clusters), virtual collaboration environments (VREs), federated identity systems, orchestration middleware and data lakes (Table 12.1) (CNR-ISTI, 2024; IRPPS CNR, 2024; Open Science Italia, 2024b).

Glossary of infrastructures

- **Research Infrastructure (RI)**: an organized structure capable of providing resources, data, and services for advanced research.
- **Data Lake**: large digital archive that allows the preservation of heterogeneous data in raw format, accessible and analyzable in a flexible way.
- **VRE (Virtual Research Environment)**: a digital platform that integrates tools, data and resources for remote collaboration of research teams.
- **Identity Federation**: a set of protocols and technologies for federated digital identity management, essential for securely accessing shared resources.

### *12.1.2 Infrastructure Models: From the Autarkic Laboratory to the Federated Digital Ecosystem*

Historically, research was linked to laboratories run by individual groups or institutions, often with duplicate resources and tools, accessible to a small audience, and difficult to interoperate with. In the last 30 years, the exponential growth of the amounts of data produced (genomic sequencing, climate data, social surveys, satellite images, etc.) and the digitization of procedures have made the transition to

**Table 12.2** Building blocks of modern RIs

| Component | Function | Current technologies and frameworks | Current examples |
|---|---|---|---|
| Advanced computing | Data processing, simulations | HPC, Cloud, GPU, Edge | Leonardo (CINECA), Google AI Platform |
| Storage and repository | Storage and access | Ceph, BeeGFS, S3, Zenodo, Dataverse | Zenodo, FOSSR, OpenAIRE |
| Scientific networking | Low-latency data transport | GARR, GÉANT, spine-leaf, VPN, SDN | GARR Cloud, PRACE |
| Middleware and orchestration | Resource coordination | OpenStack, Kubernetes, Docker | EOSC, FOSSR, Kubernetes clusters |
| Governance | Role/policy management, compliance | IAM, RBAC, data stewardship | WSO2 IS, AARC Blueprint, ISO/IEC 27001 |

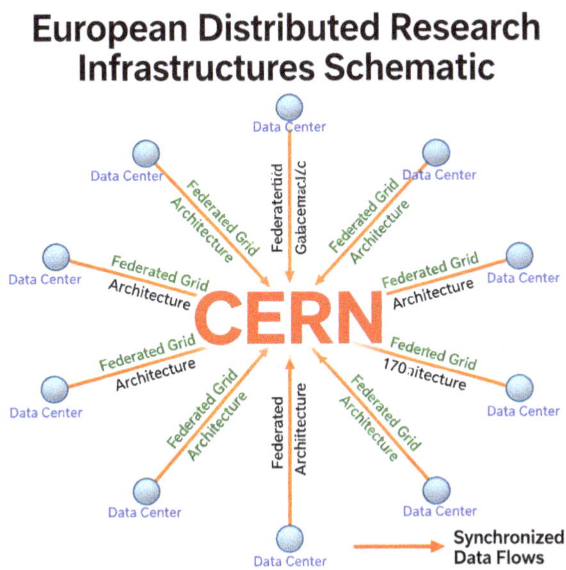


**Fig. 12.1** The case of pan-European distributed RIs

"federated infrastructure ecosystems" inevitable (Table 12.2, Fig. 12.1) (Di Giorgio & Reale, 2023; FOSSR, 2024; FOSSR Project, 2024).

CERN, the world's largest scientific infrastructure, is based on more than 170 globally distributed data centers in a federated Grid architecture. Through the Worldwide LHC Computing Grid (WLCG), more than 2 PB of data are processed, synchronized and made available to the international scientific community (WLCG official) every day.

**Table 12.3** Comparison between "Closed" vs. "Open Science" infrastructure objectives

| Objective | Closed RI (pre-Open Science model) | Open RI/FAIR (contemporary model) |
| --- | --- | --- |
| Access to data and services | Restricted, affiliates only | Open, multi-actor |
| Documentation | Often absent or incomplete | Rich, standard formats, open metadata |
| Interoperability | Limited (proprietary protocols) | High (Standard API, Common Languages) |
| Transparency | None or limited | Public logging, audits |
| Governance | Centralized | Distributed or federated |
| Long-term sustainability | Non-priority (project funding) | Central (energy policies, federation budgets) |

### *12.1.3 Paradigm Transitions: Open Science and FAIR Principles*

In recent years, Open Science has redefined the purposes and organizational models of infrastructures: not only technological efficiency, but openness, collaboration, transparency, social inclusion and reusability of research products. Even the main regulatory bodies, such as UNESCO and the European Commission, have codified these values in the FAIR (Findable, Accessible, Interoperable, Reusable) principles (Table 12.3) (INFN, 2023; INRIM, n.d.; OGS NODC, 2021; SBA Unisalento, n.d.; University of L'Aquila, n.d.; Wikipedia Contributors, 2024a).

The implementation of the FAIR principles requires technological and organizational choices: the use of DOIs for digital objects, multi-level metadata, open licenses (e.g. Creative Commons), linked data and interoperable data discovery services via API (Fig. 12.2) (Kumar et al., 2024; Mons et al., 2017; Wilkinson et al., 2016).

FAIR infrastructure allows the researcher to: quickly identify multidisciplinary datasets through global data catalogs; Access data, analysis tools and the computing environment with federated credentials; Reuse pipelines that have already been validated (e.g., open-source data cleaning tools); Submit new data for automatic validation through FAIR-enabling workflows.

The social impacts are obvious: faster peer-review, increased citation of datasets, democratized access to science, involvement of non-academic actors (policy makers, NGOs, citizen scientists) (Brandes & Young, 2024; Open Research Europe, 2021; Rainey et al., 2023).

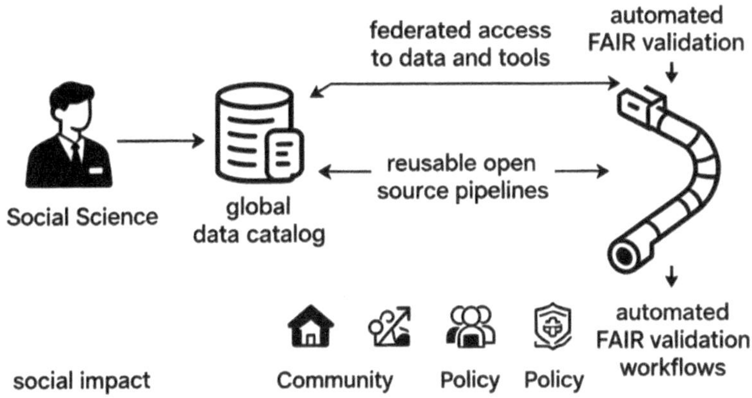


**Fig. 12.2** FAIR in practice: how science is changing

## *12.1.4 Strategic Objectives and Challenges of RIs for Open Science*

Modern RIs have a series of strategic objectives:

- **Open access, review and exploitation of data**
  The adoption of centralized and distributed repositories allows the download, navigation and citation of data and results, with positive effects on the transparency of public research and scientific reproducibility (European Commission, 2025; Open Science Italia, 2024a; University of Padua, n.d.).
- **International collaboration and disciplinary integration**
  RIs play a systemic role in fostering interdisciplinary cooperation: humanities, biomedicine, physics and computer science can share tools, workflows, analysis environments and methodologies, thanks to common APIs and semantic mappings between ontologies (Danese, 2024; InterNO Collective, 2022; University of Milano-Bicocca, 2024).
- **Environmental, social and economic sustainability**
  Energy-intensive infrastructures (HPC, massive storage) must now respond to climate challenges: energy efficiency (PUE less than 1.2), intelligent load balancing, modularity of structures also to reduce e-waste.
- **Training, inclusion and enhancement of skills**
  RIs promote courses, summer/winter schools, hackathons and communities of practice that enable researchers, data stewards, students and professionals to use advanced tools, knowing the risks (cybersecurity, privacy, bias) and the potential of new technologies (INVALSI, 2024; Scuola Normale Superiore (SNS), 2023; University of Bologna, 2025).

**Fig. 12.3** The ethical and social challenges of open science

- **Regulatory compliance (GDPR, NIS2, digital accessibility, gender & diversity)**
  The inclusion of privacy and security rules (data protection by design & by default) and the adoption of gender-inclusive policies are increasingly central, also to obtain public/EU accreditation and funding.
- **Traceability and recognition of scientific production**
  Thanks to DOIs, logs, audit trails and automatic attribution systems, RIs allow full recognition, including academic recognition, of the various products (datasets, codes, workflows, open publications, reports), favoring new evaluation metrics (Fig. 12.3).

In addition to the obvious advantages, open science and the expansion of RIs pose new challenges: how to ensure the protection of sensitive data in healthcare, how to prevent mass surveillance with interoperable datasets, how to incentivize openness without penalizing intellectual authorship (Casò, 2022; European Commission, CORDIS, 2024; NextGenHeritage, 2025; University of Florence, n.d.).

## 12.2 Components of FOSSR RI Architecture

From the general framework on the evolution and significance of research infrastructures, we move on to a more technical description of their components, with particular attention to the architecture of open science-oriented RIs.

### *12.2.1 Technical Architecture: Physical and Virtual Infrastructure*

Traditionally, social researchers have relied on desktop computers or local servers with limited computing and storage capacity. This approach is inadequate in the face of the increasing availability of large and complex data sets (big data), such as those from social media, large-scale surveys, administrative records, and digitized texts. Analyzing this data requires computing power and storage capacity that only HPC and cloud computing architectures can efficiently offer.

The FOSSR RI architecture embodies the principles of distributed innovation, leveraging both advanced physical facilities and modular cloud solutions to deliver scalability, reliability, security, and interoperability.

The adoption of a technological infrastructure that integrates cloud datacenters and high-performance computing (HPC) architectures offers significant advantages for researchers in the social sciences, overcoming the limitations of traditional computational approaches and opening new frontiers for the analysis of complex data.

These two technologies create a powerful, flexible, and collaborative research ecosystem.

1. **Access to Advanced Computing Resources**: Researchers can access high-end computing resources on demand, such as servers with multi-core CPUs and specialized GPUs (e.g., the Nvidia H100), without the need to purchase and maintain expensive hardware. This is crucial for applying computationally intensive techniques such as the simulation of complex social models or in the AI field, machine learning, and deep learning.
2. **Scalability and Flexibility**: Cloud architecture allows you to scale out resources according to the needs of your project. A researcher can launch hundreds of virtual machines for large-scale analysis and release them once the job is done, paying only for what they use. Orchestration platforms such as OpenStack and Kubernetes make it easy to manage complex computing environments in an automated and reproducible way.
3. **Simplified Collaboration and Sharing**: Virtual Research Environments (VREs), such as the one hosted in Pisa, are one of the most significant advantages. They offer pre-configured digital workspaces with analytics tools such as Jupiter Hub and RStudio, shared storage, and access to common data. This allows geographically distributed research teams to collaborate in real time on the same project, sharing data, code, and results in a secure and controlled environment.
4. **Large-Scale Data Analytics**: The combination of high-performance storage (such as BeeGFS and Ceph, with capacities greater than 1.6 PB) and low-latency networks (such as Rockport) is critical for big data analytics. Social researchers can, for example, analyze the entire archive of a social media platform or process decades of textual data for computational linguistics studies, tasks that are not achievable with traditional infrastructures.
5. **Reproducibility and Transparency of Research (FAIR)**: The infrastructure actively supports the FAIR (Findable, Accessible, Interoperable, Reusable) principles. Through unified portals, guided workflows for data publication and the assignment of persistent identifiers such as DOIs, it is ensured that research is transparent, verifiable and that data can be easily reused by other scholars, amplifying scientific impact.

**Table 12.4** Characteristics of the FOSSR federated RI

| Infrastructure | Quantity/capacity | Distinctive notes |
|---|---|---|
| Total servers | >200 | Advanced CPUs, GPUs, high RAM |
| Storage | >1.6 PB | Block+object (BeeGFS/Ceph) |
| GPU | >50 H100 | Deep learning/simulation |
| NAS PowerScale | Multi-tier | VRE Shared Storage |
| Networks | 100 Gbps (GARR) | Intra/inter-datacenter, VPN/HPC |

6. **Democratization of Access**: By providing unified access through federated Single Sign-On (SSO) systems with university credentials, the FOSSR infrastructure lowers technical and financial barriers. Researchers from smaller or underfunded institutions can also access world-class tools and resources, fostering a fairer and more inclusive research ecosystem (Table 12.4).

## *12.2.2 Connectivity and Advanced Networking*

The architecture ensures that huge amounts of data can travel quickly and smoothly between research centers. For more complex analyses, which require the collaboration of many processors, it ensures that they can "talk" to each other almost instantaneously, making it possible to search on vast datasets (the so-called "data-intensive projects") that would be impossible on a normal computer.

The connection between these nodes is guaranteed by a "spine-leaf" network architecture and relies on the 100 Gbps GARR backbone For High Performance Computing (HPC) activities, it uses low-latency network solutions such as Rockport, essential for scientific projects that require intensive data processing.

The following describes how these "libraries" (data centers) communicate with each other and how the super-powerful computers within them collaborate for the most complex analyses.

- **Spine-leaf architecture and backbone GARR at 100 Gbps**. By analogy with a road network. The "GARR backbone" is the main highway that connects our libraries throughout Italy. It is a special highway, reserved for research, and it is incredibly fast (100 Gbps), like a high-speed train that carries a huge number of books (data) in a very short time. The "Spine-leaf" architecture is like a super-efficient system of highway junctions within each city/library. Instead of having a single long avenue where everyone gets bottled up, this system ensures that every computer can reach any other computer in the data center with the shortest and fastest path possible. This eliminates data traffic bottlenecks.
- **High Performance Computing (HPC) and low latency networking (Rockport)**. Imagine having to do an analysis that requires 100 researchers to read and comment on the same paragraph of a book simultaneously. To do this, they need to communicate with each other instantly, without any delay. HPC is a team of 100 researchers working together as a single super-brain. "Low-latency

networking" (such as Rockport) is a technology that enables instantaneous communication. "Latency" is the delay. Having low latency is like talking face-to-face instead of a video call that freezes all the time. This absence of delay is critical because, for complex social simulations or big data analysis, computers must continuously exchange small pieces of information to keep calculations "consistent" and fast.
- **Seamless integration of external resources via secure VPNs**. Suppose you need access to a confidential document stored in one of these special libraries from your office or home. A VPN (Virtual Private Network) is like a private, armored tunnel you create from your computer to your library. No one from the outside can see what you are carrying. This allows you to work on sensitive data in the infrastructure in total security, as if you were physically sitting there. The integration is "transparent" because, once connected, you don't notice the complexity of the network: everything works in a simple and straightforward way.

### *12.2.3 Cloud Layers and Virtual Environments*

The entire hardware infrastructure that supports research computing—servers, storage, and network systems—can be imagined as a large repository of digital building materials. Alone, these components represent a set of unassembled resources. The cloud layer is an intelligent system that organizes and transforms these materials into functional and customized workspaces for researchers.

The cloud layer orchestrates computational and storage resources, enabling the creation of Virtual Research Environments (VREs) on both public and private cloud infrastructures. Each research group operates within an independent and secure environment, known as a tenant. All computational nodes are interconnected and managed through the OpenStack platform, which allows for instant provisioning of virtual machines, Docker containers, and Kubernetes clusters.

These virtual environments provide immediate access to analytical tools such as JupyterHub, RStudio, and virtual desktops for simulation and data analysis. Automation within these environments is ensured by standard APIs and configuration tools such as Terraform and Ansible, which enable the creation of reproducible and reliable workflows (Table 12.5).

### *12.2.4 Cloud Layers and Virtual Research Environments*

The entire hardware infrastructure that supports research computing- servers, storage, and network systems can be imagined as a large repository of digital building materials. Alone, these components represent a set of unassembled resources. The cloud layer is an intelligent system that organizes and transforms these materials into functional and customized workspaces for researchers.

**Table 12.5** Technologies of the FOSSR federated RI

| Technology | Description |
|---|---|
| OpenStack | Cloud IaaS federation, multi-tenant |
| Kubernetes | Container and microservices orchestration |
| Docker | Containerization of apps and tools |
| JupyterHub/Lab | Multi-user interactive analytics environments |
| Ansible/Terraform | Automation, provisioning and updates |

The cloud layer orchestrates computational and storage resources, enabling the creation of **Virtual Research Environments (VREs)** on both public and private cloud infrastructures. Each research group operates within an independent and secure environment, known as a *tenant*. All computational nodes are interconnected and managed through the **OpenStack** platform, which allows for instant provisioning of virtual machines, Docker containers, and Kubernetes clusters.

These virtual environments provide immediate access to analytical tools such as **Jupiter**, **RStudio**, and virtual desktops for simulation and data analysis. Automation within these environments is ensured by standard APIs and configuration tools such as **Terraform** and **Ansible**, which enable the creation of reproducible and reliable workflows.

| Technology | Description |
|---|---|
| OpenStack | Federated, multi-tenant Cloud Infrastructure (IaaS) |
| Kubernetes | Orchestration of containers and microservices |
| Docker | Application containerization |
| Jupyter Hub/Lab | Multi-user interactive analytics environment |
| Ansible/Terraform | Automation, provisioning, and system updates |

**Federated Nodes in OpenStack**

The term *federated* refers to a coordinated system of independent units that operate under shared management. A useful analogy is that of a university system comprising multiple campuses. Each campus (node) maintains its own facilities and staff but functions under a unified administrative structure that manages resources and recognizes shared credentials. Similarly, OpenStack acts as the central coordination system of a federation of data centers located, for example, in Pisa, Naples, or Turin. To the researcher, computational resources are offered as a single, unified infrastructure—independent on the servers' physical location.

**Instant Provisioning of Virtual Machines, Docker Containers, and Kubernetes Clusters**

Depending on the nature and scale of a research project, the cloud infrastructure can provide different types of virtual environments:

- **Virtual Machines (VMs):** Comparable to receiving a fully equipped private office, a VM offers an isolated computing environment where the researcher can install software and conduct experiments independently.
- **Docker Containers:** These represent lightweight, portable units—similar to pre-packed toolboxes—designed for specific tasks. For instance, a container might already include statistical software such as R and its necessary libraries. Containers start quickly and ensure computational reproducibility across systems.
- **Kubernetes Clusters:** For large-scale projects requiring coordination among multiple containers, Kubernetes functions as an automated manager. It allocates tasks, ensures communication between containers, and manages recovery in case of failure.

**Virtual Research Environments (VREs) and Tenant Concept**

A VRE can be envisioned as a dedicated digital research department created for a specific research group. It may consist of multiple virtual offices (VMs), shared laboratories, and collaborative data archives. The concept of a *tenant* ensures that each VRE operates in complete isolation, guaranteeing data confidentiality and access control.

**On-Demand Research Tools**

Within the VRE, researchers can request specialized digital instruments such as JupyterHub, which functions as an interactive computational notebook integrating code, visualizations, and documentation; and RStudio, which provides a comprehensive environment for statistical analysis. "On demand" indicates that these tools are automatically deployed and ready for immediate use without any installation effort.

**Automation with Terraform and Ansible**

Automation tools streamline the deployment and maintenance of research environments:

- **Terraform** defines the architectural blueprint of an environment, specifying computational resources, network configurations, and system structures. It can automatically create multiple identical environments following this predefined design.
- **Ansible** acts as the configuration manager, entering each environment to install and configure all necessary software packages based on predefined scripts.

Together, these tools make the creation of research environments an **automated, fast and above all reproducible process**, eliminating human errors and ensuring that each researcher works in identical conditions.

### 12.2.5 *Logical Architecture: Workflows, Platforms, and Services*

The logical architecture defines the workflows, platforms, and services offered to researchers.

- **Data Services and Marketplaces**: A single portal centralizes access to FAIR data catalogs, discovery tools, and software repositories and analytics notebooks. Data search is facilitated by visual interfaces, RESTful APIs, and semantic queries (SPARQL). The system manages clear licensing policies and tracks the provenance of data, assigning persistent identifiers such as DOIs and ARKs.
- **IAM System**: Identity and access management (IAM) is handled by WSO2 Identity Server20. This system supports Single Sign-On (SSO) and is compatible with standards such as SAML and OpenID Connect, allowing federation with university Identity Providers. Access is governed by multi-level role-based control (RBAC).
- **Monitoring and Audit**: The infrastructure is constantly monitored. Prometheus and Grafana are used for asset telemetry and predictive analytics23. OpenSearch handles structured logging for analyzing security events and auditing compliance with regulations such as GDPR and NIS2. Dedicated dashboards show performance indicators (KPIs) related to SLAs, energy efficiency (PUE), and user engagement (Table 12.6).

**Table 12.6** Example of workflow for FAIR publishing

| Step | Activity | Tools involved |
|---|---|---|
| Upload | Upload files to the portal | Portal FOSSR, SSO |
| Enrichmen | Metadata entry/validation according to FAIR schema | Guided forms, semantic mapping |
| Licensing | License choice (CC-BY, CC0, etc.); Compatibility check | Portal, validator |
| Review | Automated/Checklist-Based Audit and Check by Data Stewards | Validator, workflow di review |
| Publication | DOI/ARK assignment, inclusion in catalogs, Zenodo/OpenAIRE publication | API, OAI-PMH, Zenodo interface |

### 12.2.6 *FOSSR System Technical Specifications*

Below are the characteristics of the system implemented in the FOSSR project.

**Servers**
The beating heart of the system is more than 200 high-end servers. These can be seen as the computational workforce of the infrastructure. Each server is equipped with multi-core CPUs, i.e. "brains" capable of simultaneously performing a vast number of complex calculations, and a huge amount of RAM, which acts as a large work desk to manipulate large datasets in real time. These are joined by more than 50 Nvidia H100 GPUs, specialized units that drastically accelerate the typical operations of artificial intelligence and complex simulations, such as the recognition of patterns within thousands of texts or images.

**Storage**
The total data storage capacity exceeds 1.6 PB, a volume comparable to hundreds of billions of pages of documents. This immense archive, or storage, is not a simple container, but an intelligent system. A part, based on technologies such as BeeGFS, is optimized for ultra-fast access to data, which is essential during the active analysis phases. Another part, which uses Ceph, is designed for maximum security: it automatically creates multiple copies of each piece of data and distributes them between different machines, ensuring that no information can be lost due to hardware failure.

**NAS**
Network Attached Storage (NAS) systems provide workspaces for researchers. They offer individual home directories, which function as private and secure repositories for each user. They also provide shared storage for Virtual Search Environments (VREs), acting as collaborative worktables where entire teams can access and edit the same project files in a coordinated and secure manner.

**Backup**
The infrastructure is also protected by a robust backup system. This system acts as an insurance policy for research data. Through hierarchical copies and multiple geo-replications, it ensures that a secure version of each piece of data is kept in multiple physical locations. This strategy ensures business continuity and the ability to fully restore information even in the event of unforeseen or critical events in one of the data centers.

## 12.3 Interoperability and Integration

In the previous sections, the architectural structure and the main technological layers of the infrastructures have been outlined. In this section, the dimension of interoperability, a key element to allow cooperation and integration between systems and research communities, is considered.

Interoperability is indeed a strategic enabler for interdisciplinary research, allowing seamless integration of diverse data and expertise, while empowering evidence-based public policies that address complex societal challenges.

## 12.3.1 Fundamentals of Interoperability in Modern RIs

In the context of contemporary research infrastructures, interoperability represents the ability of systems, platforms, software and data to be effectively exchanged, understood, reused and integrated by different actors regardless of their origin, discipline or nationality. It is a key concept of open science, since the availability of data alone is not enough without tools, standards, and metadata that allow their real sharing and enhancement (Almeida et al., 2011; European Committee for Interoperable Systems [ECIS], 2022; Molinaro, 2025; Wikipedia Contributors, 2024b).

Dimensions of interoperability:

- **Technical**: ability of applications and services to communicate via standard protocols, common data schema, public APIs (Data.europa.eu, 2024; FAIR-Impact.eu, 2024; van der Zwaan et al., 2024).
- **Semantics**: commonality of meaning; use of reference ontology (e.g. DDI for social data, Dublin Core for bibliographic resources, SKOS for thesaurus)
- **Organizational**: harmonization of procedures, access policies and workflows across bodies, countries or disciplines
- **Legal/Ethics**: License negotiation, regulatory compliance, and shared governance policies (Table 12.7, Fig. 12.4) (Morando, 2013).

The European Open Science Cloud has established harmonised guidelines for the federation of Europe's leading RIs. In this way, a survey of social data collected by CESSDA in Finland can be immediately aggregated with environmental data from LifeWatch in Spain, or economic data from Eurostat, thanks to the cross-mapping

**Table 12.7** Main interoperability layers, related standards and instruments, and typical applications

| Level | Standard/instrument | Typical application |
|---|---|---|
| Syntactic | CSV, XML, JSON, HDF5 | Data exchange, repository |
| Semantic | RDF, OWL, SKOS, DDI, DCAT | Linked data, metadata |
| Protocol | OAI-PMH, REST, SWORD | Harvesting data, API |
| Identity | SAML, OAuth2, OpenID Connect | Single Sign-On, federation |

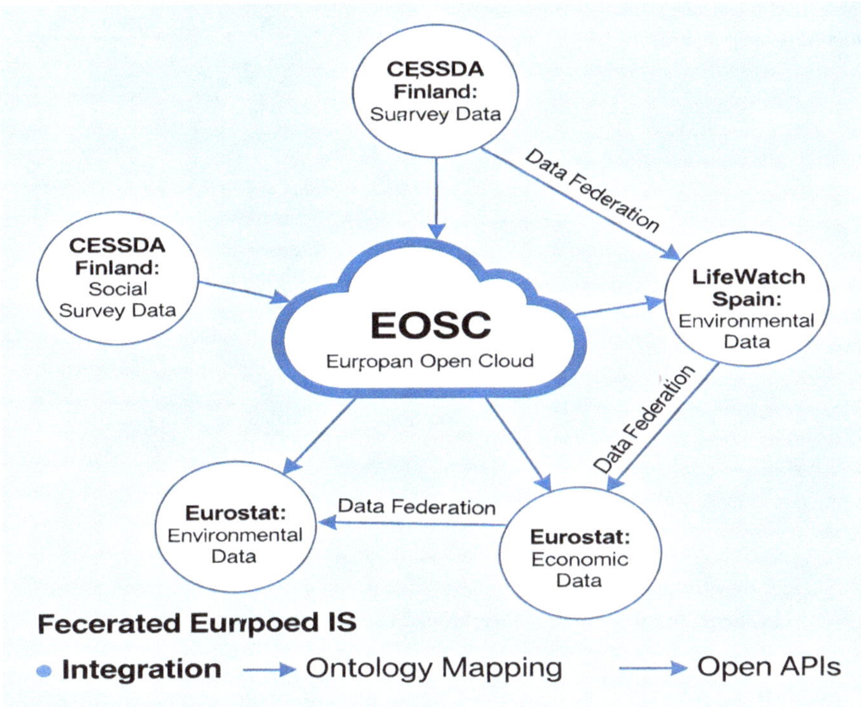


**Fig. 12.4** EOSC interoperability

of ontologies and open APIs, with the entire supply chain accessible to accredited users from multiple countries [ref. EOSC].

### *12.3.2 System Integration: Practical Solutions in Large Consortia and FOSSR*

1. *Vertical and horizontal integration*
   (a) **Vertical**: between assets and tools of the same domain (e.g. sociological surveys integrated with ISTAT demographic databases, visual analytics and open historical archives)
   (b) **Horizontal**: between heterogeneous assets (e.g. sociological survey data, satellite images, integrated genomic databases for studies on the impact of the environment, society and health)

   Middleware tools (e.g., open-source ETL such as Apache NiFi), data mapping services, and metadata normalization ensure that datasets from the various nodes are homogeneous and machine actionable.

**Table 12.8** Data integration workflows between RIs

| Phase | Key activities | Instruments |
|---|---|---|
| Discovery | Dataset discovery in external catalogs | OpenAIRE, CKAN, DCAT |
| Normalization | Local/external data schema adaptation | ETL, mapping ontologies |
| Aggregation | Dataset unification, deduplication | Data lake, Spark |
| Analysis | Integration into collaborative workflows | Jupyter, RStudio |
| Publication | Standard format output and links to provenance | Zenodo, OAI-PMH |

2. *FOSSR and the harmonization of flows*

   In FOSSR, interoperability is achieved through:

   (a) Multi-level metadata according to FAIR/ISO19115 scheme
   (b) Ontologies and vocabularies for socioeconomic data (e.g. ISCO-08, NACE Rev.2 classifications)
   (c) RESTful API for federated access and semantic search
   (d) Federated SSO (with university IdPs, CESSDA...)
   (e) Crosswalk tool to map legacy metadata with FAIR metadata (Table 12.8).

3. *Ontology and Linked Data*

   The infrastructure supports the creation and reuse of open ontologies (OWLs, RDF Schemas) that allow:

   (a) automatic semantic enrichment of data;
   (b) inference of hidden relationships in distributed information assets;
   (c) enabling cross-functional search and automatic discovery of resources through semantic engines (e.g. ElasticSearch with RDF plugins, Virtuoso, GraphDB);
   (d) even external parties can then hook new sets to the same nodes via APIs and drag-and-drop visual interfaces (Fig. 12.5).

A researcher uploads a survey to FOSSR: the metadata (author, measured variables, period, target population, methodology) are automatically enriched through a mapping with the DDI-Lifecycle scheme, the dataset is linked to similar international surveys and is inserted directly into the FOSSR knowledge graph;

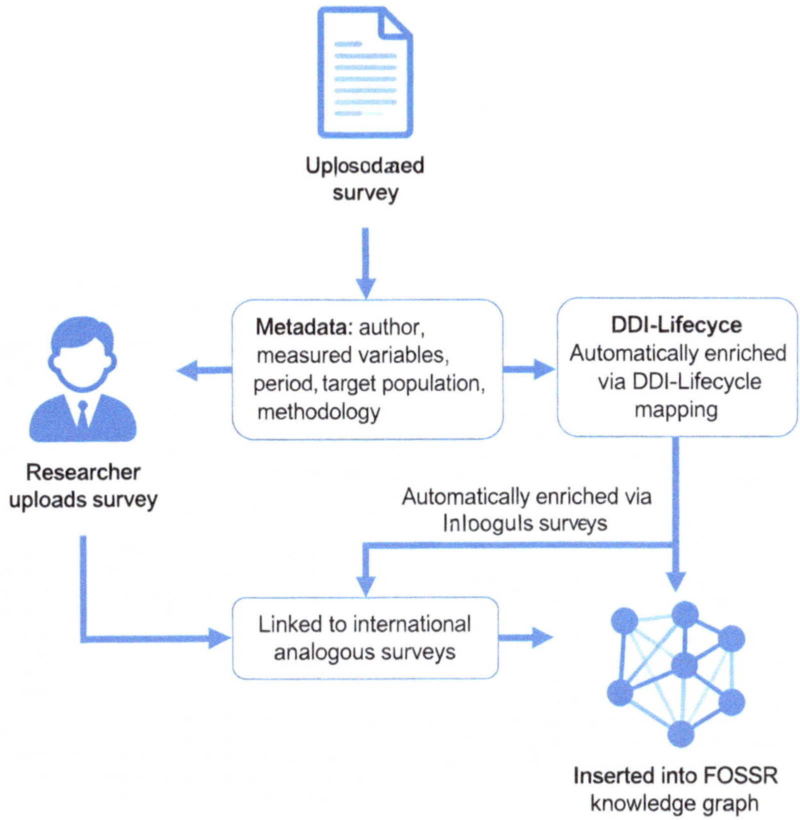


**Fig. 12.5** Survey metadata enrichment and integration into the FOSSR knowledge graph

### *12.3.3 Organizational Policies for Integration and Advanced Case Studies*

1. Internal organization and workflows
   FOSSR operating units work on:
   (a) Data policy federation submitted by the ethical/legal board
   (b) Automatic integration toolkit (batch and real-time) for uploading normalization, cleaning, enrichment and publishing
   (c) Centralized catalogs, automatic indexing, digital object identification services (DOI/ARK/Handle).

2. Partnerships and real case studies

   ***Example CESSDA and FOSSR***

   The federation between FOSSR and CESSDA allows Italian users direct access to open European surveys via SSO, maintaining GDPR policies and data localization according to national legislation.

   ***Example Open AIRE and FOSSR***

   Through OAI-PMH harvesting, FOSSR publishes and makes discovery-capable also on platforms such as Open AIRE, increasing the international reach of Italian social datasets.
3. Critical issues and future scenarios

   Critical issues remain:

   (a) Lack of perfect standardization across all domains (continuous community convergence, field testing, transdisciplinary pilot projects needed)
   (b) Need for advanced training for data stewards and workflow managers
   (c) The risk of lock-in and technological obsolescence: the FOSSR contrasts with continuous migration to open solutions, modularization, and a shared annual update roadmap.

## 12.4 Scalability and Flexibility

Scalability and long-term sustainability are tightly linked in a Research Infrastructure. The ability to efficiently expand services and integrate new technologies ensures that the infrastructure remains relevant, cost-effective, and capable of supporting evolving scientific needs over time.

Therefore, having in mind the fundamentals and practices of interoperability, it becomes essential to address the issue of scalability, i.e. the ability of RIs to adapt to increasing loads, new technological requirements, and evolving scientific contexts.

### *12.4.1 Introduction to Scalability in Research Infrastructures*

Scalability represents the ability of a research infrastructure to accommodate an increasing amount of work (users, data, computational processes) without losing performance, reliability or consistency in governance, and without the need to redesign the entire system (AppMaster, 2025; Lenovo, 2025; Moko, 2025).

Unlike traditional systems, modern RIs must have both scalability:

1. **Vertical**: Enhancement of internal resources to a single node (addition of CPU, RAM, latest generation GPU, expansion of storage capacity at rack/server level)
2. **Horizontal**: addition of new nodes (servers, remote datacenters, specialized clusters), federated based on shared, compatible and synchronized policies

**Table 12.9** Computing modalities, key advantages, and typical applications

| Modality | Advantages | Typical application |
|---|---|---|
| Cloud bursting | Elasticity, pay-per-use costs, speed | Peak-use analysis, batch projects |
| Container (K8s) | Agile scaling microservices, easy orchestration | Workflow analytics, data ingestion, API |
| Edge computing | Decentralized processing, reduced latencies | IoT sensors, distributed data analysis |

### *12.4.2 Scaling Mode: Cloud, Container, Edge*

The cloud-native approach, increasingly adopted in RIs, makes dynamic scalability possible, i.e. the ability to allocate or release resources in response to demand, at optimized costs and with very short provisioning times (Table 12.9) (Clust-ER Innovate, 2023; EconomyUp, 2025; Hewlett Packard Enterprise, 2025; Oracle, 2025).

### *12.4.3 Infrastructure and Software Flexibility*

Flexibility in an RI infrastructure is about the ability to quickly adapt to:

- New data types or multidisciplinary flows (e.g. textual data, images, streaming from IoT, genomics...)
- New laws, regulations and policies (e.g. GDPR update, NIS2 standard inclusion, energy DNSH compliance)
- Changes in the composition of the user community (e.g. openness to new institutions, students, industry partnerships)
- Evolution of analytical tools (upgrade/modularity of Jupyter environments, ML library, AI/Bio/Stats plugin integration)

Key Solutions:

- Service modularization (microservices, public and private RESTful APIs)
- Continuous deployment (CICD, automation pipeline with Ansible/Jenkins/Gitlab)
- Plug-and-play architectures: ability to integrate new environments or enable specialized services without downtime (example: addition of interoperable Visual Analytics platform) (IdeaPM, 2025).

### *12.4.4 Scalability Traceability and Benchmarking*

All scaling activities are tracked via:

- Self-calculated KPIs (resource usage metrics, response times, quota occupied, SLAs)
- Advanced reporting available on real-time dashboards (Grafana, custom PROM-Q)
- Logging automatic provisioning, deployment e incident for audit and strategic CAPEX/OPEX (Table 12.10, Fig. 12.6)

The new frontiers include the creation of **digital twins** of entire infrastructures (digital twins for simulations of capacity planning, energy impact, simulated failovers) and the experimentation of **serverless computing** to automate job analytics on even unstructured data.

**Table 12.10** Target vs. typical performance benchmarks for scalability and service metrics in federated research infrastructures

| KPI scalability | Target FOSSR | International medium |
|---|---|---|
| Node add time | <10 min/node | <30 min/node |
| Storage expandability | +100 TB/month without downtime | +10%/year typical |
| SLA availability | >99.95% | 99.9% (media EOSC) |
| Orchestration latency | <60 s/startup JupyterLab | 2–5 min (without adv. orchestra) |

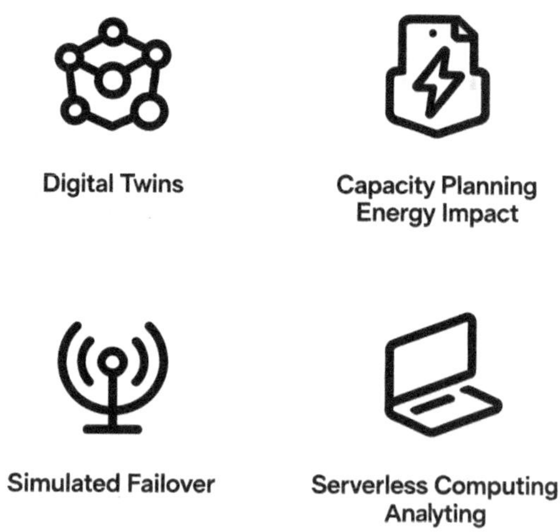


**Fig. 12.6** Future prospects: super-scalability and digital twins

## 12.5 Security and Privacy

As infrastructure expands and adapts, the issue of security and data protection is emerging as key to ensuring the reliability, compliance and long-term sustainability of RIs.

### *12.5.1 Security in Research Infrastructures: Principles and Risks*

The openness and large extension of contemporary RIs bring with them new **security challenges**: the risk of cyber-attacks (DoS, data leaks, privilege escalation, supply chain compromise), the risk of human error, the exposure of sensitive data, the need to govern permissions on a multi-tenant scale, and ever-evolving regulatory compliance (Fig. 12.7).

Data breaches and identity theft on federated services can lead to:

- Unauthorized access to open or semi-open datasets
- Malware e ransomware on private clouds
- Insider threat (abuse of administrative privileges)
- Supply chain compromise (OS/malicious software updates)
- Social engineering towards administrators (advanced phishing)

**Fig. 12.7** Top threats to RIs

**Table 12.11** Security principles, their implementation in FOSSR, and associated operational advantages

| Security principle | FOSSR implementation | Operational advantage |
|---|---|---|
| Advanced SSO and IAM | WSO2IS, SAML/OIDC, LDAP | Simplicity, traceability |
| Data encryption | HTTPS/TLS, data-at-rest encryption | Data breach mitigation |
| Tenant isolation | VRE instances, RBAC segmentation | Minimizes lateral move |
| Incident Response | Playbook, logging, backup | Speed of reaction |

Key Principles for Modern Security:

- **Security by design and by default**: setting security as a founding principle from the design phase of each component or service, with periodic review, threat modeling and continuous assessment.
- **Least privilege and advanced access control**: each user and service must have exactly the minimum authorizations necessary to operate, with timed and audited delegations.
- **Audit trail and structured logging**: every access, deployment, modification or critical use must be historicized in a way that is compatible with regulations such as GDPR, ISO/IEC 27001 (Table 12.11).

## *12.5.2 Privacy, GDPR/NIS2 and Ethical-Legal Compliance*

The management of personal data, especially in RIs that process sensitive data (health, socio-economic conditions, ethnic/religious data, etc.), is now subject to the stringent rules of the GDPR and, increasingly, also to the European NIS2 regulation on cyber security of essential networks.

- **Privacy by design & by default**: Each service from the design includes data minimization, the use of pseudonymization, access logging, granular consent tools, Data Protection Impact Assessment (DPIA) mandatory for new workflows.
- **GDPR principles**:
  - Lawfulness, transparency and fairness in processing;
  - Right to be forgotten, limitation of processing, portability;
  - Strengthened responsibility of Data Controller and Data Processor;
  - Logging and updating treatment registers.

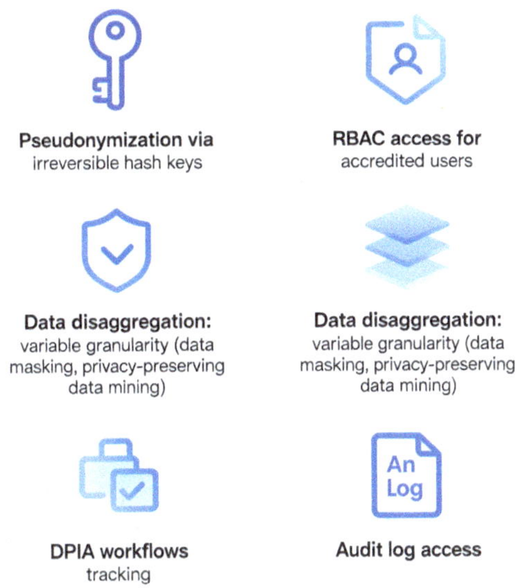


**Fig. 12.8** Case study: management of sensitive sociological data FOSSR

**Table 12.12** Compliance mapping: GDPR vs. NIS2

| Requirement | GDPR | NIS2 |
|---|---|---|
| Data consent | Explicit, documented | Integrated local policy |
| Data breach notification | <=72 h compulsory | Immediate Incident Notification |
| Audit/certification | Treatment Register | Minimum INAIL/ISO certifications |
| Safety continuity | DPO Role | Business Continuity Plan |

- **NIS2**:

  Applies to RIs defined as "essential" according to the Directive. It provides for obligations on:

  - ICT risk management and cybersecurity;
  - continuity of service;
  - mandatory accident notification;
  - mandatory security training for staff and students;
  - adoption framework and certifications (ISO/IEC 27001-2, ENS, etc.) (Fig. 12.8).

In the case of large social surveys uploaded to FOSSR (e.g., questionnaires on economic conditions, mental health, political preferences), the data are: Pseudonymized at the origin via irreversible hash keys; Made accessible only to users accredited via RBAC; Disaggregated for open publication with variable granularity, through data masking and "privacy preserving data mining" techniques; Tracked by DPIA workflows and access logs that can only be consulted by the audit body (Table 12.12).

In general, security and controlled accessibility are complementary dimensions of a Research Infrastructure and must be balanced, ensuring robust protection without hindering authorized data sharing and collaboration.

## 12.6 Overcoming Barriers to Open Data

Finally, a reflection on the barriers that hinder the full adoption of Open Data, addressing both the cultural and technical and legal dimensions that influence the path towards a truly open science (Open Science Italia, 2024c).

### *12.6.1 Cultural Barriers: Resistance, Training, Incentives*

Despite the apparent theoretical simplicity, many barriers to the adoption of open data are still cultural in nature:

1. Fear of losing control, primacy or data-centric "competitive advantage";
2. Academic resistance to valuing datasets as research outputs equal to publications;
3. Poor training on licenses, FAIR models and open tools;
4. Incentives that are misaligned with traditional evaluation parameters (Fig. 12.9).

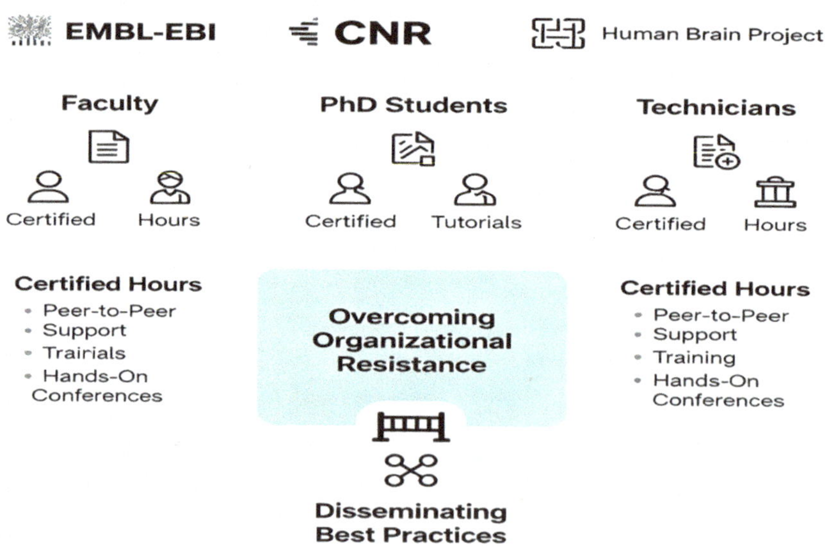


**Fig. 12.9** Best practice: "Open Science Champion" program

Many institutions (e.g., EMBL-EBI, CNR, Human Brain Project) promote ambassadors or open science champions: professors, doctoral students and technicians with dedicated hours (congruous, certified) in peer-to-peer support, curatorship of tutorials, training and hands-on conferences to overcome organizational resistance and disseminate best practices.

### *12.6.2 Technical Barriers: Standards, Tools, Interoperability*

- Legacy data in proprietary/obsolete formats;
- Lack of automation pipeline for conversion and metadata;
- Obsolete or insufficient storage for big data and long-term preservation;
- Lack of data stewards and support functions in FAIR automation;
- Fragmentation of workflows at national level or across disciplines.

Solutions:

- Investments in infrastructure updates (hardware and software);
- Automated mapping tool;
- "One-stop" platforms for data steward training, development of conversion microservices, and semantic data validators.

### *12.6.3 Legal, Ethical and Political Barriers*

- Uncertainty regarding the intellectual property of data produced in public-private collaboration (PPP);
- Complexity in international compliance (multi-jurisdiction, data location, copyright, data at ethical risk such as gen(-omics), religious, political data, etc.);
- Restrictive national regulations on population data storage.

Examples:

- In Italy, not all social surveys can be made open, opinions from the Privacy Guarantor and supplementary policies from the Digital Agency are needed (Fig. 12.10, Table 12.13) (Agency for Digital Italy (AgID), 2024).

In general, Research Infrastructures act not only as technological and scientific enablers but also as agents of cultural change, shaping practices, norms, and collaborative behaviors across the scientific community and beyond.

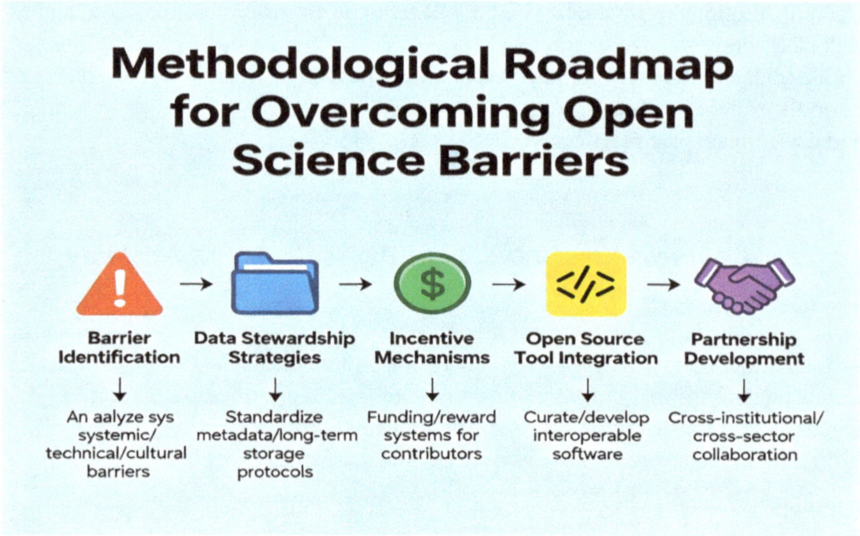


**Fig. 12.10** Methodological pathway to overcome open science barriers

**Table 12.13** Success/criticality indicators in open data adoption

| Barrier type | Exceeding KPIs | Unresolved issue |
|---|---|---|
| Cultural | % of teach-ers/researchers trained | Absence of champi-ons/disseminators |
| Technique | % dataset FAIR-validation | Legacy Stor-age/Documentation |
| Legal/Ethics | Transparent policies and audits | Lack of institutional interlocutors |

## 12.7 Conclusions

Research infrastructures are undergoing a profound transformation driven by the exponential growth of data, increasing technological complexity, and the rise of Open Science as a scientific, political, and cultural paradigm. The chapter has shown that modern Research Infrastructures are no longer mere facilities or collections of tools; they are federated, distributed, and highly specialized digital ecosystems where interoperability, security, sustainability, governance, and ethical responsibility are as essential as hardware and software themselves.

FOSSR (Fostering Open Science in Social Science Research) strengthens Italy's participation in key European research infrastructures (e.g., CESSDA-ERIC, SHARE-ERIC, RISIS) by integrating their national nodes into a unified Open Science Cloud, enhancing access to high-quality social science data, innovative tools, and services, and promoting interoperable, collaborative research aligned with European open science policies.

The FOSSR case demonstrates that a contemporary Research Infrastructure must rely on:

- integrated, scalable HPC–cloud infrastructures;
- automated, virtualized environments (VREs, containers, orchestrators);
- FAIR-oriented data and metadata services;
- interoperable identity and access management systems;
- transparent, auditable workflows governed by shared policies.

At the same time, persistent challenges remain against fragmented standards, heterogeneous regulatory frameworks, shortages of specialized expertise, and insufficient institutional incentives to fully embrace open data. Overcoming these obstacles requires coordinated investment in training, automation, semantic technologies, digital culture, and harmonized policy frameworks.

Future Research Infrastructures must be not only technologically resilient, but also open, inclusive, sustainable, and capable of rapidly adapting to evolving scientific and regulatory contexts. In this sense, the convergence of FAIR principles, distributed cloud architectures, AI, advanced security models, and federated governance represents the most promising trajectory for building a truly integrated, trustworthy, and socially beneficial European scientific infrastructure.

**Acknowledgment** Special thanks for the preparation of this book chapter to Simona Sada, for her constant support in promoting and monitoring the development of all tasks in line with the FOSSR project schedule.

## References

Agency for Digital Italy (AgID). (2024). *Open data and research infrastructures: The AgID guidelines*. Retrieved from https://open-science.it/ri-e-linee-guida-agid

Almeida, F., Oliveira, J., & Cruz, J. (2011). Open standards and open source: Enabling interoperability. *International Journal of Software Engineering & Applications, 2*(1), 1–11. https://doi.org/10.5121/ijsea.2011.2101

AppMaster. (2025). *Ricerca e sviluppo sulla scalabilità*. Retrieved from https://appmaster.io/it/glossary/ricerca-e-sviluppo-sulla-scalabilita-ricerca-e-sviluppo

Brandes, P., & Young, J. (2024, May 16). Open-access papers draw more citations from a broader audience. *Science*. https://doi.org/10.1126/science.z613h0x

Burnard, L., Dacos, M., & Mounier, P. (Eds.). (2012). *Du literary and linguistic computing aux digital humanities*. OpenEdition Press. Retrieved from https://books.openedition.org/oep/1749

Casò, R. (2022, January 22). *Dati aperti della ricerca o proprietà intellettuale?* Retrieved from https://www.robertocaso.it/2022/01/22/dati-aperti-della-ricerca-o-proprieta-intellettuale/

Clust-ER Innovate. (2023, October). *SCABIS—White paper*. Retrieved from https://innovate.clust-er.it/wp-content/uploads/2023/10/SCABIS.pdf

CNR-ISTI. (2024, March 5). *Le infrastrutture di ricerca per l'Open Science al CNR*. Retrieved from https://www.isti.cnr.it/it/comunicazioni/notizie/2551-le-infrastrutture-di-ricerca-per-l-open-science-al-cnr

Danese, M. (2024). *Open Data per i Beni Culturali*. CNR Edizioni. Retrieved from https://www.cnr.it/sites/default/files/public/media/attivita/editoria/9788880805946_5953_digitale.pdf
Data.europa.eu. (2024, April 23). *Embracing open standards for an open data ecosystem*. Retrieved from https://data.europa.eu/en/news-events/news/embracing-open-standards-open-data-ecosystem-interoperability-across-europe
Di Giorgio, S., & Reale, E. (2023, October 23). FOSSR, l'Open Science Cloud italiano per le scienze sociali. *GARRnews*. Retrieved from https://www.garrnews.it/internazionale/fossr-l-open-science-cloud-italiano-per-le-scienze-sociali
EconomyUp. (2025). *Scalabilità nel cloud: come gestire la crescita*. Retrieved from https://www.economyup.it/innovazione/scalabilita-nel-cloud/
European Commission. (2025). *Strategia europea per i dati*. Retrieved from https://digital-strategy.ec.europa.eu/it/policies/open-data
European Commission, CORDIS. (2024, July 16). *Strumenti per una scienza aperta responsabile ed etica*. Retrieved from https://cordis.europa.eu/article/id/451296-tools-to-achieve-responsible-and-ethical-open-science/it
European Committee for Interoperable Systems (ECIS). (2022). *Interoperability & open standards*. Retrieved from https://www.ecis.eu/open-standards/
FAIR-Impact.eu. (2024). *Technical and semantic interoperability—Cross-domain use cases*. Retrieved from https://fair-impact.eu/technical-and-semantic-interoperability-cross-domain-use-cases
FOSSR. (2024). *Fostering Open Science in Social Science Research*. Retrieved from https://www.fossr.eu
FOSSR Project. (2024). *Cosa facciamo?* Retrieved from https://www.fossr.eu/cosa-facciamo/
Hewlett Packard Enterprise. (2025). *Che cos'è la scalabilità del cloud?* Retrieved from https://www.hpe.com/it/it/what-is/cloud-scalability.html
IdeaPM. (2025). *Come costruire un'infrastruttura IT scalabile*. Retrieved from https://ideapm.it/come-costruire-uninfrastruttura-it-scalabile/
INFN. (2023). *Open Science in pillole*. Retrieved from https://web.infn.it/openscience/open-science-in-pillole/
INRIM. (n.d.). *Open Science*. Retrieved from https://www.inrim.it/it/ricerca/open-science
InterNO Collective. (2022). *Collettivo InterNO. Ricerca partecipata e dati aperti*. Retrieved from https://iris.unive.it/retrieve/2e62689c-5647-4e59-8cb1-fe02dfadfc11/collettivo_INTERNO.pdf
INVALSI. (2024, May 17). *Accessibilità e trasparenza. Gli obiettivi dell'Open Science*. INVALSIopen. Retrieved from https://invalsiopen.it/accessibilita-trasparenza-obiettivi-open-science/
IRPPS CNR. (2024). *Infrastruttura FOSSR*. Retrieved from https://www.irpps.cnr.it/ricerca/infrastruttura-fossr/
Kumar, P., Singh, V. K., & Sharma, A. (2024). Investigating FAIR data principles compliance in Horizon Europe projects: A focus on health and environmental sciences. *Heliyon, 10*(15), e34538. https://doi.org/10.1016/j.heliyon.2024.e34538
Lenovo. (2025). *Scalabilità. Glossario*. Retrieved from https://www.lenovo.com/it/it/glossary/scalling/
Moko. (2025). *L'importanza della scalabilità dei servizi di app e web*. Retrieved from https://www.moko.it/it/news/limportanza-della-scalabilita-dei-servizi-di-app-e-web
Molinaro, M. (2025). *Standards and interoperability* [Presentation slides]. INAF. Retrieved from https://indico.ict.inaf.it/event/2870/contributions/18609/attachments/9174/18880/Standards_Interoperability.pdf
Mons, B., Neylon, C., Velterop, J., Dumontier, M., da Silva Santos, L. B., & Bourne, P. E. (2017). Revisiting the 'FAIR' data guiding principles for scientific data management. *Communications of the ACM, 60*(11), 40–42. https://doi.org/10.1145/3135441
Morando, F. (2013). Legal interoperability: Making Open Government Data Compatible with Businesses and Communities. *JLIS.it, 4*(1) Retrieved from https://doi.org/10.4403/jlis.it-8608

Mortara, A., & Scramaglia, R. (Eds.). (2023). *AM-RS volume lumi*. Retrieved from https://apeiron.iulm.it/retrieve/c6e485df-8451-4fe5-a1dc-f205fa04f14d/AM-RS%20VOLUME%20LUMI%2010-07-23%20DEF%20seconde%20bozze.pdf

NextGenHeritage. (2025). *Open Science: la scienza aperta a tutti, una grande sfida*. Retrieved from https://www.nextgenheritage.it/open-science-la-scienza-aperta-a-tutti-una-grande-sfida/

OGS NODC. (2021). *Open Science*. Retrieved from https://nodc.ogs.it/about/openscience?-1.-localelist-0-localelink

Open Research Europe. (2021). *Open Research Europe*. Retrieved from https://open-research-europe.ec.europa.eu/articles/5-250

Open Science Italia. (2024a, May 22). *The National Plan for Open Science*. Retrieved from https://open-science.it/en/article?rpk=289720

Open Science Italia. (2024b, October 16). *Infrastrutture condivise per la ricerca multi-scala nelle scienze della vita e della Terra*. Retrieved from https://open-science.it/article?rpk=309364

Open Science Italia. (2024c, August 23). *Superare le barriere alla condivisione dei dati*. Retrieved from https://open-science.it/article?rpk=302464

Oracle. (2025). *Cloud adoption framework: Era della scalabilità*. Retrieved from https://docs.oracle.com/it-it/iaas/Content/cloud-adoption-framework/era-scalability.htm

Rainey, L., van der Meer, P., & Kater, G. (2023). FAIR data sharing: An international perspective on why and how research data should be shared. *Data & Policy, 5*, e30. https://doi.org/10.1017/dap.2023.23

Salvatori, E. (Ed.). (2021). *AIPH 2020—Book of abstract*. Italian Association of Public History. Retrieved from https://iris.unito.it/retrieve/e27ce435-7306-2581-e053-d805fe0acbaa/BoA_AIPH2020_v_1_5.pdf

SBA Unisalento. (n.d.). *Cos'è la scienza aperta*. Retrieved from https://sba.unisalento.it/cos-%C3%A8-la-scienza-aperta

Scuola Normale Superiore (SNS). (2023). *Open Science nei progetti di ricerca*. Retrieved from https://www.sns.it/it/guida/open-science-nei-progetti-di-ricerca

University of Bologna. (2025). *Open Science*. Retrieved from https://www.unibo.it/it/ricerca/open-science

University of Florence. (n.d.). *Dati FAIR, dati sensibili e privacy*. http://www.unifi.it/it/ricerca-e-innovazione/ricerca/scienza-aperta-ateneo/dati-fair-dati-sensibili-e-privacy

University of L'Aquila. (n.d.). *Cosa si intende per Open Science*. Retrieved from https://www.univaq.it/include/utilities/blob.php?item=file&table=allegato&id=6991

University of Milano-Bicocca. (2024). *Osservatorio open data*. Retrieved from https://ogd.sociologia.unimib.it/osservatorio-open-data/

University of Padua. (n.d.). *Open Science*. Retrieved from https://biblio.unipd.it/en/digital-library/about-publishing/open-science

van der Zwaan, H. J. J., Dros, M. J., & van Hage, W. R. (2024). Towards the development of interoperable open data ecosystems. *Proceedings of the 17th international conference on pervasive technologies related to assistive environments* (pp. 469–476). https://doi.org/10.1145/3660507.3664062

Wikipedia Contributors. (2024a, November 9). *Open Science*. Wikipedia. Retrieved from https://it.wikipedia.org/wiki/Open_science

Wikipedia Contributors. (2024b, October 22). *Web interoperability*. Wikipedia. Retrieved from https://en.wikipedia.org/wiki/Web_interoperability

Wilkinson, M. D., Dumontier, M., Aalbersberg, I. J., Appleton, G., Axton, M., Baak, A., Blomberg, N., Boiten, J.-W., da Silva Santos, L. B., Bourne, P. E., Bouwman, J., Brookes, A. J., Clark, T., Crosas, M., Dillo, I., Dumon, O., Evelo, C. T., Finkers, R., Gonzalez-Beltran, A., et al. (2016). The FAIR Guiding Principles for scientific data management and stewardship. *Scientific Data, 3*, Article 160018. https://doi.org/10.1038/sdata.2016.18

# Chapter 13
# Governance and Collaboration for Impact

**Daniele Bruschi, Diana D'Alterio, Daniela De Gregorio, Antonio De Lorenzo, Alessia Fava, Maria Elisa Rosati, Massimiliano Saccone, and Marco Sprocati**

## 13.1 Introduction

Research infrastructures (RIs) have assumed an increasingly central role within contemporary knowledge systems, reflecting their strategic relevance in sustaining scientific progress and innovation across disciplinary domains. Beyond providing technological resources or data services, RIs operate as complex ecosystems in which governance frameworks, operational practices, and broader societal expectations intersect and co-evolve (Gutleber, 2026). Within the Social Sciences and Humanities (SSH), this complexity becomes even more pronounced. RIs are expected not only to support scientific research, but also to enable collaboration across institutions, disciplines, and communities, while adhering to the principles of openness, transparency, and long-term sustainability.

D. Bruschi (✉) · M. Saccone
Department of Social Science and Humanities, Cultural Heritage—CNR (DSU-CNR), National Research Council of Italy, Rome, Italy
e-mail: daniele.bruschi@cnr.it; massimiliano.saccone@cnr.it

D. D'Alterio · D. De Gregorio · A. De Lorenzo
Institute for Mediterranean Studies—CNR (ISMED-CNR), National Research Council of Italy, Naples, Italy
e-mail: diana.dalterio@ismed.cnr.it; daniela.degregorio@ismed.cnr.it; antonio.delorenzo@cnr.it

A. Fava · M. Sprocati
Institute for Research on Sustainable Economic Growth—CNR (IRCrES-CNR), National Research Council of Italy, Rome, Italy
e-mail: alessia.fava@cnr.it; marco.sprocati@cnr.it

M. E. Rosati
Institute of Cognitive Sciences and Technologies—CNR (ISTC-CNR), National Research Council of Italy, Rome, Italy
e-mail: mariaelisa.rosati@cnr.it



G. Cerulli, E. Reale (eds.), *Research Infrastructures for Open Science in Social Science Research*, https://doi.org/10.1007/978-3-032-29575-0_13

Understanding how research infrastructures operate therefore requires moving beyond a strictly technological perspective. Their effectiveness depends on the interplay between institutional constraints and their capacity to generate value for both scientific communities and society at large. Governance mechanisms, resource coordination, regulatory compliance, and impact generation do not constitute separate dimensions; rather, they form an integrated system that shapes the infrastructure's overall performance and resilience.

FOSSR, conceived as a national research infrastructure dedicated to supporting open and collaborative research in the social sciences, embodies these dynamics. Its model integrates technological innovation with a governance architecture designed to engage a diverse set of stakeholders—including research institutions, policymakers, and public actors—and mirrors broader European efforts to promote open science, interdisciplinary collaboration, and evidence-based policymaking.

This chapter examines the FOSSR initiative through a systemic perspective that highlights the interactions between governance structures, operational constraints, and impact generation. By analysing these interconnected dimensions, the chapter proposes a conceptual framework for understanding how research infrastructures evolve within complex institutional environments and how they produce scientific and societal value.

## 13.2 Multi-Stakeholder Governance Model: The Living Architecture of FOSSR

Within the Social Sciences and Humanities (SSH) domain, recent governance trends highlight a strong commitment to long-term sustainability planning, the seamless incorporation of digital technologies, and the design of more sophisticated strategies for public engagement. Increasingly, institutions are also prioritising collaborative approaches that enhance transparency and foster interdisciplinary dialogue, recognising these elements as essential to addressing emerging societal challenges. Taken together, these orientations reflect a broader shift towards governance models that are more adaptive, inclusive, and future-oriented (ESFRI, 2024). To better understand these emerging governance trends, it is useful to situate them within the broader scholarly debate on how governance has been conceptualised across different contexts.

Governance has long been a subject of research in many different forms. it is an important concept in innovation and knowledge sharing networks, particularly in relation to their effectiveness (Zyzak, 2024). O'Toole and Meier (2003) define "governance" as the production and regulation of rules, norms and actions within a network. According to Moore (2021), governance differs from management, as it does not concern the day-to-day operations of an organisation. Rather governance is more strategic and refers to the structures and values that shape an organisation's work, including the accountability and oversight of structures and values. Powell

(1990) characterises governance as a "distinct form of coordinating economic activity." Similarly, Lijun and Wei (1998) describe governance as "the way the rules, norms and actions are produced, sustained, regulated and held accountable." In this sense, governance encompasses both the coordination of activities within a network and the processes through which the norms and rules enabling such coordination are produced, maintained, and subjected to accountability (Neelis, 2020).

Organisation studies have identified comparable governance mechanisms, often described as tight (or crisp) and loose (or fuzzy) governance (Butler et al., 1998; Hofman et al., 2017). While tight governance promotes structure, clarity and formalised coordination within a network, loose governance favours flexibility and encourages more active participation among its members. These two modes influence network effectiveness in different ways: tight governance tends to enhance efficiency yet may become restrictive in dynamic or rapidly evolving contexts (Weick, 1976). Conversely, loose governance can foster adaptability, although insufficient guidance may also generate uncertainty among actors. The inherent tension between efficiency and adaptability underscores the need for an integrated approach capable of balancing both dimensions to ensure overall network effectiveness (Butler et al., 1998). In this light, the long-term sustainability of research infrastructures depends on governance arrangements that are simultaneously robust and adaptable, and grounded in trust and growing forms of mutuality. According to the European Open Science Cloud Association (EOSC, 2017), such a governance model should be guided by the principles of representability, proportionality, accountability, inclusiveness and transparency, ensuring that decision-making processes remain both legitimate and responsive over time. These considerations provide a coherent analytical bridge to the case of FOSSR, where such governance principles are concretely operationalised within a multi stakeholder research ecosystem.

Entering the FOSSR ecosystem—the Italian Open Cloud for Social Science Research—means encountering far more than a technological platform. FOSSR is, at its core, a collective endeavour: a shared environment where researchers, organisations, and communities come together to reshape how social science knowledge is produced, shared, and mobilised within contemporary society.

At the heart of this initiative lies a distinctive governance architecture—purposefully multi-stakeholder—designed to incorporate and balance the perspectives of the diverse actors involved in its development. Because it hinges on shared resources and on decision-making processes that engage multiple constituencies (researchers, policymakers, industry representatives and the public), a collaborative governance model was identified as the most appropriate approach for these contextual specificities (Ostrom, 1990; Poteete, 2010; Jürgens et al., 2024). The model derives its dynamism from a constellation of values that define the infrastructure's identity. These values are not abstract statements of intent; they constitute the foundational principles upon which FOSSR's scientific, organisational, and ethical framework is built.

Together, these values form the ethical and operational compass of FOSSR: a commitment to ethical and accountable research practices; equitable and transparent data governance; recognition that collaborative networking is not a secondary

**Fig. 13.1** FOSSR purpose, vision and mission

element but a precondition for scientific vitality; an innovation oriented mindset that challenges established boundaries; sustained attention to environmental and institutional sustainability; comprehensive adoption of Open Science principles; and the continuous promotion of diversity, equality, and inclusion. Taken collectively, these principles nurture an institutional culture in which scientific rigour in data practices coexists with social responsibility and openness, enabling a deeper understanding of the complex realities of contemporary society.

Anchored in these guiding principles, FOSSR has articulated a coherent strategic framework for its long-term development (see Fig. 13.1).

Its purpose is to develop tools and resources that enable scholars to systematically investigate and interpret Italy's evolving economic and social landscape. This purpose is further articulated in FOSSR's vision, which aims to cultivate an open ecosystem in which disciplinary expertise, research communities, and data infrastructures are meaningfully integrated to support rigorous evidence-based research and informed policy-making.

These orientations are operationalised through a concrete and ambitious mission: the establishment of the first Italian Open Cloud dedicated to the social sciences, with completion targeted for 2026. The project's guiding principle—"Join FOSSR: empower your social science research"—encapsulates this institutional commitment, expressing its aspiration toward openness, capacity-building, and empowerment.

Regarding the implementation of FOSSR's mission, it is organised around a strategic architecture designed to manage the critical transition from project inception to full institutional consolidation. The years 2024–2026 represent a decisive phase in this evolution. As the National Recovery and Resilience Plan (NRRP) funding approaches its conclusion, the infrastructure is moving beyond its startup phase and progressively establishing itself as a stable and sustainable institutional actor. This transition is guided by six closely interconnected strategic lines that collectively shape FOSSR's trajectory.

1. A first line of action concerns the transformation of FOSSR from an NRRP-funded project into a sustainable structure capable of ensuring long-term governance and financial continuity. The objective is to convert an initiative initially supported by extraordinary public investment into a lasting research infrastructure equipped with clear, reproducible, and transparent management processes. Securing services continuity beyond the initial investment requires the devel-

opment of robust sustainability models combining public funding, institutional collaboration, and potential contributions from the scientific community. This transition therefore marks a shift from a project-based approach to a firmly institutional perspective.

2. Closely linked to this goal is the establishment of a dedicated legal entity capable of representing FOSSR both nationally and internationally. An autonomous legal form will allow the infrastructure to operate with full administrative, governance, and negotiating capacity. This step is essential for strengthening visibility, participating effectively in European networks, formalizing agreements, and managing service provision with transparency and accountability. A clear legal framework also provides long-term stability and facilitates the integration of new partners.
3. A further strategic priority concerns dissemination and outreach to scholars, institutions, and policymakers. Effectively communicating the opportunities and results generated by FOSSR is crucial for expanding its impact and fostering the adoption of open and sustainable research practices. Activities in this domain include communication initiatives, training programmes, and engagement actions aimed at raising awareness among diverse audiences. Through this proactive approach, FOSSR positions itself not only as a provider of services but also as an agent of cultural transformation within the national and international research landscape.
4. Benchmarking and networking with research infrastructures in Italy and abroad constitute another essential line of action. Systematic comparison with other infrastructures enables FOSSR to assess the effectiveness of its organisational and technological solutions while identifying best practices and areas for improvement. Networking activities support participation in European consortia, the creation of strategic alliances, and integration within established international ecosystems, thereby situating FOSSR within a rapidly evolving global context.
5. Another crucial dimension of the strategic framework involves clustering user communities to align services with the diverse needs that characterise contemporary research. The user base is highly heterogeneous in terms of disciplines, methods, and levels of digital maturity, and therefore requires flexible and tailored services. Clustering enables the identification of homogeneous groups of researchers and institutions, facilitating the design of tools and pathways adapted to their specific needs. Through this approach, the infrastructure strengthens its role as a responsive and inclusive support system attentive to the diversity of research practices.
6. Finally, FOSSR places strong emphasis on fostering transdisciplinarity and innovation, particularly through the integration of technological advancement with practices of social innovation. This line of action recognises that contemporary societal challenges demand approaches capable of overcoming traditional disciplinary boundaries and fostering cross-domain collaboration. By encouraging experimental methodologies, supporting emerging technologies, and promoting the co-creation of knowledge, FOSSR aims to cultivate an environment conducive to developing shared solutions to complex societal needs.

### 13.2.1 FOSSR Business Model Canvas

The FOSSR Business Model Canvas provides a comprehensive analytical framework that outlines the fundamental components required for the functioning and long-term sustainability of the infrastructure. Beyond simply listing elements, it offers a structured means of visualizing how FOSSR generates value for its diverse user communities and how this value is produced, delivered, and maintained over time.

At the core of the canvas are the key actors—both internal and external—whose collaboration enables the development and continuous evolution of FOSSR. These include research institutions, service providers, technological partners, and the communities engaged in open research practices. The model also identifies the activities and resources required to sustain the infrastructure, ranging from technological development and data stewardship to expert consultation, training programmes, and governance mechanisms. Together, these components articulate what is operationally necessary for FOSSR to function as a national Research Infrastructure.

Central to the canvas is the value proposition, which defines the specific benefits FOSSR offers to its target users: reliable open-science services, expert support, shared tools, and a coordinated environment that promotes sustainable research practices. This value is framed in relation to user needs, which vary widely across disciplines, institutions, and levels of digital maturity.

The canvas further maps the relationships FOSSR establishes with its users, highlighting mechanisms for engagement, support, and long-term community building. It also identifies the channels through which services, information, and training opportunities are delivered, including digital platforms, institutional partnerships, and outreach activities.

The business model additionally addresses the financial dimension, outlining the elements that contribute to long-term economic sustainability beyond the initial funding phase. This includes resource planning, diversified funding streams, and the alignment of financial strategies with the broader mission of fostering open, accessible, and high-quality research.

Overall, the FOSSR Business Model Canvas offers a clear and consolidated overview of the infrastructure's operational ecosystem. It helps identify the prerequisites for delivering high-value services and clarifies the roles of tools, experts, and researchers who contribute to FOSSR's mission as a Research Infrastructure (Fig. 13.2).

### 13.2.2 A Governance Woven from Many Voices

FOSSR brings together an unusually diverse ecosystem that includes CNR institutes, universities, research centres, ministries and public administrations, private

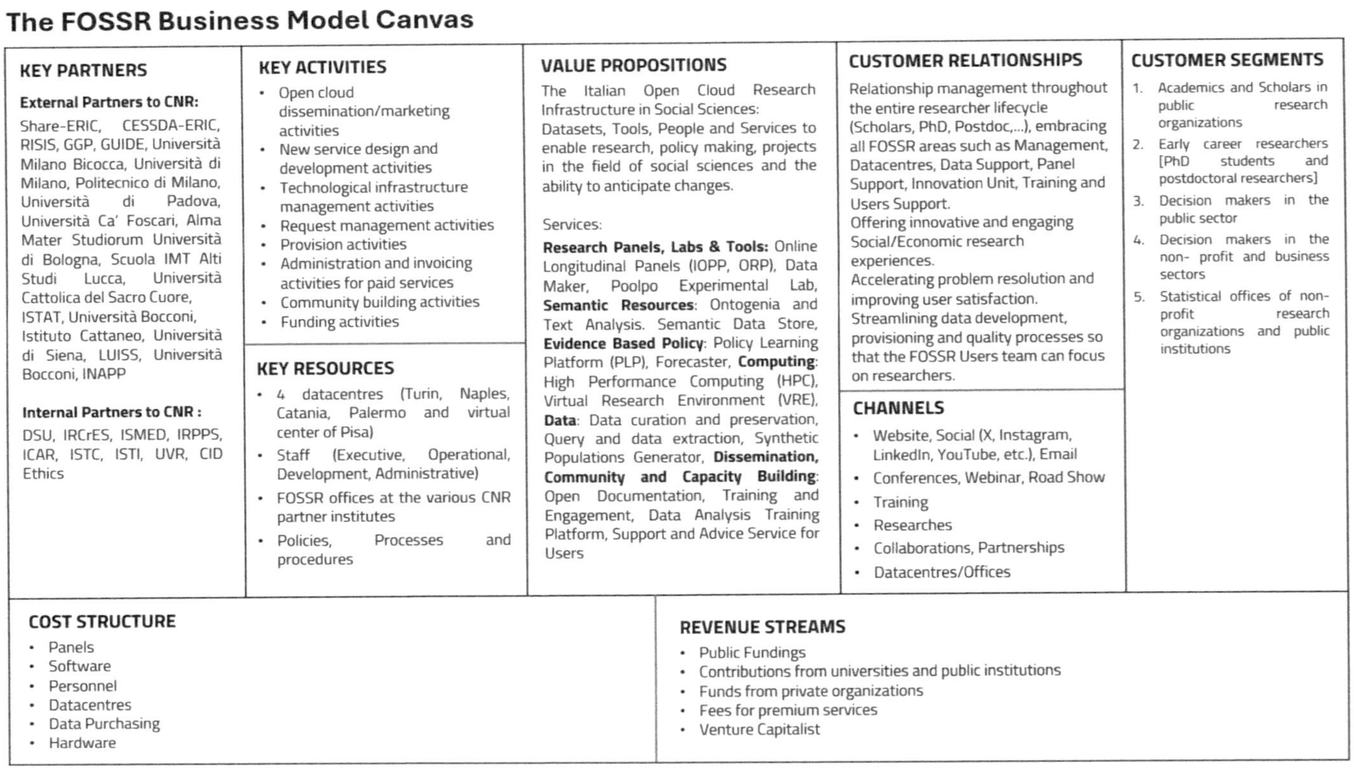


**Fig. 13.2** FOSSR business model canvas

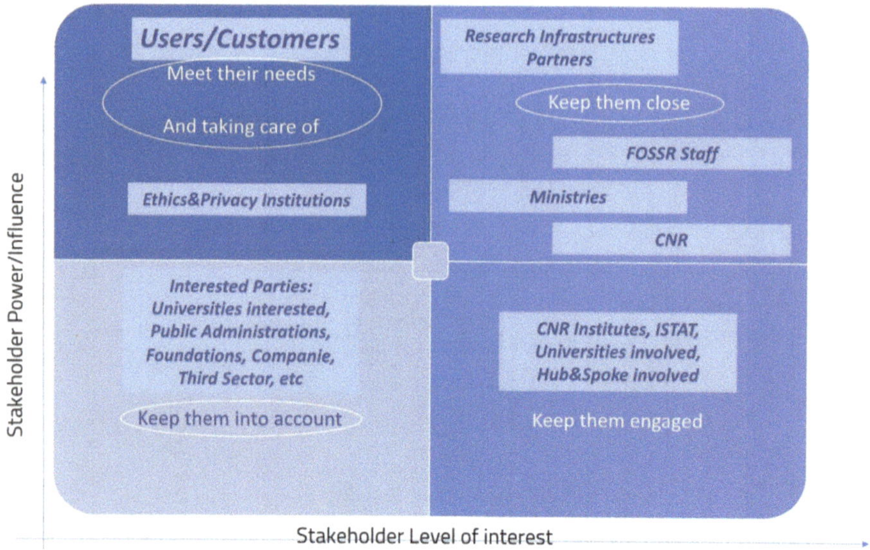


**Fig. 13.3** FOSSR stakeholders matrix

actors, third-sector organisations, NRRP Hub & Spoke ecosystems, and international partners. To navigate this complexity, FOSSR adopts a structured stakeholder-mapping approach based on two core dimensions: level of influence and degree of interest.

This analysis identifies four groups:

- **Keep them close**: actors with high influence and high interest (RI partners, FOSSR staff, ministries, CNR).
- **Meet their needs**: high influence but lower interest (users/customers, ethics and privacy institutions).
- **Keep them engaged**: lower influence but strong interest (participating CNR institutes, institutional partners).
- **Keep them in view**: low influence and low interest (Stakeholder Advisory Board members).

This framework is not merely descriptive; it directly informs communication strategies, partnership development, and broader strategic decisions (Fig. 13.3).

A clear understanding of who interacts with a research infrastructure is essential for shaping services that are both effective and inclusive. Because FOSSR's mission requires engagement with a wide and heterogeneous community—each group characterised by specific practices, expectations, and levels of readiness—stakeholder mapping becomes a foundational step for designing tools, support mechanisms, and policies able to respond to the evolving landscape of social science research.

**Table 13.1** FOSSR typology of users/customers

| Tipology of users and descriptions | |
|---|---|
| Category | Description |
| Academics and scholars in public research organizations | An academic is a member of a university or college who teaches or does research. A research scholar is a college student or graduate who works on projects in a specific field for a university or organization. As a research scholar, he works with professors and other professionals in his field of study and focuses on uncovering new information that can be published in academic or trade journals |
| Early career researchers (PhD students and postdoctoral researchers with less than 5–8 years of post-PhD experience) | A postdoctoral fellow, postdoctoral researcher, or simply postdoc, is a person professionally conducting research after the completion of their doctoral studies (typically a PhD). Postdocs most commonly, but not always, have a temporary academic appointment, sometimes in preparation for an academic faculty position |
| Decision makers in the public sector | A decision maker is someone who creates ideas and plans, especially those carried out by a government or public institution. A mayor, a school board, a corporation's board of directors, and Minister are all policy makers. Policy refers to the plans that a government or public institution follows |
| Decision makers in the non-profit and business sectors | A non-profit or business decision maker is the person or group of individuals who is responsible for making strategically important decisions based on several variables, including time constraints, resources available, the amount and type of information available and the number of stakeholders involved |
| Statistical offices of non-research organizations and public institutions | A non-profit or public institution that collects and studies detailed information about a country or local economy |

User identification is central to this process. FOSSR serves a broad range of stakeholders, including:

- academics and scholars,
- early career researchers,
- public-sector decision-makers,
- actors from the nonprofit and business sectors,
- statistical offices.

Understanding user types and volumes enables targeted service design, efficient resource allocation, stronger collaboration, enhanced user experience, more relevant policy development, and more robust impact assessment (Tables 13.1 and 13.2).

**Table 13.2** Strategic targeting of FOSSR users/customers

| User segmentation for strategic targeting | |
|---|---|
| Category | Description |
| Academics and Scholars in public research organizations (included public and private universities) | It is estimated that there are 18,543 researchers in public and private universities (Source: ISTAT 18/01/2025)<br>It is estimated that there are: Area 13—Economics and Statistics: 5858 academics Area 14—Political and Social Sciences: 2046 academics TOTAL: 7904 academics (Source: to date: 18/01/2025, taken from the MUR portal 'Cerca Università') |
| Early career researchers (PhD students and postdoctoral researchers) | It is estimated that Early career researchers in Social Sciences are: 1352 (Source: Open data—MUR 2023) |
| Decision makers in the public sector | Considering different levels of government (national, regional and local) we can estimate 3000 public policy makers |
| Decision makers in the non-profit and business | Considering the companies that draw up the sustainability report, it is estimated that in 2025 there will be 7.800 (Source: https://www.eutekne.info)<br>While for the Third Sector there are estimated to be 1403 researchers (Source: ISTAT 18.01.2025) |
| Statistical offices of non-research organizations and public institutions | ISTAT |

### 13.2.3 *Scientific Prospects Beyond the NRRP Horizon*

As FOSSR approaches the end of the NRRP phase, the infrastructure enters a stage in which the foundations established through initial investments must evolve into long-term scientific development. This transition requires not only continuity of the services already in place, but also the capacity to anticipate emerging needs in the social sciences and integrate innovative research practices. The following directions outline how FOSSR plans to expand its scope, strengthen its scientific relevance, and position itself as a key actor within national and international research ecosystems in the years ahead.

In the next phase, FOSSR aims to broaden the Italian Open Science Cloud by extending its coverage to a wider range of social science disciplines, ensuring that researchers across fields can benefit from shared resources and interoperable services. At the same time, the infrastructure intends to consolidate and expand international cooperation, deepening relationships with research networks and infrastructures abroad to foster methodological alignment and knowledge exchange.

A central priority will be the enhancement of data quality through a more systematic implementation of the FAIR principles, enabling research outputs that are transparent, reusable, and machine-actionable. This effort will be accompanied by the integration of new digital and real-time data sources, which are increasingly necessary for analysing fast-moving social phenomena. Building on this enriched data environment, FOSSR plans to develop advanced analytical tools, including applications of artificial intelligence, machine learning, and simulation techniques, thereby increasing its ability to support complex modelling and predictive research. These innovations will ultimately enable real-time policy evaluation and contribute to more effective evidence-based policymaking across institutional levels.

Ensuring sustainability in this new phase will depend on securing diversified funding streams, implementing more resilient financial strategies, fostering continuous skills development among staff, and achieving full integration into both national and European scientific frameworks. Together, these elements will ensure that the infrastructure remains robust, future-oriented, and capable of supporting the evolving needs of the research community.

In parallel with scientific and technological development, FOSSR will intensify its engagement with the public and with key societal actors. This will be pursued through educational programmes, outreach events, workshops, focus groups, and structured dialogue with civil society. Such activities are essential for promoting open-science literacy, strengthening public trust in scientific evidence, and ensuring that research practices remain aligned with the expectations and needs of broader communities. Collaboration with a diverse range of stakeholders—from government institutions to nongovernmental organisations—will further reinforce the societal relevance of FOSSR's mission and enhance the infrastructure's ability to respond to emerging social challenges.

Supporting this long-term evolution also requires a robust organisational architecture. FOSSR envisages a structure articulated across multiple levels of governance and operation. At the strategic level, a Supervisory Board will provide overall direction and oversight, while a dedicated Secretariat will support decision-making processes and ensure coordination across the infrastructure. Day-to-day management will be entrusted to a Management Board composed of functional managers responsible for translating strategic objectives into operational actions. These governance bodies will be complemented by specialised operational units tasked with cloud coordination, the management of longitudinal data, innovation in data analysis, training activities, user support, and administrative functions. Taken together, this organisational model is designed to balance scientific ambition with long-term operational stability (Fig. 13.4).

Personnel constitute the cornerstone of this institutional stability. Recognising their centrality, FOSSR has developed comprehensive policies aimed at attracting, developing, and retaining highly qualified professionals. These policies prioritise the creation of clear and appealing career pathways within the research-infrastructure sector, support exchange programmes that enable staff to acquire diverse expertise

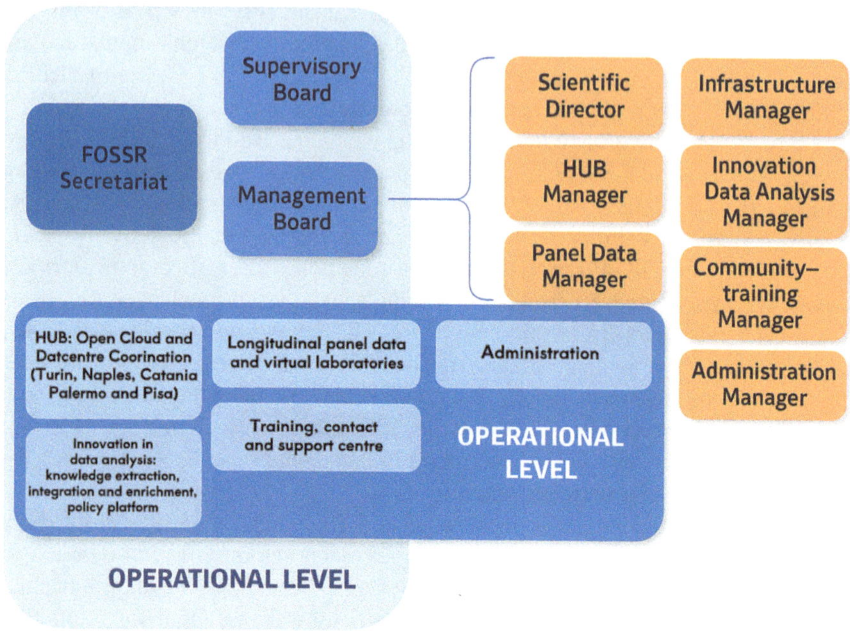


**Fig. 13.4** FOSSR Organizational structure after NRRP (a first hypothesis)

and build international networks, and advocate for stronger institutional and national recognition of research-infrastructure careers as a legitimate and valued professional trajectory. They are complemented by a firm commitment to gender balance and equality across all organisational levels. Through these integrated measures, FOSSR seeks not only to recruit competent personnel but to cultivate a skilled, diverse, and deeply committed community capable of sustaining and advancing a world-class research infrastructure over the long term.

## 13.3 Constraint Management

Constraint management prioritizes identifying and managing the limited factors that restrict system performance rather than optimizing isolated activities (Cox & Spencer, 1997). Rooted in the Theory of Constraints (TOC), it conceptualizes organizations as systems governed by bottlenecks that may be physical, organizational, regulatory, or behavioural. Goldratt and Cox (1984) define five focusing steps that guide this approach: identifying the constraint, exploiting it, subordinating other activities to it, elevating it, and reassessing the system to prevent inertia. Emphasis is placed on throughput and flow protection, particularly in complex and regulation-driven environments where delays and inefficiencies can quickly propagate.

Originally derived from Optimized Production Technology in the late 1970s, TOC became widely known in industrial operations (Watson et al., 2007) and subsequently expanded into logistics, performance measurement, and structured problem solving (Spencer & Cox, 1995). Throughput Accounting shifted attention from local efficiency to system-level output, while logical thinking processes provided systematic diagnostic tools. Goldratt later applied TOC to project environments through Critical Chain Project Management (Goldratt, 1997), highlighting time as a primary constraint.

As TOC matured, it evolved into a strategic governance paradigm for complex systems where constraints are often intangible and linked to administrative capacity, regulatory compliance, or stakeholder alignment. Its integration with Lean, Six Sigma, and digital tools increasingly supports real-time bottleneck detection and constraint management in knowledge-intensive and highly regulated environments. In this perspective, TOC offers a conceptual framework for improving performance in interdependent systems operating under uncertainty and rigid regulation—conditions that are typical of public research infrastructures.

Within research infrastructures, constraint management becomes central to ensuring sustainability and scientific excellence. These infrastructures are capital-intensive, long-lived systems that operate at technological frontiers and involve multiple stakeholders (Hallonsten, 2020), which amplifies the challenge of identifying and addressing constraints. They function as dynamic ecosystems that integrate digital resources, human capital, and advanced technologies within European networks. Constraint management therefore acquires a strategic role in supporting adaptation to financial, technological, and social limits. It involves identifying limiting factors and balancing scope, time, cost, quality, resources, risk, and IT systems across the project lifecycle. Relevant domains include strategic planning, risk assessment, data governance, business models, and access policies.

Research on large projects further clarifies the nature of constraints in these contexts. Miller and Lessard (2000) distinguish between "hard" constraints—technical and financial—and "soft" constraints—institutional and political—with the latter often determining project outcomes. Flyvbjerg et al. (2003) relate megaproject overruns to cognitive and governance biases, while Shenhar and Dvir (2007) argue that high-complexity projects require adaptive and flexible approaches, a principle that applies equally to research infrastructures.

These dynamics become particularly evident in projects funded under the NRRP and managed within the regulatory framework of the National Research Council. In such projects, quality encompasses scientific outcomes as well as compliance with regulatory, administrative, and time-related requirements. In multi-actor infrastructures, dominant constraints are often non-technical and include deadlines, administrative capacity, governance structures, and coordination mechanisms. TOC principles support flow protection and systemic alignment in these contexts. Regulation (EU) 2021/241 and Decree-Law No. 77/2021 (converted into Law No. 108/2021) define quality through milestone achievement, expenditure correctness, traceability, verifiability, and timely implementation. Ensuring consistency

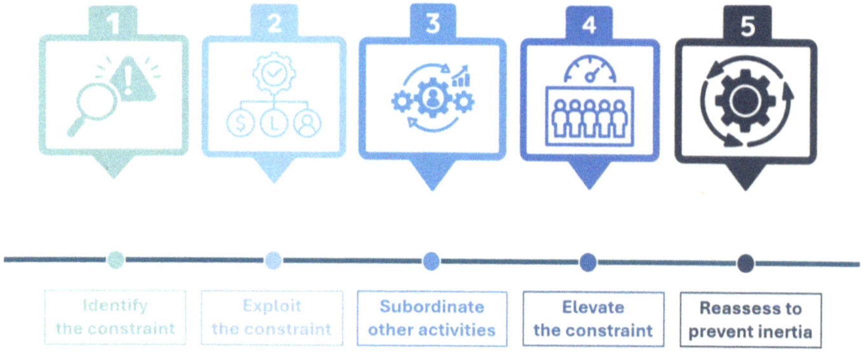


**Fig. 13.5** The five focusing steps in TOC (source: authors' reworking image starting from Brown, 2026)

between activities, outputs, and objectives is another key indicator of project quality. Economic quality further requires compliance with eligibility and reporting rules, while procurement compliance under Legislative Decree No. 36/2023 ensures the integrity of processes. In this environment, constraint management becomes a core component of quality assurance.

Time constraints also play a decisive role in European-funded projects, where strict deadlines create conditions of "time scarcity." Time compression generates trade-offs between cost, quality, and risk (Stalk & Hout, 1990), and in NRRP implementation, the need for speed must be balanced with administrative rigor and stakeholder consultation. Project teams respond to these pressures through pacing strategies and synchronization with external cycles (Ancona et al., 2001). Aligning institutional decision processes, procurement timelines, and EU milestones requires carefully structured temporal coordination.

Another systemic factor shaping project performance is administrative capacity, understood as the combination of skills, procedures, resources, and organizational culture. As noted by Painter and Pierre (2005), administrative capacity frequently constrains public policy implementation. In Italy, hiring freezes, generational turnover, and limited digitization have produced structural deficits. Institutional fragmentation and overlapping competences further slow implementation and increase transaction costs (North, 1990), pressures that are intensified under the NRRP. Relatedly, the concept of "capability traps" (Andrews et al., 2017) highlights how reforms may inadvertently reduce effective capacity, generating additional bureaucracy and procedural formalism. Overcoming administrative constraints therefore requires not only investments in training and resources but also process redesign, clearer responsibilities, and improved incentive structures (Fig. 13.5).

### *13.3.1 Italian PNRR Architecture for Research and Its Main Constraints*

The Italian National Recovery and Resilience Plan (PNRR), approved in 2021, allocates 191.5 billion euros for 2021–2026, with approximately 11.44 billion euros devoted to Mission 4, "Education and Research". Within this mission, Component 2, "From Research to Business", provides substantial support for research infrastructures through several complementary investment lines. These initiatives include the upgrading of existing ESFRI and national facilities, the creation of new infrastructures in fields related to the digital and ecological transitions, the development of advanced computational and data infrastructures, and the reinforcement of innovation and technology transfer mechanisms. The overarching objectives are to align Italian facilities with European standards, build capacity in emerging scientific domains, and strengthen linkages between public research and industry.

The governance architecture underpinning these investments is inherently complex. The Italian Ministry of University and Research (MUR) exercises overall strategic oversight, while major public research organisations—such as CNR, INFN, INAF, and INGV—serve as implementing entities, frequently in partnership with universities and other stakeholders. European institutions supervise transnational components, and an interministerial "Control Room" coordinates implementation at the national level. Although this multi-tiered structure facilitates accountability, it simultaneously generates coordination challenges, procedural heterogeneity, and potential misalignment across institutions characterised by divergent organisational cultures and administrative capacities.

A defining feature of the PNRR is the extreme compression of implementation timelines. EU regulations require all funds to be committed by 2023 and spent by August 2026, forcing research infrastructures—typically characterised by 10–15 year development cycles—to be delivered within 4–5 years. Milestones such as tender finalisation, contract award, start of construction or installation, intermediate functional steps, and full operationalisation must all occur within these rigid deadlines, with non-compliance risking delays or funding reductions. Time thus becomes the dominant constraint, pushing project leaders toward mature technological solutions, accelerated administrative procedures, simplified partnerships, and rapid recruitment and training strategies that may not fully align with long-term research needs.

At the same time, PNRR projects must operate within a dense and often rigid Italian regulatory framework. Public procurement rules, requiring extensive transparency and competition procedures, can produce significant delays between planning and delivery. Construction and installation activities must undergo planning compliance checks, environmental and heritage evaluations, and safety certifications, procedures that can take months or even years, particularly in protected or historic areas. Restrictions on public recruitment—such as mandatory open competitions, contractual limits, and rigid pay structures—further constrain the ability of institutions to hire specialised personnel or compete internationally.

Additional obligations related to safety, data protection, hazardous materials, and environmental compliance require highly specialised documentation and expertise, generating further delays and administrative burden.

Market dynamics introduce additional constraints. The simultaneous launch of numerous PNRR-funded initiatives across different sectors has created high demand for specialised equipment and professional skills, resulting in price increases, extended delivery times, and shortages of critical expertise. Global supply chains for advanced scientific instrumentation are highly concentrated and exposed to geopolitical volatility, and dependence on components such as semiconductors or specialised optics increases exposure to disruptions. Italy also faces structural shortages of data scientists, software engineers, advanced technicians, and cybersecurity experts, exacerbated by long-standing brain drain and insufficient technical training pathways.

Administrative capacity emerges as a systemic bottleneck. Many institutions lack the staff and specialist competences needed for complex project management, reporting obligations, and compliance with EU regulations. Years of hiring freezes and an ageing workforce have reduced organisational resilience, while the additional workload generated by the PNRR contributes to overload, errors, and delays. Skills in EU financial rules, digital reporting systems, and inter-institutional coordination are unevenly distributed, and the need for training competes with ongoing operational demands. Multi-partner projects require harmonisation of procedures and information systems, further complicating implementation.

Finally, significant technical constraints arise from the need to integrate diverse hardware and software components, often sourced from multiple suppliers and expected to interface with legacy systems and international standards. Integration risks can generate delays, cost overruns, or performance compromises. Dependence on specialised scientific software introduces uncertainties linked to development cycles, customisation needs, and licensing costs. Cybersecurity requirements impose additional architectural and monitoring needs, and balancing security with accessibility is particularly challenging in research environments. Looking beyond 2026, the long-term sustainability of the infrastructures represents another major concern. PNRR funds cover capital expenditure but seldom provide resources for operational costs—such as staff, maintenance, energy, consumables, or software licences—which may represent 10–20% of initial investments annually. Temporary contracts funded through the PNRR generate uncertainty and turnover, unless stabilisation plans are developed early. Moreover, the integration of new facilities into scientific ecosystems requires the gradual establishment of user communities, access policies, governance structures, and peer-review mechanisms—elements that demand time and resources but are not fully reflected in milestone-driven frameworks, raising the risk of underutilisation after the PNRR cycle ends.

Table 13.3 summarises the main categories of constraints affecting PNRR-funded actions, outlining the associated risks, the corresponding control and mitigation measures, and the relevant regulatory references that govern compliance and implementation.

**Table 13.3** Management of constraints within the risk and quality management framework

| Constraint | Associated risk | Control/mitigation measures | Regulatory references |
|---|---|---|---|
| Time constraint (milestones and targets) | Delays in achieving milestones, with risk of funding suspension or revocation | Detailed planning aligned with PNRR milestones; periodic progress monitoring; early-warning mechanisms and corrective actions | Regulation (EU) 2021/241; Decree-Law No. 77/2021, converted into Law No. 108/2021 |
| Scope constraint | Deviation from approved objectives; non-recognition of results | Systematic consistency checks between activities, outputs, and objectives; control of project variations; decision traceability | Regulation (EU) 2021/241; Funding agreements |
| Overall budget constraint | Budget overruns or inefficient allocation of resources | Periodic financial progress monitoring; alignment between physical progress and expenditure; priority review | Regulation (EU) 2021/241; Decree-Law No. 77/2021 |
| Eligibility of expenditure constraint | Disallowance of costs during audits; recovery of funds | Ex-ante eligibility verification; complete and traceable documentation; internal compliance checks | Regulation (EU) 2021/241; National PNRR guidelines |
| Procedural constraint (procurement and purchasing) | Operational delays; litigation; procedural irregularities | Application of the Public Procurement Code; early planning of procedures; administrative and specialist support | Legislative Decree No. 36/2023 |
| Regulatory and governance constraint | Non-compliance with transparency and control requirements; audit findings | Continuous alignment with regulatory provisions; procedural updates; internal audits | Regulation (EU) 2021/241; Decree-Law No. 77/2021 |
| Organizational constraint (human resources) | Insufficient operational | Clear allocation of responsibilities; skills planning; workload monitoring | General regulations on public sector organization |

### *13.3.2 How Constraint Management Has Been Implemented in FOSSR Project*

The implementation of the FOSSR project offers a concrete illustration of how constraint management can be operationalised within a large-scale research infrastructure funded under the PNRR framework. From the very beginning, the project team encountered constraints that could not be addressed through conventional schedule optimisation or resource redistribution alone. Consequently, FOSSR progressively adopted a constraint-oriented management logic aimed at safeguarding overall project flow within rigid regulatory and administrative conditions.

A central element supporting this approach was the adoption of a dedicated internal management platform specifically designed to enable integrated constraint monitoring (https://pm.fossr.eu/). The platform served as a unified governance environment, allowing for the systematic identification and documentation of constraints across all project dimensions—time, scope, organisation, compliance, reporting, and regulatory obligations. It also ensured continuous visibility over emerging interdependencies, assessment of potential impacts on milestones and territorial commitments, traceable documentation of mitigation measures, and alignment between operational decisions and PNRR regulatory requirements. Rather than treating constraints as isolated disruptions, this infrastructure enabled a flow-oriented and compliance-driven governance model in which each decision was evaluated for its systemic effects.

Against this backdrop, the following examples illustrate how individual constraints were managed during the project lifecycle:

- **Constraint 1—Time Constraint (Milestones and Targets)**
  Strict compliance with the milestones and targets defined under Regulation (EU) 2021/241 and Decree-Law No. 77/2021 rapidly emerged as a critical constraint. To safeguard the approved timeline, the project team carried out an internal rescheduling exercise that realigned operational activities without altering the official milestone structure.
- **Constraint 2—Organisational Constraint (Partner Withdrawal)**
  During April–June 2023 (bimesters 3 and 4), the withdrawal of partner UO9 (Bari Research Area) created a significant organisational discontinuity, particularly for Work Package 7. The governance responded by reassigning responsibility for these activities to ICAR (UO7), thereby preserving continuity and preventing disruption of the work package's outputs.
- **Constraint 3—Scope Constraint Linked to Project Duration**
  Between bimesters 4 and 5, a structural constraint emerged due to the incompatibility between the project's duration (30 months) and the minimum length of doctoral programmes (36 months). As timeline extensions were not permitted under PNRR rules, the constraint was managed at the level of project scope. The number of doctoral positions under Work Package 8 was reduced from 20 to 11, ensuring alignment with the approved schedule while safeguarding the project's training objectives and compliance with territorial investment obligations.
- **Constraint 4—Procedural and Administrative Constraint**
  In bimester 8, the entry into force of the new Public Procurement Code (Legislative Decree No. 36/2023) introduced a procedural constraint with immediate effects on procurement workflows. Rather than accelerating procedures at the risk of non-compliance, the project management opted for a controlled operational pause until internal processes and documentation were fully adapted to the

new regulatory framework. This decision exemplifies a compliance-prioritising approach in which procedural legitimacy takes precedence over execution speed.

- **Constraint 5—Reporting and Traceability Constraint**
  Throughout the initial phases, the delayed activation of the national GEA reporting platform represented an external constraint beyond the project's control. To mitigate its impact, FOSSR established internal systems for tracking activities, expenditures, and documentation, thereby ensuring continuous traceability and preparedness for retrospective reporting.
- **Constraint 6—DNSH (Do No Significant Harm) Constraint**
  Compliance with the DNSH principle, as required by Regulation (EU) 2021/241, represented a pervasive constraint governing all procurement and investment activities. DNSH verification influenced the selection of eligible technologies, the formulation of technical specifications, supplier eligibility criteria, and the timing of procurement procedures due to ex-ante checks.
- **Constraint 7–Minimum 40% Allocation of Investments to Southern Italy**
  The obligation to allocate at least 40% of investments to Southern Italy constrained the geographical distribution of infrastructures and activities. This requirement influenced decisions regarding the localisation of data centres, redistribution of tasks following the partner withdrawal, and assessment of alternative technical options. Notably, after the withdrawal of the Bari unit, the project reassigned the affected activities to another eligible southern site, thereby preserving the required territorial balance.
- **Constraint 8—Gender Balance in Recruitment (≥40% Female Participation)**
  The requirement to ensure a minimum of 40% female participation in recruitment introduced a further non-negotiable constraint. Beyond shaping recruitment outcomes, it influenced the design of the procedures themselves. Inclusive language, bias-reducing selection mechanisms, and continuous monitoring across reporting periods were adopted to ensure compliance.

## 13.4 Impact Evaluation of FOSSR Network

Over the past decades, the societal impact of research activities has become a topic of growing interest within research evaluation and science policy literature, encompassing contributions from both the scientific, technological, engineering, and mathematical (STEM) domains and the social sciences and humanities (SSH). This growing attention reflects the increasing expectation that research should address societal challenges and engage responsibly with society (Sivertsen & Meijer, 2025).

Despite this broad interest, no shared terminology or standardized methodology currently exists to support the definition and evaluation of research impacts. What is evident, however, is that the diversity and breadth of impacts require the use of a wide range of information sources and analytical approaches to adequately capture, measure, and monitor them (Reed et al., 2021). In this respect, the OECD's definition of impact as "the extent to which the intervention has generated or is expected to generate positive or negative, intended or unintended, higher-level effects" (OECD, 2021) underscores both the open-ended and temporally extended nature of impact processes. Moreover, impact may concern different audiences, including researchers, citizens, and governments, at the local, national, or global level (Dekker, 2019).

Within SSH disciplines in particular, several approaches have been developed to address the specific challenges associated with societal impact assessment. These approaches are grounded in the recognition that the impact of social science research on policy and practice is not readily captured through standard quantitative metrics, such as bibliometric indicators or citation counts. In this context, Meagher et al. (2008) propose the Flows of Knowledge approach, a model aimed at identifying and understanding the processes through which knowledge circulates, is debated, and is potentially taken up within policy-making and practice contexts.

Similarly, Spaapen and van Drooge (2011), noting the lack of robust instruments to measure the final impact of research activities, advance the Productive Interactions model. This framework conceptualizes social impact as a non-linear outcome emerging from dynamic interactions and joint efforts between academic researchers and societal actors, thereby promoting an evaluation approach oriented toward learning rather than mere accountability and reporting.

Building on these perspectives, Muhonen et al. (2020) argue that in many SSH research contexts impact is neither linear nor immediate and is often difficult to attribute to individual research outputs. They contend that focusing solely on interactions does not fully explain why some research generates impact while other research does not. To address this limitation, they introduce the concept of impact pathways, understood as cumulative, non-linear processes that connect interactions, contextual conditions, and change over time.

Further contributions emphasize the need for methodological pluralism in impact assessment. Reale et al. (2018) argue that, given the limitations associated with indicators in SSH research, effective impact assessment practices typically rely on the integration of narrative approaches with qualitative indicators and complementary quantitative measures. This combination allows for a more nuanced understanding of the multidimensional and context-dependent nature of complex societal phenomena. In line with this view, Molas-Gallart and Tang (2011) suggest that assessment methods should prioritize processes over outcomes, as this makes it possible to identify how relevant research is conducted and how, or whether, it is ultimately applied in practice. For systematic and comprehensive reviews of the literature on research impact assessment, see Bornmann (2013), Penfield et al. (2014), Pedersen et al. (2020), Smit and Hessels (2021), and Lykke et al. (2023).

These conceptual and methodological challenges are further compounded in the context of research infrastructures (RIs). As highlighted by Kolar et al. (2023), no uniform methodology currently exists to assess the impact of RIs, resulting in largely unstandardized approaches that hinder comparability and benchmarking. Moreover, research infrastructures are highly heterogeneous and therefore cannot be adequately evaluated using a single method or a fixed set of indicators. Emphasizing the complexity of the relationship between activities and impact, van Drooge (2018) stresses the existence of a long causal chain linking research processes to societal effects. Accordingly, assessing the impact of research infrastructures requires a focus on the underlying processes that lead to results and generate outcomes, rather than on final impacts alone.

Research infrastructures are not created as ends in themselves, but rather to generate positive enhancements in the lives and opportunities of the communities they target. Qiao et al. (2016) argue that RIs promote the advancement of scientific knowledge, stimulate technological innovation, support business competitiveness, and create new training and employment opportunities. As such, research infrastructures act as key drivers of socio-economic transformation, generating a wide range of multidimensional and interconnected impacts that contribute to the overall development of society. The knowledge produced by research infrastructures and their user communities can stimulate innovation and contribute to addressing major societal challenges, including climate change, health, energy, and ageing (Kolar et al., 2023). In addition, RIs enhance the capacity of regions to attract investment and foster international cooperation. Policymakers and funding agencies widely recognize that research, and research infrastructures in particular, generate impacts beyond the scientific domain and play a crucial role in supporting innovation-oriented policies (Ribeiro, 2021; Zakaria et al., 2021; Cao et al., 2025). Moreover, Vignetti (2021) considers RIs as unique learning environments. The ongoing demand for emerging skills—such as metadata management, semantics, ontologies, and digital resource stewardship—actively promotes the development of advanced, specialized scientific and technological expertise.

Consequently, assessing the critical contributions of research infrastructures to society and the economy has become increasingly important, alongside growing pressure to evaluate how RIs contribute not only to research but to society at large (Hajdinjak, 2019). This requires a multidimensional approach that goes beyond traditional research metrics (e.g. publications, citations, patents).

Instead, assessment frameworks must consider how RIs generate broader societal value, stimulate innovation, support policymaking, and contribute to regional cohesion and sustainable development (OECD, 2019). In this context, Catalano et al. (2021) suggest distinguishing between direct users of RIs—those who access facilities or participate directly in research projects—and indirect users, who benefit from research outcomes more broadly.

In line with this perspective, Griniece et al. (2020) argue that research infrastructures, in addition to their scientific impact, generate a large variety of socio-economic impacts that can be grouped into four major impact areas: (1) impact on human resources; (2) impact on the economy and innovation; (3) impact on society; and (4) impact on policy. While all four areas are relevant across different types of research infrastructures, the relative emphasis placed on each impact area may vary depending on the characteristics of the infrastructure, such as whether it is physical or virtual, single-sited or distributed, and whether it operates in the social sciences, humanities and arts, or in the natural sciences and engineering

**Fig. 13.6** Impact areas of FOSSR network

(Fabre et al., 2021). Catalano (2021), in examining the societal impact generated by RIs, distinguishes two subcategories: a) Outreach impacts, which refer to the contribution of RIs to the broader public. This dimension is specifically associated with outreach initiatives and public engagement activities that enhance citizens' awareness and understanding of scientific issues; b) Societal impacts, which pertain to the role of RIs in improving individual and collective wellbeing. These impacts are expressed through tangible improvements in the quality of life of individuals who directly benefit from the outputs and services generated by the RIs.

Considering the research infrastructures (RIs) involved, and the research activities carried out within FOSSR network, Fig. 13.6 provides a reference framework of the main impact areas that FOSSR, with its specific features, can generate.

Finally, FOSSR research infrastructures play a crucial role not only in contributing to the achievement of the 17 Sustainable Development Goals (SDGs) defined by the United Nations, but also in effectively interpreting, monitoring, and implementing them. Figure 13.7 shows the contributions that the RIs of the FOSSR network generate to some of the 17 SDGs.

**Fig. 13.7** Contributions of FOSSR network to the SDGs

In conclusion, research infrastructures play a pivotal role in enabling high-quality research and generating multidimensional impacts that extend well beyond the scientific domain. Their contribution emerges through complex, non-linear processes that involve interactions, knowledge flows, and long-term pathways of change. As the literature shows, capturing these dynamics requires methodological pluralism and assessment frameworks capable of integrating qualitative and quantitative evidence. The FOSSR network exemplifies this complexity, demonstrating how RIs can support human capital, innovation, societal, environmental, and policy impact areas, including contributions to the SDGs. Continued investment in adaptable yet robust evaluation approaches is therefore essential to fully understand and enhance the transformative potential of research infrastructures, ensuring comparability while respecting the specificities of diverse RIs.

## 13.5 Conclusion

The analysis presented in this chapter shows that the functioning of a research infrastructure cannot be reduced to its technological capabilities or to the volume of outputs it generates. Infrastructures such as FOSSR operate instead as complex socio-technical systems where governance arrangements, operational constraints, and impact processes continuously interact. Their effectiveness depends on the capacity to coordinate these dimensions while responding to institutional requirements, stakeholder expectations, and evolving research practices.

The FOSSR case demonstrates how a multi-stakeholder governance model can provide the strategic orientation needed to align diverse actors around shared objectives and values. Through structured decision-making, stakeholder engagement, and long-term planning, governance offers the framework within which the infrastructure's activities are defined and prioritised. At the same time, administrative, regulatory, and organisational constraints must be managed carefully to ensure that implementation remains coherent, efficient, and sustainable. In this perspective, constraints are not merely obstacles but integral components of the infrastructure's operational logic: by identifying and addressing the factors that most strongly influence project flow, the system can remain stable while still evolving.

Ultimately, the broader value of a research infrastructure becomes visible through the impacts it generates across scientific, institutional, and societal domains. These outcomes do not emerge from isolated actions but from the cumulative interactions between the infrastructure, its users, partner institutions, and the wider research ecosystem. Recognising and governing these interdependencies is therefore essential for ensuring that research infrastructures can translate their strategic mission into meaningful and lasting impact.

Ensuring that research infrastructures can truly fulfil their mission therefore requires not only robust technological systems, but governance models capable of transforming collaboration into impact—turning complexity into a strategic asset and enabling infrastructures to act as generative forces within the research ecosystem.

## References

Ancona, D. G., Okhuysen, G. A., & Perlow, L. A. (2001). Taking time to integrate temporal research. *Academy of Management Review, 26*(4), 512–529. https://doi.org/10.2307/3560239

Andrews, M., Pritchett, L., & Woolcock, M. (2017). *Building state capability: Evidence, analysis, action*. Oxford University Press.

Bornmann, L. (2013). What is societal impact of research and how can it be assessed? A literature survey. *Journal of the American Society for Information Science and Technology, 64*(2), 217–233. https://doi.org/10.1002/asi.22803

Brown, L. (2026). *Theory of constraints in project management: Comprehensive guide*. Retrieved February 26, 2026, from https://www.invensislearning.com

Butler, R. J., Price, D. H. R., Coates, P. D., & Pike, R. H. (1998). Organizing for innovation: Loose or tight control? *Long Range Planning, 31*(5), 775–782. https://doi.org/10.1016/S0024-6301(98)00082-X

Cao, Z., Zhang, L., Wang, Z., Li, C., & Sivertsen, G. (2025). How does scientific research generate impact beyond academia? Cross-disciplinary comparison based on REF impact cases. *Humanities and Social Sciences Communications, 12*(1856), 1–17. https://doi.org/10.1057/s41599-025-06129-4

Catalano, G. (2021). Thinking how to define and measure impacts of RIs. In H. P. Beck & P. Charitos (Eds.), *The economics of big science* (Science policy reports) (pp. 109–126). Springer.

Catalano, G., López, G. G., Sánchez, A., & Vignetti, S. (2021). From scientific experiments to innovation: Impact pathways of a synchrotron light facility. *Annals of Public and Cooperative Economics, 92*(3), 447–472. https://doi.org/10.1111/apce.12322

Cox, J. F., & Spencer, M. S. (1997). *The constraints management handbook*. CRC Press. https://doi.org/10.4324/9781003579137

Dekker, R. (2019). Impact of social science data services. In B. Maegaard, R. Pozzo, A. Melloni, & M. Woollard (Eds.), *Stay tuned to the future. Impact of research infrastructures for social sciences and humanities* (pp. 111–119). Olschki Editore.

European Open Science Cloud (EOSC). (2017). *EOSC declaration*. Retrieved February 26, 2026, from https://www.ouvrirlascience.fr/wp-content/uploads/2018/11/eosc_declaration.pdf

European Strategy Forum on Research Infrastructures—ESFRI. (2024). *ESFRI landscape analysis 2024*. Retrieved February 26, 2026, from https://landscape2024.esfri.eu/media/coqdoq0q/20240604_la2024.pdf

Fabre, R., Egret, D., Schöpfel, J., & Azeroual, O. (2021). Evaluating the scientific impact of research infrastructures: The role of current research information systems. *Quantitative Science Studies, 2*(1), 42–64. https://doi.org/10.1162/qss_a_00111

Flyvbjerg, B., Bruzelius, N., & Rothengatter, W. (2003). *Megaprojects and risk: An anatomy of ambition*. Cambridge University Press.

Goldratt, E. M. (1997). *Critical chain*. North River Press.

Goldratt, E. M., & Cox, J. F. (1984). *The goal: A process of ongoing improvement*. North River Press.

Griniece, E., Angelis, J., Reid, A., Vignetti, S., Catalano, J., Helman, A., Barberis Rami, M., & Kroll, H. (2020). *Guidebook for socio-economic impact assessment of research infrastructures*. Retrieved February 26, 2026, from https://doi.org/10.5281/zenodo.3950043

Gutleber, J. (2026). Research and technology infrastructures as strategic capability systems. *EPJ Research Infrastructures, 10*(1), 1–9. https://doi.org/10.1007/s41781-026-00158-7

Hajdinjak, M. (2019). *A practical guide: Assessment of socio-economic impacts of research infrastructures*. Retrieved February 26, 2026, from https://dtp.interreg-danube.eu/uploads/media/approved_project_output/0001/32/0b698b634cc4cc3df75dd303bdc3917f5ed6e2af.pdf

Hallonsten, O. (2020). Research infrastructures in Europe: The hype and the field. *European Review, 28*(4), 617–635.

Hofman, E., Halman, J. I. M., & Song, M. (2017). When to use loose or tight alliance networks for innovation? Empirical evidence. *Journal of Product Innovation Management, 34*(1), 81–100. https://doi.org/10.1111/jpim.12325

Jürgens, A., Tedeschi, G., D'Errico, G., Kilian, K., Zawadzki, K., Daniel, O., Leibfried, A., Poschet, G., Lau, L., & Helm-Petersen, N. (2024). Navigating the frontier: Research infrastructures, core facilities and a new paradigm at European Universities. *Cogent Education, 11*(1), 2365613. https://doi.org/10.1080/2331186X.2024.2365613

Kolar, J., Lutz, G., Angelieva, K., Angelis, J., Brecko, B., Chamberlain, M., Guittet, E., Karayannis, F., Plaskan, J., Ryan, M., Sobczak, D., & Wenzel-Constabel, P. (2023). *Assessment of impact of RIs*. ESFRI Policy Brief. Retrieved from www.esfri.eu/sites/default/files/ESFRI_Impact_Policy_Brief_23052023.pdf

Lijun, Y., & Wei, S. (1998). *New humanism and global governance*. World Scientific Publishing. https://doi.org/10.1142/10882

Lykke, M., Amstrup, L., Hvidtfeldt, R., & Pedersen, D. B. (2023). Mapping research activities and societal impact by taxonomy of indicators: Uniformity and diversity across academic fields. *Journal of Documentation, 79*(5), 1049–1070. https://doi.org/10.1108/JD-06-2022-0131

Meagher, L., Lyall, C., & Nutley, S. (2008). Flows of knowledge, expertise and influence: A method for assessing policy and practice impacts from social science research. *Research Evaluation, 17*(3), 163–173. https://doi.org/10.3152/095820208X331720

Miller, R., & Lessard, D. L. (2000). *The Strategic management of large engineering projects: Shaping institutions, risks, and governance*. MIT Press.

Molas-Gallart, J., & Tang, P. (2011). Tracing 'productive interactions' to identify social impacts: An example from the social sciences. *Research Evaluation, 20*(3), 219–226. https://doi.org/10.3152/095820211X12941371876706

Moore, S. (2021). *Exploring models for community governance*. https://doi.org/10.5281/zenodo.4730687

Muhonen, R., Benneworth, P., & Olmos-Peñuela, J. (2020). From productive interactions to impact pathways: Understanding the key dimensions in developing SSH research societal impact. *Research Evaluation, 29*(1), 34–47. https://doi.org/10.1093/reseval/rvz003

Neelis, M. L. (2020). *Tight and loose governance in innovation and knowledge sharing networks. A necessary configuration for network effectiveness*. Retrieved February 26, 2026, from https://arno.uvt.nl/show.cgi?fid=152014

North, D. C. (1990). *Institutions, Institutional Change and Economic Performance*. Cambridge University Press.

O'Toole, L. J., & Meier, K. J. (2003). Bureaucracy and Uncertainty. In B. C. Burden (Ed.), *Uncertainty in American Politics*. Cambridge University Press.

OECD. (2019). *Reference framework for assessing the scientific and socio-economic impact of research infrastructures*. OECD Science, Technology and Industry Policy Papers, No. 65, OECD Publishing. https://doi.org/10.1787/3ffee43b-en

OECD. (2021). *Applying Evaluation Criteria Thoughtfully*. OECD Publishing. https://doi.org/10.1787/543e84ed-en

Ostrom, E. (1990). *Governing the commons: The evolution of institutions for collective action*. Cambridge University Press.

Painter, M., & Pierre, J. (2005). Unpacking policy capacity: Issues and themes. In M. Painter & J. Pierre (Eds.), *Challenges to state policy capacity*. Palgrave Macmillan. https://doi.org/10.1057/9780230524194_1

Pedersen, D. B., Følsgaard Grønvad, J., & Hvidtfeldt, R. (2020). Methods for mapping the impact of social sciences and humanities—A literature review. *Research Evaluation, 29*(1), 4–21. https://doi.org/10.1093/reseval/rvz033

Penfield, T., Baker, M. J., Scoble, R., & Wykes, M. C. (2014). Assessment, evaluations, and definitions of research impact: A review. *Research Evaluation, 23*(1), 21–32. https://doi.org/10.1093/reseval/rvt021

Poteete, A. R. (2010). *Working together: Collective action, the commons, and multiple methods in practice*. Princeton University Press.

Powell, W. (1990). Neither market nor hierarchy. *Research in Organizational Behaviour, 12*(1), 295–336. https://doi.org/10.1007/978-3-658-21742-6_108

Qiao, L., Mu, R., & Chen, K. (2016). Scientific effects of large research infrastructures in China. *Technological Forecasting and Social Change Journal, 112*, 102–112. https://doi.org/10.1016/j.techfore.2016.07.029

Reale, E., Avramov, D., Canhial, K., Donovan, C., Flecha, R., Holm, P., Larkin, C., Lepori, B., Mosoni-Fried, J., Oliver, E., Primeri, E., Puigvert, L., Scharnhorst, A., Schubert, A., Soler, M., Soòs, S., Sordé, T., Travis, C., & Van Horik, R. (2018). A review of literature on evaluating the scientific, social and political impact of social sciences and humanities research. *Research Evaluation, 27*(4), 298–308. https://doi.org/10.1093/reseval/rvx025

Reed, M. S., Ferré, M., Martin-Ortega, J., Blanche, R., Lawford-Rolfe, R., Dallimer, M., & Holden, J. (2021). Evaluating impact from research: A methodological framework. *Research Policy, 50*, 104147. https://doi.org/10.1016/j.respol.2020.104147

Ribeiro, M. (2021). Towards a sustainable European research infrastructures ecosystem. In H. P. Beck & P. Charitos (Eds.), *The economics of big science, science policy reports* (pp. 7–14). Springer.

Shenhar, A. J., & Dvir, D. (2007). *Reinventing project management: The diamond approach to successful growth and innovation*. Harvard Business School Publishing.

Sivertsen, G., & Meijer, I. (2025). Evaluating and improving the societal impact of research. In G. Sivertsen & L. Langfeldt (Eds.), *Challenges in research policy. Evidence-based policy briefs with recommendations* (SpringerBriefs in political science) (pp. 21–28). Springer.

Smit, J. P., & Hessels, L. K. (2021). The production of scientific and societal value in research evaluation: A review of societal impact assessment methods. *Research Evaluation, 30*(3), 323–335. https://doi.org/10.1093/reseval/rvab002

Spaapen, J., & van Drooge, L. (2011). Introducing 'productive interactions' in social impact assessment. *Research Evaluation, 20*(3), 211–218. https://doi.org/10.3152/095820211X12941371876742

Spencer, M. S., & Cox, J. F. (1995). Optimum production technology (OPT) and the theory of constraints (TOC): Analysis and genealogy. *International Journal of Production Research, 33*, 1495–1504. https://doi.org/10.1080/00207549508930224

Stalk, G., & Hout, T. M. (1990). *Competing against time: How time-based competition is reshaping global markets*. Free Press.

van Drooge, L. (2018). *Impacts of infrastructures—In the eyes of the beholder*.https://doi.org/10.5281/zenodo.1402957

Vignetti, S. (2021). Designing a research infrastructure with impact in mind. In H. P. Beck & P. Charitos (Eds.), *The economics of big science. Science policy reports* (pp. 79–84). Springer. https://doi.org/10.1007/978-3-030-52391-6_11

Watson, K. J., Blackstone, J. H., & Gardiner, S. C. (2007). The evolution of a management philosophy: The theory of constraints. *Journal of Operations Management, 25*(2), 387–402. https://doi.org/10.1016/j.jom.2006.04.004

Weick, K. E. (1976). Educational organizations as loosely coupled systems. *Administrative Science Quarterly, 21*(1), 1–19. https://doi.org/10.2307/2391875

Zakaria, S., Grant, J., & Luff, J. (2021). Fundamental challenges in assessing the impact of research infrastructure. *Health Research Policy and Systems, 19*(1), 119–127. https://doi.org/10.1186/s12961-021-00769-z

Zyzak, B. (2024). Importance of managerial networking for innovation in governance networks. *Nordic Journal of Innovation in the Public Sector, 3*(1), 1–20. https://doi.org/10.18261/njips.3.1.1

# Chapter 14
# Enhancing Skills, Building Capacity: The FOSSR Approach to Training in Social Science Research Infrastructures

**Andrea Orazio Spinello, Serena Fabrizio, and Claudia Pennacchiotti**

## 14.1 Introduction

The mission of Research Infrastructures (RIs), including those in the Social Sciences, goes beyond providing access to advanced research tools and services. Among their aims is to foster a cultural shift in scientific practices and behaviors by promoting openness, data sharing, and the use of technologically advanced research services (Kleiner et al., 2013; ESFRI, 2020). Indeed, RIs embody the principles of a "new path for science"—that engages not only scholars but also the wider community of stakeholders in scientific knowledge—grounded in the richness and circulation of massive quantities of data (*data-intensive science*, Hey et al., 2009), the capacity to make data and research outputs accessible at every level (*Open Science*, Boulton et al., 2012), and the enhanced ability to collaborate across networks to address complex scientific challenges (*networked science*, Nielsen, 2011). Thus, RIs constitute complex ecosystems in which, as Latour would say, the production of knowledge depends as much on technological infrastructures (conceived as full-fledged actors, albeit non-human) as on human, social, and institutional relations (Latour, 1987, 2005).

Social studies of science have long emphasized that the spread of practices within epistemic communities, especially innovative ones, is strongly dependent on social processes such as education, mentoring, and apprenticeship. This is

A. O. Spinello (✉) · S. Fabrizio
CNR-IRCrES—Research Institute on Sustainable Economic Growth, National Research Council of Italy, Rome, Italy
e-mail: andreaorazio.spinello@cnr.it; serena.fabrizio@cnr.it

C. Pennacchiotti
CNR-IRPPS—Institute for Research on Population and Social Policies, National Research Council of Italy, Rome, Italy
e-mail: claudia.pennacchiotti@cnr.it



G. Cerulli, E. Reale (eds.), *Research Infrastructures for Open Science in Social Science Research*, https://doi.org/10.1007/978-3-032-29575-0_14

particularly relevant in the context of RIs, where the effectiveness of both the material and immaterial resources they provide (tools, data, practices, values) ultimately depends on the capability of individuals to recognize their value and use them competently. Much like scientific paradigms, which sustain themselves through the training of new practitioners (Kuhn, 1962), RIs rely on training to cultivate competent user communities capable of exploiting their potential and embedding them into scientific routines. This is even more true for RIs operating in an Open Science context. Here the researcher is called upon not only to act as a producer of data but also as a mediator, custodian, and innovator within a plural and interconnected cognitive ecosystem where processes of co-creation of knowledge occur, transforming science into a collective endeavor that integrates technical expertise with contextual knowledge (Funtowicz & Ravetz, 1993). Thus, *training initiatives* within RIs serve not only educational and sustainability purposes but also an essential sociological function: they nurture the *human dimension* of the infrastructure, which complements and animates its technical systems. Indeed, infrastructure data and services have no intrinsic value or meaning; they become truly functional only when they are "learned as part of membership" within a community—when they exist in an ecosystem of people, practices, technologies, institutions, material objects, and relationships (Star & Ruhleder, 1996; Borgman, 2015). In other words, RIs can achieve their full potential only *when a broad set of skilled users is formed and socialized around them.*

In this Chapter, we examine the role of training in the context of the FOSSR RI, from improving data and service expertise to expanding the number and diversity of users. The FOSSR capacity-building strategy serves as a paradigmatic example of an integrated and multi-level approach that combines a diverse range of formats, i.e. traditional online courses, participatory sessions based on constructivist learning principles, and higher education programs developed in collaboration with Italian universities. Through the provision of free training opportunities and academic scholarships, the FOSSR project, funded under the Italian National Recovery and Resilience Plan (NRRP), sought to equip current and future researchers with the skills and culture needed to leverage RIs in the social sciences, also promoting more equitable access. This effort is particularly needed in the Italian context where social science scholars and practitioners are still in the early stages of transitioning to a knowledge production model based on shared RIs (Spinello, 2020).

This contribution is structured as follows. Section 14.2 will situate training initiatives in RIs within the broader framework of research policies aimed at strengthening Open Science. Section 14.3 will then examine in detail the integrated, multi-level design of the FOSSR training portfolio. This is followed by Sect. 14.4, which presents the implementation of the training initiatives, and Sect. 14.5 that will discuss key result indicators and feedback indications. Finally, Sect. 14.6 will draw conclusions.

## 14.2 The Strategic Value of Training Activities Within Research Infrastructures

In European and international research policy frameworks, training is widely recognized both as a strategic investment for RIs and as an operational necessity to ensure their long-term social and scientific sustainability. Training initiatives directly strengthen users' technical and methodological capabilities, thus expanding access to and use of research data and services provided by RIs (ESFRI, 2020; European Commission, 2024).

**Building Capacity for Open and Data-Intensive Science**
The OECD Global Science Forum identifies human capabilities as a determinant of scientific success in data-driven research, calling for the development of digital skills among researchers and support personnel (OECD, 2020). In this vision, RIs serve as *knowledge hubs* where training, data management, and research practice converge (ESFRI, 2020). The RI commitment to train users in FAIR data management, computational methods, and Open Science practices not only improves the quality and reproducibility of research but also strengthens the analytical capacity of epistemic communities, particularly in the social sciences, where attitudes toward openness often remain cautious (Berkowitz & Delacour, 2022).

The *European Charter for Access to Research Infrastructures* explicitly includes education and training among the functions that facilitate access and equitable participation. It encourages RIs to integrate capacity development into their broader missions of excellence, innovation, and societal relevance (European Commission, 2024). Also, OECD promotes coordinated approaches to foster a digitally competent research workforce by aligning education systems, funding bodies, and RIs around shared objectives of capacity building and digital transformation (OECD, 2020).

However, the adoption of Open Science remains constrained by persistent skills gaps and limited institutional incentives. In order to address these shortcomings, it is necessary to integrate data literacy, ethics, and openness into RI training and operational frameworks, as well as promote peer-to-peer learning models within research organizations.

**Expanding and Diversifying the User Community**
Training, especially if it is accessible at no cost and without geographical or technological barriers, also plays a strategic role in expanding access to RIs and democratizing participation in the research process. By empowering users with the skills needed to navigate advanced research ecosystems, it reduces barriers to entry for early-career researchers, interdisciplinary scholars, and underrepresented communities. The *European Charter for Access to Research Infrastructures* reaffirms this principle, identifying user training as a key support measure for promoting equitable access and long-term engagement with infrastructure services (European Commission, 2024). In the Social Sciences, where computational and data-driven approaches are still unevenly adopted, training helps reduce disciplinary disparities

by providing researchers with analytical and methodological skills (Kleiner et al., 2013).

The democratizing function of training extends beyond academia. Many RIs within the *European Strategy Forum on Research Infrastructures* (ESFRI) have developed training models that actively engage policymakers, industry professionals, and civil society actors. The involvement of these groups amplifies the social impact of RIs, enabling non-academic users to interact and contribute to knowledge production. This expansion is consistent with UNESCO's call for Open Science to promote "the open involvement of social actors" and foster the integration of scientific knowledge into public decision-making (UNESCO, 2021).

Training within RIs therefore serves as a means for social engagement and dialogue between science and society. Initiatives aimed at policymakers, civil servants and citizen communities help bridge the gap between scientific production and the social application of data, promoting capacity development for evidence-based decision-making (OECD, 2020).

## 14.3 Design of the FOSSR Training Portfolio

Creating enabling environments for RIs means acting on conditions that place researchers' competences at the center (UNESCO, 2021; Wehn et al., 2024). These competences extend beyond disciplinary expertise to include making data and practices accessible, collaborative, and transparent and embracing open data, open access, open infrastructures, and public engagement as evidenced by the EU Working Group on Skills for Open Science. From this perspective, training and lifelong learning become transformative (Mezirow, 1991; Sterling, 2001), forming individuals able to critically inhabit knowledge networks. Open Science thus represents not only a shift in research practices but a broader educational and cultural opportunity fostering inclusivity, epistemic citizenship, and social innovation (Peters et al., 2020).

Building on these principles, the FOSSR project, which ultimately aims to promote open science in social science research, developed a multi-level training architecture conceived as an integrated ecosystem connecting learning forms, audiences, and engagement levels into a coherent capacity-building strategy (Spinello & Fabrizio, 2025). The portfolio includes a diversified range of learning initiatives aimed at capacity-building. It integrates opportunities for an immediate involvement in RI-encouraged practices, scientific co-design and collaboration and major engagement within academic programs (Fig. 14.1). At the foundational level, *Online Training Courses* provide knowledge on open, reusable resources introducing Open Science, FAIR data, and responsible research, establishing a shared conceptual baseline. *Participatory Sessions*, which include two formats—Learning Sessions and Action Research Sessions—form the transformative core, engaging participants in co-design, interdisciplinary dialogue, and experiential learning. At the advanced level, *Higher Education Programmes* (a University Master Programme and funded

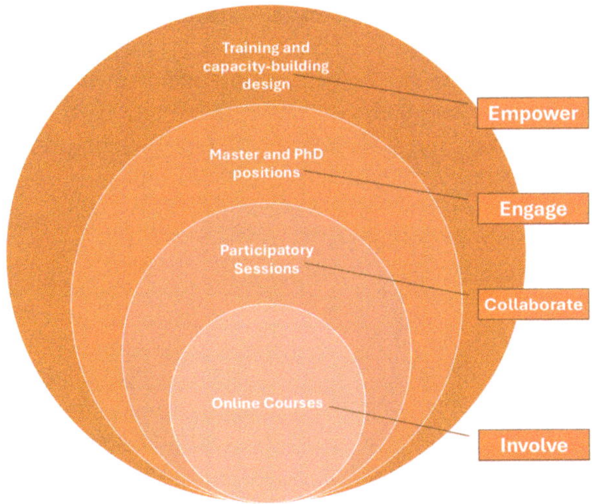


**Fig. 14.1** The FOSSR training multi-level approach. Source: Spinello and Fabrizio (2025)

PhD positions) are designed to train a new generation of social data scientists, in collaboration with academic institutions.

Figure 14.1 illustrates the coherence among three interconnected levels of the training and capacity-building design: a foundational level (Involve), a participatory level (Collaborate), and an institutional level (Engage). These are framed by an overarching 'empower' level, which defines the overall purpose of the approach. These levels enable recursive feedback loops that sustain innovation and learning, reflecting a shift from *training for research infrastructures* to *training through research infrastructures*, where participants are involved, collaborate, and engage across different stages by co-developing tools and critically reflecting on their usability (Spinello & Fabrizio, 2025).

### *14.3.1 Online Training Courses*

The role of the Online Training Courses (OTCs) is to enhance the engagement of researchers, students and practitioners, contributing to bridging the gap between the potential of the FOSSR RI and the basic competencies of the researchers who are expected to use it. With this aim, they represent an opportunity for participants to interact with FOSSR researchers who are developing the infrastructure and its services, to engage with some of the major goals related to the FOSSR project's mission (Cf. Chap. 5) and the issues emerging from the core of the project itself. Participants are called to reflect on them and acquire the skills needed to access, manage, use and exploit data in the environments developed according to rigorous standards of quality, reproducibility and ethical integrity.

The courses, lasting generally 2 days, are designed to focus on two main priority areas: (1) a deep understanding of different tools, techniques and methodological approaches to social research to address innovative research questions in data-intensive contexts, (2) a comprehensive knowledge of data management, curation, documentation and preservation throughout their lifecycle. Each course incorporates a FOSSR case study to contextualize the learned concepts within an empirical framework. Moreover, in line with Open learning and Open knowledge principles, to guarantee a wider impact and to support accessibility and inclusiveness, the educational resources and documents associated to each online course are freely available on the FOSSR Zenodo Cloud, allowing no-cost access (Butcher, 2011) and re-use by others (UNESCO, 2019). Together, all these components, contribute to building a sustainable community of practice capable of fully leveraging the potential of data-driven social research within the infrastructure ecosystem and in which collaborative approaches and collective intelligence are prioritized in the knowledge creation process.

Delving deeper into the two priority areas of the OTCs, in the first one specific advanced methodologies for data collection and data analysis, and advanced statistical methods and techniques are explored. The aim is to enhance social scientists' use of quantitative approaches in particular related to the use of the FOSSR RIs for surveys, advanced methodologies for data collection and data analysis (e.g. use of longitudinal data, spatial models, text mining) based on the most recent solutions in statistical modelling, complex modelling, deep learning. OTCs falling into the second priority area are devoted to increase social scientists' skills and competences related to make data sharable and compliant with FAIR principles, GDPR rules, data organization, data documentation, legal and ethical constraints, data preservation and standards that facilitate the semantic and technical interoperability among systems and organizations. Regardless of whether the course falls into one of the two priority areas, the format was designed to be *fully online*, not only for pedagogical reasons but also to maximize the inclusivity and accessibility of the training opportunities offered.

As a primary consideration, in designing the format for OTCs, the learning environment was regarded as a key aspect in the learning process. Indeed, drawing on Latour's perspective (2005), pedagogical interactions and knowledge production are shaped by the learning environment adopted, which is acknowledged as an actor in its own right, highlighting the collective nature of agency in the educational context. The online learning environment is, thus, not a mere host of learning activities, but actively mediates the relationships that are built among participants (Fenwick & Edwards, 2010). Under this conceptual umbrella, online courses allow to design learner-centered environments where advanced methodological and technical competences can be enhanced (Garrison et al., 2000) supported by flexible and inclusive learning frameworks (Laurillard, 2013; Bates, 2015). As evidenced by Garrison et al. (2000), online training, through its interactive components such as, for example, a well balanced mix of frontal/theoretical lessons and more interactive activities like discussion forums and collaborative assignments, allows participants to interact with peers activating processes of knowledge co-construction, peer-to-peer knowledge exchange and fostering inquiry-oriented learning, while at the same time contributing to building the community of practice.

In this perspective, the virtual learning environment adopted, where technologies facilitate collaborative, flexible learning and the open sharing of educational materials through the Zenodo cloud enhances the democratization of knowledge access (Inamorato dos Santos et al., 2016), provides a space of 'creative training' where the trainers stimulate the trainees to reflect on their data needs and research questions.

### *14.3.2 Participatory Sessions*

The design of the Participatory sessions (PSs) combines collaborative learning and action research approaches to promote shared knowledge creation and transformative reflection among researchers, students, and societal stakeholders. This approach follows the principles outlined by the ESFRI (2020), which emphasizes the need for training strategies that not only build methodological expertise but also foster socially relevant and collaborative research practices. The participatory framework is articulated into two complementary formats—Learning Sessions (LS) and Action Research Sessions (ARS)—conceived as iterative and interconnected training spaces. Both are grounded in constructivist pedagogy and informed by the concept of knowledge co-creation (Reed & Rudman, 2023), encouraging participants to move from individual knowledge acquisition toward collective problem-solving. This dual structure fosters interdisciplinarity, inclusivity, and reflexivity, enabling participants to bridge academic research with societal challenges.

The learning process underpinning the PSs follows a three-phase logic: *learning about*, *learning through*, and *learning with*. Participants first *learn about* theoretical and methodological frameworks; they then *learn through* experimentation and collaborative application; finally, they *learn with* others by engaging in co-reflection and co-design. This progression cultivates not only technical expertise but also meta-cognitive and relational skills essential for collective inquiry.

LS are designed as intensive 2-day events, combining conceptual lectures with collaborative exercises and peer discussions. Each session follows a modular sequence: (1) theoretical framing led by researchers and practitioners, (2) group work and hands-on application, and (3) collective reflection and synthesis. This design promotes engagement and critical dialogue across disciplinary boundaries while reinforcing participants' capacity to use Social Science RIs tools in analytical and policy-oriented contexts.

ARS have been developed across multiple meetings, following iterative reflection–action cycles. Participants co-design conceptual and operational outputs, applying action research methods to test solutions in their own professional settings. This cyclical process of reflection, planning, and experimentation allows participants to internalize Open and Citizen Science principles and to critically explore how infrastructures can be shaped to meet diverse informational and analytical needs. The approach recalls the notion of stakeholder engagement for societal impact (Reale et al., 2019), highlighting the potential of participatory methodologies to enhance the transformative capacity of research. The ARS are examined in a specific section of the Chap. 15 from a complementary perspective, which provides a more detailed account of the action research methodology adopted and its role within the broader community building and FOSSR stakeholders engagement strategy.

Both LS and ARS are grounded in prior capacity-building experiences within European RIs, particularly those developed under the RISIS RI (Fabrizio et al., 2023). They move beyond traditional training formats by positioning participants as co-creators of knowledge rather than passive recipients. Through iterative reflection-action loops, they are encouraged to challenge assumptions about research practices, recognize the social dimensions of data use, and rethink infrastructures as collective resources. By positioning infrastructures as living ecosystems co-shaped by users, the sessions foster a more democratic and sustainable model of research capacity building.

Each session involves a diverse community of participants—researchers at various career stages, doctoral candidates, students, and stakeholders from public institutions, civil society organizations, and local administrations. Facilitators, typically experienced researchers, play a dual role as subject-matter experts and moderators of group dynamics. They guide discussions, ensure balanced participation, and support collaborative learning through structured exercises such as participatory mapping, needs assessment, and scenario development. Hybrid delivery formats, combining in-person and online interaction, ensure broad accessibility and geographical inclusion, while digital collaboration tools support real-time co-production and cross-institutional communication. Participant selection prioritizes gender balance, disciplinary diversity, and equitable regional representation, in line with Open Science principles of inclusivity (UNESCO, 2021). Finally, they are offered free of charge to eliminate economic barriers to participation, reflecting the broader principle of open and equitable access to advanced research education.

The intended outcome is to strengthen participants' confidence in handling data, a deeper understanding of collaboration, and an increased awareness of how Open Science principles can be applied in their research activities. Facilitators gain insights into participants' evolving needs, supporting the continuous refinement of training content and pedagogical tools. From this perspective, participatory learning operates as a dynamic exchange fostering mutual learning and strengthening links between capacity building, methodological innovation, and community development.

### 14.3.3 Higher Education Programmes

Through training opportunities linked to higher education programmes, the FOSSR project aims to cultivate a *new generation of researchers* capable of exploiting the opportunities offered by the increasingly data-intensive research environment. Thus, FOSSR have collaborated with Italian universities to promote advanced training programs that combine disciplinary knowledge with cutting-edge methodological training. Strategic agreements have been established between the National Research Council of Italy (CNR, the institution managing the FOSSR project) and leading academic institutions to create postgraduate programs—such as a dedicated University Master Programme and several doctoral positions—which represent a long-term investment in human capital and the sustainability of an open and collaborative research ecosystem.

**University Master Programme**

The rapid expansion of data, algorithms, and computational models requires social scientists to combine a solid theoretical foundation with advanced skills in statistics, data science, and programming. This transformation requires greater attention to the design of academic curricula in the social sciences, where a gap often persists between the quantitative skills required by contemporary research and those actually taught. Recent reports indicate that many European programs still struggle to systematically integrate advanced quantitative methods, big data analysis, and programming skills into traditional social science courses (Ferrie et al., 2022).

With the aim of creating an opportunity to train highly skilled professionals capable of improving the innovation capacity in the Social Sciences, FOSSR has funded a second-level University Master Programme (EQF[1] Level 8) in Social Data Science (SDS) at the University of Milano-Bicocca, delivered online.[2] This academic institution was identified as particularly well-suited for its role, together with the CNR, as the Italian national hub for the CESSDA European Research Infrastructure, one of three European infrastructures strengthened under the FOSSR project. The SDS Master programme has been designed to offer advanced training in quantitative methods, programming, and data science applied to the social sciences, directly connecting academic teaching with the data, resources, and expertise of social science RIs. By integrating modules in advanced statistics and computational techniques with applied projects that address substantial societal challenges, the programme aimed to equip graduates with the interdisciplinary tools needed to address complex social issues through collaborative and data-intensive approaches. Students trained in data science can design tools to improve data accessibility, develop methodologies for analyzing large-scale datasets, and promote the adoption of FAIR data principles.

**Doctoral Positions**

Funding doctoral positions aligned with RIs' missions supports the advancement of methodological and practical innovation, as doctoral researchers are often at the forefront of developing new techniques, adapting computational tools to social

[1] The acronym refers to the European Qualifications Framework, adopted at the European level to facilitate the comparability of qualifications across countries and education systems. Level 8 is the highest on the scale.

[2] Website: https://sds.sociologia.unimib.it

**Table 14.1** Doctoral positions funded by the FOSSR project in the 39th Italian Doctoral Cycle

| Positions activated | PhD program | University | Years |
|---|---|---|---|
| 1 | Social and Political Science | Bocconi University | 4 |
| 2 | Social Sciences and Economics | Sapienza University of Rome | 3 |
| 1 | Philosophy, Science, Cognition and Semiotics | University of Bologna | 3 |
| 1 | Political Science | University of Catania | 3 |
| 1 | Computer Science | University of Catania | 3 |
| 1 | Economy Sociology, Organization and Labor | University of Milan "Statale" | 4 |
| 2 | Social Sciences and Statistics | University of Naples Federico II | 3 |
| 1 | Sustainability: Economics, Environment, Management and Society | University of Trento | 3 |

Source: FOSSR project documentation (De Gregorio et al., 2024, 2025)

research, and analyzing the broader societal implications of open data. Support for doctoral studies in areas such as computational social sciences, quantitative methods, and Open Science therefore ensures the continuous renewal of expertise in these strategically important fields. The impact of PhD scholarships may extend well beyond academia: graduates specializing in computational social sciences and Open Science are increasingly sought after by government, industry, and nonprofit organizations (Kesari et al., 2023). In this sense, investing in doctoral training yields substantial returns for both the research ecosystem and society at large.

Thus, FOSSR funded ten PhD scholarships within the 39th Italian doctoral cycle, distributed across seven Italian universities, covering the initial phase coinciding with the project duration (Table 14.1). The remaining part of the 3- or 4-year programs was funded by the CNR and/or partner universities through complementary funding, thus ensuring their sustainability. These doctoral fellowships, hosted by the universities enable doctoral students to pursue research projects directly relevant to the FOSSR data, methods and services.

### *14.3.4 Transversal Values of the FOSSR Capacity-Building Framework: Inclusiveness and Gender Balance*

**The Inclusive Approach**

The overall learning framework of the FOSSR has been designed to ensure broad accessibility with the OTCs and PSs offered free of charge and the Higher Education Programmes covered by scholarships. Rather than functioning as an exclusive advanced training for researchers, the initiatives were designed to enable interaction among multiple actors within the research ecosystem (senior and early-career researchers, doctoral candidates, postgraduate students, and representatives from public institutions, data service providers, and civil society organizations) in a way aligned with the objectives of each specific type of initiative. This approach reflects a pedagogical strategy to support the emergence of interdisciplinary and intersectoral networks capable of sustaining Open Science practices and translating RIs into socially relevant resources. Moreover, situating learning within emerging communities of practice, in line with open learning and open education initiatives, this approach fosters deeper engagement, and empowers learners as active agents in their educational journeys (Wenger et al., 2002).

However, as evidenced by the NRRP's Component 2 of Mission 4, which funded the FOSSR project, realizing this potential requires sustained attention to issues related to the territorial cohesion and the structural conditions necessary to support the creation of vibrant and sustainable knowledge communities throughout the country. With the aim of contributing to reduce regional inequalities and overcome economic and temporal barriers (Bates, 2019) while simultaneously strengthening the research and innovation ecosystem, the online and hybrid formats designed offer the opportunity to involve heterogeneous research communities that are geographically dispersed and institutionally diverse. At the same time, this strategy enables participation from researchers based in institutions or regions with limited access to face-to-face training opportunities (Laurillard, 2013; Bates, 2015). In this way, it concretely contributes to the creation of collaborative learning ecosystems, where participants regardless their geographical location, can engage in peer learning, share practices and co-construct knowledge. This process is central to the development of shared standards for data curation and research methodology (Wenger, 1998; Salmon, 2011), and to democratize access to training opportunities and promote equitable participation in RIs (ESFRI, 2020; UNESCO, 2021).

**Gender Balance**

In line with the recommendations outlined in the Gender Equality Plan of the FOSSR project, the design of the different formats placed particular emphasis on gender equity as a cross-cutting principle of the training activities. Rather than treating gender balance as a quantitative outcome, the training initiatives embedded inclusivity at every stage of their planning, implementation, and evaluation. This approach aligns with the Open Science values of accessibility and fairness, and with international frameworks (UNESCO, 2021; Wehn et al., 2024) that recognize gender equality as essential to the responsible governance of RIs.

The strategies adopted for the selection of participants and for communication were developed to attract participants of all genders by using inclusive language in calls for participation, neutral visual materials, and open dissemination channels through both academic and professional networks. The online and hybrid formats also contributed to this objective by lowering participation barriers often experienced by those with family or caregiving responsibilities, allowing flexibility in attending and engaging in the activities.

The conceptual framing of gender balance within the FOSSR training also extended to include awareness-raising on the social dimensions of data production and use. Discussions around Open Science and data ethics incorporated examples of gender bias in datasets and analytical models, inviting participants to critically reflect on inclusivity in their own research practices. Furthermore, the commitment to gender-sensitive participation was connected to the broader formative goal of promoting inclusive epistemologies—that is, ways of producing and validating knowledge that recognize diversity in perspectives, experiences, and expertise. The participatory structure, based on small interdisciplinary groups, fostered dialogue and mutual learning among individuals with different professional trajectories and gendered experiences of academia.

Finally, in particular within the PSs, facilitation methods were specifically designed to encourage equitable participation and to prevent dominance by particular groups or voices. Moderators received guidance on inclusive communication and adopted techniques such as structured turn-taking, breakout group discussions, and anonymous contribution tools to ensure that all participants could contribute equally.

## 14.4 Implementation of the Training Initiatives

This section presents how the capacity-building strategy was effectively implemented throughout the FOSSR project, through the various initiatives. A distinction will be made between the OTCs and PSs activated and the establishment of university programs developed in collaboration with several Italian universities.

**Online Training Courses and Participatory Sessions**

Between October 2023 and June 2025, FOSSR delivered six OTCs and four PSs. Together, they represented the most visible direct contact point between the developers of the FOSSR infrastructure—acting as instructors, facilitators, and mediators—and its emerging user community.

The six OTCs were held entirely online in a synchronous format, for a total of 74 h of structured training (Table 14.2). They attracted participants from universities, research institutions, and social science professionals. A first series of three courses (OTCs 1–3) focused on the Research Data Management (RDM) Cycle and the principles of FAIR and Open Science. Participants were guided through the full data lifecycle—from data collection and documentation to preservation, licensing, and dissemination—through examples drawn from the CESSDA RI and Italian social-science archives. Practical modules introduced tools for approaching data management plans, curating metadata, implementing GDPR-compliant data-handling practices, and addressing ethical and legal challenges in data sharing. A dedicated course on semantic interoperability expanded this framework, allowing participants to experiment with the integration of heterogeneous datasets through RDF models, Linked Open Data, SPARQL querying, and ontology design. The

**Table 14.2** Overview of the OTCs delivered within the FOSSR project (October 2023–June 2025)

| ID number | Title | Topics | Hours | Format |
|---|---|---|---|---|
| OTC 1 | Data Lifecycle and Architectures in the Social Sciences | Methods and Practices for High-Quality Data Production in Social Research | 12 | Online |
| OTC 2 | Managing Data Within the Social Science Infrastructures: the Role of FOSSR | FAIR Data Management and Privacy Policies In Social Research | 12 | Online |
| OTC 3 | From Open Data to Open Knowledge Graphs: The Role of Semantic Technologies | Semantic Technologies and Knowledge Graphs for Open Data Integration | 12 | Online |
| OTC 4 | Exploring Research Infrastructure Data Through Advanced Statistical Applications | Data-Driven Research and Open Science in Social Sciences | 10 | Online |
| OTC 5 | Tools and Methods for Analysing Complex Science, Technology, and Innovation Systems | Advanced Data Analytics (Network Science, Bayesian Networks, Machine Learning, Spatial Models) | 18 | Online |
| OTC 6 | Designing and Implementing Longitudinal and Panel Surveys | Methods and Practices for Longitudinal Data in Social Research | 10 | Online |

Source: FOSSR project documentation (De Gregorio et al., 2024, 2025)

second series of OTCs (4–6) shifted from foundational principles to applied data analytics and computational approaches for social-science research. These courses explored topics such as machine-learning for social data, text and network analysis, and longitudinal-data methodologies. They also offered an overview of the data resources available through European and Italian RIs, positioning FOSSR within this broader ecosystem. Each session alternated lectures with collaborative group exercises and discussions, encouraging peer learning and cross-institutional dialogue.

In parallel, four PSs—comprising two Learning Sessions (LSs) and two Action Research Sessions (ARSs)—activated the experiential and dialogic dimension of the training initiatives (Table 14.3). Conducted primarily in hybrid format, they functioned as collaborative laboratories where participants were encouraged to critically reflect on the use of RI resources and fostered to co-design and

**Table 14.3** Overview of the PSs delivered within the FOSSR project (December 2023–May 2025)

| Type | Title | Topics | Hours | Format |
|---|---|---|---|---|
| LS | Designing Socio-Economic Policy Evaluation: learning through FOSSR | Policy Design and Evaluation Methods | 8 | Hybrid |
| ARS | Transformative Paths in Research Practices: Co-Developing Social Science Infrastructures | Action Research for Transforming Social Science practices | 11 | Hybrid |
| LS | Data Analysis in the era of Large Language Models within FOSSR | Data Analysis with Large Language Models | 8 | Hybrid |
| ARS | Participatory and Reflexive Engagement to Co-Define the Impact of FOSSR Research Services | Collaborative Evaluation and Co-Development of RI Services for SSH | 13 | In-person |

Source: FOSSR project documentation (De Gregorio et al., 2024, 2025)
*LS* Learning Session; *ARS* Action Research Session

experiment with the use of FOSSR data and services in concrete research and policy contexts. The LSs focused on two central themes: the use of RIs for policy evaluation and socio-economic analysis, and the methodological challenges and opportunities of Large Language Models (LLMs) for the social sciences. The first LS engaged researchers, data professionals, and civil servants in working groups analyzing real policy-assessment cases through FOSSR services, while the second LS, encouraged critical discussion of the potential and risks of AI applications for social research and infrastructure design. The ARSs deepened this participatory approach by transforming collective reflection into practical implications in utilizing RIs. The first ARS guided interdisciplinary teams in developing micro-projects connecting FOSSR data with transformative paths in research practices. The second ARS concluded the cycle with a reflective session focused on the operational use of FOSSR RI. Participants developed mini-projects aimed at improving the usability and interoperability of RIs services, providing feedback for future enhancement.

**University-Level Initiatives**

The establishment of the University Master Programme in Social Data Science (SDS) at the University of Milano-Bicocca, at the end of summer 2023, marked a major step in translating the project's vision into the training of a new generation of researchers. Conceived through an agreement between the CNR and the University, the Master reflects the project's vision of combining disciplinary depth in the social sciences with the technical and ethical literacy required for data-intensive research. The 2-year, second-level programme (120 ECTS[3]) was entirely funded by FOSSR and offered free of charge.

The curriculum—comprising approximately 750 hours of lectures and laboratory work—combined modules in social-science theory and methodology with intensive technical and computational training. Year 1 included courses on research design, statistics and R, Python programming, relational and non-relational databases, digital sociology, social network analysis, linguistics and computational semantics, logic and causal reasoning, and introductory AI for social research. Year 2 added modules on Data, Power and Society; Law, Ethics and Data Governance; Big Data and AI for Evaluation Research; Digital Methods; Data Visualisation. In addition, the programme featured a 32-h seminar series delivered by FOSSR partners, covering advanced and cross-cutting topics such as semantic knowledge graphs, privacy and ethics in RIs, agent-based modelling, multi-agent systems, and the use of LLMs for data cleaning and ontology development. Every student completed a 150-h internship or project work with public or private organizations and produced a final thesis applying data-science methods to an empirical problem in the social sciences.

At the highest level of university education, FOSSR strengthened Italy's social science research ecosystem by funding ten doctoral positions (starting in the academic year 2023–2024) (Cf. Par. 14.3.3). These positions were established through bilateral agreements between CNR institutes participating in the FOSSR partnership (IRCrES, IRPPS, and ISTC) and seven Italian universities—Trento, Sapienza University of Rome, Bocconi University, University of Milan "Statale", University of Bologna, University of Catania, and University of Naples "Federico II".

The selection of doctoral projects prioritized strong alignment with FOSSR's mission and thematic priorities. The funded projects cover a wide range of research topics, including: adaptation and innovation to climate change using micro-level data; text-mining and machine-learning analysis; evaluation of territorial policies; social effects of migration in Europe; agent-based modelling of long-term care preferences; human-algorithm interaction modelling; creation of evaluation-data repositories for evidence-based policy; development of decision-support systems in healthcare; algorithmic awareness; and ontology-based knowledge-graph generation (see Table 14.4).

[3] The acronym ECTS stands for European Credit Transfer and Accumulation System and is a standardized system in the European Union for measuring the workload of university students.

**Table 14.4** Research projects carried out by PhD candidates funded by FOSSR

| Gender of the PhD candidate | Research topic |
|---|---|
| M | Climate Change and Extreme Events: Micro-Level Economic Impacts Across the Energy System |
| M | Mapping Sustainability Discourses in Italian PhD theses. A Data-Driven Analysis Using FOSSR Infrastructures |
| F | Evaluating Integrated Territorial Development Strategies. Approaches, methodologies, and evidence |
| F | How Migration Reshapes Europe: Enforcement, Family Formation, and Interethnic Contact |
| M | Exploring Preferences, Sustainability, and Demographic Impact of Long-Term Care Policies: a Conjoint analysis and Agent Based Modeling Approach |
| M | Through interactions I learn to be: a Free Energy Principle exploration of the development of self and world models through interactions with predictive algorithms |
| F | Exploring, Building, and Enhancing Evaluation Data for Open Science and Evidence-Based Policy: The Case of the Fund for Combating Child Educational Poverty |
| M | The SDO Framework: a Data Science Approach to Estimate Readmission Rates |
| F | Investigating Algorithmic Awareness: Reflections, Tools, and Intervention Perspectives |
| F | Integrating LLM capabilities with Graph-Based Evidence for Effective Author Disambiguation |

Source: FOSSR project documentation (De Gregorio et al., 2025)

## 14.5 Key Participation Indicators and Feedback from the Participants

This section presents a set of key participation indicators and participants feedback aimed at capturing the short-term implications of the FOSSR training activities. By combining descriptive participation data with quantitative evaluation data and open feedbacks, the analysis provides an integrated overview of engagement patterns, perceived quality, and early signals of effectiveness.

**Key Results on Participation in OTCs and PSs**

Overall, the FOSSR training activities recorded a high level of participation and engagement. Across the full portfolio of OTCs and PSs, a total of 398 participations were registered, corresponding to 281 unique participants, indicating that a high share of participants engaged in more than one activity. This participation pattern emerges primarily across OTCs, while PSs functioned more as targeted formats.

The distribution of participants by type of organization indicates the broad institutional reach of the training activities and their capacity to engage heteroge-

**Fig. 14.2** Number of training participants (OTCs and PSs) by type of organization. Source: Database of participants in OTCs and PSs (N = 398)

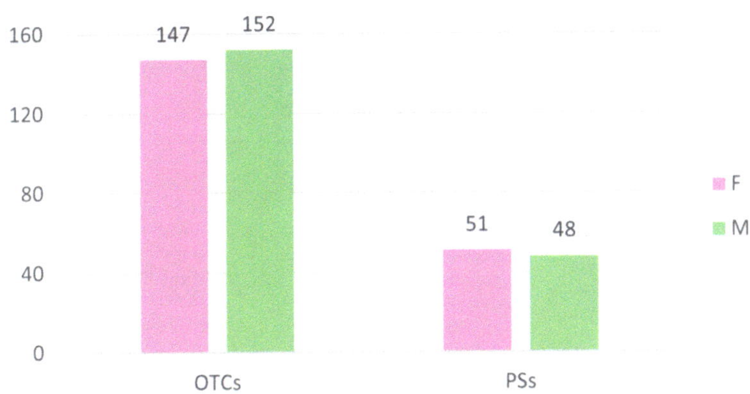


**Fig. 14.3** Training participants in OTCs and PSs by gender. Source: Database of participants in OTCs and PSs (N = 398)

neous research and policy communities (Fig. 14.2). Nearly half of the participants came from CNR institutes. A strong level of participation was also recorded from the universities confirming the broad interest generated by the topics addressed. Approximately 10% of participants have an international background, highligthing the considerable interest generated even in cross-border contexts. This pattern reflects the inclusive nature of OTCs, which were designed to maximize accessibility and sectoral diversity.

From a socio-demographic perspective, participation showed a good level of gender balance, with 50.3% of participants identifying as male, 49.7% as female (Fig. 14.3). The balanced participation observed suggests that the design and

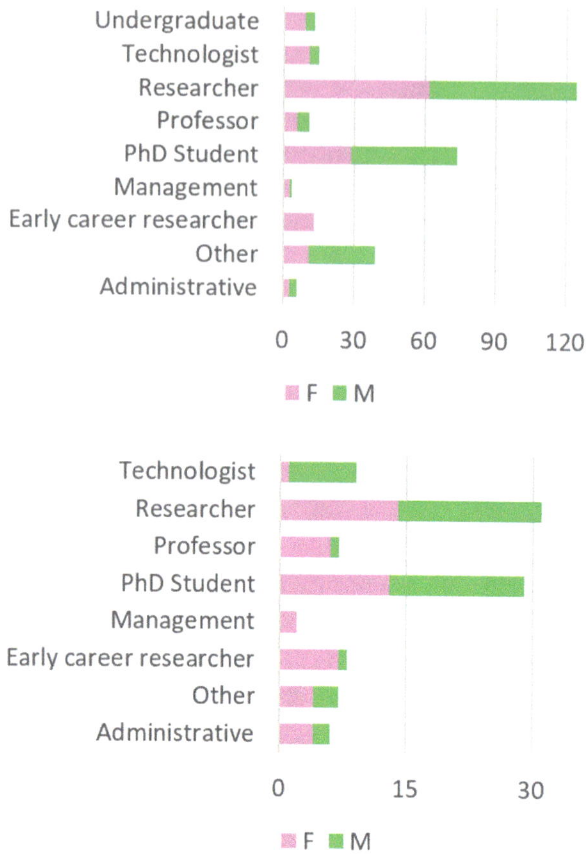


**Fig. 14.4** Number of training participants in OTCs (**a**) and PSs (**b**) by position and gender. Source: Database of participants in OTCs (N = 299) and PSs (N = 99)

delivery of the training activities were effective in lowering structural and cultural barriers to access, contributing to a more inclusive learning environment and supporting the development of diverse communities of practice around RIs.

In term of career stage, both OTCs and PSs mainly engaged researchers and PhD students, indicating the central role of these profiles within the FOSSR training activities. Gender participation appears overall balanced across positions, with no marked structural differences between men and women. As shown in Fig. 14.4a, b, OTCs attracted participants from a wide range of professional positions and career stages, whereas PSs mainly engaged a smaller, more stable group of researchers and practitioners, reflecting the higher level of commitment required by participatory and action-oriented training activities.

Focusing only on academic participants (131), the Fig. 14.5 shows a balanced geographic distribution across Italian universities, with Central Italy accounting for the largest share (42%), followed by Southern (37%) and Northern universities (21%). This geographic balance is primarily driven by participation in OTCs, which reduced territorial barriers through online delivery.

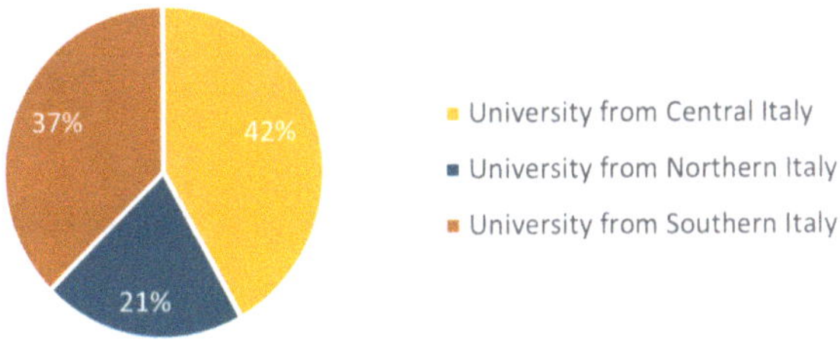


**Fig. 14.5** Geographic distribution of academic participants (OTCs and PSs). Source: Database of participants in OTCs and PSs (N = 131)

In terms of career stage, PhD students represent the largest group, followed by researchers and professors, indicating a strong involvement of both early-stage and established academic profiles. Participation by type of training highlights that OTCs attracted a broader academic audience across all positions, while PSs were more selectively attended, particularly by PhD students and researchers, consistent with their intensive and co-creative design.

**Participants Feedback from OTCs and PSs and Short Term Implications**
The assessment of the FOSSR training activities focuses on a limited set of short-term indicators aimed at capturing participants' engagement, perceived quality, and early signals of effectiveness.

Considering the specific characteristics of the training portfolio, to measure the early impact generated we relied on dimensions related to: (1) participants' satisfaction levels, (2) the incidence of individuals who attended more than one course (3) diversity of participants' sectors of origin, as an indicator of the ability to foster dialogue across different areas of society.

An important dimension of the training activities concerns how they were experienced by participants. Participants feedback from OTCs and PSs was collected through post-training evaluation questionnaires combining Likert-scale questions and open-ended responses. The overall satisfaction was high—in particular, participants reported high levels of appreciation on the clarity of the objectives (82%), the organizational features (77%), and the interest stimulated on the subjects (76%). Moreover, 82% expressed high appreciation for the consistency of the course with its description and for the overall course organization (see Fig. 14.6).

When given the opportunity to express their opinions in an open-ended question, participants of OTCs highlighted several particularly appreciated aspects: the instructors' expertise, the specificity and depth of the content covered, and the inclusion of numerous practical examples. Considering the opinions related to PSs, respondents particularly valued interaction, hands-on activities, and collaborative learning, while also indicating the need for longer durations and more time to develop group work and discussion.

Participation redundancy is a relevant short-term indicator of engagement continuity, as it reflects participants' willingness to return to and invest in multiple training opportunities rather than attending isolated activities. Specifically, 83 participants, corresponding to 29.5% of all unique participants, attended more than

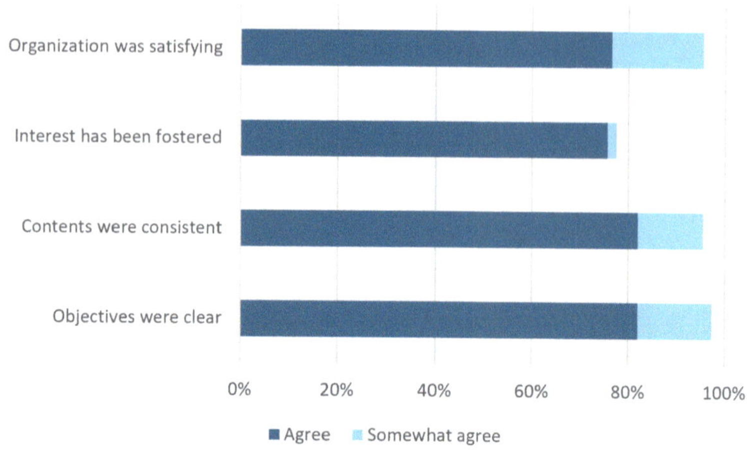


**Fig. 14.6** Participants feedback from post training questionnaire evaluations (OTCs and PSs). Source: Database of participants in OTCs and PSs (N = 398)

one training activity. This redundancy rate highlights that a substantial share of participants followed more than one learning opportunity within the FOSSR training portfolio.

As previously evidenced, participants to training activities represent a variety of sectors, among them research (48%), higher education (39%), other public administrations, private sector, NGOs. Such a variety is key to generating two different effects: to disseminate common skills across different sectors of society in the specific areas addressed, providing a shared language from which to engage, exchange ideas, create synergies and enhance social engagement and dialogue between science and society; to provide an opportunity for meeting and exchanging experiences and ideas, foundational elements for building interdisciplinary communities.

**Participation and Feedback from the University Master Programme**

The University Master Programme in SDS helped create a pool of young professionals capable of supporting methodological innovation, improving data management, and developing new technical solutions. Out of the 26 admitted students (16 men and 10 women), 22 attended the Master regularly (13 men and 9 women), and held their university title at the end of the 2-year program. Although the University Master Programme was held in Milan, its online delivery allowed for broad participation: the share of participants from Lombardy is less than 20%, but participation from outside the region remained predominant. The concentration in Lazio (six students) indicates strong participation from Central Italy, with a broad distribution also in the South and the Islands (Campania, Basilicata, Sicily).

The data collected through the evaluation questionnaires administered to students at the end of the programme reveal a very high overall appreciation for both the

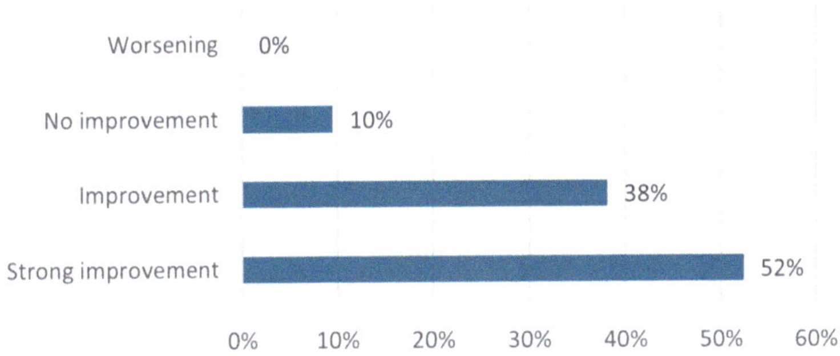


**Fig. 14.7** Perceived variation in skill levels from the beginning to the end of the University Master Programme. Source: Master SDS evaluation data

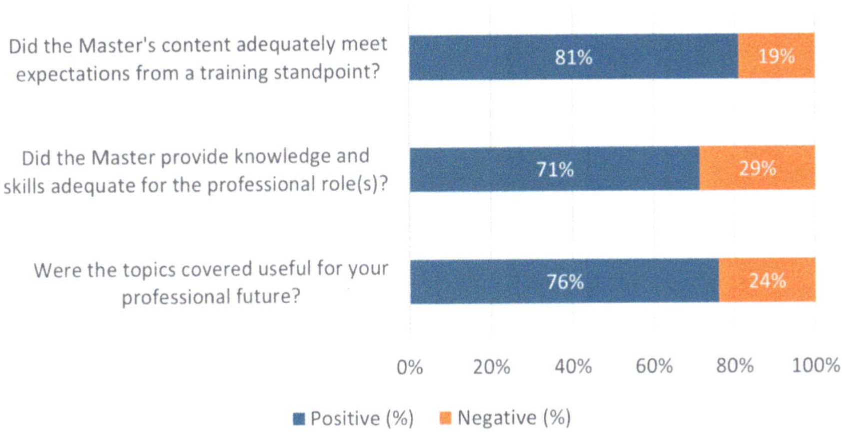


**Fig. 14.8** Evaluations of training quality and knowledge acquisition in the University Master Programme. Source: Master SDS evaluation data

educational impact and the quality and relevance of the content offered. Nearly all students reported significant benefits from the programme (Fig. 14.7): over half of participants (52%) reported a significant improvement in their skills, while a further 38% noted a clear improvement. None reported a decline, and only 10% perceived no change. Evaluation of the course content was also overwhelmingly positive (Fig. 14.8). Four students out of five felt the University Master Programme met their educational expectations, while 71% rated the skills provided as appropriate for their current or future professional roles. Furthermore, 76% considered the topics covered useful for their professional careers. The emerging picture is one of a valued learning experience with clear added value for students' professional growth.

## 14.6 Conclusions

Training is not an ancillary service of RIs, but rather it is one of the essential preconditions for their effectiveness and their capacity to shape scientific practices. The multilevel training strategy adopted by FOSSR, characterized by the combination of diverse types of initiatives—online courses, participatory sessions, university programmes—, on the one hand, aimed to address skill gaps required for innovative, high-quality social science research, and on the other, promoted the active involvement of potential users in the co-design of data services and resources. At the same time, the initiatives have sought to cultivate a new generation of researchers who do not only possess greater methodological expertise but are also committed to a contemporary and open approach to scientific research. The decision to design such a structured training framework represents a strategic choice that directly addresses the specific weaknesses of the Italian social sciences context, where awareness of RIs, quantitative culture and the habit of working with shared data require a broader widespread in the Social Sciences sector (Spinello, 2020).

The analysis of participation patterns reveals that the FOSSR training portfolio engaged a broad audience, respecting gender balance and paying attention to territorial disparities. The combination of different formats in multiple training events has addressed the diverse needs and career stages of different communities. High satisfaction levels also suggest that the training opportunities were perceived as relevant and worthy of engagement.

The experience described in this Chapter suggests that the training mission, widely advocated within RIs, can be made operational building strategies that can address diverse but complementary objectives. A systemic approach can be the path to strengthening the overall effectiveness of RIs and to conceptualizing research services as open, reflexive environments in which developers and users jointly engage in experimenting with new ways of producing and using social science data. Finally, it demonstrates that structured collaboration between RI and universities, experimented through the University Master Programme in SDS and co-funded doctoral scholarships, offers a viable approach for integrating Open Science and advanced methods into university programs.

In addition to the described initiatives, and in line with ESFRI's vision (2017), the FOSSR project has also invested in improving the excellence of RI internal staff, recognizing it as a key condition for medium- and long-term sustainability (ESFRI, 2017). As part of the broader strategy outlined in this document, FOSSR has complemented its training activities targeted to the users with additional courses specifically for FOSSR staff, aimed at strengthening both technical and managerial skills among those responsible for managing the infrastructure. The organization of a Winter School and a Summer School focusing on leadership and team building, strategic management of research infrastructures, service and data management, and innovation project management has further expanded and consolidated the overall training ecosystem (De Gregorio et al., 2025).

For the future, the validity and robustness of the FOSSR capacity-building strategy will depend on its ability to be accompanied, over time, by systematic monitoring capable of capturing the relationship between training activities and the evolution of research practices and the use of infrastructure services. Furthermore, sustainability remains the most sensitive issue: funding for a University Master programme and PhD scholarships represents a significant investment, but it is vulnerable to disruption unless it is absorbed into ordinary budgets.

Despite these challenges, in the short term, FOSSR's investment in training has led to a widespread culture of Open Science and the promotion of the quantitative dimension in the Social Sciences. The OTCs have helped spread expertise on FAIR data, documentation, standards, and interoperability; the PSs have made the connections between methodological choices and the social uses of data more explicit; Higher Education Programmes are developing professional profiles capable of navigating statistical modeling, programming, and theoretical reflection. Taken together, these initiatives have helped to nurture a community of practice that cuts across institutions, regions and generations.

## References


Bates, A. W. (2015). *Teaching in a digital age: Guidelines for designing teaching and learning*. Tony Bates Associates.

Bates, A. W. (2019). *Teaching in a digital age: Guidelines for designing teaching and learning* (2nd ed.). Tony Bates Associates.

Berkowitz, H., & Delacour, H. (2022). Opening research data: What does it mean for social sciences? *M@n@gement, 25*(4), 1–15.

Borgman, C. L. (2015). *Big data, little data, no data: Scholarship in the networked world*. MIT Press.

Boulton, G., Campbell, P., Collins, B., Elias, P., Hall, W., Laurie, G., O'Neill, O., Rawlins, M., Thornton, J., Vallance, P., Walport, M., & Wilsdon, J. (2012). *Science as an open enterprise*. The Royal Society. https://royalsociety.org/topics-policy/projects/science-public-enterprise/report/

Butcher, N. (2011). *A basic guide to Open Educational Resources (OER)*. Commonwealth of Learning and United Nations Educational, Scientific and Cultural Organization, UNESCO.

De Gregorio, D., De Lorenzo, A., Fabrizio, S., Spinello, A. O., Tudisca, V., & Valente, A. (2024, April). *D8.3 First Report on initiatives related to capacity building and training (online courses, learning session and action research session, higher education courses)*. NRRP-RI Project FOSSR—Fostering Open Science in Social Science Research. https://doi.org/10.5281/zenodo.15090390

De Gregorio, D., De Lorenzo, A., Fabrizio, S., Pennacchiotti, C., Spinello, A.O., & Tudisca, V. (2025, June). *D8.5 Second Report on initiatives related to capacity building and training (online courses, learning session and action research session, higher education courses)*. NRRP-RI Project FOSSR—Fostering Open Science in Social Science Research.

ESFRI. (2017). *Long-term sustainability of research infrastructures*. ESFRI Scripta Volume II ISBN PDF: 978-88-901562-8-1.

ESFRI. (2020). *Making science happen. A new ambition for research infrastructure in the European research area*. ESFRI White Book. https://www.esfri.eu/sites/default/files/White_paper_ESFRI-final.pdf

European Commission. (2024). *European charter for access to research infrastructures: Principles and guidelines for access and related services*. European Commission.
Fabrizio, S., Reale, E., & Spinello, A. O. (2023). *Building a stronger community in STI studies for effective impact: The experience of RISIS*. RISIS Policy Brief 15. https://doi.org/10.5281/zenodo.11276785
Fenwick, T., & Edwards, R. (2010). *Actor-network theory in education*. Routledge.
Ferrie, J., Wain, M., Gallacher, S., et al. (2022). *Scoping the skills needs in the social sciences to support data-driven research*. Technopolis Group.
Funtowicz, S. O., & Ravetz, J. R. (1993). Science for the post-normal age. *Futures, 25*(7), 739–755.
Garrison, D. R., Anderson, T., & Archer, W. (2000). Critical inquiry in a text-based environment: Computer conferencing in higher education. *The Internet and Higher Education, 2*(2–3), 87–105.
Hey, T., Tansley, S., & Tolle, K. (Eds.). (2009). *The fourth paradigm: Data-intensive scientific discovery*. Microsoft Research.
Inamorato dos Santos, A., Punie, Y., & Castaño-Muñoz, J. (2016). *Opening up education: A support framework for higher education institutions*. JRC Science for Policy Report, EUR 27938 EN. https://doi.org/10.2791/293408
Kesari, A., Kim, J. Y., Shah, S., Brown, T., Ventura, T., & Law, T. (2023). Training computational social science PhD students for academic and non-academic careers. PS. *Political Science & Politics, 57*(1), 101–106.
Kleiner, B., Renschler, I., Wernli, B., Farago, P., & Joye, D. (Eds.). (2013). *Understanding Research Infrastructures in the Social Sciences*. Seismo Press.
Kuhn, T. S. (1962). *The structure of scientific revolutions*. University of Chicago Press.
Latour, B. (1987). *Science in action: How to follow scientists and engineers through society*. Harvard University Press.
Latour, B. (2005). *Reassembling the social: An introduction to actor-network-theory*. Oxford University Press.
Laurillard, D. (2013). *Teaching as a design science: Building pedagogical patterns for learning and technology*. Routledge.
Mezirow, J. (1991). *Transformative dimensions of adult learning*. Jossey-Bass.
Nielsen, M. (2011). *Reinventing discovery: The new era of networked science*. Princeton University Press.
OECD. (2020). *Building digital workforce capacity and skills for data-intensive science*. OECD Science, Technology and Industry Policy Papers, No. 90.
Peters, M. A., Jandric, P., & McLaren, P. (Eds.). (2020). *Open science and education*. Springer.
Reale, E., Fabrizio, S., & Morettini, L. (2019). Stakeholders' role to produce impact from social science research: What lessons for evaluation? *fteval Journal for Research and Technology Policy Evaluation, 48*, 143–151.
Reed, M. S., & Rudman, H. (2023). Re-thinking research impact: Voice, context and power at the interface of science, policy and practice. *Sustainability Science, 18*, 967–981.
Salmon, G. (2011). *E-moderating: The key to online teaching and learning* (3rd ed.). Routledge.
Spinello, A. O. (2020). Le infrastrutture di ricerca nelle scienze sociali: uno studio di caso su utilizzo ed effetti nella produzione scientifica. *Welfare e Ergonomia, 1*(2019), 67–78. https://www.francoangeli.it/riviste/Scheda_rivista.aspx?IDArticolo=65717
Spinello, A. O., & Fabrizio, S. (2025). Integrated capacity-building approach to address societal challenges through social science research infrastructures. *Societal Impacts, 6*, 100140. https://doi.org/10.1016/j.socimp.2025.100140
Star, S. L., & Ruhleder, K. (1996). Steps toward an ecology of infrastructure: Design and access for large information spaces. *Information Systems Research, 7*(1), 111–134. https://doi.org/10.1287/isre.7.1.111
Sterling, S. (2001). *Sustainable education: Re-visioning learning and change*. Green Books.
UNESCO. (2019). *Recommendation on Open Educational Resources (OER)—Supporting universal access to information through quality open learning materials*. UNESCO.

UNESCO. (2021). *Recommendation on open science*. United Nations Educational, Scientific and Cultural Organization.

Wehn, U., Ajates, R., Mandeville, C., Somerwill, L., Kragh, G., & Haklay, M. (2024). Opening science to society: How to progress societal engagement into (open) science policies. *Royal Society Open Science, 11*, 231309.

Wenger, E. (1998). *Communities of practice: Learning, meaning, and identity*. Cambridge University Press.

Wenger, E., McDermott, R., & Snyder, W. (2002). *Cultivating communities of practice: A guide to managing knowledge*. Harvard Business School Press.

# Chapter 15
# Communication, Engagement and Community Building: Enabling the Use of Research Infrastructures

**Serena Fabrizio, Rita Giuffredi, Erica Rizziato, Alessandra Maria Stilo, Elisa Storace, and Valentina Tudisca**

## 15.1 Introduction

In today's Open Science landscape, the way research is shared through open Research Infrastructures (RIs) and made accessible to the public is evolving beyond traditional dissemination practices. This shift is occurring in parallel with transformations in the models and roles assigned to science communication, as well as in the physiognomy of the contemporary system of knowledge production and of its interplay with the societal context.

Open Science is characterised by the emphasis on knowledge circulation across disciplinary boundaries and institutional contexts, hybridisation of knowledge production, and shifting values, concerns and requests made to academia by the public. Research communication is required to evolve towards the recognition of diversified audiences, blurred boundaries between science and society, and work to foster shared epistemologies based on co-production (Jasanoff, 2004b; Trench, 2008), in order to achieve effective and meaningful engagement.

S. Fabrizio (✉) · R. Giuffredi · E. Rizziato · A. M. Stilo
CNR-IRCrES - National Research Council of Italy, Research Institute on Sustainable Economic Growth, Rome, Italy
e-mail: serena.fabrizio@cnr.it; rita.giuffredi@cnr.it; erica.rizziato@cnr.it; alessandramaria.stilo@cnr.it

E. Storace
CNR-UVR - National Research Council of Italy, Technology transfer office, Rome, Italy
e-mail: elisa.storace@cnr.it

V. Tudisca
CNR-IRPPS - National Research Council of Italy, Institute for Research on Population and Social Policies, Rome, Italy
e-mail: valentina.tudisca@cnr.it



G. Cerulli, E. Reale (eds.), *Research Infrastructures for Open Science in Social Science Research*, https://doi.org/10.1007/978-3-032-29575-0_15

In the context of Research Infrastructures, understood as a socio-technical objects, it is critical to adequately recognise the importance of the social component. This dimension encompasses the individuals and organisations involved in designing, operating, and governing the infrastructure, as well as those who access its resources or interact with it as users, contributors, or stakeholders.

Within this perspective, communication does not constitute an end, nor is part of the primary missions of a Research Infrastructure. However, it plays an important role to support coordination, mutual understanding, and interaction among different actors, thereby facilitating access, use, and meaningful integration of the infrastructure resources within research and policy contexts.

From a broader epistemological perspective, contributions from Science and Technology Studies have shown how scientific knowledge and practices increasingly emerge from interactions among heterogeneous social actors and institutional contexts (Gibbons et al., 1994; Jasanoff, 2004b; Ziman, 2000). Although these contributions primarily address knowledge production rather than the design of Research Infrastructures, they offer a useful conceptual background for understanding the relational conditions under which knowledge is produced and mobilised in open and distributed research environments. Within this context, attention to communicative and relational dimensions supports access, coordination, and effective use of Research Infrastructures (RIs), contributing to their practical relevance and usability by enabling their uptake and sustained use through the development of a robust and aware community of users.

The chapter examines communication and engagement practices implemented within the FOSSR Research Infrastructure as interrelated components of a broader process of interaction between RI developers, potential users, and stakeholders. The different sections address complementary dimensions, from communication and dissemination activities to more participative formats. Within this perspective, both participatory practices and monitoring tools are discussed as part of a coherent approach to understand how relationships and learning processes are built and sustained within an Open Research Infrastructure. The chapter is organised as follows. Section 15.1 introduces the overall framing and rationale of the chapter. Section 15.2 outlines the conceptual foundations of the FOSSR approach to communication and community building. Section 15.3 describes the main communication, community-building, and stakeholder engagement actions implemented within the FOSSR framework. Section 15.4 presents the adoption of an innovative Action Research methodology with the aim of fostering the creation of a community among partners and stakeholders, to promote the generativity of the project and improve its social impact. The aim was also to experiment with expanding the competencies of those involved, to broaden the vision of FOSSR's potential. Section 15.5 regards the system of KPIs (Key Performance Indicators) and of the early engagement indicators used to monitor communication performance and engagement dynamics and discusses their role within a phased evaluation perspective. Section 15.6 concludes the chapter.

## 15.2 The FOSSR's Approach to Communication, Community Building and Stakeholders' Engagement

The evolution of science communication theory in recent decades provides a critical lens to interpret the transformations impacting Open Science Research Infrastructures. Initially, at the beginning of the '80 s, the prevailing paradigm of science communication was the "Public Understanding of Science" model, promoted by scientific and public Institutions to reduce the disengagement of the public from science, predicated to be attributable to an absence, or "deficit", of scientific knowledge (Bodmer, 1985; Miller, 2004). This deficit was theorised to be remedied through the provision of adequate injections of scientific knowledge.

However, this model has been criticised by the academic community for its technocratic and paternalistic assumptions, and for its failure to adequately value the importance of social, cultural, value-related and political dimensions of public engagement with science (Davies & Horst, 2016; Jasanoff, 2003). In response, scholars have developed a reflection pivoting on public dialogue and participation, emphasising the role of context in learning, the role of non-formal epistemologies in the understanding and resolution of science-based issues, and models aimed at co-producing knowledge (Funtowicz & Ravetz, 1993; Jasanoff, 2004b; Wynne, 1992).

Particularly, in the social sphere, new practices for creating knowledge and communication have been developed through participatory approaches, including Action Research, which consists of a cyclical process of planning, action, and reflection on the results of the action. This approach generates a communication vision that extends beyond content and is inspired by the opportunity for transformative practices, creating spaces for the reflexive adaptation of projects, meaning-making and the creation of genuine value. In Action Research, the relationship between subject and object is intersubjective; both are social actors, the product and producer of processes and knowledge based on a mutual relationship (Lewin, 1972; French & Bell, 1998, Reason & Bradbury, 2001, 2008, 2015). The conceptual framework grounding the new Action Research methodology is addressed and detailed in Sect. 15.4.

Dialogic and participatory models of science communication are in alignment with the principles of Open Science, as both are aimed at fostering a paradigm change in research, heading towards the direction of a more democratic incorporation in social contexts (Hecker et al., 2018; Jasanoff, 2004a). In both cases, communication role extends beyond the mere dissemination of knowledge to the public, towards the facilitation of an engagement among researchers, policymakers, civil society, and communities. This approach is of particular significance for Research Infrastructures (RIs), whose identity as collaborative, cross-disciplinary platforms is as relevant as the technical one.

Building on this relational understanding of communication, recent contributions in research impact assessment have further conceptualised how interactions themselves become mechanisms through which research generates social relevance.

Some approaches (Molas-Gallart & Tang, 2011) focus on the dynamic interplays between researchers and societal stakeholders as key mechanisms through which research generates socially relevant outcomes. In this framework, *productive interactions*, whether direct (e.g. meetings and workshops), indirect (e.g. reports, policy documents, shared artefacts), or financial (e.g. collaborative funding arrangements), are conceptualised as relational processes through which knowledge produced in research contexts acquires relevance beyond academia. This perspective offers a possibility for understanding how communicative and participatory activities within Research Infrastructures may contribute to the emergence of socially meaningful forms of interaction, and to the generation of impact.

The FOSSR communication approach was conceived as an integral component of the infrastructure's strategic assets, contributing to the coordination, alignment, and interaction of its multiple actors. In this sense, FOSSR meta-infrastructure is considered as a complex socio-technical system, in which technical components, organisational arrangements, and human practices are tightly interwoven (Hughes, 1987). Within such systems, communication plays a central and dynamic role in enabling interoperability, shared understanding, and collective sense-making across institutional and disciplinary boundaries.

Prior to the initiation of the communication activities, a SWOT (Strengths, Weaknesses, Opportunities and Threats) analysis (Reale & Fabrizio, 2024) was performed to inform the design of the FOSSR communication and engagement strategy, assessing the initial assets and potential pitfalls specifically related to visibility, uptake, and use of the Research Infrastructure. The analysis emphasised that FOSSR could rely on the demonstrated effectiveness of existing Research Infrastructure communities (notably CESSDA ERIC, SHARE ERIC and RISIS) as consolidated ecosystems, as regards the access requests to datasets and the impact produced in terms of projects and publications. Furthermore, all involved partners could rely on robust competencies in the activities connected to RI development, as well as on consolidated past experiences in designing and managing training and PhD activities. Conversely, the analysis identified the necessity to concentrate efforts on the integration of tools, internal and external networking, and on the effective use of resources. This highlighted the importance of actively engaging researchers and stakeholders in a cohesive and stable manner to foster knowledge circulation and the full exploitation of resources.

In light of these considerations, the FOSSR project was conceived with the objective of mobilising knowledge-intensive resources as the Open Cloud, thereby serving as a formidable intermediation layer among data and services producers (who also simultaneously play the role of actual users of the RI's developing ecosystem), archives, and potential users from the diverse stakeholder groups.

Further opportunities identified through the SWOT analysis concerned the role of communication in supporting innovation and awareness, particularly in relation to emerging methodologies for data collection and analysis and to the development of semantic knowledge graphs, which require shared understanding and coordinated interaction among diverse user communities.

Similarly, the development of longitudinal and panel data, historically underutilised in the Italian research context, was identified as a communication challenge as much as a technical one, requiring targeted actions to raise awareness and foster adoption among researchers and institutional users.

Finally, the SWOT analysis drew attention to potential threats relevant for communication and engagement strategies, including geographical disparities within Italy, institutional fragmentation, uneven awareness among SSH scholars, and the challenge of ensuring long-term visibility and use of the Research Infrastructure beyond the NRRP-funded phase.

### *15.2.1 The FOSSR Audience*

Communication priorities are primarily shaped by the needs of those actors who are directly involved in the production, use, and institutional uptake of research outputs.

In this respect, core scientific communities constitute the primary reference audience of FOSSR. Researchers, doctoral candidates, and early-career scholars represent the main potential users of infrastructural services, data, and tools, and their sustained engagement is essential for ensuring the scientific relevance, methodological robustness, and continuous development of the infrastructure. Communication towards these communities is therefore closely intertwined with access to resources and services, training, capacity building, and opportunities for feedback, rather than being limited to dissemination for visibility purposes (see Fig. 15.1).

Alongside academic potential users, policy makers and institutional stakeholders represent a second, strategic audience for the Research Infrastructure (RI). Communication addressed to this group is oriented towards facilitating the uptake and interpretation of research outputs, supporting evidence-informed decision-making, and reinforcing the legitimacy of public investment in large-scale RIs. In this context, communicative practices are closely connected to policy-oriented formats, such as targeted workshops, policy briefs, and dedicated sessions designed to align infrastructural resources with policy needs.

The differentiated articulation of communication priorities also opens the space for more intensive forms of engagement. Sustained interaction with core scientific communities and policy-oriented stakeholders creates the conditions for moving beyond information provision and structured dialogue towards processes of shared problem framing, mutual learning, and reflexive adaptation of research practices.

This strategy followed a progressive model of stakeholder engagement adapted to the context of RIs, articulated in four sequential phases: inform, involve, collaborate, and engage (Fabrizio et al., 2023). The temporal evolution of communication activities mirrors the project own development, from a top-down approach in 2023 to a more horizontal and participatory model during 2024–2025.

At the *Inform* and *Involve* levels, indicators primarily capture the performance of communication activities aimed at awareness-raising and initial participation,

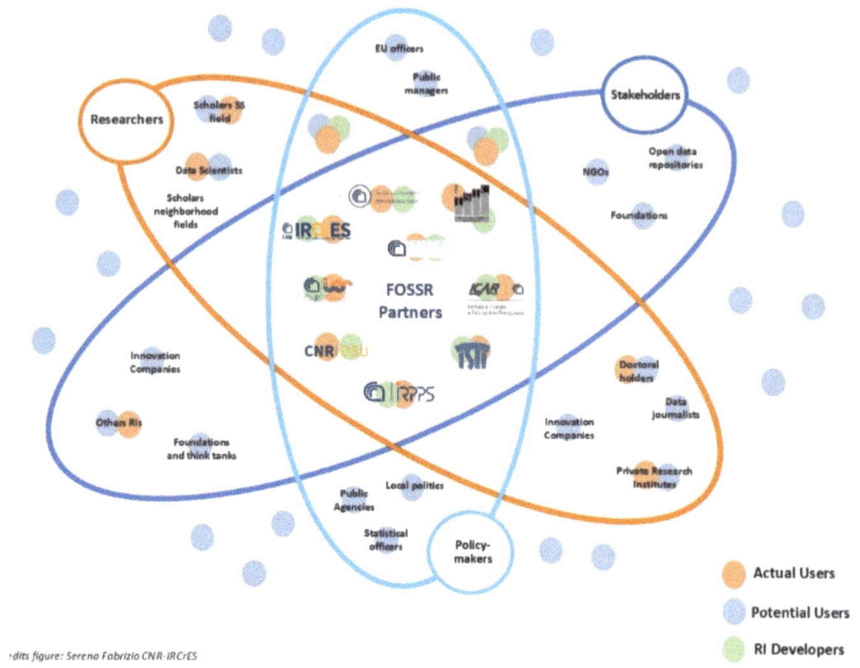


**Fig. 15.1** The FOSSR "galaxy"

such as website access, downloads, attendance at events, and first interactions with project outputs. These indicators document the capacity of FOSSR to reach and mobilise potential users.

More advanced levels, particularly *Collaborate*, provide the interpretative space to account for qualitative shifts in interaction, where engagement moved beyond participation towards co-design and reflexive exchange. It is at this level that the project generated its most tangible outcomes to date, in the form of design-oriented improvements resulting from iterative interaction between services developers and potential users within Action Research activities. Such outcomes correspond to what the literature describes as internal or organisational forms of impact, where learning and adaptation occur within the infrastructure itself rather than through external uptake (Fabre et al., 2021; Mayernik et al., 2017).

The *Empower* level, while conceptually relevant for long-term infrastructural sustainability, is here treated as a perspective dimension. Indicators associated with governance participation or strategic alignment are interpreted as early signals of potential future engagement.

From this perspective, communication is not limited to supporting access, visibility, or legitimacy, but contributes to the emergence of collaborative dynamics in which researchers and institutional actors jointly reflect on infrastructural needs, research workflows, and governance arrangements. Such dynamics rely on selective, stable, and context-sensitive interactions, rather than on symmetrical engagement across all audiences, and are especially relevant for Research Infrastructures operating in open, distributed, and policy-relevant research environments.

Communication addressed to wider, non-specialist audiences plays a more limited and complementary role supporting objectives of transparency and public visibility, contributing to broader reflections on the societal relevance of publicly funded research. Scholarly discussions on the public communication of science have highlighted the importance of such practices in sustaining trust and institutional legitimacy, particularly in domains where public accountability is central (Benessia et al., 2016; Irwin, 2015; Jasanoff, 2003, 2005; Wynne et al., 2007).

## 15.3 Community Building and Stakeholder Engagement for RIs: Main Issues and Actions Developed

The FOSSR communication strategy was designed as a coherent, multi-channel framework structured around three interconnected dimensions:

(a) institutional and informational presence through the project website;
(b) relational and narrative presence across social media platforms;
(c) dialogical and participatory presence through a diversified offer of events.

In the first phase, FOSSR communication activities were designed to achieve visibility and recognition, in a context where other analogue research-based initiatives were already present or under development.

The starting point of the process was the group of participants involved in the project kick-off meeting and the initial core of the FOSSR research team, comprising approximately 70 contacts.

Objectives of immediate importance for the FOSSR communication strategy were relation-building and knowledge exchange among all infrastructure actors, and the promotion of a smooth and constant circulation of information within the internal project community, alongside the more traditional broadcasting paradigm, focused on transmitting information and gaining visibility.

### *15.3.1 Informing, Documenting and Establishing a Narrative*

FOSSR digital communication strategy focused on two main channels: social media and the website.

#### 15.3.1.1 Social Media Profiles: Visibility, Proximity, and Narrative

The project's social media profiles—Facebook, LinkedIn, YouTube and initially Twitter, later replaced by Instagram following an editorial reorientation—were the first communication tools activated.

The social media strategy was grounded in three operational principles:

(a) integration with the overall communication framework;
(b) editorial continuity, with regular weekly publications maintaining a consistent format and tone; and
(c) differentiation across platforms, through the adaptation of language and formats to specific audiences.

On Facebook, communication emphasized the broader community by publishing event-related content, photographic reports, and outreach materials for a general audience. LinkedIn adopted a professional and institutional register, targeting researchers, partner organizations, and policymakers, with an emphasis on project results, calls, and collaborations (e.g., #FOSSRpeople). Twitter and later Instagram have been used for more immediate, visually driven communication targeting younger audiences and doctoral researchers. The YouTube channel targets a broad audience, including both specialists and people with a general interest in Open Science, and consequently the proposed contents are highly segmented: out of the forty videos uploaded, more than half (23) are interviews, just over a quarter (11) are complete recordings of events, while the remaining six (6) are explanatory videos focusing on aspects of the project or related scientific concepts (e.g., DOI, FAIR data).

The social media channels provide a means of presenting the "human dimension" of FOSSR—researchers, personal stories, and shared experiences—thereby fostering a sense of belonging and identification within the FOSSR community (Davies et al., 2019). In this way, social communication played a central role in the Involve phase, facilitating relationships among the project's stakeholders and with the broader public.

#### 15.3.1.2 The Website: Informing, Documenting, and Connecting

The official project website[1] was conceived as both an informational hub and a public archive of FOSSR's activities. The primary target groups identified for the website included:

(a) social science researchers seeking data, tools and services;
(b) others research infrastructures, institutions, and policymakers engaged in developing the national infrastructure;

[1] www.fossr.eu.

(c) a wider variety of stakeholders such as students, doctoral candidates, and the scientific communities interested in open-science practices.

The architecture was designed to ensure accessibility, transparency, and continuity, presenting project objectives, services and technical developments, events and outcomes, and promoting training and dissemination activities. The website was articulated into a limited number of core sections covering project information, the Open Cloud, community-building activities, scientific outputs, and news and events. In particular, the Open Cloud section functions as a central access point to data, services, and methodological resources. This modular organisation supports intuitive navigation and allows different user groups—such as researchers, policymakers, and infrastructure developers—to access relevant content efficiently.

The iconographic style—based on images of contemporary architecture—was selected to provide visual coherence and to evoke for FOSSR the metaphors of an ambitious building under construction, built with the contribution of many actors, open to the exchanges with the world and articulated on the interconnection and networking of researchers and societal actors. Moreover, the choice of architectural structures had the advantage of evoking the study of people's social behaviours, which is at the heart of social sciences.

## 15.3.2 *Developing Dialogue and Grounding Participation*

Among FOSSR's primary objectives, community building was fostered through a diversified offer of events, including in-person, online, and hybrid formats. These events were designed to leverage the full range of involvement formats, encompassing both the more traditional settings, online seminars, through events targeting specific communities, like policy maker sessions, until formats based on full engagement of participants, such as Action Research sessions. A series of FOSSR Café was also incorporated into the original event planning, with the objective of facilitating informal interactions and conversation among the FOSSR research team. In Appendix (Table 5), we collected the main information related to all the events organized.

### 15.3.2.1 The FOSSR Café: A Dialogical Dimension

One of the most effective tools for community building within FOSSR has been the FOSSR Café format, launched in 2024 as an informal and participatory space for dialogue. The Cafés have been targeted at the project internal community, comprising doctoral students and young researchers (identified as promising actors for the development of the infrastructure since the design phase), researchers, and technologists involved in the development of the RI. The Cafés were intended to promote mutual understanding, listening, and a reflective space for the RI.

The inclusion of these cafes was particularly designed to provide a space for younger members of the community, with the intention of enhancing community-building. Participants were invited to share experiences, expectations, and working tools through a "representative object" symbolizing their individual contribution to the community. Inspired by knowledge cafes and by the methodology behind science cafes (Lefika & Mearns, 2015; Powell, 2010) this approach was chosen to encourage dialogue and knowledge circulation among FOSSR staff members, whose home Institutes are distributed across Italy, promoting collective identity and project interdisciplinarity while maintaining a relaxed and informal setting. Participants were brought together to introduce their profiles and exchange ideas, developing soft skills related to sociality, such as those of team and community building. For many project participants, the FOSSR Café experience was an opportunity to get to know their colleagues and make themselves known to them, building trust in an informal setting. The FOSSR Cafés functioned as laboratories of communicative experimentation, where the institutional language of research infrastructures was opened to conversation, storytelling, and direct participation. Between 2024 and 2025, eight FOSSR Café sessions were held, with an average of 20 participants per session.

#### 15.3.2.2 Seminars/Webinars and Demonstration Sessions

Within the online communication initiatives, we planned two categories of events—webinars and seminars—organized through a similar participatory approach, but targeting different groups and pursuing distinct aims. Even though the two formats blurred to a certain extent during the development of the activities, the distinction made in the design phase reveals some fine details of the articulation of publics—and hence adequate formats—hypothesized for the FOSSR audience.

Online seminars were targeted to an academic audience—researchers from universities and public research centres, university students, including but not limited to FOSSR research teams—and had the main aim of promoting the exchange of research ideas and questions, presenting methods and findings developed by FOSSR thematic network, building a shared knowledge background and activating a collective process of knowledge co-creation that nourished the techno-scientific decisions taken within the project. Indeed, seminars were not conceived to transmit consolidated knowledge, but to foster an informed debate on problematic research issues that required a deep and wide exchange of points of view among scholars from different fields to achieve transdisciplinary solutions. This aspect was stressed by the format chosen, including 1–2 invited/selected speakers working in FOSSR research field followed by a roundtable composed by 4–10 panellists selected to nourish the debate, and leaving the audience the possibility to contribute via chat.

Among the topics considered as suitable were, e.g., building the FOSSR Italian Online Probability Panel (IOPP), other existing research infrastructures, with special attention to those connected to FOSSR, theoretical models underlying the main international social surveys and their possible evolution, and FOSSR virtual panels.

Online webinars were targeted not only to academics, but to a larger audience, including also researchers working in the private sector, practitioners, and various kinds of social actors/stakeholders, e. g., policy makers, officers, administrative staff, associations, and companies. The webinars were intended to give visibility to the project and discuss specific tools and services developed within FOSSR to investigate economic and societal changes, thereby increasing awareness about their public availability and collecting inputs and feedback from civil society to foster their usability in different contexts and ensure their alignment to the needs, values, and expectations of society, as envisaged by the European Responsible Research and Innovation framework.

Moreover, as a complement to the webinars, during the last two editions of the FOSSR Days—annual event aimed at presenting and discussing the project achievements—a new format was introduced to showcase FOSSR services in a practical and operational way: Demonstration Sessions, conceived as hands-on activities designed to involve participants in a direct experimentation with available tools and services.

Structured around a "tour" of the services and concrete application cases, these two sessions allowed participants to explore functionalities and workflows with the support of experts, respectively focusing on FOSSR Virtual Research Environment and Open Cloud and Marketplace. Within the engagement framework adopted in the chapter, Demonstration Sessions represent a transition point from involvement to early forms of collaboration, where participants actively interact with services and contribute feedback to their further development.

All the events were delivered through a Teams platform in Italian, the related written materials being prepared in English to encourage interest beyond the national context and made available on the project cloud via Zenodo together with the video recordings also posted on the project YouTube channel.

Moreover, we conducted an ongoing evaluation activity to improve the quality of the events, submitting evaluation questionnaires to participants to gather information about their appreciation levels and, for the seminars, also asking a discussant from the scientific community feedback.

Both seminars and webinars were conceived as events where dissemination and scientific research overlap: with reference to the FOSSR framework of community building and stakeholder engagement they were aimed to realize not only the "inform" and "involve" level, but also the "collaborate" dimension. Indeed, while giving visibility to the project, seminars offered wide academic audiences—also external to FOSSR partnership—the opportunity of contributing to address FOSSR scientific issues and challenges, informing and nourishing the techno-scientific decisions to be taken within the project; in particular, with reference to the development of the IOPP, to the Agent-based modelling and to the FOSSR Open Cloud. In the case of webinars, tools and innovations developed by the projects were presented and collectively debated: the Policy Learning Platform, targeted to policy makers, and the FOSSR IOPP in the startup phase, debated among international research communities that revolve around other European Online Probability Panels.

#### 15.3.2.3 Policy Dialogue: Policy Brief and Policymakers' Sessions

FOSSR has identified several key audiences (see Sect. 15.2), including policymakers and institutional actors represent a distinct and strategic reference public. The relevance of FOSSR research streams to this audience is twofold: first, these streams are targeted at gathering socio-economic data regarding key societal issues, and to the development of methodological advancements in data collection; secondly, they monitor, interpret, and offer advanced interpretation tools of general trends related to relevant socio-political development that are relevant to policy design, implementation, and evaluation.

In line with the differentiated articulation of publics adopted by the project, communication with policy makers was conceived not as a generic outreach activity, but as a targeted form of institutional engagement, calibrated to the roles, constraints, and informational needs of actors involved in decision-making processes.

Specifically, FOSSR aimed to engage with officers from all levels of policy implementation, including government bodies at both the national and local levels. The primary strategy adopted to establish and consolidate these interactions built upon pre-existing relational capital developed within European Research Infrastructures RIs (RISIS, CESSDA, SHARE), with the subsequent expansion of these networks through a snowball approach and by means of devoted communication tools.

The two principal instruments conceived to provide content and stimulate dialogue with policy officers were the Policymakers Sessions and the Policy Brief series which should be read as complementary components of a single engagement strategy. Both tools were developed to translate research results into policy-relevant knowledge, adopting a language, format, and narrative style suited to the time constraints and operational logics of policy actors, while preserving analytical rigour. In this perspective, policy briefs functioned as *boundary objects*, enabling a first level of interaction by framing complex evidence in a concise and accessible form, supported by visual elements and infographics to facilitate rapid interpretation.

The Policy Briefs were published as six-page booklets, with a coordinated cover illustrated with cover images that metaphorically evoked the contents. Following the dissemination of the Policy Briefs to the designated target audience, the identical content was presented and discussed in concise two-hour webinars, designated as "Policymakers sessions". These webinars were specifically targeted at policymakers and enriched by the presence of a discussant, who played a role in commenting on and animating the debate, chosen to ensure scientific rigour and enhance clarity.

Each Policymakers Session was strategically positioned as the opening event of the annual FOSSR Days, reinforcing the connection between policy dialogue and the broader scientific and community-oriented activities of the Research Infrastructure. This design choice contributed to situating policy engagement within the wider communicative framework.

Policy Briefs and Policymakers Sessions were structured around substantive policy questions emerging at the intersection of data availability, methodological innovation, and policy evidence. Among the recurrent themes addressed were data-driven policy learning and ex-ante policy evaluation, the use of advanced analytical techniques such as text mining and causal inference to support policy design, and the production of high-quality, high-frequency individual data for monitoring social and economic change.[2]

These topics were selected not only for their scientific relevance, but also for their direct applicability to ongoing policy challenges, including the evaluation of public programmes, the alignment of research funding with societal goals, and the anticipation of policy impacts in contexts of uncertainty.

Focusing policy dialogue on concrete thematic domains contributed to grounding interaction in shared problem spaces, facilitating discussion on how research infrastructures can support policy learning processes, enhance the usability of evidence, and strengthen institutional capacities for evidence-informed decision-making.

## 15.4 A New Action Research Methodological Approach to Generate Impact on the Community

The Action Research sessions are part of the participatory sessions of the FOSSR project, which aimed to promote shared knowledge creation and transformative reflection among researchers, students, and societal stakeholders.

In the FOSSR context, Action Research was used in an innovative way, as described below, with the aim of fostering the creation of a community among partners and stakeholders to promote the generativity of the project and improve its social impact. In this sense, the aim was to experiment with broadening the competencies of those involved to expand the vision of FOSSR's potential.

The Action Research methodology is a type of research that complements traditional scientific research. It is characterised by its ability to generate knowledge about the dynamic reality of socio-economic systems by activating the actors in the field to investigate the critical issues they experience and transform them. It proposes the transformation of social systems, using certain elements of the descriptive-analytical tradition, but focusing on transformative and interactive processes (Lewin, 1972; French & Bell, 1998, Reason & Bradbury, 2001, 2008, 2015).

In Action Research, the relationship between subject and object is intersubjective; both are social actors, the product and producer of processes based on a mutual

[2] Details and agendas are available at the pages: https://www.fossr.eu/en/eventi/fossr-days-opportunities-from-italys-first-open-cloud-for-social-sciences/ (First Policy makers session, October 16th, 2023); https://www.fossr.eu/eventi/fossr-days-2024-policy-makers-session/ (Second Policy makers session, October ninth, 2024); https://www.fossr.eu/eventi/fossr-days-2026-policy-makers-session-high-quality-high-frequency-individual-data-production-in-italy-innovation-introduced-by-fossr/ (Third Policy makers session, February four, 2026).

relationship. Here, the empirical object no longer has a passive role, but an active one, as does the researcher, who is no longer just an observer.

Action Research becomes an essential approach for studying complex systems, considered, as Edgar Morin argues, to be a set of heterogeneous variables, both subjective and objective, which can only be understood by studying their interaction; it is not possible to understand a complex system by abstracting its variables and studying them as isolated from the situation from which they originate.

Kurt Lewin (1972), who first formalised the forms of Action Research, defines it as: "research that, by comparing the conditions and effects of various forms of social action and research, produces social action. Research that only produces books is not sufficient".

Action Research is based on a spiral of steps, each of which consists of a cyclical process of planning, action, and reflection on the results of the action.

In the international debate, in the last 25 years, two critical issues have emerged that needed to be addressed in order to develop various Action Research practices: improving the quality of interactions and being able to transform the contexts in which the critical issues to be addressed emerge (Reason & Bradbury, 2001, 2008, 2015, Rizziato, 2014).

During a long-term Action Research project by CNR-IRCrES, a methodology was developed that brought significant innovations to these two critical issues: the methodology for horizontal leadership and integrated organisations (HOLIO), which forms the basis of a CNR spin-off company.

It proposes a paradigm shift regarding traditional approaches to change in organisational and territorial contexts, overcoming the reductive rationalistic visions of the positivist approach with a transdisciplinary and multidisciplinary approach. It is based on a systemic and evolutionary vision of the individual and the organisation and on a generative approach to development, characterised by transformative learning dynamics. The methodology has also been applied to innovation in the management of complex projects, to the renewal of university teaching, and to placement (Rizziato, 2010, 2020; Rizziato, 2017; Rizziato, 2022a, b; 2024; Scardicchio, 2019).

The person is considered as a system, characterized by the dimensions through which they relate to reality-cognitive, emotional, and volitional-guided by a biographical leitmotif toward the realization of their own identity (Morin in Ceruti, 2017; Morin, 1993; Campbell et al., 1982; Mounier, 1955; Assagioli, 1977; Lievegoed, 1979; Kelly, 2004; Maslow, 1954). This becomes visible in the activation of a transformative "intention" toward one's personal constructs, often unconscious, derived from one's biography and constituting the source of the recurring critical issues the individual faces. Neuroscience has shown that the power of intention in interactions has a transformative nature (Rizzolatti & Sinigaglia, 2006; Tomasello, 2005; Siegel, 2001; Poli, 2014; Bateson, 1993; Rohen, 2007). From this arises a new form of responsibility: that of one's own intentionality and how it manifests in the thought-forms that guide our feeling and acting. It involves adopting an evolutionary attitude that enables the identification and transformation of the constructs that inspire the automatisms underlying our recurring criticalities, thereby consciously renewing our implicit epistemologies.

The organisation/project is seen as a social structure, both closed and open, according to the vision of philosopher Edgar Morin, for whom it is "what determines a system from different elements, and therefore constitutes a unity at the same time as it constitutes a multiplicity", capable of imposing constraints on the parts, as well as "bringing out qualities that would not exist without such an organisation". It is an autonomous system of relationships, but one that is constantly connected to the outside world. It defines its identity, its raison d'être, in serving a customer/beneficiary through a product or service (Morin, 2002; Novara, 2008; Novara in Rizziato, 2010; Senge, 1990; Lievegoed, 1973; Bekman, 2007, 2010; Varela et al., 1991; Luhmann, 2001).

Organisational/project health is linked to the fact that personal and organisational/project identities are connected by an evolutionary synergy, guided by a mutual generation of meaning that is both subjective and collective.

For this reason, the HOLIO methodology proposes the creation of a "horizontal space" as a development infrastructure, to initiate systemic interactions by overcoming vertical functional logics (or projects excessively fragmented into activities), which have often been the source of the critical issues to be addressed.

It consists of two groups, which are fundamental to initiating new forms of work: that of the responsible (staff) and that of those called upon to take concrete action to create new processes (developers). The two groups work through regular meetings using a transformative learning method (TRASE—Systemic Evolutionary Training) and an exploratory, experimental approach that allows for the creation of new competencies and new processes, constantly focusing attention on the added value for the beneficiary.

The starting point of the process is the formulation of development questions, designed to orient activities toward the beneficiary and overcome self-referential logic. These development questions must be shared with those impacted by the critical issues and reoriented to broaden perception and the reference system's scenario, so that innovation becomes sustainable because it is generated by the actors who will have to implement it. They differ from problem-solving questions, which narrow the view of the system's complexity, often leading to illusory solutions because they are disconnected from the reality that needs to be transformed.

The HOLIO methodology was applied in the FOSSR context to maximize social impact by co-generating project activities with the involvement of partners and stakeholders. To this end, a development process was created, organized into two sessions of 2 days each, one week apart: the first session took place in March 2024 and the second in May 2025.

The responsible and operational staff (developers) were brought together in a horizontal space, conceived as a development infrastructure, in which the groups reflected and worked on how to optimize impact on the beneficiary, who was analysed and divided into different categories.

On the first day of the first session, which involved several beneficiaries and stakeholders, the project's development questions were explored, focusing on the impact on beneficiaries from a systemic perspective. The work was carried out in groups, within which the questions were reformulated several times. Finally, concrete steps were defined to explore, together with the stakeholders and beneficiaries not present at the meeting, the possibilities of redefining the questions themselves and gathering ideas to generate the innovations envisioned by the project.

The development questions were particularly useful for shifting the focus from problem-solving tasks to be carried out to problem setting, i.e., a systemic and shared awareness of the scenario in which the innovations envisioned by the project are to be implemented.

The groups worked with the TRASE approach of transformative learning, defined as an alternating cycle between reflecting on what one aims to achieve, identifying possible steps to explore/experiment with real opportunities for innovation, and implementing those steps. The method highlights the participants' interactive habits and the potential improvements achievable through the renewal of their implicit personal epistemologies, according to the needs that emerge from focusing on the beneficiary during the process.

The TRASE pathway of the HOLIO methodology articulates reflective and future-oriented phases through specific dialogue and movement exercises (MOV-CORE), which stimulate imaginative and intuitive thinking, enabling the expansion and sharing of the reference scenario. This allows the conscious co-creation of new processes.

The pathway is focused on action-rhythmic and generative, characterized by creative initiative in relation to the complexity of the context. People are valued as an "active part" of the system: they are not considered a "resource" like any other, which would render them de-subjectified. On the contrary, they are called to act as individuals.

The groups worked in parallel on the development of new processes and new competencies suited to complex contexts: horizontal leadership competencies for the systemic and evolutionary development of organizations, territories, and projects. Horizontal leadership is not defined by leading people, but by leading oneself (self-leadership) and the processes in which the people involved can act responsibly toward a common goal. The competencies that characterize horizontal leadership enable systemic-evolutionary thinking, perception, and action, making forms of social creativity possible.

The proposed transformative learning approach has a constructivist foundation (Mezirow, 2003) and is inspired by recent developments in neuroscience, particularly studies on neuroplasticity (Siegel, 2001; 2010; Damasio, 1995; Doidge, 2007). It is characterized by a multi and trans disciplinary approach that combines an analytical, formal, and quantitative dimension with a descriptive, phenomenological, and qualitative one, and specifically proposes working on the transformative potential of intention.

The second day of the first session of the FOSSR program, held after one week, involved sharing the results of the explorations, defining new questions, and articulating them for a dynamic design of the outcomes to be pursued, which enabled the co-generation of ideas emerging from the shared development questions. Dynamic design is an important element of the HOLIO methodology, as it allows a shift from development questions to a mode of co-designing-together with key stakeholders-what is intended to be achieved. It is defined through seven interconnected perspectives (called the 7 Beacons), allowing for the experimentation of the innovation to be realized.

After about a year, the main FOSSR services had been prototyped, and the two-day process was repeated, starting from development questions on how to optimize these services to maximize their impact on beneficiaries.

During the process, some horizontal leadership competencies were exercised, which proved to be very significant in changing the perspective of the working group and reviewing processes.

In this regard, it is believed that, in general, horizontal leadership competencies can be considered as new competencies for social researchers who wish to work with Action Research in social contexts aimed at optimising impact, as has been the case for FOSSR research infrastructures.

Furthermore, as a follow-up to the Action Research sessions emerged that:

- the Action Research sessions helped expand and solidify the concept of co-creation with stakeholders and users, stimulating new systemic competencies in the definition of FOSSR services;
- for many participants, the path clarified how Action Research can support the development of FOSSR's soft infrastructure, moving beyond the data dimension alone;
- the work on the development question and the dynamic design approach with the "7 Beacons" allowed the group to focus collectively on beneficiaries, broadening the audience and assisting in co-designing with a focus on maximizing the impact of FOSSR's offerings. Consequently, it was possible to share a working principle centred on the actual use of the prototyped services, allowing for their refinement;
- some services and platforms had been designed for researchers and research institutions, but their potential for community activation had been underestimated. In this regard, the exploratory logic of the "next step" was considered particularly useful for concretely defining work phases and clarifying easily achievable short-term goals;
- for many, the proposed approach was seen as a valuable methodology for future use as well.

The innovative experimentation of Action Research Sessions within the framework of an RI was considered one of the most original contributions to the transformative development of FOSSR into a socially robust Research Infrastructure, based on knowledge co-production and with the ability to engage in reflexivity.

In alignment with the engagement framework, the Action Research sessions positioned FOSSR at the upper stages of the engagement continuum-primarily within the *Collaborate* and *Engage* dimensions by enabling participants to influence decision-making processes, service development, and long-term organisational learning. This represents one of the most innovative elements of the FOSSR engagement model, moving from participation to shared responsibility and co-construction.

## 15.5 Monitoring Communication Performance and Engagement with Potential Users

The development of a system of Key Performance Indicators (KPIs) is a crucial step for monitoring the progress and effectiveness of a Research Infrastructure. In the case of FOSSR the KPI framework was designed with a specific focus on the performance of communication and outreach activities. In this sense, engagement is conceived as a preparatory dimension, aimed at familiarising relevant audiences with the infrastructure and supporting the gradual construction of a community that may later evolve into an active user base once the cloud-based environment becomes available. In this section, we present an overview of main results emerging from the implementation of these indicators and discuss how they have supported a clearer understanding of the project reach, visibility, and interactions with relevant audiences and stakeholders.

While traditional performance metrics proved appropriate for documenting communication activities, it also became evident that a meaningful assessment of infrastructural impact would require conditions that are not yet in place within FOSSR, such as stable user communities and integrated service use. This distinction between performance monitoring and impact assessment is widely acknowledged in the literature on Research Infrastructures, which highlights how impact can only be meaningfully assessed once infrastructures reach a sufficient level of maturity and sustained use (Fabre et al., 2021; Mayernik et al., 2017).

Our approach aligns with recent debates within the European Research Infrastructure landscape, particularly those fostered by ESFRI (European Strategy Forum on Research Infrastructures) and the ERIC (European Research Infrastructure Consortium) Forum, which underscore the need for flexible, domain-sensitive, and development-stage-aware indicator systems (ESFRI Working Group on Monitoring, 2019). Comparative analyses of KPIs across Research Infrastructures show that no single set of metrics can adequately reflect the diversity of missions, services, and communities involved, especially in early or transitional phases (Kolar et al., 2019). This could be particularly relevant for Social Science Research Infrastructures, where patterns of use, citation, and impact tend to emerge more slowly and in less standardised forms.

Within FOSSR, the assessment of communication and community-building activities was guided by a combined system of quantitative indicators and a qualitative interpretative framework represented by the Engagement Chart (see Sect. 15.2). In the current phase of the infrastructure development, this dual approach was designed to document the performance of communication activities and early forms of engagement with potential users. This combination reflects recommendations in the RI evaluation literature to complement quantitative metrics with interpretative frameworks capable of capturing relational and processual dimensions of infrastructural development (Mayernik et al., 2017).

From a quantitative perspective, the KPIs defined in the Communication Strategy (Reale & Fabrizio, 2024) tracked the main dimensions of dissemination and visibility: website accesses and visits; downloads of newsletters, policy briefs, and training materials; uploads and downloads on Zenodo; number of social media posts, followers and interactions; number of media mentions; and the growth of mailing lists and contact bases. These indicators provide evidence of the capacity of communication actions to reach relevant audiences and sustain a regular flow of content across channels.

Complementing these performance indicators, the KEIs included the number of events organised—such Training, Seminars and Webinars and Networking Events (General Conference, FOSSR Café)—the number and profiles of participants, the recurrence of participation across multiple activities, interactions with stakeholders and policymakers, and the emergence of expressions of interest or co-designed initiatives. These indicators trace how potential users progressively move from passive contact to more active forms of involvement in the project communication and dialogical activities, consistent with approaches that interpret engagement as a gradual and relational process (Mayernik et al., 2017).

Looking ahead, the challenge is to move from measuring communication performance and early engagement towards forms of assessment that may become meaningful once stable conditions of infrastructure use are in place. This implies going beyond documenting how many potential users interact with the Research Infrastructure, towards understanding how such interactions may eventually translate into enhanced research capabilities, informed decision-making, and the uptake of scientific resources beyond academic circles. In this perspective, reflections on next-generation indicators are necessarily prospective and point to the need for indicator systems capable of integrating quantitative and qualitative dimensions, considering the pathways through which Research Infrastructures may contribute to societal outcomes, and reflecting core Open Science values such as openness, interoperability, and inclusiveness(ESFRI Working Group on Monitoring, 2019).

To clarify the conceptual framework Fig. 15.2 illustrates the distinction between KPIs (communication performance), KEIs (early engagement with potential users), situating current indicators within a pre-operational phase of the Research Infrastructure; while Action Research represents the only context in which design-oriented internal impacts can currently be observed.

The KPI and KEI framework adopted within FOSSR was conceived as evolvable. When stable conditions of use are in place, the same framework may be progressively extended to capture engagement with services and patterns of actual use, allowing for a clearer distinction between potential and established users. In this sense, current indicators contribute to documenting the early consolidation of a community that is already familiar with FOSSR and may therefore be more readily oriented towards active use of the infrastructure in its next phase.

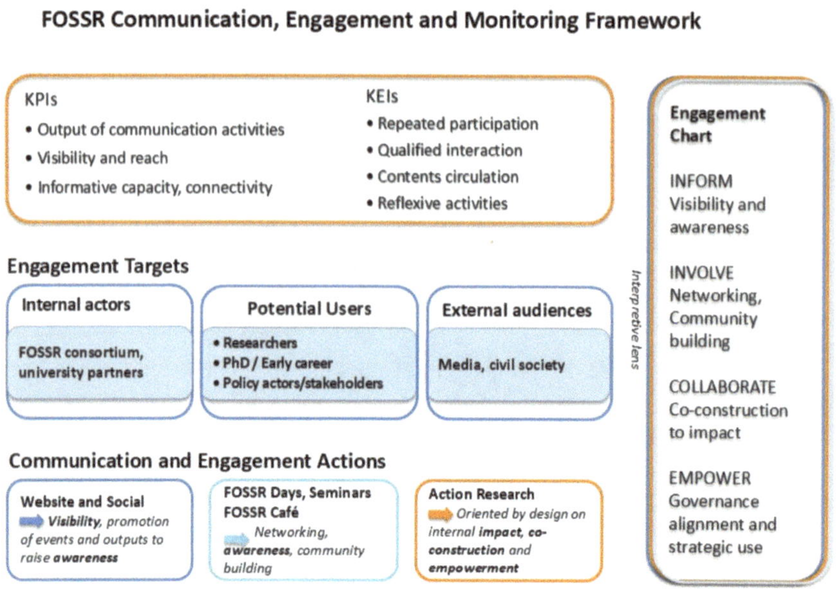


**Fig. 15.2** Conceptual scheme for monitoring communication performance and early engagement in FOSSR. *Source*: CNR-IRCrES elaboration

### *15.5.1 Preliminary Results from Communication and Early Engagement Indicators*

This section provides an overview of the performance of FOSSR communication and outreach activities and of early engagement dynamics involving potential users. While individual metrics are discussed in detail below, this section introduces the overall logic through which the results should be read and interpreted (Table 15.1).

The results are organised to reflect the progression from the ability of the project to reach relevant audiences, then to sustain interaction over time, and finally to mobilise a community of potential users through differentiated formats and channels.

Quantitative indicators first describe the scale and continuity of communication activities and their reach across target audiences. They are followed by engagement-oriented indicators that shed light on participation patterns, recurrence of involvement, and interaction within more participatory formats, such as Action Research activities.

**Table 15.1** Main indicators on community building and stakeholder engagement in FOSSR

| Indicator category | Indicator | What it captures | Target |
|---|---|---|---|
| KPI | Communication and training events organised | Volume and continuity of communication activities | Potential users; stakeholders |
| KPI | Participants in events and sessions | Reach of communication and outreach actions | Potential users |
| KPI | Website access, downloads, and social media interactions | Visibility and circulation of project content | External audiences; potential users |
| KPI | Dissemination activities by FOSSR members | Effort in scientific and policy dissemination | Scientific and policy audiences |
| KEI | Recurrence of participation across activities | Continuity of interest over time | Potential users |
| KEI | Participation in interactive formats | Transition from exposure to active involvement | Selected potential users |
| KEI | Feedback and co-design contributions | Reflexive interaction influencing service design | Potential users; project team |

#### 15.5.1.1 Overview of the Main Performance Results

As of October 2025, 30 months from the start of the project, communication activities display a steady and cumulative growth across digital channels, events, and policy-oriented outputs, reflecting the consolidation of a recognisable presence within emerging community of potential users.

The project website, comprising 25 active pages, recorded over 22,000 unique visitors by October 2025 with an average annual growth rate exceeding 60%. Over time, the most visited sections shifted from general informational pages (e.g. Home, What We Do) towards event-related and community-oriented content, in line with the progressive movement along the engagement trajectory described earlier (Table 15.2).

Social media activity followed a comparable pattern. Between 2023 and October 2025, almost 100 posts and audio-visual contents were published with a regular frequency of one to two updates per week. The combined number of followers across platforms reached approximately 1750, corresponding to an annual organic

**Table 15.2** Growth of FOSSR Communication (2023–2025)

| Indicator | 2023 | 2024 | 2025 (Oct.) | Notes |
|---|---|---|---|---|
| Unique website visitors | ≈8000 | ≈17,000 | ≈22,000 | Continuous increase, with peaks corresponding to major events (e.g., FOSSR days) |
| Most visited pages | Home, what we do, news | News /Events, FOSSR days | Community building | Increasing interest in participatory and community-related content |
| Social media posts | 45 | 68 | 72 (cumulative) | Consistent publishing rate (1-2 posts per week) |
| Total followers (fb + linkedin + ig) | ≈450 | ≈1100 | ≈1750 | Annual organic growth exceeding 60% |

*Source*: CNR-IRCrES elaborations from website and social media statistics

growth rate above 60%. As discussed in relation to KPI indicators, these figures are interpreted as signals of sustained attention and content circulation, rather than as evidence of deep engagement.

Communication performance is also reflected in the scale and continuity of project events. By October 2025, a total of 21 events had been organised, involving 1447 participants overall. These events, ranging from conferences and policy-oriented sessions to online seminars and capacity-building initiatives, represent the main arenas in which early engagement with potential users was activated, in line with the objectives outlined in the engagement framework.

The circulation of research outputs further complements this picture. By October 2025, 33 materials were uploaded to Zenodo, accounting for nearly 5000 downloads, while policy briefs were downloaded 382 times. Together with the growth of the mailing list to 743 contacts, these indicators document the capacity of communication activities to sustain information flows and maintain regular contact with academic and institutional audiences (Table 15.3).

Overall, these results provide a coherent overview of communication performance consistent with the documenting of the conditions under which a community of potential users has been progressively developed, informed, mobilised, and stabilised, thereby laying the groundwork for future engagement once integrated services become fully operational.

**Table 15.3** Key Engagement Indicators (2023–2025)

| Dimension | Indicator | October 2025 |
|---|---|---|
| Events and participation | Number of events organised | 21 |
| | Number of participants at events | 1447 |
| Publications and materials | Materials uploaded on Zenodo | 33 |
| | Materials downloaded from Zenodo | 4983 |
| Policy-oriented outputs | Policy briefs downloaded | 382 |
| Mailing and contacts | Mailing list contacts | 743 |

*Source*: CNR-IRCrES elaborations from database of events and participants

#### 15.5.1.2 Overview of FOSSR Community, Events Participation and Engagement Traces

Participation data highlight the central role of events as drivers of early engagement within FOSSR. The predominance of online participation reflects the pre-operational phase and a strategy aimed at maximising accessibility and reach (KPI).

The following analyses are based on a database originally comprising 975 records (registered participants to all events organized during the project). The dataset was systematically cleaned, missing information was completed where possible, and organisational affiliations and job positions were harmonised through a recoding process. The resulting core dataset of 899 validated contacts was subsequently analysed to explore the composition and characteristics of the FOSSR community developed to date, starting from the participants involved in the project kick-off meeting held in November 2022.

The distribution shown by Fig. 15.3 highlights the central interest by universities and public research organisations, with researchers and doctoral candidates representing the largest groups across all organisational types.

Gender distribution appears relatively balanced across positions, with a slight prevalence of female participation, particularly among early-career profiles (Fig. 15.4).

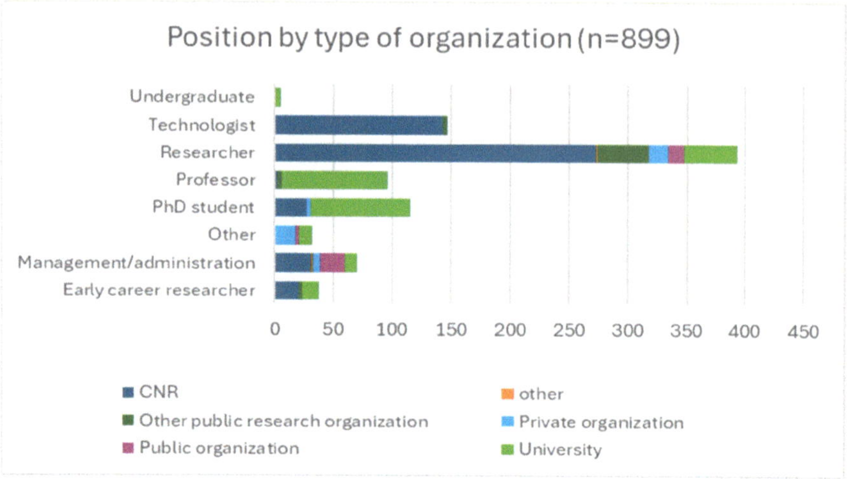


**Fig. 15.3** Position by type of organization. Source: CNR-IRCrES elaborations from database of events and participants

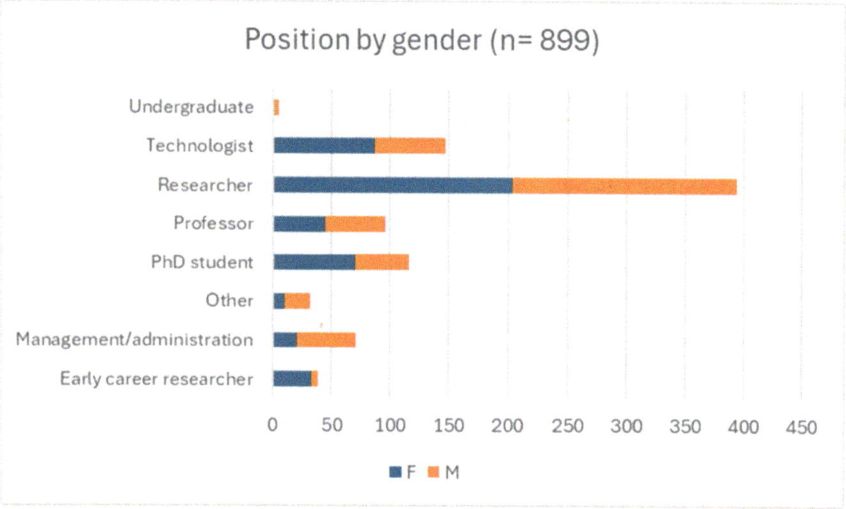


**Fig. 15.4** Position by gender. *Source*: CNR-IRCrES elaborations from database of events and participants

Networking activities[3] show the highest participation levels (Fig. 15.5), indicating strong demand for capacity building and peer interaction and acting as

[3] Event categories were derived through the aggregation of different activity formats into broader analytical categories. In particular, Networking encompasses general conferences, FOSSR cafés, and the kick-off meeting; Dissemination covers seminars, webinars, and service demonstration sessions; and Policy dialogue refers to dedicated sessions with policymakers. Participation counts

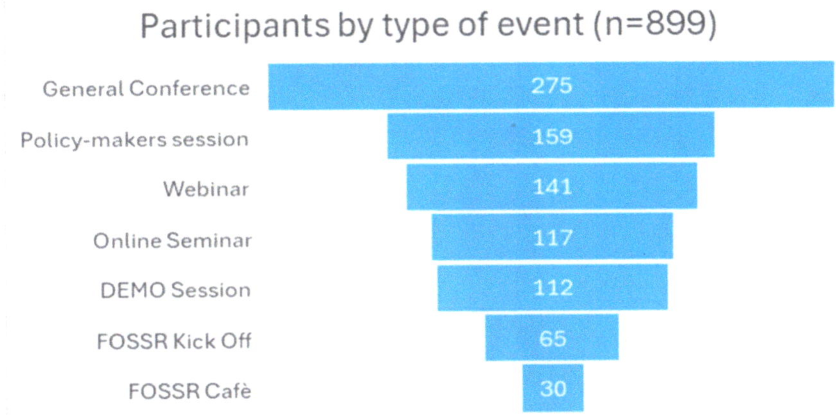


**Fig. 15.5** Participants by type of event. Source: CNR-IRCrES elaborations from database of events and participants

early signals of sustained engagement (KEI). Participation in seminars/webinars and policy dialogue further suggests the ability to address both scientific and institutional audiences through differentiated formats.

Gender participation remains broadly balanced across event categories, suggesting inclusiveness in the design of communication and engagement formats (Fig. 15.6).

Early-career researchers and PhD candidates show the highest levels of participation (Fig. 15.7), indicating strong interest in capacity-building and community-oriented activities.

Among 481 unique participants, 175 individuals took part in more than one project activity, resulting in a participation redundancy rate of 36.4%. This level of recurrence provides evidence of sustained engagement over time and suggests the progressive consolidation of a core community actively involved in FOSSR communication and participatory initiatives.

Finally, feedback questionnaires collected from 110 participants indicate a very high level of satisfaction with the FOSSR events. The average overall rating is 4.6 out of 5, with most respondents assigning the highest scores (5 or 4). Moreover, 87 participants explicitly stated that the events met their expectations, while only two negative responses were recorded. Qualitative comments highlight, in particular, the relevance of the topics and the quality of the organisation, while suggestions for improvement mainly concerned the duration of some sessions.

---

consider registered participants for Networking, Dissemination, and Policy dialogue events, while for Training activities only selected participants were included, in line with the admission procedures foreseen for these formats.

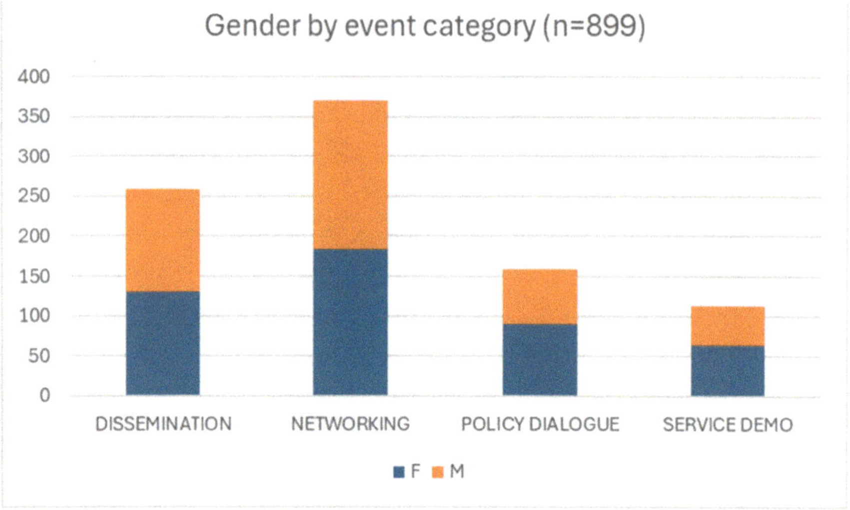


**Fig. 15.6** Gender distribution by event category. *Source*: CNR-IRCrES elaborations from database of events and participants

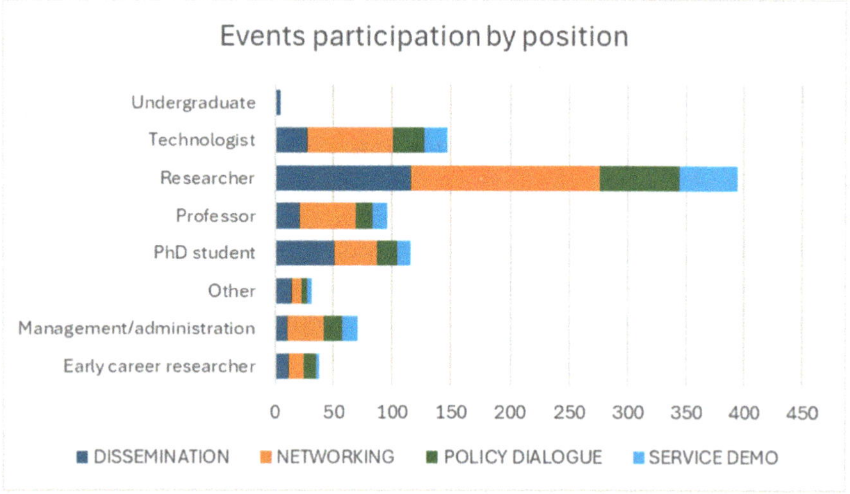


**Fig. 15.7** Events participation by position. *Source*: CNR-IRCrES elaborations from database of events and participants

Overall, the data align with the progressive engagement framework discussed in the chapter, linking visibility, involvement, and early forms of collaboration.

## 15.6 Conclusions

The FOSSR communication experience illustrates how a research infrastructure can construct and consolidate its public identity through a balanced interplay of institutionality and openness, informational rigor and community-oriented practices. The analysis presented in this chapter shows how website, social media channels, and participatory event formats operate as an integrated communicative ecosystem: the first ensures informational continuity and transparency, the second enhances visibility and accessibility, and the third fosters dialogue, interaction, and awareness.

Beyond describing communication tools and activities, the chapter highlights their functional role in supporting the use, uptake, and development of infrastructural services. Communication within FOSSR thus emerges as a mechanism that connects access to resources, capacity building, and feedback processes, rather than being limited to dissemination for visibility purposes.

In perspective, the communication strategy aims to consolidate the FOSSR community, broaden participation, and promote the transition from passive user to active member—that is, a researcher who not only accesses the platform but also contributes to events, governance, and service co-design.

The measurable outcomes—growth in audience size, increased participation, and improved quality of interaction—confirm that communication within FOSSR functions not as a secondary dissemination activity but as a constitutive dimension of open research.

From a policy and decision-making perspective, the FOSSR experience suggests that communication and engagement strategies can provide significant signals for understanding early patterns of adoption, user needs, and relational dynamics within Research Infrastructures. The use of KPIs and early engagement indicators offers decision makers and infrastructure managers a monitoring framework to inform strategic choices, resource allocation, and the design of participatory mechanisms, particularly in pre-operational and transitional phases.

The various follow-ups to the Action Research actions further demonstrated the importance of reflexive and beneficiary-oriented approaches to reassess objectives, recalibrate activities, and strengthen internal learning processes. Feedback emerging from these participatory settings also highlighted the relevance of social research competences as a key asset for initiatives aimed at involving heterogeneous stakeholders and generating value at multiple levels.

Looking forward, sustaining community commitment beyond the project lifetime will require the gradual institutionalization of engagement mechanisms and governance practices to support long-term contributions, ownership, and shared accountability. Future developments may include the refinement of engagement indicators, the integration of communication data into broader evaluation frameworks, and the consolidation of participatory spaces as stable components of Research Infrastructure governance.

# Appendix

List of events organised in the frame of the Communication Work Package (Table 15.4):

**Table 15.4** List of organised events (2022-2026)

| Event | Date | Title | People involved |
|---|---|---|---|
| Kick off meeting | 25/11/2022 | FOSSR—fostering Open Science in social science research | 8 speakers, 1 moderator |
| Online Seminar | 11/18/2023 | "Building the Italian online probability panel" | 2 speakers, 7 panelists, 1 moderator |
| Online Seminar | 01/23/2024 | "Agent-based modeling: Contributions for the social sciences and FOSSR" | 2 speakers, 6 panelists, 1 moderator |
| Online Seminar | 04/29/2024 | "Open cloud and knowledge integration for empowering social sciences" | 2 speakers, 7 panelists, 1 moderator |
| Webinar | 02/19/2025 | "The FOSSR policy learning platform: A tutorial" | 3 speakers, 2 discussants |
| Webinar | 05/05/2025 | "European online probability panels (EOPPs): Opportunities for social research" among OPPs | 12 speakers/panelist |
| Policymakers session | 16/10/2023 | Data driven policy learning: The role of FOSSR | 1 speaker, 2 discussants, 1 moderator |
| Policymakers session | 09/10/2024 | Text mining in and for policy-making within FOSSR | 2 speakers, 2 discussants, 1 moderator |
| Policymakers session | 04/02/2026 | High-quality, high-frequency individual data production in Italy: Innovation introduced by FOSSR | 4 speakers, 3 discussants, 1 moderator |
| Demo session | 11/10/2024 | The FOSSR virtual research environment | 3 speakers, 1 moderator |
| Demo session | 06/02/2026 | The FOSSR cloud infrastructure and marketplace | 3 speakers, 1 moderator |
| General Conference | 17/10/2023 | FOSSR conference - fostering Open Science in social science research | 13 speakers, 1 moderator |
| General Conference | 10/10/2024 | FOSSR general conference - fostering Open Science in social science research | 15 speakers, 1 moderator |
| General Conference | 05/02/2026 | FOSSR final general conference - achievements, tools, and future perspectives for Open Science in the social sciences | 52 speakers, 6 moderators, 2 discussants |

## References


Assagioli, R. (1977). *L'atto di volontà*. Astrolabio.

Bateson, G. (1993). *Verso Un'Ecologia della Mente*. Adelphi.

Bekman, A. (2007). The methodology of evidential. In J. J. Boonstra & L. Caluwè (Eds.), *Intervening and changing: Looking for meaning in interactions* (pp. 29–45). Wiley.

Bekman, A. (2010). *The horizontal leadership book*. Alertverlag.

Benessia, A., Funtowicz, S., Guimarães Pereira, Â., Ravetz, J. R., Saltelli, A., Strand, R., & van der Sluijs, J. P. (2016). *The rightful place of science: Science on the verge*. Consortium for Science, Policy and Outcomes at Arizona State University.

Bodmer, W. F. (1985). *The Public Understanding of Science: Report of a Royal Society Ad Hoc Group Endorsed by the Council of the Royal Society.*

Campbell, D., Elgin, D., Harman, W., Hastings, A., Markley, O., Matson, F., O'Regan, B., & Schneid, L. (1982). *Changing image of the man*. Stanford Research Institute, Pergamon Press.

Ceruti, M. (2017). *Il tempo della complessità*. Raffaello Cortina.

Damasio, A. (1995). *L'errore di Cartesio. Emozione, ragione e cervello umano*. Milano: Adelphi

Davies, S. R., Horst, M. (2016). The changing nature of science: Academic capitalism, Entrepreneurial Universities and PR. In *Science communication*. London: Palgrave Macmillan. https://doi.org/10.1057/978-1-137-50366-4_5

Davies, S. R., Halpern, M., Horst, M., Kirby, D., & Lewenstein, B. (2019). Science stories as culture: experience, identity, narrative and emotion in public communication of science. *JCOM, 18*(05), A01. https://doi.org/10.22323/2.18050201

Doidge, N. (2007). *The brain who change itself*. New York: Penguin book

ESFRI Working Group on Monitoring. (2019). *Monitoring of research infrastructures performance: A report from the ESFRI Working Group on Monitoring*. European Strategy Forum on Research Infrastructures (ESFRI). https://www.esfri.eu

Fabre, R., Egret, D., Schöpfel, J., & Azeroual, O. (2021). Evaluating the scientific impact of research infrastructures: The role of current research information systems. *Quantitative Science Studies, 2*(1), 42–64. https://doi.org/10.1162/qss_a_00111

Fabrizio, S., Reale, E., & Spinello, A. O. (2023). Policy Brief, Issue 15/ Building a stronger community in STI studies for effective impact: the experience of RISIS (Versione 1). *Zenodo*. https://doi.org/10.5281/zenodo.11276785

French, W. L., & Bell, C. H. (1998). *Organisation development: Behavioral science. Intervention for organisational improvement*. Englewood Cliff.

Funtowicz, S., & Ravetz, J. (1993). Science for the post-normal age. *Futures, 25*(7), 739–755. https://doi.org/10.1016/0016-3287(93)90022-L

Gibbons, M., Limoges, C., Nowotny, H., Schwartzman, S., Scott, P., & Trow, M. (1994). *The new production of knowledge: The dynamics of science and research in contemporary societies*. SAGE.

Hecker, S., Haklay, M., Bowser, A., Makuch, Z., Vogel, J., & Bonn, A. (2018). *Citizen science: Innovation in Open Science, society and policy*. UCL Press. https://doi.org/10.14324/111.9781787352339

Hughes, T. P. (1987). The evolution of large technological systems. In W. E. Bijker, T. P. Hughes, & T. Pinch (Eds.), *The social construction of technological systems* (pp. 51–82). MIT Press.

Irwin, A. (2015). Citizen science and scientific citizenship: Same words, different meanings? In B. Schiele, J. L. Marec, & P. Baranger (Eds.), *Science communication today* (pp. 29–38). Presses Universitaires de Nancy.

Jasanoff, S. (2003). Technologies of humility: Citizen participation in governing science. *Minerva, 41*(3), 223–244. https://doi.org/10.1023/A:1025557512320

Jasanoff, S. (2004a). Science and citizenship: A new synergy. *Science and Public Policy, 31*(2), 90–94. https://doi.org/10.3152/147154304781780064

Jasanoff, S. (2004b). *States of knowledge: The co-production of science and the social order*. Routledge.

Jasanoff, S. (2005). *Designs on nature: Science and democracy in Europe and the United States*. Princeton University Press.
Kelly, G. (2004). *La psicologia dei costrutti personali*. Raffaello Cortina.
Kolar, J., Ahlgren, P., & Sørensen, M. P. (2019). Towards key performance indicators of research infrastructures. *arXiv preprint*. https://arxiv.org/abs/1910.00304
Lefika, P. T., & Mearns, M. A. (2015). Adding knowledge cafés to the repertoire of knowledge sharing techniques. *International Journal of Information Management, 35*(1), 26–32. https://doi.org/10.1016/J.IJINFOMGT.2014.09.005
Lewin, K. (1972). *I conflitti sociali*. FrancoAngeli.
Lievegoed, B. C. J. (1973). *Developing organisation*. Tavistock Publications.
Lievegoed, B. C. J. (1979). *Phases, crisis and development in the individual*. Rudolf Steiner Press.
Luhmann, T. (2001). *Sistemi sociali. Fondamenti di una teoria generale*. Il Mulino.
Maslow, A. (1954). *Motivation and personality*. Harper, Row.
Mayernik, M. S., Hart, D. L., Maull, K. E., & Weber, N. M. (2017). Assessing and tracing the outcomes and impact of research infrastructures. *Journal of the Association for Information Science and Technology, 68*, 1341–1359. https://doi.org/10.1002/asi.23721
Mezirow, J. (2003). *Apprendimento e trasformazione*. Milano: Raffaello Cortina.
Miller, J. D. (2004). Public understanding of, and attitudes toward, scientific research: What we know and what we need to know. *Public Understanding of Science, 13*(3), 273–294. https://doi.org/10.1177/0963662504044908
Molas-Gallart, J., & Tang, P. (2011). Tracing "productive interactions" to identify social impacts: An example from the social sciences. *Research Evaluation, 20*(3), 219–226. https://doi.org/10.3152/095820211X12941371876706
Morin, E. (1993). *Introduzione al pensiero complesso*. Sperling & Kupfer.
Morin, E. (2002). *Il metodo 5: L'identità umana*. Raffaello Cortina.
Mounier, E. (1955). *Rivoluzione personalista e comunitaria*. Edizioni di Comunità.
Novara, F. (2008). *Si può guarire l'organizzazione? Esperienze professionali, proposte metodologiche e teoriche, rivista Psicologia Sociale 1/2008*. Il Mulino.
Novara, F. (2010). Le ragioni del progetto. In E. Rizziato (Ed.), *Etica dello sviluppo organizzativo e senso del lavoro: verso un approccio europeo*. FrancoAngeli.
Poli, E. (2014). *Anatomia della guarigione*. Anima Edizioni.
Powell, M. (2010). Science Café. In *Encyclopedia of science and technology communication* (pp. 689–690). SAGE Publications. https://doi.org/10.4135/9781412959216
Reale, E., & Fabrizio, S. (2024). *FOSSR Deliverable 9.1 - Dissemination and communication plan (Version 1)*.https://doi.org/10.5281/zenodo.13970700.
Reason, P., & Bradbury, H. (2001, 2008, 2015). *Handbook of action research: Participative inquiry and practice*. Sage.
Rizziato, E. (2010). *Etica dello sviluppo organizzativo e senso del lavoro. Verso la definizione di un approccio europeo*. FrancoAngeli.
Rizziato, E. (2014). *La ricerca-azione: un approccio per comprendere ed interagire con i processi delle dinamiche socio-economiche. Working Paper 26/2014*. CERIS-CNR. http://www.ceris.cnr.it/ceris/workingpaper/2014/WP_26_RIZZIATO.pdf
Rizziato, E. (2017). *Horizontal organization and leadership: A generative approach for an ethic development in complex systems book of proceedings international conference*. Euromed. https://emrbi.org/wp-content/uploads/2020/09/EuroMed-10-2017.pdf
Rizziato, E. (2020). *Verso un umanesimo della vita organizzativa: generare sviluppo nella complessità con la leadership orizzontale*. Francoangeli, collana AIF.
Rizziato, E. (2022a). *Contributi di Nemmo, E. e Vetrano, G. Lo sviluppo locale: un approccio sistemico e generativo con la leadership orizzontale. Quaderni IRCrES n.15*. CNR-IRCrES. https://doi.org/10.23760/2499-6661.2022.15
Rizziato, E. (2022b). *Leadership orizzontale e organizzazioni integrate: rendere costruttiva la complessità in Sviluppo & Organizzazione, Sezione accreditata AIDEA (Accademia Italiana di economia aziendale), n.304 Marzo/Aprile 2022*. Este ISSN 0391-7045.

Rizziato, E. (2024). *Toward a humanism in organizations. Horizontal leadership and consciousness*. Roma: CNR Edizioni. http://doi.org/10.23760/TowardsHumanism-2024. ISBN (ed. digitale) 978 88 8080 628 8

Rizzolatti, G., & Sinigaglia, C. (2006). *So quel che fai. Il cervello che agisce e i neuroni specchio*. Raffaello Cortina.

Rohen, J. W. (2007). *Functional morphology: The dynamic wholeness of the human organism*. Adonis Press.

Scardicchio, A. C. (2019). *Complessità delle organizzazioni, complessità della formazione. Report di studio qualitativo ed analisi ermeneutica del Modello TRASE - IRCRES/CNR-IMO. Working Paper 1/2019*. IRCrES-CNR.

Senge, P. (1990). The fifth discipline. In *The art and practice of the learning organization*. New York: Doubleday Currency.

Siegel, D. J. (2001). *La mente relazionale. Neurobiologia dell'esperienza interpersonale*. Raffaello Cortina.

Siegel, J. (2010). *Mindsight*. Milano: Raffaello Cortina.

Tomasello, M. (2005). *Le origini culturali della cognizione umana*. Il Mulino.

Trench, B. (2008). Towards an analytical framework of science communication models. In *Communicating science in social contexts* (pp. 119–135). Springer. https://doi.org/10.1007/978-1-4020-8598-7_7

Varela, F. J., Thompson, E., & Rosch, E. (1991). *The embodied mind: Cognitive science and human experience*. MIT Press.

Wynne, B. (1992). Misunderstood misunderstanding: Social identities and public uptake of science. *Public Understanding of Science, 1*(3), 281–304. https://doi.org/10.1088/0963-6625/1/3/004

Wynne, B., Felt, U., Callon, M., Gonçalves, M., Jasanoff, S., Jepsen, M., Joly, P.-B., Konopasek, Z., May, S., Neubauer, C., Rip, A., Siune, K., Stirling, A., & Tallacchini, M. (2007). *Taking European Knowledge Society Seriously. Report of the Expert Group on Science and Governance to the Science, Economy and Society Directorate, Directorate-General for Research, European Commission.*

Ziman, J. (2000). *Real science: What it is and what it means*. Cambridge University Press.

# Part III
# Theoretical Perspectives and Methods

# Chapter 16
# Collaborative Research Models

**Massimiliano Assante and Elisa Molinaro**

## 16.1 Introduction

Collaborative research is increasingly organised through shared digital and organisational arrangements rather than through informal coordination alone. In many domains, particularly in the Social science domain, collaboration may depends on the ability to securely access and combine heterogeneous data, to execute analyses in reusable computational environments, to document provenance and workflows, and to share results in ways that support verification and reuse. These requirements have moved infrastructures and platforms from the background to the centre of research practice, shaping not only teamwork, rather, shaping also how research outputs are produced, validated, and made actionable.

This chapter deals with collaborative research models through the perspective of Open Science and Research Infrastructures. The focus is willingly operational: how collaboration is implemented in practice through Virtual Research Environments (VREs) and Research Infrastructures (RIs), what governance and interoperability conditions make these systems effective, and what lessons can be derived for building open and sustainable collaboration in Social Science. Section 16.2 present sand explores interdisciplinary collaboration in the Social Science, highlighting how the digital transformation could help reshaping research practices and epistemic cultures. Section 16.3 discuss the role of Research Infrastructures in fostering durable partnerships through governance, federation, and stewardship. Section 16.4 examines the lessons learned and emerging models for Open Social Science, with a focus on interoperability, ethics, skills, and sustainability. The chapter concludes

M. Assante (✉) · E. Molinaro
CNR-ISTI (Institute of Information Science and Technologies), National Research Council of Italy, Pisa, Italy
e-mail: massimiliano.assante@cnr.it; elisa.molinaro@cnr.it



G. Cerulli, E. Reale (eds.), *Research Infrastructures for Open Science in Social Science Research*, https://doi.org/10.1007/978-3-032-29575-0_16

by reflecting on future directions for collaborative research in the Collaborative Research Models landscape.

## 16.2 Interdisciplinary Collaboration in Social Sciences

Interdisciplinary collaboration has become a defining characteristic of twenty-first-century science. The growing complexity and interdependence of global challenges, climate change, demographic transition, digital transformation, and sustainability, have exposed the limits of workinf in silos. Social sciences, traditionnaly focussed with interpretive and qualitative analysis, are now called to interact continuously with computational, natural, and engineering sciences. These collaborations not only to integrate diverse methodologies, rather they also aims to produce shared frameworks of understanding that connect the human and technological dimensions of knowledge. In this evolving research landscape, interdisciplinarity is no longer a mere aspiration, rather it is an operational necessity that reshapes how questions are given, how data are interpreted, and how scientific value is assessed.

The digital transformation of research has been accelerated by the emergence of data-driven research[1] and e-Infrastructures,[2] through which knowledge is generated, verified, and disseminated. The exponential growth of heterogeneous datasets, administrative records, large-scale surveys, digital traces from online platforms, sensor-derived observations, and geospatial data, has expanded the evidentiary base of the social sciences. Data previously treated as "accessory" have become central to theory building, while computational methods have blurred the boundary between empirical description and simulation. This evolution has created new dependencies between social scientists and experts in computer science, data engineering, statistics, and informatics. Addressing complex phenomena such as misinformation, climate adaptation, or migration dynamics now demands hybrid teams fluent in both social interpretation and algorithmic reasoning. Interdisciplinary collaboration thus operates simultaneously as a technical process of integration and as a cultural redefinition of what counts as legitimate knowledge.

From a European perspective, the Open Science movement has established the institutional and political conditions required for this paradigm shift. The *European Open Science Cloud (EOSC)* provides a federated structure for connecting Research Infrastructures across domains, ensuring that data, tools, and services circulate beyond disciplinary and national borders. EOSC promotes a "federation of infrastructures" model in which interoperability, transparency, and shared governance replace isolated national systems. This model acknowledges that

[1] Research that use data analysis as its foundation to find insight, patterns and generate new knowledge.

[2] Short term for electronic Infrastructure, comprising a set of ICT based resources (e.g. networks, grids, data centres, collaborative environments).

scientific knowledge is a common good and that its effective reuse depends on trust, accountability, and open standards.

Within this framework, the social sciences are progressively reintegrating into the wider research ecosystem. They contribute interpretive, normative, and contextual expertise that complements the quantitative orientation of data-intensive research, while simultaneously adopting new computational methodologies, from natural-language processing to network analysis and agent-based modelling. However, integration within the EOSC federation requires the reconfiguration of legacy data infrastructures that evolved around national statistical offices, thematic archives, and stand-alone repositories. It demands harmonised metadata, cross-domain ontologies, and shared protocols for privacy, ethics, and intellectual-property management.

The shift toward such integrated infrastructures is not merely technical; it involves what philosophers of science call a change in *epistemic practices,* the collective routines through which knowledge is produced and validated. In the social sciences, these practices historically revolved around surveys, interviews, and case studies. Today, they increasingly involve algorithmic reasoning, high-performance computing, and collaborative workflows executed on distributed platforms. The EOSC framework thus provides both the political and technical scaffolding for a deeper epistemic transformation.

The concept of the *Virtual Research Environment (VRE),* also known as *Virtual Laboratory (VLab),* addresses these requirements. A VRE is an online system designed to support and enhance collaboration among researchers. It provides shared access to data, tools, computational resources, and communication services, enabling teams to work together efficiently even when they are distributed across different institutions or disciplines., across institutional and disciplinary boundaries. Unlike traditional portals or repositories, VREs are process-oriented and community-specific: they adapt dynamically to the evolving needs of their users and to the methodologies of their domains.

Candela (2013) first defined a VRE as "a web-based, community-oriented, comprehensive, flexible, and secure working environment conceived to serve the needs of modern science." This definition emphasises that VREs are *socio-technical* systems, they combine technical infrastructure with social organisation. They embody the principles of co-creation, allowing researchers not merely to consume services but to participate in their configuration and governance. In this sense, VREs serve as boundary infrastructures that translate between epistemic cultures, providing a space where heterogeneous practices, experimental, computational, interpretive, can coexist and interact.

Technologically, a VRE provides authenticated access to distributed resources, enabling researchers from multiple domains to work together on shared datasets and analytical pipelines. It ensures traceability of results through provenance tracking, enforces reproducibility through workflow versioning, and supports data governance through fine-grained access control. In the social sciences, these features are crucial for enabling the comparison of diverse methodologies—quantitative, qualitative, and computational, within a common and transparent analytical framework.

The state of the art in VRE design reflects the convergence of several technological paradigms:

- *Cloud computing and containerisation* (e.g. Kubernetes, Docker) provide elasticity and scalability for data processing and workflow execution, enabling dynamic allocation of computational resources.
- *Federated identity and access management* (e.g. eduGAIN, EOSC AAI) ensure secure and seamless access across institutions, preserving user identity while respecting privacy and compliance frameworks.
- *FAIR* principles (Wilkinson, 2016) and linked-data technologies support machine-actionable metadata and integration with external catalogues and knowledge graphs, enhancing the findability and contextualisation of data.
- *Interactive analytics environments* such as JupyterLab, RStudio Server, or Galaxy are now embedded directly into VREs, providing a ready-to-use interface for computation and visualisation across programming languages and analytical models.
- *Collaboration and communication services*, including integrated wikis, dashboards, and persistent digital identifiers (DOIs, ORCID), foster transparency and attribution in multi-partner projects.

In practice, these capabilities turn a VRE into a virtual laboratory where data, methods, and interpretations evolve collectively. They allow distributed research teams to build workflows that link computational models, visual analytics, and interpretive commentary, thus bridging the gap between quantitative and qualitative reasoning.

Several major European initiatives have been instrumental in the evolution and operationalisation of these environments. Among the most mature is the *D4Science* (Assante et al., 2019) *infrastructure*, developed and operated by Institute of Information Science and Technologies (ISTI) of the Italian National Research Council (CNR). D4Science enables on-demand creation of domain-specific VREs that federate data, computation, workflows, and social tools. It underpins projects such as Blue-Cloud (Schaap, 2022) (marine science), SoBigData (Grossi, 2018) (social mining), AGINFRA (Assante, 2020), (environmental science) and the European Research Infrastructure for Science, Technology and Innovation Policy Studies (RISIS). D4Science architecture is based on the gCube system (Assante, 2018), a comprehensive suite of software components that allows the creation of VREs by composing services, data, and user-specific tools through a highly modular and scalable infrastructure. As documented in *Virtual Research Environments Co-creation: The D4Science Experience* (Assante et al., 2023), the co-design of services and data catalogues with user communities enhances adoption and sustainability. Each participating project contributes new functionalities to the shared platform, resulting in cumulative innovation and a collective sense of ownership.

A significant recent contribution to the evolution of VREs is represented by the *VRE-Hub initiative at CERN*, developed to serve as a collaborative environment for high-energy-physics communities and beyond. CERN VRE-Hub[3] provides an open-source platform that enables the creation of community-driven workspaces for sharing data, workflows, and applications. It extends the collaborative ethos of the Worldwide LHC Computing Grid (WLCG) into a user-centric ecosystem where researchers can seamlessly connect distributed computing resources, repositories, and software environments. The CERN VRE-Hub exemplifies a new wave of lightweight, modular, and standards-compliant infrastructures that can be rapidly deployed across communities. Built with open-source components, it emphasises composability: researchers can instantiate new VREs for specific projects, integrate containerised applications, and connect external data services through APIs. The Hub's design follows the principles of *as-a-service* provisioning, not only compute-as-a-service, but *collaboration-as-a-service*. It implements a federated identity layer compatible with EOSC AAI,[4] enabling cross-infrastructure authentication and authorisation.

Among both D4Science and CERN VRE-Hub innovative aspects it is worth to notice the integration of collaborative notebooks (JupyterLab, RStudio) with workflow orchestration and version-controlled storage. Researchers can reproduce analyses, share parameter settings, and document results within a single interface. Moreover, they incorporates continuous-integration pipelines, ensuring that software dependencies remain updated and analyses reproducible over time, addressing one of the persistent challenges of computational research.

For the social sciences, the CERN VRE-Hub provides a reference model for implementing interoperable, open-source VRE frameworks adaptable beyond the physical-sciences domain. Its modularity and emphasis on open standards make it suitable for integration with data repositories managed by social-science infrastructures such as CESSDA-ERIC, SHARE-ERIC e RISIS. By lowering the technical barriers to collaboration, it fosters methodological innovation, enabling social researchers to perform large-scale simulations, apply natural-language processing, or run complex statistical models in cloud-native environments. Equally important, the CERN experience demonstrates the institutional dimension of VRE sustainability. By embedding the VRE-Hub within the organisational and governance structure of CERN, the initiative secures long-term support, professional maintenance, and alignment with international standards. This approach mirrors the broader European trend of integrating VREs within enduring research infrastructures rather than treating them as project-based artefacts. It ensures continuity, scalability, and interoperability with continental frameworks such as EOSC.

Other platforms also illustrate the diversity and maturity of VRE design. The EVER-EST project[5] developed a research-object-centric VRE architecture for Earth Observation communities, allowing data, code, and workflows to be bundled and published with full provenance. This object-oriented model aligns with the

[3] https://vre-hub.github.io/.

[4] AAI: Authentication and Authorization infrastructure.

[5] https://ever-est.eu.

principles of data stewardship and supports reuse across research contexts. CyVerse[6] in the USA provides cloud-based VRE services for life sciences, integrating data management, workflow execution, and remote access to large-scale datasets.

Beyond their technical sophistication, VREs serve as catalysts for *epistemic integration,* the alignment of diverse modes of inquiry into shared practices of reasoning and validation. In social-science contexts, this integration is particularly challenging because it involves reconciling statistical inference, computational modelling, and qualitative interpretation. VREs provide the operational scaffolding for such reconciliation by offering transparent and traceable workflows. Through provenance metadata and shared analytical notebooks, they make the research process itself a subject of collective reflection.

As noted by Assante et al. (2019) in *Enacting Open Science by D4Science*, the openness promoted by VREs is not limited to data access; it extends to methodological transparency and participatory governance. The design of a VRE becomes a form of social negotiation where diverse actors, *i.e.* researchers, developers, data managers, and policy makers, align their expectations and responsibilities. This socio-technical negotiation ensures that infrastructure development is responsive to community needs while adhering to ethical and legal constraints. Moreover, VREs enhance *epistemic accountability*: the ability of researchers to explain, reproduce, and justify their analytical choices. By embedding provenance tracking and reproducibility features, VREs transform accountability from a post-hoc exercise into an integral component of research. In interdisciplinary collaborations, where differences in method and interpretation often generate friction, such accountability mechanisms serve as a common language that bridges epistemic cultures.

Despite their success, VREs face enduring challenges. The first concerns *interoperability at scale*. Technical interoperability, *i.e.* aligning APIs, metadata, and authentication protocols, is relatively well understood while semantic and organisational interoperability remain more difficult. Each discipline employs its own conceptual frameworks and data vocabularies. Achieving genuine integration requires the development of shared ontologies and crosswalks that preserve disciplinary specificity while enabling translation. Initiatives like EOSC's Interoperability Framework and the Research Data Alliance (RDA) Vocabulary Services IG provide some reference models, but implementation across communities is uneven. A second challenge involves *sustainability and funding*. Many VREs are developed within the timeframe of European projects, with limited post-project maintenance. Long-term viability demands hybrid funding mechanisms combining institutional support, user-community contributions, and alignment with national infrastructures. Open-source licensing and modular design mitigate obsolescence, but professional maintenance and governance remain essential. A third issue concerns *usability and digital literacy*. Advanced infrastructures risk being under-utilised if researchers lack the skills to operate them effectively. Continuous training, documentation, and community engagement are thus integral

[6] https://cyverse.org.

to VRE success. Programs such as SoBigData's Training Academy[7] hosted at the University of Pisa and EOSC Skills and Training Catalogue[8] from the HORIZON EUROPE Skills4EOSC[9] exemplifies efforts to try closing this gap.

Emerging technological trends promise to redefine VRE functionality. Artificial Intelligence (AI) and its sub discipline in particular, Machine Learning and Deep Learning are increasingly integrated into VREs to automate metadata generation, detect anomalies, recommend analytical workflows, and support intelligent data discovery. Semantic technologies and knowledge graphs enhance the contextualisation of data, while natural-language interfaces simplify user interaction. The incorporation of *edge computing* and *federated learning* will enable privacy-preserving analytics on distributed datasets, a capability particularly relevant to social-science research involving sensitive information.

At the same time, ethical and legal considerations are gaining prominence. The European General Data Protection Regulation (GDPR) has established rigorous standards for data protection, consent, and accountability. VREs must therefore implement advanced access-control policies, anonymisation pipelines, and audit trails to ensure compliance. Beyond legal compliance, however, VREs also embody ethical commitments to fairness, inclusivity, and responsible innovation. Their design choices influence who can participate in research, whose knowledge counts, and how results are communicated to society.

The evolution of VREs is steering research toward what might be termed *collaborative knowledge ecosystems*. These ecosystems transcend the boundaries of single infrastructures, linking data, methods, and communities through interoperable services. In the social sciences, this transformation is particularly consequential. By providing access to computational resources and large-scale datasets, VREs empower researchers to tackle questions that were previously beyond reach: modelling urban mobility, mapping disinformation networks, analysing social resilience to climate shocks, tracing atmospheric pollution, or tracing innovation flows across regions. At the same time, by embedding ethical and participatory frameworks, VREs preserve the interpretive and reflexive strengths of the social sciences. They allow quantitative analysis and qualitative understanding to inform one another within transparent, collaborative workflows.

Ultimately, Virtual Research Environments represent both a technological and a cultural innovation. Technologically, they integrate distributed computing, storage, and analytics into seamless collaborative systems. Culturally, they institutionalise openness, trust, and co-creation as fundamental principles of scientific practice. Their success will depend not solely on software robustness but on their capacity to nurture communities of practice that sustain the spirit of interdisciplinary cooperation.

---

[7] https://sobigdata.unipi.it.

[8] https://www.skills4eosc.eu/participate/skills4eosc-training-courses.

[9] https://cordis.europa.eu/project/id/101058527/it.

## 16.3 Role of Research Infrastructures in Fostering Partnerships

Research Infrastructures (RIs) are the backbone of modern collaborative science. They do not merely provide computational capacity, data storage, or connectivity; they constitute the institutional and cultural frameworks through which science organises collective intelligence. As *socio-technical systems*, RIs integrate human expertise, organisational structures, and digital resources into coherent ecosystems of cooperation. They enable continuity in scientific production, promote responsible governance of data, and support the translation of research outcomes into societal and policy impact. By embedding principles of trust, accountability, and stewardship within their operation, RIs transform ad hoc collaborations into long-term communities of practice and sustain knowledge creation beyond project cycles. RIs play a decisive and multifaceted role in shaping the collaborative environments that enable interdisciplinary and transdisciplinary science and cultivates shared epistemic and governance practices that sustain cooperation over time.

In the European context, RIs have evolved into key instruments of scientific integration. Originating from the large physical infrastructures of the twentieth century, such as CERN, EMBL,[10] and GÉANT,[11] that pioneered shared facilities for experimental science, the concept has broadened with the digital transformation of research. Today's infrastructures include both *hard* and *soft* components: distributed computing networks, metadata frameworks, semantic registries, authentication and authorisation infrastructures (AAIs), and human networks that mediate access, governance, and training. The European Commission's strategic investment in RIs through ESFRI roadmaps and Horizon Europe has institutionalised this dual function: infrastructures are not only technical artefacts but community-building frameworks that define how research collaboration is organised, validated, and sustained.

The social sciences have been profoundly affected by this evolution. Once dependent on national data archives and bespoke survey platforms, they are now embedded within distributed infrastructures that connects survey data, administrative records, behavioural traces, and textual corpora. This shift has expanded the boundaries of what counts as a research infrastructure. Platforms such as CESSDA-ERIC, SHARE-ERIC, and CLARIN provide access to harmonised datasets and tools for comparative social analysis, while new-generation infrastructures, SoBigData, RISIS, and FOSSR itself, connect these resources to advanced computational frameworks and machine-learning capabilities. The integration of high-performance computing, real-time data streams, and semantic web technologies has created a new model of the *data-rich social science laboratory*.

[10] https://www.embl.org.

[11] https://geant.org.

At the heart of this transformation lies the mission of RIs to convert fragmented and heterogeneous research outputs into coherent, accessible, and reusable assets. By operationalising the *FAIR principles* (Findable, Accessible, Interoperable, Reusable), infrastructures ensure that knowledge circulates freely and responsibly. Persistent identifiers, harmonised metadata, provenance tracking, and federated access policies enable the discoverability and reuse of scientific resources across disciplines and borders. Federated identity management solutions such as *eduGAIN* and *EOSC AAI* allow researchers to authenticate once and access a broad portfolio of services across Europe, carrying with them a persistent digital identity that guarantees compliance and security. These technical frameworks are complemented by governance mechanisms that uphold ethical and legal standards, enabling collaboration among diverse institutional actors.

Yet the importance of RIs extends beyond their technical sophistication. They function as *boundary infrastructures*, interfaces where multiple epistemic cultures meet and negotiate meaning. Within these hybrid spaces, social scientists seeking interpretive understanding interact with data engineers developing scalable architectures and with policy analysts translating evidence into actionable insight. RIs facilitate such interactions through shared ontologies, standardised interfaces, and interoperable services, fostering what has been called "productive heterogeneity": a condition in which methodological diversity becomes an engine for innovation rather than a source of fragmentation.

The European *Open Science Cloud (EOSC)* represents the culmination of this trajectory toward federation and interoperability. Conceived as a *meta-infrastructure*, EOSC interconnects national, thematic, and e-infrastructure nodes into a unified ecosystem that supports the circulation of data, tools, and services across the continent. Within EOSC, domain-specific infrastructures such as *ELIXIR and EMBL* (life sciences), *BBMRI-ERIC* (biobanking), and the *Blue-Cloud Digital Twin of the Ocean* operate as functional nodes that both consume and contribute services. This federated constellation replaces the centralised architectures of the past with a distributed yet coherent network governed by common policies, standards, and trust frameworks.

The *EOSC Federation*, formalised through the *EOSC Federation Handbook*[12] published in 2025, marks a decisive step in institutionalising this model. The Federation is built around *Nodes*: national, thematic, or e-infrastructure entities, that serve as user-entry points to the EOSC ecosystem. Each Node integrates its own and third-party service, ensuring that local communities contribute to and benefit from the shared European infrastructure. The Federation's design embodies a *system-of-systems* philosophy: distributed but interoperable, locally governed but globally aligned. The first wave of Candidate Nodes was identified through a Europe-wide consultation in 2025, inaugurating a continuous process of accreditation and expansion that will progressively populate the European knowledge commons.

[12] https://zenodo.org/records/14999577.

This federated approach transforms RIs into platforms for strategic collaboration. Rather than competing for visibility or funding, infrastructures within EOSC operate as interdependent components of a continental ecosystem. Shared authentication, accounting, and interoperability standards create a digital trust fabric that extends from individual research groups to entire disciplines. As the EOSC Federation grows, it will increasingly serve as the *connective tissue* linking data producers, service providers, and end-users in an integrated workflow of open and reproducible research.

The *FOSSR* Research Infrastructure demonstrates how national initiatives can strengthen their ecosystems while aligning with continental frameworks. Funded through Italy's National Recovery and Resilience Plan, FOSSR builds upon D4Science to deliver interoperable VREs for social-science communities, supporting secure data management, reproducible analysis, and training consistent with the *EOSC Skills Agenda*. It broadens access to advanced computational tools and curated datasets, democratising participation in data-intensive social research. Such initiatives exemplify the inclusive ethos of Open Science, ensuring that the benefits of digital transformation reach diverse communities of researchers.

In the policy domain, the *RISIS* Research Infrastructure (Research Infrastructure for Science, Technology, and Innovation Policy Studies) provides another model for collaborative research. By interlinking databases on publications, patents, research projects, and institutions, RISIS generates evidence to support innovation and science-policy studies. Built upon principles of ethical use and controlled access, it demonstrates how technical integration and governance design can jointly foster trust and policy relevance. RISIS's long-term partnership model, uniting data producers, analysts, and policy-makers, bridges the gap between knowledge creation and decision-making, transforming data into actionable intelligence.

Globally, similar dynamics can be observed in the US *NSF's Cyberinfrastructure for Sustained Scientific Innovation (CSSI)* in the United States and in the *NIH Data Commons*. These initiatives converge with European approaches around shared goals: to create reusable, interoperable, and community-driven frameworks for multidisciplinary collaboration. The emergence of such global alignment indicates the gradual formation of an international infrastructure commons, a distributed ecosystem where knowledge, standards, and services circulate across borders under the principles of openness and reciprocity.

Beyond their technological achievements, RIs have become vehicles for embedding *Open Science* principles into institutional workflows. They transform openness from a rethorical aspiration into an operational reality through technical mechanisms, data catalogues, DOI registration, workflow publishing, and open APIs, and through governance structures that ensure transparency and accountability. Steering boards, user committees, and advisory councils engage diverse stakeholders in setting priorities, balancing openness with privacy, and aligning innovation with ethical and legal norms.

At the same time, infrastructures have emerged as powerful *engines of capacity building*. They not only provide access to data and tools but also cultivate the digital and analytical skills required to use them effectively. Initiatives like the EOSC Skills and Training Programme[13] or SoBigData's Training Academy[14] contribute to the professionalisation of data stewardship and reproducible research, ensuring that future generations of researchers can thrive in open, data-intensive environments. This investment in human capital reinforces the sustainability of RIs by creating knowledgeable and empowered user communities.

Sustainability itself is a defining dimension of successful infrastructures. Unlike time-bounded projects, RIs are conceived for permanence and continuous evolution. Their governance typically combines national funding, European co-investment, and in-kind contributions from partners, ensuring resilience to economic and political fluctuation. Through this distributed ownership model, infrastructures function as *repositories of collective memory*, preserving data, workflows, and expertise across generations of researchers. In doing so, they transform transient collaborations into enduring, institutionalised networks of shared knowledge. Technological innovation continues to redefine the operational logic of RIs. The adoption of *microservices*, *container orchestration*, and *continuous-integration pipelines* allows for modular deployment and rapid responsiveness. During the COVID-19 pandemic, these infrastructures enabled infrastructures to mobilise data portals and modelling platforms within weeks, supporting public-health decision-making. The same agility now underpins responses to climate change, energy transition, and societal resilience. RIs are thus not static systems but adaptive ecosystems capable of evolving in step with scientific and policy imperatives.

Crucially, the contemporary paradigm of research infrastructure is *participatory and co-creative*. Users are no longer passive consumers but active partners in design and governance. Co-creation methodologies, iterative feedback, agile development, and open community forums, ensure that infrastructures evolve according to the practical needs of researchers and societal actors. This participatory governance enhances legitimacy, usability, and long-term adoption, turning infrastructures into living institutions grounded in collective agency. Inclusivity and equity remain guiding principles. By lowering barriers to access technological, financial, and geographical RIs democratise participation in the production of knowledge. Federated models allow institutions in less-resourced regions to leverage continental-scale services without duplicating costly infrastructures. The EOSC Federation explicitly promotes this equal-access philosophy, supporting the creation of a level playing field where all researchers can engage in data-driven science.

In summary, Research Infrastructures are evolving into federated ecosystems that integrate technology, governance, and culture to sustain interdisciplinary partnerships. They institutionalise openness and accountability, align scientific ambition with societal responsibility, and enable Europe to act as a unified actor in the global knowledge economy. These infrastructures will constitute the scaffolding of the next generation of collaborative, inclusive, and impact-oriented science. In doing so, they redefine what partnership means in the age of Open Science: not a

[13] https://www.skills4eosc.eu/participate/skills4eosc-training-courses.

[14] https://sobigdata.unipi.it.

temporary alliance of convenience, but a sustained, federated, and reflexive process of co-creation aimed at advancing collective understanding and societal well-being.

## 16.4 Lessons and Emerging Models for Open Social Science

The experiences accumulated through Virtual Research Environments and Research Infrastructures over the last decade offer a rich laboratory for thinking about the future of open and collaborative social science. Rather than being isolated technical projects, initiatives such as,SoBigData, RISIS, FOSSR, and the emerging EOSC Federation have collectively generated a set of practices, design patterns, and governance models that can be seen as *emerging archetypes* of how interdisciplinary, data-intensive social research may be organised in the coming years.

This section tries suggest some of these lessons into a set of interconnected themes: the socio-technical design of collaboration, the centrality of interoperability, the embedding of ethics and law into infrastructure, the role of training and capacity building, and the conditions for long-term sustainability. Taken together, these themes point toward a model of *open social science* in which infrastructures and communities co-evolve, and in which VREs function as operational interfaces between methods, domains, and institutions.

One of the clearest lessons is that *collaboration must be designed as a socio-technical process*. The success of a VRE or RI cannot be reduced to its technical robustness or performance metrics; it depends equally on governance, user engagement, and institutional alignment. Digital Infrastructures such as D4Science have demonstrated that co-design and co-creation are not optional "add-ons" but structural features of sustainable platforms. The most widely used services and workflows are often those that emerged from iterative dialogue between developers and domain researchers, where scientific objectives and infrastructural capabilities were negotiated and refined over multiple cycles. In this perspective, a VRE is not a finished product delivered to a passive community but a *negotiated space* that evolves with its users. Requirements are not simply "gathered" at the beginning of a project; they emerge from practice, as researchers attempt to apply tools to real problems and encounter limitations, frictions, or new opportunities. Agile development, continuous feedback, and regular usability assessments become crucial mechanisms for aligning infrastructure development with scientific goals. This approach also has important institutional implications: funders and host organisations need to recognise that a substantial part of infrastructure work consists in *facilitating communication*, not merely in writing code or operating servers.

*A second, closely related lesson* concerns *interoperability and openness* as non-negotiable preconditions for collaborative science. At the technical level, open standards for metadata, access control, provenance, and identity management are essential if infrastructures are to communicate and exchange resources. Without shared protocols, *each platform risks becoming a silo*, and the effort invested in data curation and software development cannot be multiplied across domains. The

*FAIR* principles have been instrumental in articulating this requirement; they have helped shift the focus from local optimisation to global reusability.To this end, technical interoperability is only one layer. *Semantic interoperability* is equally important and far more difficult. Social science data may be deeply infused with theory: concepts like "household," "migration," or "innovation" are molded by legal systems, administrative practices, and scholarly disputes. Linking datasets across nations or fields thus demands not only common metadata standards but also conceptual mappings that clearly articulate differences and partial equivalences among categories. Here, crafting shared vocabularies, ontologies, and crosswalks emerges as a core intellectual endeavor, rather than a mere technical exercise. It requires ongoing collaboration between subject-matter experts, data curators, and infrastructure builders. Open social science thus depends on a multi-layered notion of interoperability: not only can systems "talk to each other," but the data they exchange can be interpreted meaningfully in different contexts. Infrastructures like RISIS, which link bibliometric data, patent records, and project databases, illustrate how difficult and yet how fruitful this work can be. Their experience suggests that semantic alignment is an ongoing process rather than a one-off task; it must be continuously revised as new data sources, policy needs, and analytical methods emerge.

*A third major lesson* concerns the embedding of ethical and legal dimensions into infrastructure design. Social science research often deals with personal, sensitive, or otherwise delicate information: health records, education trajectories, employment histories, or digital traces of online behaviour. The entry into force of the General Data Protection Regulation has raised the bar for compliance, requiring explicit consent procedures, clear purpose limitation, and strong safeguards against misuse. In open-science contexts, where the aim is to facilitate data sharing and reuse, this introduces apparent tensions between openness and privacy, transparency and protection. VREs and RIs have responded to this challenge by integrating privacy-by-design and ethics-by-design principles into their architectures. Access-control policies have become more granular, allowing differentiated access levels for different user groups. Secure "data enclaves" and remote-analysis environments permit researchers to run computations on sensitive data without direct download, thus reducing disclosure risks. Anonymisation and pseudonymisation pipelines are combined with rigorous governance procedures, including data-access committees, audit trails, and compliance documentation.

The experience of SoBigData, for example, shows that it is possible to enable cross-institutional research on mobility traces or social media data in ways that respect both legal constraints and ethical concerns. However, these solutions are not purely technical: they depend on continuous ethical reflection and institutional commitment. Codes of conduct, ethics guidelines, and training in responsible data use must accompany the deployment of technical safeguards. In this sense, VREs and RIs become arenas where the normative frameworks of open social science are debated, interpreted, and operationalised. Closely related to ethics and law is the issue of epistemic accountability. VREs that support provenance tracking, workflow versioning, and reproducible execution environments allow researchers to document not only their results but the entire process leading to those results. In interdisciplinary settings, where disagreements about methods and assumptions are frequent, this capability acquires special value: it provides a common reference point for discussion. Instead of debating abstractly whether a particular model is "appropriate," collaborators can inspect the concrete sequence of steps, parameter choices, and data transformations implemented in a workflow. Accountability thus becomes embedded in the infrastructural fabric of research, rather than being relegated to narrative descriptions in publications.

*A fourth set of lessons* revolves around training, capacity building, and the redistribution of expertise. The deployment of Research Infrastructures does not automatically translate into their effective use. Without adequate digital skills, researchers may perceive them as opaque or intimidating, and infrastructures risk being under-utilised or misused. Yet, when paired with robust capacity building, these infrastructures can powerfully disseminate cutting-edge methods and narrow disparities in capability across institutions and regions. Successful projects have recognised that training is not a peripheral activity but a core function of infrastructures. FOSSR, SoBigData and other initiatives have invested in summer schools,[15] workshops, and online courses that combine conceptual introductions to Open Science with hands-on training on specific tools, workflows, and datasets. These activities are often designed as collaborative learning environments, where participants work on shared problems and exchange expertise across disciplinary boundaries. Over time, such practices contribute to the emergence of new professional profiles, such as data stewards, research software engineers, digital curators, that are crucial for sustaining open social science. They also help shift academic cultures by valorising not only publications but also the production of reusable datasets, workflows, and software components.

*A fifth lesson* concerns sustainability and long-term institutional commitment. Many VREs and RIs were initially created within the framework of time-bounded projects; when funding ended, the risk of discontinuity was acute. It has become increasingly clear that infrastructure cannot be treated as a temporary deliverable; it requires structural funding models, clear governance structures, and integration into institutional strategies. The federated model adopted by D4Science, combining national support, European projects, and in-kind contributions, offers one example of how to move beyond purely project-based logic. Open-source software licences, shared maintenance responsibilities, and transparent decision-making processes further contribute to resilience. At the same time, sustainability has a social dimension: infrastructures endure when communities perceive them as indispensable and feel a sense of ownership. Co-creation, responsiveness to user needs, and visible support for scientific careers (for example through citation of datasets and workflows) all play a role in cultivating this sense of ownership. Infrastructures that merely deliver services without engaging with the evolving agendas of their communities risk becoming obsolete or marginal.

[15] https://summerschool2025.sobigdata.eu, https://summerschool2024.sobigdata.eu.

*These lessons together point toward an emerging model of federated, Open Science ecosystems.* Instead of centralising all resources in a single monolithic platform, Europe and other regions are converging on a distributed configuration in which multiple infrastructures serve specific communities while adhering to shared principles and interoperability frameworks. The EOSC Federation is perhaps the most explicit articulation of this model: national and thematic nodes act as entry points for communities, while cross-cutting e-infrastructures provide generic capabilities for identity management, storage, computing, and monitoring. Within this ecosystem, collaborations are no longer episodic or confined to single projects. Researchers may move across VREs and infrastructures over the course of their careers, bringing with them digital identities, methodological preferences, and epistemic commitments. Data collected in one project can be *reused, recombined, and reinterpreted* in others, provided that provenance and licensing conditions are respected. Workflows developed in one domain, for example for spatial analysis or text mining, *can be adapted to other domains* with relatively modest effort. Over time, this ongoing exchange of data, methods, and expertise may helps forge a common methodological toolkit for open social science.

To conclude, one of thes challenges ahead is to continue refining these infrastructures in ways that remain attentive to power asymmetries, ethical dilemmas, and the evolving needs of society. If this challenge is met, open social science will emerge not just as a methodological option, but as a robust and legitimate mode of inquiry for understanding and shaping the twenty-first century.

## 16.5 Conclusions

This chapter has described collaborative research models in the Social Science through "the lens" of Open Science practices, Virtual Research Environments, and Research Infrastructures. Across its sections, it has shown that collaboration is no longer sustained primarily through informal coordination or short-lived project arrangements, but increasingly through durable socio-technical systems that integrate data, computation, governance, and communities. VREs emerge as operational instruments that translate Open Science principles into everyday research practice, while Research Infrastructures provide the institutional continuity, stewardship, and trust frameworks required to sustain collaboration over time.

A key insight is that effective collaboration depends on the alignment of technical interoperability, organisational governance, and epistemic practices. Interdisciplinary work in the social sciences requires more than shared access to data and tools; it demands transparent workflows, traceable analytical processes, and shared conventions for interpretation and validation. By embedding provenance tracking, reproducibility mechanisms, and controlled access policies, VREs and federated infrastructures help reconcile methodological diversity with accountability. In doing so, they support a form of openness that is responsible rather than indiscriminate, particularly important when dealing with sensitive or personal data.

From a policy and decision-making perspective, the collaborative models have clear implications. Public institutions increasingly rely on complex analytical pipelines to inform policy choices in areas such as climate adaptation, innovation policy, social resilience, and demographic change. Infrastructures that enable reproducibility, auditability, and reuse enhance the credibility of scientific evidence and strengthen the link between research and policy. Federated approaches such as the EOSC Federation further amplify this value by reducing fragmentation, promoting interoperability across national and thematic boundaries, and enabling coordinated investment in shared capabilities.

The chapter also highlights that the sustainability of collaborative research models is inseparable from capacity building and governance. Skills development, professional roles such as data stewards and research software engineers, and participatory governance mechanisms are not ancillary components but core conditions for long-term success. Without sustained institutional commitment and community engagement, even technically advanced infrastructures risk underutilisation or obsolescence.

Looking ahead, several trajectories will shape the evolution of collaborative Open Social Science. The integration of AI-driven services promise to enhance discovery, automation, and analytical support, but will require renewed attention to transparency and explainability. Privacy-preserving computation and federated analytics are likely to become central for enabling collaboration on sensitive data at scale. At the same time, evaluation and incentive systems will need to evolve to recognise data, workflows, and infrastructure contributions as legitimate scholarly outputs, reinforcing the cultural foundations of openness.

In conclusion, we believe that collaborative research models grounded in Virtual Research Environments and Research Infrastructures represent a mature and credible pathway toward more transparent, reusable, and societally relevant Social Science. Their continued development should prioritise federation over centralisation, governance alongside technology, and community co-creation as a guiding principle. In this way, Open Science can move beyond aspiration and become a stable, institutionalised mode of knowledge production that supports both scientific advancement and informed decision making.

## References

Assante, M. C. (2018). The gCube system: Delivering virtual research environments as-a-service. *Future Generation Computer Systems*, 445–453.

Assante, M. B. (2020). Realizing virtual research environments for the Agri-food community: The AGINFRA PLUS experience. *Concurrency and Computation Practice and Experience*.

Assante, M., Candela, L., Castelli, D., Cirillo, R., Coro, G., Frosini, L., & Sinibaldi, F. (2019). Enacting open science by D4Science. *Future Generation Computer Systems*, 555–563.

Assante, M., et al. (2023). Virtual research environments co-creation: The D4Science experience. *Concurrency and Computation: Practice and Experience, 35*(18), e6925. https://doi.org/10.1002/cpe.6925

Candela, L. C. (2013). Virtual research environments: An overview and a research agenda. *Data Science Journal.*

Grossi, V. R. (2018). Data science at SoBigData: The European research infrastructure for social mining and big data analytics. *International Journal of Data Science and Analytics*, 205–216.

Schaap, D. A. (2022). Blue-cloud: Exploring and demonstrating the potential of Open Science for ocean sustainability. In *International workshop on metrology for the sea; learning to measure sea health parameters (MetroSea)* (pp. 198–202). IEEE.

Wilkinson, M. D. (2016). The FAIR guiding principles for scientific data management and stewardship. *Science Data.*

# Chapter 17
# Computational Social Science

**Rocco Paolillo, Giusy Giulia Tuccari, Sara Zuppiroli, Carmelo Fabio Longo, Giovanni Cerulli, Antonio Zinilli, Lorenzo Giammei, Andrea Giovanni Nuzzolese, Francesco Poggi, Misael Mongiovì, and Miguel Ceriani**

## 17.1 Introduction

Computational Social Science is a broad term that encompasses a variety of disciplines and methods. It covers a variety of aspects, from the usage of advanced technologies and large amount of data, to the focus on distributed dynamics of collective action. However, each declination of the term converges on the interdisciplinary effort this field requires and its role to understand the complexity

R. Paolillo (✉)
Institute for Research on Population and Social Policies, National Research Council (CNR-IRPPS), Rome, Italy
e-mail: rocco.paolillo@cnr.it

G. G. Tuccari · M. Mongiovì
Department of Mathematics and Informatics, University of Catania, Catania, Italy

Institute of Cognitive Sciences and Technologies, National Research Council (CNR-ISTC), Catania, Italy
e-mail: giusy.tuccari@istc.cnr.it; misael.mongiovi@unict.it

S. Zuppiroli · A. G. Nuzzolese · F. Poggi
Institute of Cognitive Sciences and Technologies, National Research Council (CNR-ISTC), Bologna, Italy
e-mail: sara.zuppiroli@cnr.it; andreagiovanni.nuzzolese@cnr.it; francesco.poggi@cnr.it

C. F. Longo
Institute of Cognitive Sciences and Technologies, National Research Council (CNR-ISTC), Catania, Italy

G. Cerulli · A. Zinilli
Research Institute on Sustainable Economic Growth, National Research Council (CNR-IRCRES), Rome, Italy
e-mail: giovanni.cerulli@cnr.it; antonio.zinilli@cnr.it



G. Cerulli, E. Reale (eds.), *Research Infrastructures for Open Science in Social Science Research*, https://doi.org/10.1007/978-3-032-29575-0_17

of societies. The emergence of the discipline within the mainstream of the social sciences developed in parallel with the strengthening of the Open Science movement. Research infrastructures provide an essential support to Computational Social Science by enabling large-scale data curation and integration, offering research services, and promoting collaboration and training across diverse disciplines. This chapter describes how FOSSR can support this field as a meta-infrastructure, presenting some services and experiences related to the topic. The chapter is organized as follows. Section 17.2 provides an introduction to the field of Computational Social Science and delves into the benefits of research infrastructures to the discipline; Sect. 17.3 narrows to the opportunities of FOSSR as a meta-infrastructure covering several aspects of Computational Social Science; Sect. 17.4 lists some detailed experiences and services in Computational Social Science research that were developed within the project, showing the potential usage and benefit for the field. Topics include Data Integration and Disambiguation, Knowledge Graphs, Agent-based Modeling and Multi-Agent Systems, Machine Learning, Network Science and Bayesian Networks. The chapter closes with the Conclusions in Sect. 17.5 where a synthesis of the case studies is provided to highlight the strategic role the FOSSR meta-infrastructure can have for Computational Social Science in the national context and beyond, delving also into reflections for sustainability of training of human capital.

## 17.2 Computational Social Science and Research Infrastructures

The position paper by Lazer et al. in 2009 and the manifesto proposed by Conte et al. in 2012 are considered historically the first mentions to Computational Social Science. Especially in Lazer et al. (2009), this was referred to as an emerging field derived from the progress of technologies at that time and their growing presence in daily activities such as the Internet. The term *computational* referred to the heavy usage of ICT technologies to collect and analyze data at unprecedented large scales, providing new venues for data-driven social sciences. However, a few years later, the manifesto proposed by Conte et al. (2012) added another layer of meaning to Computational Social Science, as a tool to understand the underlying mechanisms of the interconnected society described by those data. The

L. Giammei
National Institute for Public Policy Analysis (INAPP), Rome, Italy
e-mail: l.giammei@inapp.gov.it

M. Ceriani
Institute of Cognitive Sciences and Technologies, National Research Council (CNR-ISTC), Rome, Italy
e-mail: miguel.ceriani@cnr.it

term *computational* here was referred to building explanatory models of human and collective behaviour. The need for an interdisciplinary expertise was evident already in these first contributions. Nowadays, the term *computation* refers to a wide category including both formal models, simulations, network analysis and information extraction, supporting interdisciplinary collaboration in understanding societal complexity (Cioffi-Revilla, 2014).

Lazer et al. (2020) specifically point to the supporting role of data and research infrastructures when revising obstacles and opportunities of Computational Social Science, more than a decade after their seminal work. The contribution was written out of the grown recognition of the field and technologies associated. Recommendations involve developing data infrastructures strengthening collaborations with policymakers and citizen participation, while establishing ethical and legal frameworks for the management of data. As a matter of fact, these aspects reflect the progress of the Open Science movement occurred in the years before. These include culture of sharing in academia (Denden & Abed, 2025), together with the promotion of Open Science from government agencies (Burgelman et al., 2019; Hallonsten, 2020), and the need of reusable data for orienting policy work (OECD, 2015). Research infrastructures can serve a fundamental role in connecting researchers from different fields promoting open and collaborative science, aligning with the recommendation to nurture "computationally literate social scientists and socially literate computer scientists" (Lazer et al., 2009, p. 722). In addition, research infrastructures provide technical support through the management of large amounts of data and services that support interdisciplinary work. We show in the next paragraph how FOSSR aligns with these recommendations when providing support for computational social scientists. After describing some general premises, we provide actual experiences and description of services to the case.

## 17.3 The Potential of FOSSR for Computational Social Science

As a meta-infrastructure for research in the social sciences, FOSSR provides an array of opportunities for diverse aspects of Computational Social Science. These span from data curation, data extraction and synthesis, to methods of artificial intelligence for policy advice, open-access dissemination, and capacity building for social researchers. The availability of a large amount of data to integrate and elaborate is at the core of Computational Social Science, whether in the form of text-as-data or numeric data. A key concept in this regard is that of Big Data, as vast amounts of data supposed to cover wider knowledge of society and requiring tailored technologies and practices to be processed and analyzed (Boyd & Crawford, 2012; Laney et al., 2001). Research infrastructures guarantee the 4 V requirements for using Big Data (Avazpour et al., 2016): volume of data, variety of topics, velocity in data delivery, and veracity of information. However, the interest of social and computational scientists is that data are not just big, but rather meaningful to the research questions they want to pursue (Bouyousfi & Ouedraogo, 2025) and easy to integrate in transparent procedures of analysis (Krasmann, 2020). To this aim, a critical resource provided by FOSSR is to guarantee protocols for data curation, data extraction and the semantic representation of knowledge elaborated from data. These instruments adhere to the FAIR principles (Wilkinson et al., 2016) (Findable, Accessible, Interoperable, Reusable) to assure readability of data between machines and computational methods, together with transparent sharing within the scientific community as described by Lazer et al. (2020).

Research services are the core of research infrastructures as socio-technical systems, to facilitate the critical usage of computational methods by social scientists. The main declination of this approach is the development of software-as-a-service (*SaaS*) to facilitate the application of data to different methods without the requirement of technical dependencies or expertise by researchers (Demchenko et al., 2022). This approach is adopted by European macro research infrastructures such as the European Open Science Cloud (EOSC), or infrastructures specific in terms of context of application such as the European Digital Twin of the Ocean (European-DTO) or scientific topics such as the European Strategy Forum on Research Infrastructures (ESFRI) (ESFRI, 2020; Hallonsten, 2020). FOSSR also adopts this strategy when delivering its services. However, the peculiarity of the project is to build a research infrastructure with the clear aim to support social scientists. This facilitates its development as a socio-technical system better able to reply to the needs, practices and questions of a specific community (Bail, 2024; Fecher et al., 2021). Another peculiarity of FOSSR is that it primarily responds to the needs of the Italian society, particularly within the framework of the National Recovery and Resilience Plan (NRRP) from which the project originated. This translates into data collected that are representative of the national population (see IOPP, ORP and POOLPO), that combined with computational methods such as the extraction of synthetic populations or policy testing can provide insights specific to the national context. Finally, FOSSR actively invests on the capacity-building and training of current and future generations of social researchers, facilitating the interdisciplinary effort and participation required by Computational Social Science (Lazer et al., 2009; Yarkoni et al., 2021). This topic is however addressed in other chapters of the book and out of reach in this one. In the next section, we show detailed experiences of research and services that fall into the paradigm of Computational Social Science and specific methods of application developed in the FOSSR context.

## 17.4 Case Studies and Services for Computational Social Science

As show in Fig. 17.1, we map methods of Computational Social Science to the services provided by FOSSR as a meta-infrastructure. We follow a cycle from data

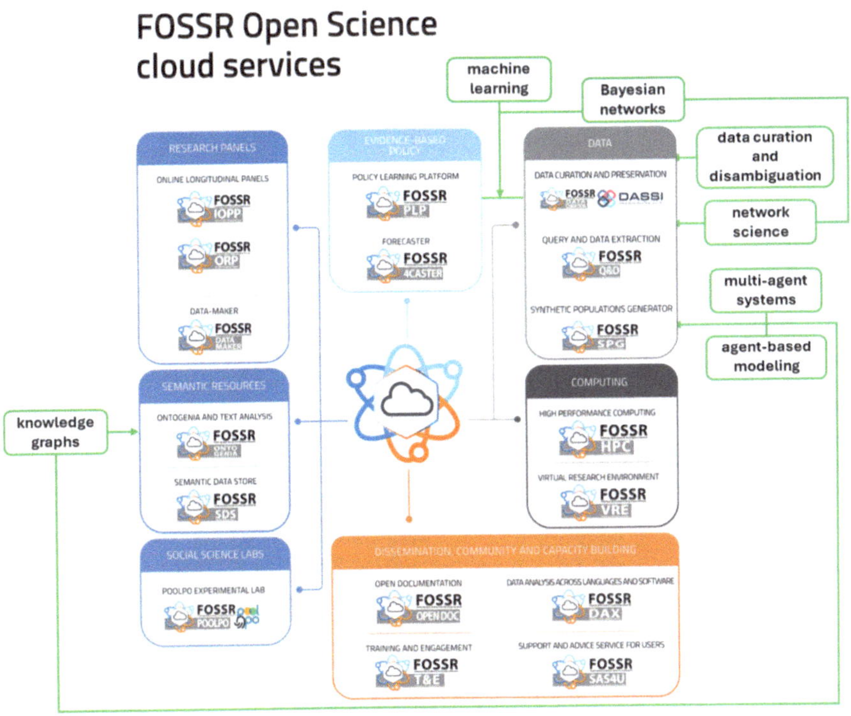


**Fig. 17.1** Mapping of Computational Social Science methods (in green) to the frame of FOSSR resources at the time of writing (Image concept and visual design by Rita Giuffredi, with support from Serena Fabrizio, Alessandra Maria Stilo, and Elisa Storace (FOSSR Communication Team))

integration and knowledge formalization, to integration in computational methods and their application, until more complex dimensions of network analysis. The aim of this section is to illustrate concrete examples of how the FOSSR infrastructure can be applied to research in Computational Social Science or policy advice.

### *17.4.1 Data Integration and Disambiguation*

Integrating heterogeneous research data remains one of the central challenges in Computational Social Science. Scientific information is distributed across a wide range of heterogeneous sources—bibliographic databases, institutional registries, funding archives, and patent repositories—each characterized by distinct metadata structures and standards. Achieving interoperability among these systems requires resolving inconsistencies, linking equivalent entities, and ensuring that data referring to the same real-world objects can be integrated into a coherent representation. We provide an example of integrating data concerning citation information, co-authorship networks and academic careers in the Italian context, whose results are used for another case study in computational modeling described later in the Sect. 17.4.3. The case study revolves around obstacles to the integration process arising from the absence of unique and persistent identifiers for individuals. Authors are typically represented by their names, affiliations, or partial metadata, which often vary across sources. The absence of standardized identifiers represents a major challenge for the integration of heterogeneous research information systems—ranging from bibliographic databases to those tracking academic careers and institutional roles (Martini et al., 2022), as well as databases covering patents (Morrison et al., 2017), research evaluation processes (Bologna et al., 2023), grant funding (Jacob & Lefgren, 2011), and doctoral training (Zinilli et al., 2025).

This challenge falls within the broader domain of entity resolution (Christophides et al., 2021), which aims to identify and reconcile records that refer to the same real-world entity across different data sources. Among the challenges involved in integrating heterogeneous research data, Author Name Disambiguation (AND) remains particularly critical (Kim et al., 2014; Smalheiser & Torvik, 2009). This task concerns the accurate identification of individual researchers across bibliographic and institutional datasets, ensuring that each author record correctly corresponds to the real-world person it represents. Ambiguity in author identification arises from two main sources, i.e. homonymy, when different researchers share the same name, and synonymy, when a single author appears under multiple name variants due to spelling variations, transliterations, or changes in institutional affiliation (Gomide et al., 2017). Such inconsistencies fragment author profiles, lead to publication misattributions, and distort bibliometric indicators, ultimately compromising the reliability of research evaluation and the validity of data-driven analyses in scientometrics.

To address this challenge, we introduce the LLM-enhanced Engine for Author Disambiguation (LEAD) (Tuccari et al., 2025), a hybrid framework specifically developed to establish reliable correspondences between academic career records from CercaUniversità—the official registry of Italian academic staff, covering careers from 2000 to the present—and their corresponding author profiles in Scopus. Scopus provides bibliographic metadata and citation information, while CercaUniversità offers official records on the academic careers of Italian researchers and professors. This task falls within the subproblem of cross-source author name disambiguation, where a single academic record may correspond to multiple candidate Scopus Author IDs (AUIDs) due to string-matching ambiguities and inconsistencies in bibliographic metadata.

LEAD combines three complementary sources of evidence, each capturing a different dimension of similarity across heterogeneous data. Citation-based evidence is provided by Bibliographic Coupling (BC) (Kessler, 1963; Maltseva & Batagelj, 2024), which measures the overlap between cited references and offers a strong, interpretable signal of intellectual proximity between authors. Collaboration-based evidence is derived from the co-authorship network through Label Spreading (LS) (Sattari & Zamanifar, 2018; Zhou et al., 2004), which propagates field labels from confirmed matches to neighboring authors and thus embeds collaboration patterns and disciplinary proximity into the disambiguation process. Finally, semantic evidence is extracted from textual metadata using a Large Language Model (LLM), which evaluates the conceptual coherence between candidate profiles on the basis of titles, keywords, and affiliation information. These components are orchestrated in a selective two-stage pipeline designed to maximize robustness while controlling the computational cost associated with LLM inference. In the first stage, BC is applied to all candidate pairs and serves as the primary decision mechanism. Pairs whose citation-overlap score exceeds a reliability threshold (0.15 on the extended 8-year citation network) are directly accepted as correct matches. Notably, BC alone achieves strong results, with 94.7% F1 and 93.2% accuracy, confirming its strength as a baseline. Only pairs with scores below this threshold are considered hard cases and further analyzed in the second stage. Disambiguation at this stage is performed by an LLM (Llama 3.1 70B Instruct) in zero-shot mode (i.e., without task-specific training) on a richly structured prompt. Alongside textual metadata (keywords and titles), the model receives (i) information derived from LS, which estimates the compatibility between the candidate author and the expected scientific area, and (ii) detailed statistics from BC, such as the proportion of shared references. In this way, the LLM reasons jointly over semantic content and structural context, focusing its capacity exclusively on the most ambiguous instances.

For comparison, we also evaluated an LLM-enriched configuration, in which the language model is applied uniformly to all candidate pairs rather than selectively. This variant serves to quantify the computational trade-off between a comprehensive LLM-based disambiguation and the selective strategy implemented in LEAD. The framework was evaluated on a manually annotated gold standard of 606 highly ambiguous cases —including homonyms working at the same university in closely related disciplines—drawn from the Italian academic system. Results demonstrate that LEAD achieves the best overall performance, with an F1 score of 96.7% and an accuracy of 95.7%, significantly outperforming all alternative approaches. In comparison, Label Spreading (LS) reached an F1 of 86.3% and an accuracy of 81.8%, Bibliographic Coupling (BC) achieved 94.7% and 93.2%, the LLM-only approach 93.6% and 92.1%, and the LLM-enriched configuration 94.7% and 93.2%. LEAD achieves these results with substantially reduced computational costs, requiring only 1842 seconds compared to 5381 seconds for the full LLM approach and 4602 seconds for the LLM-enriched variant. This selective strategy preserves the efficiency of Bibliographic Coupling, while substantially improving performance on difficult homonymy and synonymy cases. The findings confirm that Bibliographic Coupling emerges as the fastest and strongest single-source method, providing both high precision (96.6%) and recall (92.9%) with minimal computational overhead (1.88 seconds). However, its integration with semantic reasoning through selective LLM application allows LEAD to resolve the remaining hard cases that structural evidence alone cannot handle, such as authors with sparse publication records or limited citation overlap.

These results demonstrate that integrating semantic and structural signals within a selective hybrid framework provides a robust and scalable solution for cross-database author identification. Beyond the Italian context, this approach highlights the broader potential of hybrid LLM-based methods to enhance data quality, interoperability, and reliability in scientometric analyses, offering a generalizable and practical framework for improving the integration and disambiguation of research information across diverse national systems and bibliographic databases. The next paragraph describes knowledge graph as a tool to synthetize knowledge as a next step to integration and disambiguation of data.

### *17.4.2 Knowledge Graphs*

In the social sciences, the use of knowledge graphs (KGs) represents a decisive step towards the realization of the FAIR data principles—ensuring that research data are Findable, Accessible, Interoperable, and Reusable (Wilkinson et al., 2016). Through the formal representation of entities and their semantic relationships, knowledge graphs enable the integration of heterogeneous datasets and promote the systematic linking of information across disciplinary and institutional boundaries. This capability is particularly relevant to the principle of reuse, as KGs make it possible to discover and connect data that were originally produced for distinct research purposes, thereby fostering cumulative and collaborative forms of inquiry. We present a case study applied to the structure and reuse of item questionnaires conducted within the framework of the FOSSR project.

In developing our knowledge graph, we adopted an Extreme Design (XD) methodology (Blomqvist et al., 2010). Within this framework, Competency Questions (CQs) (Grüninger & Fox, 1995) are formulated at the outset to capture the essential functional requirements of our KG. Following the XD methodology, we conducted a state-of-the-art analysis to identify existing vocabularies and ontological models relevant to our domain. The goal was to ground our conceptualization in well-established standards while ensuring semantic interoperability with external resources. In this context, particular attention was given to two central components of empirical research in the social sciences:

- The general description of studies
- The structure and reuse of questionnaires

The XD methodology proved particularly effective for this task, as it promotes a continuous dialogue between conceptual modelling and domain expertise. By iteratively refining both the CQs and the ontological patterns used to address them, we ensured that the resulting knowledge graph was not only formally coherent but also aligned with the real analytical practices of social science research. This design process enabled us to map existing standards— such as Data Documentation Initiative (DDI), Research Object Model (RO), and Semanticscience Integrated Ontology (SIO)—onto a unified semantic framework, and to identify gaps where new modeling solutions were required, particularly in representing questionnaire structures and question reuse. We extend and define our ontology that allows to represent our questionnaire, where metadata from surveys are ingested, harmonised, and represented as interconnected nodes and edges. Each survey question, for instance, is modelled as a distinct entity linked to its associated variable, question type, etc. This representation allows the graph to express not only the structure of individual surveys but also the semantic proximity between elements originating from different studies. The constructed graph can then be stored and explored within a graph database, continuously enriched by the questionnaires submitted through LimeSurvey. This dynamic ingestion process transforms the knowledge graph into a living repository that evolves alongside ongoing data collection. Researchers can perform semantic queries that go far beyond traditional keyword searches. Instead of retrieving information solely on the basis of textual similarity, queries can target relationships between concepts, e.g. in the format subject-predicate-object. For instance, they can identify all questions measuring trust in institutions across multiple studies, even when those constructs are expressed through different formulations or response scales. Through this functionality, the knowledge graph becomes a dynamic discovery environment, where conceptual connections between variables emerge as the product of semantic reasoning and iterative data integration. This process directly supports the reuse of survey questions. By identifying previously validated items and their contextual metadata—such as populations, methodologies, and temporal frames—researchers can design new surveys that ensure comparability and continuity with earlier work. Consequently, knowledge graphs enable an iterative cycle of data reuse and innovation: existing instruments inform new designs, and new data enrich the semantic network.

Ultimately, the integration of ontology-driven design, graph-based representation, and semantic querying transforms the management of social science data from a static archival activity into a living ecosystem of knowledge, which aligns with the dynamic processing of computational methods. Within this ecosystem, surveys are no longer isolated artefacts but interlinked components of an evolving research infrastructure that promotes transparency, reproducibility, and cumulative scientific understanding. Beyond facilitating data integration and methodological innovation, knowledge graphs also offer a conceptual tool for the analysis of social behaviour. In particular, by representing agents, beliefs, desires, and intentions as interconnected nodes, the KG can be used to model cognitive and behavioural dynamics consistent with models of human behavior and reasoning such as the Beliefs–Desire–Intention (BDI) framework. In this sense, knowledge graphs do not merely function as infrastructures for data management, but as analytical instruments capable of bridging empirical evidence, theoretical constructs, and computational modeling in the study of social phenomena, as we show in the next paragraph delving into the methodology of agent-based and multi-agent systems.

### *17.4.3 Agent-Based Modeling and Multi-Agent Systems*

The modeling of complex systems is one of the main pillars of Computational Social Science, focusing on how system-level functioning emerges from the interactions among its components. A central notion is that of autonomous agents that constitute the system and participate in its distributed dynamics. Agents can be defined as any software objects or hardware able to process information, having their own decisional process and reacting to their environment to complete a task (Drogoul et al., 2002; Wooldridge & Jennings, 1995). The key characteristic of agents is their social ability in being able to interact and coordinate with other agents (*ibidem*). Two closely related concepts, but with subtle differences, are those of agent-based modeling and multi-agent systems (Jebraoui & Nemiche, 2025). The former is based on the emergence of social phenomena from the interaction of heterogeneous agents, the latter on the coordination of agents for the execution of a plan. Both definitions are covered by FOSSR activities.

Agent-based modeling (ABM) aims at uncovering the dynamics of complex phenomena from the bottom-up interaction of agents (Epstein & Axtell, 1996). Agents here are virtual objects able to replicate the cognitive processes and characteristics of the social actors they represent (Gilbert & Troitzsch, 2005). The focus of this approach is on the aggregated effects of the individual actions and preferences of agents in a population (Macy & Willer, 2002). Given the scholarly interest of the method, this definition of agent-based modeling generally corresponds to what is meant in Computational Social Science with the study of complex systems. Examples are Schelling (1971) model of spatial segregation or Axelrod (1997) model of cultural dissemination. One asset of the method is to focus analytically on the dynamics linking the individual decisional processes of agents and their aggregated measurable outcomes (Manzo, 2021). Initialized with information on a target society, the method is well-suited to analyse hypothetical scenarios as in the case of policy appraisal (Gilbert et al., 2018). However, a critical issue to this point is the access to the detailed information from secondary data needed to reproduce the heterogeneous characteristics of the target population at the micro-level. Access to this level of detailed information can be limited by providers, e.g. due to privacy concerns (Longo et al. 2025a), or the information can be scattered across different datasets. Synthetic populations serve to mitigate this issue, providing a series of algorithms to reproduce micro-level agents' characteristics abstracting and integrating the statistical properties of the target population retrieved from available data (Chapuis et al., 2022). To this aim, FOSSR includes the Synthetic Populations Generator service (SPG), which provides a tool to support the generation of synthetic populations integrating separate datasets referred to the same population. The service implements a generalization of the Multiple Iterative Proportional Fitting (MIPF) (Choupani & Mamdoohi, 2016), which identifies the possible integrations of different variables in input data, corrected for conditional distributions if provided. The algorithm thus estimates weights and sizes of the different joint categories that compose the synthetic population. Users can extract the level of aggregation they desire on the whole set of joint categories identified, extract and store the results. The algorithm has been tested and validated against geo-local population morbidity rate in the region Lazio.[1] The validation procedure

[1] https://www.opensalutelazio.it/salute/.

consisted of reproducing the joint categories derived from aggregated data on heart failure, hypertension, gender and age at the regional level, knowing the conditional probability of the health indicators by age. The synthetic population extracted was able to reproduce the distributions known from the empirical data, with measures such as Mean Absolute Percentage Error (MAPE) and Root Mean Square Error (RMSE) close to zero. The information extracted can be used to reproduce the heterogeneity of the population in what-if scenarios of policy.

Multi-agent systems (MAS), on the other hand, originated within the domains of software engineering and artificial intelligence (Sichman et al., 2003; Wooldridge, 2009). This perspective focuses on the cooperation among agents to achieve a common goal — which goal is the reason itself of the existence of the coordinated system (Wooldridge & Jennings, 1995). Agents in this context can be both software or hardware machines coordinated to execute the task. The main focus of research is the adherence to a common protocol of communication between agents to coordinate efficiently. Example of protocols are provided by the Foundation for Intelligent Physical Agents (FIPA), whose guidelines are followed by architectures such as JADEX (Braubach et al., 2005) or JACAMO (Boissier et al., 2013). Interoperability of data information that can be read and interpreted by interconnected agents or machines is critical, enhanced by shared semantic ontologies supported by knowledge graphs implementations as described in the previous paragraph. A step forward in this direction is represented by the Semantic Web (Berners-Lee et al., 2001), with the application of semantic structures to World Wide Web data, which can benefit data-driven computational models (Antakli et al., 2023). However, a challenge remains on assuring the communication between agents using the same ontology in open and dynamic environments. One project in FOSSR is the implementation of the Triples-to-Beliefs-to-Triples protocol (T2B2T) for the integration of the Semantic Web with MAS (Longo et al. 2025a, b) (see Fig. 17.2). The paradigm is built on the BDI architecture (Bratman, 1987; Rao & Georgeff, 1995) implemented through the SEMAS (SEmantic Multi-Agent System) framework, built atop the BDI architecture PHIDIAS (PytHon Interactive Declarative Intelligent Agent System) (D'Urso et al., 2019). The BDI architecture is a cornerstone in artificial intelligence literature to provide realistic and dynamic processes of decision making. Beliefs represent notions of the agents about the world, desires represent the ultimate state of themselves or the world to be reached, while intentions the deliberative process to fulfill desires through specific plans execution. In the first step of the process, i.e. *acquiring triple stage*, the protocol starts with a SPARQL semantic query to a remote or local ontology to feed the knowledge graphs agents are embedded with, so to interact with the world and execute their plans. The first component of the pipeline translates triples provided in Resource Description Framework (RDF) formats (subject-predicate-object) into the beliefs that compose the initial knowledge graphs of agents. In the *inference stage*, as a second step, the decisional process of agents is modeled through a series of production rules enacted from the conditioning of the desires of agents to the state of the world known through the beliefs stored in their knowledge graph.

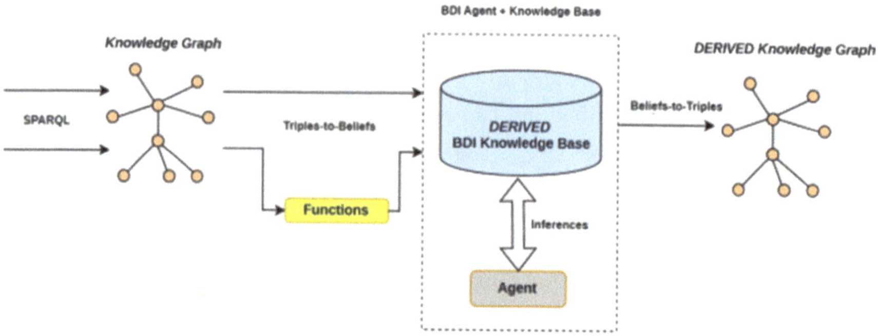


**Fig. 17.2** The T2B2T process

The third step of the pipeline concerns the *update triple stage*, generating new triples from the action taken from agents and changes in the system they can allocate. New triples are stored in the knowledge graph, which becomes a dynamic element reporting changes in the system. The protocol can be applied to mono-agent systems and multi-agent systems. In the latter case, the communication of new triples between agents is the condition for updating their knowledge graph, affecting their decisional process due to new knowledge used for inference.

T2BT2 can be applied both to virtual agents and to the interaction between machines as in the Internet of Things (IoT) through RESTful requests. As such, the protocol can be regarded both as a multi-agent system, in the sense of interactive machines coordinating to execute a plan, and as an agent-based model for social research, aimed at investigating the relationship between individual agents' decisions and system-level change. The latter was used for a study of academic mobility in the Italian context (Longo et al. 2025a, b). The study initializes the model with data disambiguated from Scopus co-authorships network as described in Sect. 17.4.1 and stored as an ontology, limiting to information at the year 2024. Agents in the model are actual scholars in the Italian academic system stored in the Scopus ontology and identified through URIs. In the scenario, scholars are initially affiliated with their actual research organization, and a selector agent must choose the offer between two other organizations, e.g. due to a job offer. The decisional process follows a preferential attachment perspective, i.e. aiming at top authors in their elective field to collaborate with (Hill, 2008; Koseoglu, 2016). Whenever top-authors are not available in either of the alternative universities, they will opt for the organization that hosts a co-author to a top-author in any other university, to whom the selector might be introduced. Figure 17.3 shows the running and results of T2B2T protocol initialized with Scopus data. It shows the state of the system before inference, reporting the affiliation of the selector scholar to one organization and the offers received. The decisional process is represented by a production rule, showing the inference produced, reporting in which university a co-author to a top-author exists and suggesting the university to select. In the final line, the new state of the system with the updated affiliation appears after the agent makes its choice.

```
Scholar: URI/authors/57201117401

PRE-INFERENCE state of the system:
Affiliation(URI/authors/57201117401,URI/organizations/60024690)
Selectionship(URI/authors/57201117401, URI/organizations/60000481)
Selectionship(URI/authors/57201117401,URI/organizations/105937250)
DECISIONAL PROCESS:
Publicationship (X) / ( CoAuthorship(Z,Y) & TopAuthorship(Y,X)
& Affiliation(Z,U) &
Selectionship(S,U) & Selectionship(S,D) & Affiliation(S,T)) >>
  [-Affiliation(S,T) ,-Selectionship(S,U), -Selectionship(S,D),
+Affiliation(S,U) ]

INFERENCE:
Author URI/authors/16021198600 at Organization
URI/organizations/60000481 is co-
author with URI/authors/55904339600 top-author in the topic
URI/topics/2003
POST-INFERENCE state of the system:
Affiliation(URI/authors/57201117401, URI/organizations/60000481)
```

**Fig. 17.3** Initialized case study with Scopus data and running of SEMAS framework in the T2B2T protocol

The method, through the comparison of what-if scenarios, can be used as an actor-based model for policy appraisal. By contrast, the next paragraph describes machine learning as a variable-based model for policy appraisal, and tools rooting in the method developed in FOSSR.

## *17.4.4 Machine Learning*

Machine learning represents one core field of Computational Social Science nowadays, with a variety of declinations and applications in various disciplines for social research (Dritsas & Trigka, 2025). Sitting at the intersection of computer science, statistics and a variety of other disciplines, machine learning concerns the automatic improvement over time of algorithms, to improve inference from data and support to decision-making under uncertainty (Jordan & Mitchell, 2015). Rather than testing with data, machine learning allows to learn from data (Bouyousfi & Ouedraogo, 2025), which is a key asset in the context of research infrastructures to support policymaking work.

FOSSR is designed to span the full spectrum of modern data-driven decision-making, from anticipating outcomes to optimizing interventions. This is reached following a layered and transparent approach, combining predictive and prescriptive analytics through two complementary digital platforms: the FORECASTER and the Policy Learning Platform (PLP). In machine learning terms, FORECASTER belongs to the domain of predictive analytics, whereas PLP operates in the field of prescriptive analytics. In predictive analytics, implemented through FORECASTER, the goal is to reduce uncertainty about future states by extracting patterns and dependencies from data, focusing on learning the data-generating process from historical observations to forecast future outcomes (Bertsimas & Kallus, 2020). FORECASTER achieves this by integrating both econometric and machine learning models—SARIMA, ETS, state-space models, Prophet, neural networks, and ensemble methods—within an automated yet customizable workflow. Prescriptive analytics, implemented through the PLP, focuses on learning optimal actions or policy rules that influence those future outcomes towards a desired direction (Bertsimas & Kallus, 2020). The PLP achieves this through counterfactual and causal inference techniques to learn optimal policies from observational data. The two platforms are methodologically connected. The FORECASTER platform is dedicated to forecasting and scenario simulation for socio-economic, demographic, and environmental time series, integrating classical econometric and modern machine learning models to predict future trends and quantify uncertainty. It thus supports anticipatory governance and ex-ante policy design by allowing users to simulate the impact of external shocks or policy changes. The PLP addresses the complementary problem of identifying optimal policies under uncertainty, employing causal inference and policy learning methods, to derive data-driven decision rules that maximize the expected social welfare. The dual design embodies FOSSR's principle of connecting statistical learning with policy intelligence. Together, they constitute the data-driven intelligence layer of FOSSR's open research infrastructure. A full treatment of the PLP—its architecture, theoretical framework, and applications to optimal policy learning, is provided in Chap. 9 of this book. Here we focus on the FORECASTER platform, describing its conceptual design, methodological underpinnings, and integration within the FOSSR infrastructure.

The FORECASTER platform is implemented entirely in R, using the Shiny framework to create an interactive and cross-platform web environment accessible through any modern browser. The architecture follows a structured six-step workflow covering data input, exploratory analysis, model estimation, validation, forecasting, and result export. Data can be uploaded in standard formats (CSV, Excel, Stata, SPSS, SAS) or accessed through the FOSSR catalogue. The software automatically recognises temporal dimensions (quarterly, monthly, weekly, daily) and allows users to define target variables and exogenous predictors. Exploratory analysis available include trend and variance inspection, autocorrelation and cross-correlation, with different levels of decomposition such as trend, seasonal or irregular, and transformations methods such as Box–Cox or log-scaling. The FORECASTER supports both an automatic mode for users, selecting suitable models based on prior diagnostics, and a guided mode allowing full manual control over model specification and parameter tuning. Measures of validation include Mean Absolute Error (MAE), RMSE, and MAPE. A distinctive feature of FORECASTER is its capability for scenario-based forecasting, where users can modify exogenous variables, such as economic indicators or policy parameters, to simulate shocks or alternative policy environments. The system compares these simulations with baseline forecasts, providing prediction intervals and graphical visualisations of uncertainty. This capability allows policy analysts to assess the potential effects of decisions before implementation, thus fostering anticipatory and risk-aware policy design. The last two paragraphs revert to the perspective of complex systems in Computational Social Science, focusing on Network Science and the causal inferences that can be derived from it.

### *17.4.5 Network Science*

Network Science emerged as an interdisciplinary field that combines theoretical and practical tools to study complex systems through their underlying network structures (Börner et al., 2007). Building on early graph-theoretical foundations—such as the Erdős and Rényi random graph model (Erdős & Rényi, 1960)—and later developments on scale-free networks and preferential attachment (Barabási & Albert, 1999), the field focuses on identifying structural patterns, explaining how networks form, and linking these structures to the processes that operate on them. Compared to traditional Social Network Analysis, Network Science places greater emphasis on universal mechanisms, model scalability, and the ability to reproduce global system properties (Zinilli, 2025). FOSSR incorporates this perspective by treating the production of knowledge as a complex, interconnected system formed by multiple types of relations. As described in Chap. 10, scientific activity generates different networks—co-authorship, project collaboration, co-patenting—each representing a distinct process but involving the same actors. FOSSR integrates these layers into a multiplex and multilayer structure, enabling researchers to analyze how mechanisms such as preferential attachment, homophily, or structural concentration operate across domains and over time. The harmonized structure of FOSSR enables the explicit modeling of such phenomena. Researchers can analyze motifs that span layers (e.g., an organization that collaborates in publications and simultaneously co-patents with project partners), investigate meso-level structures such as communities and overlapping clusters across layers, or study temporal motifs that reflect how collaborations unfold in sequences over time. Tools like Exponential Random Graph Models (ERGM), Temporal Exponential Random Graph Models (TERGM), and multilayer ERGM or Stochastic Actor-Oriented Models (SAOMs) allow these mechanisms to be expressed directly as model terms—such as cross-layer triadic closure, multiplex homophily, or temporal memory structures—moving beyond descriptive patterns toward generative explanations of the data (Zinilli & Marchi, 2020; Zinilli, 2025).

By relying on the methodological and technical expertise developed within the FOSSR community, the meta-infrastructure supports a structural and mechanistic view of the research system. It allows researchers to explore not only who collaborates with whom, but also why certain structures emerge, how collaboration patterns reinforce each other across domains, and which higher-order configurations drive the production of scientific and technological knowledge. In this way, the infrastructure aligns with the modern direction of Network Science, where the focus shifts from individual ties to the systemic, multi-level, and higher-order mechanisms that shape complex social and scientific processes. The next paragraph delves into Bayesian Networks as a method integrating the architecture of Network Science with statistical inference and causal modeling.

### *17.4.6 Bayesian Networks*

Bayesian Networks, originally formalized by Pearl (1995), provide a rigorous probabilistic framework for representing, analysing, and explaining complex systems through directed acyclic graphs. These models combine a graph, where nodes represent variables and directed edges encode conditional dependencies, with a joint probability distribution that can be factorized into conditional probability tables (Pearl, 2000). This factorization enables researchers to decompose high-dimensional uncertainty into interpretable components, clarifying how single variable interactions contribute to shaping complex data generating mechanisms. Building on foundations in probabilistic graphical modeling, Bayesian Networks research has developed structural learning algorithms capable of inferring dependency patterns directly from observational or experimental data (Kitson et al., 2023). Such algorithms, including score-based, constraint-based, and hybrid approaches, can integrate prior theoretical knowledge to constrain the search space, thereby improving computational efficiency, robustness, and interpretability of the inferred models.

This perspective is incorporated into FOSSR by viewing social and scientific phenomena as systems shaped by intertwined mechanisms and latent structures, as described in Chap. 10. The meta-infrastructure's harmonized datasets, spanning demographic patterns, labor market trajectories, educational histories, administrative registers, and research production, provide fertile ground for Bayesian Network modeling, where heterogeneous information must be jointly reasoned over. Through the explicit encoding of conditional dependencies, Bayesian Networks allow researchers to articulate and test hypotheses about the generative mechanisms underlying social processes: for example, how socioeconomic conditions mediate employment transitions, how institutional features shape collaboration and innovation, or how behavioral tendencies interact with policy interventions. Moreover, by capturing these mechanisms in a structural form, Bayesian Networks support scenario analysis, counterfactual reasoning, and uncertainty quantification, key capabilities for Computational Social Science and policy-relevant research.

Integrating Bayesian networks within the FOSSR architecture aligns with the broader mission of FOSSR: to move beyond purely descriptive analytics and foster explanatory modeling that is transparent, data-informed, and responsive to the needs of the research community. In doing so, Bayesian Networks contribute to a wider shift in Computational Social Science, where the focus is not only on identifying patterns in large-scale data but on uncovering the causal and probabilistic architectures that drive the dynamics of complex social systems.

## 17.5 Conclusions

In less than 20 years, Computational Social Science has become a recognized and expanding field within social research. Its growing popularity parallels the advances of the Open Science movement and the development of technologies that enable the interdisciplinary collaboration and innovative methods the field requires. Research infrastructures represent a key opportunity to foster this development, particularly through training of researchers and facilitating collaboration across disciplines, in addition to data curation and provision of services.

FOSSR as a meta-infrastructure offers multiple inputs for computational social scientists. In this chapter we showed some research experiences and tools developed in the context of the project out of the collaboration of computer scientists and different expertise in the social sciences from sociologists to economists. Information processing represents the foundational core of Computational Social Science. To this end, the availability of data is essential, but ensuring their interoperability and integration across different datasets is even more crucial. The disambiguation techniques developed in FOSSR and described in this chapter address this point. The semantic knowledge conveyed by knowledge graphs satisfies the need for interpretable information about the relationships among data to facilitate analyses. Bayesian networks, leveraging machine learning algorithms, add an explanatory dimension to the analysis of the relational structure of variables. Addressing how the reality represented by data came to be requires investigating the dynamics of collective social systems, as emphasized by Conte et al. (2012) already in the early years of Computational Social Science. The integration of knowledge graphs and network dynamics with computational models for decision-making as illustrated by SEMAS and the T2B2T protocol, extends this perspective to current progress in multi-agent systems. From another perspective, machine learning techniques such as those applied in the FORECASTER delve into the prediction of reliable future outcomes learning from data themselves to test policy scenarios. However, the availability of technologies risks being meaningless for social research if it is not accompanied by the expertise of researchers capable of seamlessly adapting computational methods to their scientific inquiry and collaborate with other disciplines. The investment of FOSSR on training of new generations of researchers is critical to this point.

As any research infrastructure, FOSSR has some challenges ahead, one main challenge being that of sustainability. Research infrastructures need continue investment on their technologies to be up-to-date with computational methods, together with collection of data and data curation. Data curation and services provision, together with the legal and ethical frameworks adopted, should reflect the evolving needs of the scientific communities they are meant to support. This is particularly relevant when conceiving research infrastructures as evolving socio-technical systems rather than mere data storage silos. An indication of this shift is provided by Lazer et al. (2020), when mentioning anew the ethical, legal, and social implications of research infrastructures while reflecting on the progress of Computational Social Science compared to their seminal work in 2009. This reflects the need for human capital such as researchers and administrators capable of supporting the evolving system of research infrastructures, both in their internal functioning and in their connection with the broader scientific community. The case of FOSSR within the context of the Italian NRRP is particularly relevant considering the role of research infrastructures for social sciences. The post-COVID reconstruction funding has initiated a period of change that, in many cases, has leveraged the human resources and expertise already present within national institutions involved in the project. The challenge ahead is to transform this triggering event, and a meta-infrastructure such as FOSSR, into a consolidated opportunity for the social research in the country, and implicitly aligning with the growing interest in Computational Social Science and its contributions.

## References


Antakli, A., Kazimov, A., Spieldenner, D., Rojas, G. E. J., Zinnikus, I., & Klush, M. (2023). Ajan: An engineering framework for semantic web-enabled agents and multi-agent systems. *Proceedings of the International Conference on Practical Applications of Agents and Multi-Agent Systems*, 15–27.

Avazpour, I., Grundy, J., & Zhu, L. (2016). V for variety: Lessons learned from complex smart cities data harmonization and integration. *Proceedings of the IEEE International Conference on Pervasive Computing and Communication Workshops (PerCom Workshops)*, 1–6.

Axelrod, R. (1997). Advancing the art of simulation in the social sciences. In *Simulating social phenomena* (pp. 21–40). Springer.

Bail, C. A. (2024). Can generative AI improve social science? *Proceedings of the National Academy of Sciences, 121*(21), e2314021121.

Barabási, A.-L., & Albert, R. (1999). Emergence of scaling in random networks. *Science, 286*(5439), 509–512.

Berners-Lee, T., Hendler, J., & Lassila, O. (2001). The semantic web. *Scientific American, 284*(5), 34–43.

Bertsimas, D., & Kallus, N. (2020). From predictive to prescriptive analytics. *Management Science, 66*(3), 1025–1044.

Blomqvist, E., Presutti, V., Daga, E., et al. (2010). Experimenting with eXtreme design. In P. Cimiano & H. S. Pinto (Eds.), *Knowledge engineering and knowledge management (EKAW 2010)* (pp. 120–134). Springer.

Boissier, O., Bordini, R. H., Hübner, J. F., Ricci, A., & Santi, A. (2013). Multi-agent oriented programming with JaCaMo. *Science of Computer Programming, 78*(6), 747–761. https://doi.org/10.1016/j.scico.2011.10.004

Bologna, F., Di Iorio, A., Peroni, S., et al. (2023). Do open citations give insights on the qualitative peer-review evaluation in research assessments? An analysis of the Italian National Scientific Qualification. *Scientometrics, 128*(1), 19–53. https://doi.org/10.1007/s11192-022-04581-6

Börner, K., Sanyal, S., Vespignani, A., et al. (2007). Network science. In B. Cronin (Ed.), *Annual review of information science and technology* (Vol. 41(1), pp. 537–607). Information Today.

Bouyousfi, S. E., & Ouedraogo, M. (2025). Artificial intelligence and big data-driven evaluation research and practices: A systematic literature review. *Evaluation, 31*(3), 303–330.

Boyd, D., & Crawford, K. (2012). Critical questions for big data: Provocations for a cultural, technological, and scholarly phenomenon. *Information, Communication & Society, 15*(5), 662–679.

Bratman, M. (1987). *Intention, plans, and practical reason*. Harvard University Press.

Braubach, L., Pokahr, A., & Lamersdorf, W. (2005). Jadex: A BDI-agent system combining middleware and reasoning. In R. Unland, M. Calisti, & M. Klusch (Eds.), *Software agent-based applications, platforms and development kits* (pp. 143–168). Birkhäuser.

Burgelman, J.-C., Pascu, C., Szkuta, K., Von Schomberg, R., Karalopoulos, A., Repanas, K., & Schouppe, M. (2019). Open science, open data, and open scholarship: European policies to make science fit for the twenty-first century. *Frontiers in Big Data, 2*(43).

Chapuis, K., Taillandier, P., & Drogoul, A. (2022). Generation of synthetic populations in social simulations: A review of methods and practices. *Journal of Artificial Societies and Social Simulation, 25*(2).

Choupani, A.-A., & Mamdoohi, A. R. (2016). Population synthesis using iterative proportional fitting (IPF): A review and future research. *Transportation Research Procedia, 17*, 223–233.

Christophides, V., Efthymiou, V., Palpanas, T., Papadakis, G., & Stefanidis, K. (2021). An overview of end-to-end entity resolution for big data. *ACM Computing Surveys, 53*(6), 1–42. https://doi.org/10.1145/3418896

Cioffi-Revilla, C. (2014). *Introduction to computational social science. Principles and applications*. Springer.

Conte, R., Gilbert, N., Bonelli, G., et al. (2012). Manifesto of computational social science. *European Physical Journal Special Topics, 214*(1), 325–346.

D'Urso, F., Longo, C. F., & Santoro, C. (2019). Programming intelligent IoT systems with a Python-based declarative tool. In *Proceedings of the Italian Association for Artificial Intelligence Workshops*.

Demchenko, Y., de Laat, C., Los, W., & Gommans, L. (2022). Defining platform research infrastructure as a service (PRIaaS) for future scientific data infrastructure. In B. Otto, M. ten Hompel, & S. Wrobel (Eds.), *Designing data spaces* (pp. 241–260). Springer.

Denden, M., & Abed, M. (2025). Towards promoting the culture of sharing: Using blockchain and artificial intelligence in an open science platform. *International Journal of Interactive Multimedia & Artificial Intelligence, 9*(2).

Dritsas, E., & Trigka, M. (2025). Machine learning and data science in social sciences: Methods, applications, and future directions. *IEEE Access, 13*, 105334–105352. https://doi.org/10.1109/ACCESS.2025.3578906

Drogoul, A., Vanbergue, D., & Meurisse, T. (2002). Multi-agent based simulation: Where are the agents? In *Multi-agent-based simulation II* (pp. 1–15). Springer.

Epstein, J. M., & Axtell, R. (1996). *Growing artificial societies: Social science from the bottom up*. Brookings Institution Press.

Erdős, P., & Rényi, A. (1960). On the evolution of random graphs. *Publications of the Mathematical Institute of the Hungarian Academy of Sciences, 5*, 17–61.

European Strategy Forum on Research Infrastructures. (2020, March). ESFRI White Paper. *Making science happen: A new ambition for research infrastructures in the European research area*. Retrieved November 7, 2025, from https://www.esfri.eu/sites/default/files/White_paper_ESFRI-final.pdf

Fecher, B., Kahn, R., Sokolovska, N., Völker, T., & Nebe, P. (2021). Making a research infrastructure: Conditions and strategies to transform a service into an infrastructure. *Science and Public Policy, 48*(4), 499–507.

Gilbert, N., & Troitzsch, K. (2005). *Simulation for the social scientist*. McGraw-Hill Education.

Gilbert, N., Ahrweiler, P., Barbrook-Johnson, P., Narasimhan, K. P., & Wilkinson, H. (2018). Computational modelling of public policy: Reflections on practice. *Journal of Artificial Societies and Social Simulation, 21*(1). https://doi.org/10.18564/jasss.3669

Gomide, J., Kling, H., & Figueiredo, D. (2017). Name usage pattern in the synonym ambiguity problem in bibliographic data. *Scientometrics, 112*(2), 747–766. https://doi.org/10.1007/s11192-017-2410-2

Grüninger, M., & Fox, M. S. (1995). The role of competency questions in enterprise engineering. In A. Rolstadås (Ed.), *Benchmarking—Theory and practice. IFIP advances in information and communication technology* (pp. 22–31). Springer.

Hallonsten, O. (2020). Research infrastructures in Europe: The hype and the field. *European Review, 28*(4), 617–635.

Hill, V. A. (2008). *Collaboration in an academic setting: Does the network structure matter*. Center for the Computational Analysis of Social and Organizational Systems.

Jacob, B. A., & Lefgren, L. (2011). The impact of research grant funding on scientific productivity. *Journal of Public Economics, 95*(9–10), 1168–1177. https://doi.org/10.1016/j.jpubeco.2011.05.005

Jebraoui, S., & Nemiche, M. (2025). Agent-based models and multi-agent systems: A comprehensive review of distinctions, synergies and applications. *Complex Systems, 34*(3), 10.25088/ComplexSystems.34.3.299.

Jordan, M. I., & Mitchell, T. M. (2015). Machine learning: Trends, perspectives, and prospects. *Science, 349*(6245), 255–260.

Kessler, M. M. (1963). Bibliographic coupling between scientific papers. *American Documentation, 14*(1), 10–25. https://doi.org/10.1002/asi.5090140103

Kim, J., Diesner, J., Kim, H., Aleyasen, A., & Kim, M. (2014). Why name ambiguity resolution matters for scholarly big data research. *Proceedings of the IEEE International Conference on Big Data*, 1–6. https://doi.org/10.1109/BigData.2014.7004345

Kitson, N. K., Constantinou, A. C., Guo, Z., et al. (2023). A survey of Bayesian network structure learning. *Artificial Intelligence Review, 56*(8), 8721–8814.

Koseoglu, M. A. (2016). Growth and structure of authorship and co-authorship network in the strategic management realm: Evidence from the strategic management journal. *BRQ Business Research Quarterly, 19*(3), 153–170.

Krasmann, S. (2020). The logic of the surface: On the epistemology of algorithms in times of big data. *Information, Communication & Society, 23*(14), 2096–2109.

Laney, D., et al. (2001). 3D data management: Controlling data volume, velocity and variety. *META Group Research Note, 6*(70).

Lazer, D., Pentland, A., Adamic, L., et al. (2009). Computational social science. *Science, 323*(5915), 721–723.

Lazer, D., Pentland, A., Watts, D. J., et al. (2020). Computational social science: Obstacles and opportunities. *Science, 369*(6507), 1060–1062.

Longo, C. F., Mongiovì, M., & Santamaria, D. F. (2025a). Meta-reasoning agents based on narrative-driven inference for mitigating privacy risks in multi-modal settings. In *Proceedings of the 23rd European Conference on Artificial Intelligence (ECAI 2025)*. https://doi.org/10.3233/faia250965.

Longo, C., Paolillo, R., Mongiovì, M., et al. (2025b). Bridging BDI multi-agent systems and the semantic web through the triples-to-beliefs-to-triples paradigm. In *Proceedings of the international conference on agents and artificial intelligence* (pp. 327–334). SciTePress. https://doi.org/10.5220/0013668800003985

Macy, M. W., & Willer, R. (2002). From factors to actors: Computational sociology and agent-based modeling. *Annual Review of Sociology, 28*(1), 143–166.

Maltseva, D., & Batagelj, V. (2024). Citation and bibliographic coupling between authors in the field of social network analysis. *Journal of Data and Information Science, 9*(4), 110–154. https://doi.org/10.2478/jdis-2024-0028

Manzo, G. (2021). *Research handbook on analytical sociology*. Edward Elgar Publishing.

Martini, M. C., Pelle, E., Poggi, F., et al. (2022). The role of citation networks to explain academic promotions: An empirical analysis of the Italian national scientific qualification. *Scientometrics, 127*(10), 5633–5659. https://doi.org/10.1007/s11192-022-04485-5

Morrison, G., Riccaboni, M., & Pammolli, F. (2017). Disambiguation of patent inventors and assignees using high-resolution geolocation data. *Scientific Data, 4*. https://doi.org/10.1038/sdata.2017.64

OECD. (2015). *Making open science a reality. OECD science, technology and industry policy papers, no. 25*. OECD Publishing. https://doi.org/10.1787/5jrs2f963zs1-en

Pearl, J. (1995). Causal diagrams for empirical research. *Biometrika, 82*(4), 669–688.

Pearl, J. (2000). *Causality: Models, reasoning and inference*. Cambridge University Press.

Rao, A. S., & Georgeff, M. P. (1995). BDI agents: From theory to practice. In *Proceedings of the International Conference on Multi-Agent Systems* (pp. 312–319).

Sattari, M., & Zamanifar, K. (2018). A spreading activation-based label propagation algorithm for overlapping community detection in dynamic social networks. *Data & Knowledge Engineering, 113*, 155–170. https://doi.org/10.1016/j.datak.2017.12.003

Schelling, T. C. (1971). Dynamic models of segregation. *Journal of Mathematical Sociology, 1*(2), 143–186.

Sichman, J. S., Davidsson, P., & Bousquet, F. (2003). *Multi-agent-based simulation II*. Springer.

Smalheiser, N. R., & Torvik, V. I. (2009). Author name disambiguation. *Annual Review of Information Science and Technology, 43*, 1–43. https://doi.org/10.1002/aris.2009.1440430113

Tuccari, G. G., Giammei, L., Nuzzolese, A. G., et al. (2025). LEAD: LLM-enhanced engine for author disambiguation. *arXiv preprint*. https://doi.org/10.48550/arXiv.2511.07168

Wilkinson, M. D., Dumontier, M., Aalbersberg, I. J., et al. (2016). The FAIR guiding principles for scientific data management and stewardship. *Scientific Data, 3*(1), 1–9.

Wooldridge, M. (2009). *An introduction to multiagent systems*. John Wiley & Sons.

Wooldridge, M., & Jennings, N. R. (1995). Intelligent agents: Theory and practice. *The Knowledge Engineering Review, 10*(2), 115–152.

Yarkoni, T., Eckles, D., Heathers, J. A., Smaldino, P., & Lane, J. I. (2021). Enhancing and accelerating social science via automation: Challenges and opportunities. *Harvard Data Science Review, 3*(2).

Zhou, D., Bousquet, O., Lal, T. N., Weston, J., & Bernhard, O. (2004). Learning with local and global consistency. In *Advances in Neural Information Processing Systems* (pp. 321–328).

Zinilli, A. (2025). *Elements of network science: Theory, methods and applications in Stata, R and Python*. Springer Nature.

Zinilli, A., & Marchi, M. D. (2020). Value-added in high technology and industrial basic research: A weighted network observing the trade of high-tech goods. *International Journal of Computational Economics and Econometrics, 10*(4), 398–418.

Zinilli, A., Tuccari, G. G., Poggi, F., et al. (2025). Anatomy of climate change research in Italian doctoral dissertations using a machine learning approach. *Scientific Reports, 15*(1), 38095. https://doi.org/10.1038/s41598-025-17307-4

# Conclusions: Contributing to Global and National Trends in Open Science: Challenges and Future Directions

Giovanni Cerulli • Emanuela Reale

## Introduction

The book focused on research infrastructures (RIs) for open social science research and incorporates theoretical foundations, practical insights, and a thorough examination of RIs using the case of the FOSSR project funded under the Italian National Plan of Recovery and Resilience—PNRR EC Next Generation EU.

We first set the scene of RIs for social science research in Europe and the linkages with the principles of Open Science to understand the context where data and resources devoted to social science research are developed by the different communities of scholars and then provided to the wide community of users.

Then, we focused on the case of FOSSR—Fostering Open Science in Social Science Research, analyzing its aims, structure and organization. The different research areas allow us to understand how innovation in knowledge creation can be sustained and enabled using FOSSR resources to address different issues in social science research.

In the final part of the book, we presented some of the most significant methodological, modelling, and technical developments enabled by FOSSR. These contributions demonstrate the importance of addressing new research questions through the use of RIs as strategic resources, capable of supporting the integration of large-scale datasets and the adoption of innovative data processing and analytical approaches.

To sum up, the case of FOSSR shows one example of how the RIs are evolving within the European area.


G. Cerulli, E. Reale (eds.), *Research Infrastructures for Open Science in Social Science Research*, https://doi.org/10.1007/978-3-032-29575-0

## Integration, Interoperability, and the European Evolution of RIs

The main features we can observe are the following.

First, the budget constraints and the need to reinforce the national nodes of the different infrastructures ask for a new important work of integration between different infrastructures. There are pros and cons in this solution. On the one side, there is an effort toward integrating different aims, objectives and modus operandi (rules of access, ethics, fairness, implementation of the Open Science principles) developed by each infrastructure, which can be perceived as a loss of autonomy. On the other hand, pursuing integration means to allow the implementation of new services, data and resources which supply new possibilities to the users.

The European Commission already recommended to strengthen the integration of RIs, by linking, coordinating, and harmonizing facilities, data services, and resources to enable multidisciplinary, data-intensive, and collaborative science. In the actions implemented by the Commission (see for instance the interventions through the Horizon Europe Programme), key efforts shall focus on bolstering efficiency, interoperability, and access, particularly in the European Research Area.

What FOSSR carried out is one example of three European RIs (CESSDA, SHARE and RISIS), which became five during the project's development (adding also GUIDE and GGP), and now can use integrated resources developed by their Italian nodes and by a network of other research organizations (Universities and Research Centres) that contributed to the new developments. It is not only a matter of economic efficiency, but also the possibility to integrate more scholars thus enlarging the community of producers and users.

Second, the FOSSR experience demonstrates how meta-infrastructures coordinating the national nodes of different RIs can create a stronger epistemic environment in social sciences, favoring multidisciplinary approaches and contaminations between diverse communities in the field. A further effect is that these meta-infrastructures can facilitate further coordination at European level by creating a pool of resources specifically devoted to social sciences thus overcoming barriers between ERIC and non-ERIC legal entities, and building a shared normative structure based on common standards, rules, regulations, political and social concepts.

## Future Challenges and Strategic Perspectives for Open Science Infrastructures

What future lines of evolution of RIs can we foresee for social science research? An answer is not easy to give due to the uncertainty generated by the complex geopolitical context that shall affect the actions of the European Unions and of the member countries.

RIs in the social science research suffers limitations and drawbacks of all the European infrastructures and costs that, although much lower than those of the RIs of the STEM fields, are anyhow important and ask for a permanent investment from the public government funding, as no infrastructure can be maintained by the market when operates in the Open Science paradigm.

In social science research the RIs are asked to be enablers for linking scholars with society, to supply resources inducing transformations in research activities and in society, to improve the capabilities to connecting the global with the local needs. At the same time, constraints include the difficult purpose to address new emerging topics (e.g. SDGs' related topics), the growing use of mixed methods approaches, and the overcoming of the blurring divide between quantitative and qualitative methods to deepen several items that needs exploration to formulate hypotheses, problems that the exploitation of complementarities between RIs can produce.

The National Roadmap for Open Science is another element that must be carefully considered. The key principle of Open Science—"as open as possible, as closed as necessary"—for the management of research data requires that research data and results be shared publicly to foster innovation, but that access may be limited to protect legitimate interests, such as privacy, security, commercial exploitation, or intellectual property rights. However, finding the right balance is challenging, given the difficulty of complying with the GDPR for social science research and the need to ensure inclusiveness and equity in access rules.

One final point is being aware of the technology sovereignty argument that is more and more compelling the research activities due to the need of national governments to develop, master, and control critical technologies to ensure strategic autonomy and reduce dependency on foreign actors. Data control is a key component to assure technology sovereignty, and the collaboration that RIs—inscribed in the Open Science paradigm—want to assure can be constrained by the need to prevent any foreign access to sensitive and/or strategic information.

To overcome most of the mentioned challenges, it is necessary to ensure a common space for interaction and collaboration between research groups, such as that offered by RIs. In this regard, the inclusion of meta-infrastructures such as FOSSR within the European research landscape represents an important resource to be maintained and strengthened through participation in European platforms that enable greater integration into the European ecosystem of research infrastructures, such as EOSC.

Future research must explore the significance of research infrastructures' impact and how their contribution and the free exchange of scientific resources (as in FOSSR) can be understood using indicators that capture value, and not just the performance of the infrastructures themselves. Not only the number of users and access, but the transformative capacity of RIs is also crucial for assessing their value for science and society.

Kolibri 360 GmbH
Ferdinand-Jühlke-Straße 7
99095 Erfurt, Deutschland
produktsicherheit@kolibri360.de